# SANCTUARY

# Also by Marina Warner

### FICTION

Fly Away Home (short stories)
Murderers I Have Known and Other Stories (short stories)
The Leto Bundle
Wonder Tales: Six Stories of Enchantment (ed.)
The Legs of the Queen of Sheba (libretto)
The Mermaids in the Basement (short stories)
In the House of Crossed Desires (libretto)
Indigo
The Lost Father
The Skating Party
In a Dark Wood

### NON-FICTION

Inventory of a Life Mislaid: An Unreliable Memoir
Forms of Enchantment: Writings on Art and Artists
Fairy Tale: A Very Short Introduction
Once Upon a Time: A Short History of Fairy Tale
Scheherazade's Children: Global Encounters with the Arabian Nights (ed. with Philip Kennedy)
Stranger Magic: Charmed States and the Arabian Nights
Fantastic Metamorphoses, Other Worlds: Ways of Telling the Self
Phantasmagoria: Spirit Visions, Metaphors & Media
Signs and Wonders: Essays on Literature and Culture
No Go the Bogeyman: On Scaring, Lulling and Making Mock
Monuments and Maidens: The Allegory of the Female Form
From the Beast to the Blonde: On Fairy Tales and their Tellers
Managing Monsters: Six Myths of Our Time (BBC Reith Lectures, 1994)
L'Atalante
Into the Dangerous World: Some Reflections on Childhood and its Costs
Joan of Arc: The Image of Female Heroism
Queen Victoria's Sketchbook
Alone of All Her Sex: The Myth and Cult of the Virgin Mary
The Dragon Empress: The Life and Times of Tz'u-Hsi, Empress Dowager of China, 1835–1908

### FOR CHILDREN

The Crack in the Teacup: Britain in the Twentieth Century
The Wobbly Tooth
The Impossible Day
The Impossible Night
The Impossible Bath
The Impossible Rocket

# SANCTUARY

Ways of Telling,
Ways of Dwelling

## MARINA WARNER

WILLIAM
COLLINS

William Collins
An imprint of HarperCollins*Publishers*
1 London Bridge Street
London SE1 9GF

WilliamCollinsBooks.com

HarperCollins*Publishers*
Macken House
39/40 Mayor Street Upper
Dublin 1
D01 C9W8, Ireland

First published in Great Britain in 2025 by William Collins

1

Copyright © Marina Warner 2025

Marina Warner asserts the moral right to be identified as the author of this
work in accordance with the Copyright, Designs and Patents Act 1988

A catalogue record for this book is available from the British Library

ISBN 978-0-00-834754-3

Endpapers: Sanctuary of Athena Pronaia, Delphi, Greece (*Lefteris Papaulakis / Alamy Stock Photo*).

Every effort has been made to credit material used in this book and contact
the respective copyright holder for permission. If your material has not been credited,
please contact us and we will update in future editions.

All rights reserved. No part of this publication may be reproduced, stored in a retrieval system,
or transmitted, in any form or by any means, electronic, mechanical, photocopying,
recording or otherwise, without the prior permission of the publishers.

Without limiting the author's and publisher's exclusive rights, any unauthorised use of this
publication to train generative artificial intelligence (AI) technologies is expressly prohibited.
HarperCollins also exercise their rights under Article 4(3) of the Digital Single Market Directive
2019/790 and expressly reserve this publication from the text and data mining exception.

Typeset in Garamond 3 LT Std by Jouve (UK), Milton Keynes

Printed and bound in Great Britain by CPI Group (UK) Ltd, Croydon

This book contains FSC™ certified paper and other controlled
sources to ensure responsible forest management.

For more information visit: www.harpercollins.co.uk/green

For Valentina, Din, Clelia and
Alpha
in hope, with love

This is also the aim of my explorations: examining the traces of happiness still to be glimpsed, I gauge its short supply. If you want to know how much darkness there is around you, you must sharpen your eyes, peering at the faint lights in the distance.
Italo Calvino

What hope is there of a purely secular grace?
Denise Riley

# Contents

Introduction     1

### Part One: A Kind of Freedom

1. Laws: A Brief History of Sanctuary     21

### Part Two: Sites of Memory

2. Traces: The Flight into Egypt     51
3. Relics: Helena Dreams of the Cross     78
4. Dust: The Flying House of Loreto     111
5. Bonds: The Migrant Queen     146
6. Tales: The Riddle Princess     183

### Part Three: The Shelter of Stories

7. In No Man's Land     215
8. The Map Is Not the Territory     242
9. In the Country of Words     260

Coda: Stories in Transit     290

| | |
|---|---:|
| Acknowledgements | 317 |
| Permissions | 321 |
| Illustrations | 323 |
| Notes | 327 |
| Selected Bibliography | 379 |
| Index | 395 |

# Introduction

*quo me cumque rapit tempestas, deferor hospes*
(wherever the storm drives me, I am carried as a guest)
Horace

On Saturday mornings in London in the 1950s, a neighbour's daughter would come round to take me to the 'flicks'; it was exciting to be allowed to go out with this stranger, who seemed almost grown up – she was fifteen, I think. It was a first taste of independence. We saw newsreels, mostly, but one of the features opened with an unforgettable scene: a young man in doublet and hose, his face a mask of terror, was being chased; with the hue and cry hard upon him, he seized hold of the knocker on a cathedral door and cried 'Sanctuary!' The door opened a crack, and he slipped inside. He was safe now; this was a holy place where a fugitive would find welcome and hospitality: a sanctuary.

This exciting sequence does not quite record the medieval facts – our hero may have been about to join Robin Hood's Merry Men in the green wood – but it caught the spirit of the ancient right to sanctuary, which radiates outwards from the most sacred spot inside a church, the site of the high altar, to reach the portal, where hangs a knocker, that hinges between one regime and the other, and envelops the supplicant in a protective halo. Sanctuary can be found in a temple or a chapel, a glade or a grove, a *temenos* or place apart, somewhere that is hallowed, sacred. But as in 'sanction', a word from the same root, which can mean both to approve and to forbid, sanctuary implies something to be treated with profound respect, not trifled with or defiled – in other words, *haram*, in

Islam, or taboo, itself a concept borrowed from encounters with non-European societies. In a most suggestive play on words, the geographer Marcus Doel contrasts *hollowed* ground and *hallowed* ground. Hollowed ground has been drained of meaning by violence and history's erasures; hallowed ground is filled with meaning that has been infused by tradition, ritual, tales, legends and agreed memories.

The idea of sanctuary has become synonymous in legal circumstances with asylum, a word which combines the Greek root *syl-*, from a verb meaning to seize or plunder, with the privative prefix *a-*, modifying it to mean 'not to be seized'. A sanctuary thus spans ideas of a refuge, a shelter, a retreat, even a lair, an inner sanctum, a precinct, a stronghold, a place of safety from harm and a space reserved – 'asylum' as in a mental hospital. It is an Other Place, a heterotopia. A convent of enclosed nuns is a sanctuary – for the community, to which very few are allowed admittance; yet so is a public park, one of the vital urban spaces still free and open to all. As the sculptor Antony Gormley rather grimly expressed the paradox, 'Is a refuge a prison? Is a sanctuary a cell?'

The concept of sanctuary that I am attempting to propose in this book emphatically does not stand outside society but stands inside it; it may embody certain principles that differ from mainstream values, but it aims at inclusion and belonging, sees perils of exclusion in the separatist tendencies of identity politics, and hopes instead to enclose a safe place through mixing and mingling, not dividing, segregating and isolating.

To achieve this ideal, it matters very much how such a place is perceived. How its story is told shapes the significance, the experience and the function. 'A boundary is entangled with history,' James Crawford writes in his book about borders. 'It is never simply a line, a marker, a wall, an edge. First it is an idea. An idea that is then presented as a reality. It doesn't just exist in the world. It can only ever be *made*. It can only ever be *told*.'

The ancient laws of sanctuary have prevailed in varied forms since classical Greece and biblical times, and subsequently in Anglo-Saxon and medieval Britain, until the Reformation in Europe. Many efforts continued the practice through the Vietnam war to the present day, culminating in the current vigorous movement to establish Universities and Cities of Sanctuary in different parts of the world.

Sanctuary does not only designate a reprieve that might be short-lived or a temporary suspension of the rules. It broadens into ideas of home. When arrivants reach a new place, where they hope no longer to be in danger and where they can seek asylum, the problem of estrangement remains. Taking refuge is not the same as feeling at home, of belonging. The sanctuary can be a harbour, where the fugitive can find safety, but it is not a permanent residence, even when an end to the period of homelessness is in sight and the refugee is given leave to remain. Being 'out of place' lingers: the phrase has been sensitively modified by the poet Susan Stewart to being 'lost in place'.

Homelands are fashioned over time, and imagination plays a part in making spaces where displaced persons and peoples can feel they belong, where they can find shelter and security and can dwell despite having forfeited their home, their original sites of belonging. The term 'homeland' first appears in 1627, according to the OED, and it then meant heaven. As the imperial era gathers force, homeland designates the metropole of the ruling powers or the permitted residence of the subalterns. A homeless person is said to be of no fixed abode – but home is not only the domestic address, rather it's a larger concept of country, birthplace and culture, and even status. 'Homeland' gained currency and strength in the aftermath of 9/11 when the US named its internal intelligence operations the Office of Homeland Security (in 2001) and then amalgamated twenty-two different agencies into the Department of Homeland Security (the following year). Its activities in turn inspired the successful television series *Homeland*, an intense, gripping, labyrinthine study in paranoid patriotism. The imperative to exclude therefore reverberates through the concept of home in political and public discourse, while concurrently culture is busily at work – unconsciously for the most part – weaving 'imagined communities', in the celebrated phrase of Benedict Anderson. According to this freshly vivid concept of homeland, displaced peoples and persons lie outside the homeland of others which they are attempting to enter; the boats of the suppliants – the refugees, the migrants, the *xenoi* or strangers – are the most desolating symbols of homelessness.

A sanctuary demarcates a space which some are entitled to enter, where some are allowed to dwell and which, in the interest of defending the homeland, keeps out others: the law defines the terms of admission to the sanctuary, but the law depends on a subtle mesh of custom, memory, values – whether the case is the European Community or a teenage daughter's den, which a mother may not enter without knocking.

For the dispossessed the power of place grows even stronger: yearning, nostalgia deepen. The exile, the immigrant, the asylum seeker, the travelling labourer, while wanting to make a new home, while learning the customs and contours of the place of arrival, still feels keenly the severed ties to past familiar landscapes where things were different. James Wood, in a piece he wrote about being an Englishman now living in America, coined the term 'homelooseness'. If home can be remade in the new place, borne off somehow (miraculously or by other means), then homelooseness may lessen. This perspective on homing – on home-bonding and home-making – is related to imagined communities, and tale-spinning and narrative are necessary to the process. Homelands, it turns out, are not fixed: the past is constantly being re-examined and retold. In this book, I explore the redress that acts of imagination offer.

Contradictory ideas of sanctuary compete in the general understanding of the term: on the one hand, sanctuary is a transitional process (a haven), suspending time and activity for the seeker until he or she is readmitted into society; on the other hand, it is a permanent state of safety and belonging, of recognition and harmonious acceptance (home). The spectrum of meaning similarly runs from a commons open to everyone to an enclosure owned by someone who gives or withholds permission to enter. Some sanctuaries are open and free, welcoming all. Or they may be the shrine or temple of a particular faith group and exclude others of different persuasions ('infidels'). Usage of the closely associated term 'asylum' reveals the tension at the core of sanctuary: an asylum was a place of detention, humane or otherwise in practice (the word has fallen out of favour in the medical context, but has become familiar regarding sanctuary seekers, many of whom are detained in hotels, camps, even boats, while they wait for a decision). Increasingly, in the present conditions of political tumult, sanctuary is conceived as a redoubt: the nationalist regards home and homeland as sanctuaries. Writers' studies are their sanctuaries; holiday homes (cabins, huts, even dachas) offer a similar place of retreat. Animal reserves are commonly called sanctuaries, too, for birds, for donkeys. In general, the arc of the concept of sanctuary has been bending away from a place of openness and welcome towards a private safe place, a move that is in keeping with the general growth of individualism and, with it, of atomization.

There is a poster for sale in gift shops that catches the current, private reach of the term: 'To you this may seem just a shed, but to me it's a sanctuary.'

A sanctuary has an address, a location on the map; it exists in the physical and material world, after a place has been designated a haven, by attaching a sacred story to it; the planting of relics and the practice of pilgrimage render that place special, holy, with certain powers of providing safety and shelter – as certain temples of the gods were particularly potent in this respect. Special cities were designated refuges in the Old Testament (Numbers 35: 11–24), and certain medieval abbeys, pilgrimage sites and churches accrued potent powers of protection. The meaning of sanctuary extends to take in many places of retreat – a garden or a library, for example, which is one of the reasons that public gardens and libraries are such achievements of a civil society, genuinely open, free, peaceful spaces. But I want to extend the term to mean also figurative sanctuary and fictive sanctuaries, as potential refuges and moorings and homes, which can form sites of memories and future attachments. A sanctuary is also a site of narrative, and a story makes a space in time, which is another form of refuge. The structure of narrative can also map out a different relation to territory. Most significantly in relation to today and the possibility of belonging, a sanctuary can be instituted by the consensus of the community, a complex and shifting assembly of opinion, taboos, beliefs, fears, desires and values.

A sanctuary was pronounced sacred, and its character upheld by various measures, but such sites of inviolability were above all defended by custom and verbal acts – charters, decrees, statutes, in short, laws – that declared such territory lay under a different jurisdiction, constituted by the narrative of its character and function. Memories of the past of that place, preserved through words and invested in things, things such as mementoes and relics, flowed into the accepted story. A sanctuary was thus instituted by narrative – this is the main, crucial axiom of the ancient and medieval law. I hope to show that the sacred place was made of words: its power was commonly agreed, and its sanctity observed as a result of shared notions about the rights of others and the relations of humans to higher powers. Any sacred site could be a refuge but those that became established, popular refuges were instituted by their particular story. The offer of sanctuary depends on magical thinking about danger, defilement, possible contagion between a person and a community; it has deep antecedents in Greek cult, for example, reflected in tragedies, where the underpinning memories and narrative give the place its powers.

Is the ancient and medieval practice of sanctuary, granting safety to a criminal or runaway in any way a principle that could be reconfigured for our times? Can this tradition contribute to defining the claims of nation and home, of state and citizen: declaring, this is the kind of place we live in? Or does this right belong firmly to another era? And if sanctuary is taken as a way of thinking about home, about being at home in a society, how do I make such a place, where I am not out of place? How can I find a home in the world when home has been taken from me? How does I hold on to home when it has been destroyed? How to find a way of dwelling when the habitation itself exists no longer? When the place itself has been denatured from the one you knew and lived in? How does one regain the lost place . . . *le lieu perdu*, not *le temps perdu* of Proust's title (although time always plays a part in the idea of place).

Civil wars, foreign invasions, flight from strife, famine, flood, drought and plague, the search for work, fulfilment and safety are causing mass upheavals. Migration is the defining phenomenon of our era, and the fear of migrants is becoming ever more acutely the crux of politics, although at least one scholar disputes the numbers that warrant the fear of 'invasion' and swarms. The Anthropocene is the time of the wanderer, the unhomed, the fugitive and the aspiring emigrant, the jobseeker. Some of the men and women on the move are individual dissidents; many more are the victims of conflict, racial stigmatization, social and religious intolerance, conscription into the militia of warring factions, and climate change. Many are also looking for a new life, ambitious to better their lot: as Wendy Brown has pointed out, national sovereignty collides with globalization of capital, opportunity and skills. Migrants are portrayed as 'tempest-tost', 'tired . . . poor . . . huddled masses', but they often come from the better-off sections of the countries they are leaving behind.

The issue of borders preoccupies thinkers in many fields, perhaps all fields, but most particularly governments and their leaders. The related questions of nation, culture and identity, in an era of profound and savage dislocations, of who or what belongs where, excites dangerous passions and inflames public discourse, deepening what Shakespeare calls 'your mountainish inhumanity'. Tensions are tightening between nativism and cosmopolitanism, nationalism and internationalism, with all their cultural reverberations. The stranger who travels to a new place seeking safety and a better life has become the major target of attacks, suspicion and a fundamental test of our polities and our humanity.

In this epoch of movement and flight, current legal and social measures are failing; the promoters of exclusionary and punitive policies (deportations, detention, clearing of unofficial camps in Calais and elsewhere, even the threat of death against border crossers) agree they are not stopping the flow of migration. According to the most recent figures from the United Nations High Commissioner for Refugees (UNHCR) in mid-2024, the number of 'forcibly displaced' people stands at 122.6 million, of whom 37.9 million are refugees and 68.3 million are internally displaced – and this was before President Trump came back to power, vowing mass deportations of immigrant workers. These are numbers impossible to grasp. Some 'temporary' accommodation, like the Palestinian camps Jabalya and Baddawi in Lebanon, several more in Jordan and the vast sprawl of Dadaab in Kenya, has been established for so long that these shelters have become cities, provisional, under-resourced, but home to many who have been born there. Half of the refugee population has spent around five years in exile; many have been displaced for longer, some (the more fortunate ones) for shorter periods. The average length of stay is now over a decade. Individual fates vanish into the undifferentiated mass. And there is little hope that this will change in some fundamental way in the near or distant future.

The terms used to describe those who leave their homes are many, some new-minted, all ranging from hostile to quasi-neutral and carrying, in legal and political settings, various subtexts. Strangers, foreigners, aliens, exiles, émigrés, sojourners, immigrants, migrants, displaced people, stateless people, undocumented migrants, illegals (and more unrepeatable terms). Ancient Greeks used the word *xenoi*, stranger-guests, and lived by the principle of *xenia*, hospitality. 'Refugee' designates a defined category of fugitive from war and persecution. Technically, an 'asylum seeker' is a suppliant for refugee status, a sanctuary seeker, and success in this claim will lead to protection by the host state and recognition as a refugee. At the time of writing 'forced migrants' is the preferred description among NGOs and groups to describe many seeking a better life. I prefer the little-used term 'arrivant', because it is a statement of what has happened: the person has arrived; they are with us. I came across it in Edward Kamau Brathwaite's magnum opus *The Arrivants*, a poetic trilogy that dramatizes the experience of the people who, like himself, left the Caribbean for the UK or the US after the Second World War. It implies an impetus and a spirit that does not reflect the tragic disruption of many of those displaced under duress, and for those I prefer the old term 'refugee'. The singular form of these labels helps lessen the sense of mass threat, and shapes a new, necessary structure of feeling.

The dislocations today take place near and far; many are internally displaced, living across the border of their home country in a neighbouring one. Other migrations travel over extended distances and bring about encounters between people who see one another as very different, indeed as alien: most arrivants landing on the coast of Italy having crossed the Mediterranean are young men from many different countries and languages in Asia and Africa, who have come a vast distance; they cannot melt invisibly into the crowd. The identity of the original countries of those crossing the Channel in 'small boats' changes – in 2024 Afghanistan, Iran, Syria, Eritrea and Vietnam, countries which, with the possible exception of Vietnam, are recognizably suffering from violent repression.

The majority of those who arrive in the UK will be allowed to stay: in the year ending September 2023, some 75 per cent of those seeking asylum were approved. Their continued presence arouses hostility expressed openly by some political leaders and exclusionary campaigners, who have inflamed antagonism (in the summer of 2024 in Britain, violent attacks took place against mosques and hotels where asylum seekers are housed). In terms of political approaches, the present walls and barricades against border crossers and 'small boats' waste the energies of all concerned, and rather than defeating the criminal gangs are furthering their interests, rendering sanctuary seekers vulnerable to their schemes. The numbers entering Europe are reported in lurid terms, though experts in the field explain soberly that from a historical perspective they compare favourably with major exoduses in the past. The provisions for Hong Kong nationals in 2020 and for Ukrainians in 2022 present models for an alternative to 'the hostile environment'. More legal channels for immigration need to be established; more consular offices, more efficient processing. But *Sanctuary* is not about government policy, in the UK or elsewhere. It is an attempt to identify principles that in the past underpinned ideas of a refuge and a home and could perhaps be adapted to do so today.

In this era of turmoil, a new concept of coexistence is urgently needed, which takes shape along distinctive lines, neither assimilation nor multiculturalism.

In the opening chapter, I explore, in a brief overview, the sanctuary given to fugitives in ancient Greece, and subsequently in Anglo-Saxon and medieval Britain until the Reformation, when the law was abolished, though it continued in forms that shape the present-day revivals as Universities or Cities of Sanctuary. In Chapters 2 to 6 I examine variations of effective sanctuary and the principles on which it succeeded or failed. My five case studies include, first, the Flight into Egypt (Chapter 2, 'Traces'), in which I explore the way the landscape was mapped according to the stories about the infant Jesus' experiences as a refugee from Herod, as told in many early versions, Greek, Latin, Syriac, Arabic and Ethiopic. They offer a prime example of the literature of astonishment, the genre Arabic scholars term *aja'ib*, which would include travellers' tales, folklore, fairy tale and fables, as well as, generally, *Wundermärchen* or Wonder Tales. The imprint of the legends about Jesus' presence on topography throughout southern Palestine, the Sinai desert and the Nile valley in Egypt exemplifies how a fantasy narrative can be realized, graven in rock and stone, announcing it happened here to people like ourselves. I invoke the examples of the pilgrimages in the Nile valley, to places – a cave, a spring, a tree – associated with Mary and Jesus' sojourn there during their three years' wandering while they were eluding Herod's bloodthirsty designs. Both Muslims and Christians worship at some of the same shrines, offering an example of a story – the Holy Family's stay in Egypt – that has laid out a patch or rather a meander through common ground.

In Chapter 3, 'Relics', I focus on the empress Helena and the Finding of the True Cross, splinters of which were dispersed across the empire to found sanctuaries. Material relics hallow a place; embedded in the fabric, often in the main altar, they make and define the sacred precinct. According to her richly circumstantial legend, Helena, the mother of the emperor Constantine, played a crucial role in inspiring the Edict of Milan of 313 which recognized freedom of worship, including Christianity; this decision paved the way to Theodosius later declaring, in 380, that Christianity was now the official religion of the Roman empire. According to this story, Helena had distributed the precious relics of the Cross the length and breadth of Christendom, thereby sanctifying multiple sites and profoundly transforming and Christianizing their function. This early form of networking spread and unified the faithful, as Piero della Francesca captures in his vast fresco cycle in the Cappella Maggiore of San Francesco in Arezzo. Diasporic dissemination of the wooden fragments spread the new creed through material remains to the four corners of the empire, rendering foreign parts familiar, weaving them into one story. Islamic devotions also focus on relics and relics *in situ*, though the temperature of Muslim ardour in this matter rises and falls, and popular practices and beliefs in holy sites are often censured by contemporary religious authorities.

In Chapter 4, 'Dust', I continue with the theme of bonding through suffusing imagined traces with potent meaning, but here I turn to the literal transportation of a whole home, the Santa Casa, or Holy House, where the Virgin Mary received the angel Gabriel and learned she was to become the mother of the Saviour. When travelling in the region of Palestine and neighbouring territory became more dangerous and even prohibited, on account of the ferocious hostilities between the Ottomans and Western, Christian nations, this dwelling was carried off by angels and deposited, eventually, in Loreto on the Adriatic coast in Italy.

Chapter 5, 'Bonds', takes me to my argument for a refreshed, functioning concept of sanctuary gained through imagination and the heritage of story. After examining the importance of being connected materially, through relics and mementoes, I shift the emphasis from regaining the lost place, the forsaken home, to make the case for storytelling as the binding agent between hosts and guests, incomers and residents, between strangers, and as the place where concepts of justice and *convivencia* or coexistence can be explored and developed. I revisit the famous story of Dido, who, herself a refugee – from the eastern Mediterranean – became Queen of Carthage and then gave an open-hearted welcome to Aeneas, a Trojan, in flight from the burning of his city. Troy enters my story of sanctuary and will return as a metaphor of the lost home throughout this book. Troy is the salient example of a home of the mind: few of us are Trojans, and even if we have visited Pergamon, the postulated archaeological site of the ancient city, this is not the place that burns in our minds when we hear the word 'Troy'. Troy has become a meme, a motif which scores of writers, artists, composers and cineastes have taken up as a dwelling of the mind.

In Chapter 6, 'Tales', the last in Part Two, Turandot becomes the fifth and final case study. She is a stock character in fairy tale, a riddle princess, who is eventually defeated by her prince; she has long exercised fascination for playwrights and librettists, and Puccini's treatment, left unfinished by the composer at this death in 1924, has become a dependable, popular attraction worldwide. The tale of *Turandot* is a travelling tale (Edward Said's term); it has migrated across many borders of languages and cultures, shape-shifting as to its meanings all the way. In early twentieth-century Italy it inspired a blockbuster grand opera with at its heart an aria, 'Nessun dorma' (Let no one sleep), which became a global hit when Luciano Pavarotti gave voice to it as the anthem of the 1990 football World Cup. I have chosen it for my final case study because I watched it performed in the very grand opera house in Kyiv, Ukraine, to a rapturous auditorium in which everyone there knew the arias well. This was in 2005, long before the Russian invasion in 2022, and I was struck by the opera's huge popularity with the local audience. It does not represent the rich and varied Ukrainian musical scene, especially since their country's citizens are fighting for its survival, but the story of *Turandot*'s many transformations does encapsulate the migratory and labile character of fantastic literature and its border-crossing capacities.

In Part Three, 'The Shelter of Stories', which closes the book, I continue to look at contemporary possibilities and practices of sanctuary, the ways of telling that might help build ways of dwelling, and inspire feelings of being at home in the world. 'In No Man's Land' (Chapter 7) explores the deep engagement of stories with constituting subjectivity and the long tradition of testimony in the depositions and the memoirs of migrants, arrivants, displaced people, refugees. I discuss the current emphasis on first-person witness and argue that it narrows what storytelling can achieve, limiting individual expressiveness, imprisoning the speaker/writer/witness in a unitary identity, anchored in retrospection, and failing to stimulate relations between people whom happenstance has thrown together. 'Lived experience' has become in many quarters a guarantee of value, of truth-telling and ethics, but I wish to invoke the literature of imagination, which makes space for freedom of movement, for dwelling in fantastic, speculative, hypothetical territory. Grammarians have a term – 'irrealis' – for a mood that describes things that have not happened but might happen; it is expressed chiefly in the subjunctive and conditional tenses. I want to modify this adjective into a noun, 'irreality', to differentiate a distinctive form of presence, different from the unreal or unreality, the surreal or, indeed, reality, and nuance differences in representations of experience.

The stories that institute sanctuary involve, alongside image magic, relics and mementoes, psycho-geographical mappings. In Chapter 8, 'The Map Is Not the Territory', I explore the potential of topography, literally the writing of place or, in other words, the stories inscribed in earth. 'In the Country of Words' (Chapter 9) turns to an alternative literature, less anchored in the first person and in lived experience. Can the folk and fantasy traditions worldwide – myths, legends, ballads, poems and all kinds of fictive stories or irrealities – provide alternative shelter, sites of memory, where an outcast, exile, refugee, migrant or wanderer might feel at home? Finally, in the Coda, I conclude with the work of Stories in Transit, a project in Palermo, Sicily which began in 2016, and represents a small local attempt to tell stories and foster *convivencia* and a sense of belonging.

One of the first testimonies to strike me to the heart about what was happening in the Mediterranean was the artist Isaac Julien's film *The Leopard* (2007). He filmed in Sicily, in Palermo and Lampedusa, combining a documentary record of the crossings with staged imaginary scenes of the experiences of those who made the voyage. A decade later he developed the material into *Western Union: Small Boats* (2017), a yet more intense and impassioned meditation on the fate of arrivants. He intercut dramatic re-enactments of bodies lying on the salt-baked blanched rocks of the islands, with sequences shot in the baroque grandeur of a local palace, Palazzo Valguarnera-Gangi, where Visconti had set the ballroom scene in his epic film of Giuseppe Tomasi di Lampedusa's novel *The Leopard*; Julien tracks his protagonist, his silent alter ego, a female figure, tall, black, shaven-headed, elegant, as she sweeps up flights of marble stairs and through galleries lustrous with candelabra and mirrors. The contrast with the pitiless landscape, the splintered boats, the shipwrecked arrivants, is violent. The work records events and is also unsettlingly prophetic. It awakened me then to the dangers of the sea crossings and the extremity of need. Sicily's contrasts between ancient splendour and contemporary misery vividly represent the disparity between the moneyed old world, our continuing comparative wealth and comforts, and the destitution that so many suffer around the world.

Since then, the situation in Italy has become numbingly familiar and interventions from artists frequent, sometimes deeply troubling ethically, not least the case of *Barca Nostra*, a boat in which in 2016, around 800 migrants died after a Portuguese fishing boat, attempting to rescue the passengers from sinking, accidentally rammed it. The wreck was exhibited by the Swiss artist Christoph Büchel on the quayside as an exhibit of the Venice Biennale in 2019, causing a furore over the tastelessness of setting up a death ship near elegant cafés where the urbane crowd of art lovers took refreshments. The artist and the curator defended themselves: the hulk was a relic that bore witness to the 'liquid cemetery' that the Mediterranean has become. I take a lesson from this example: displaying evidence on behalf of the sufferers may be well intentioned and have a certain effect on opinion, but those who have themselves undergone the ordeals must be heard.

Some of the ideas that have arisen in the course of my exploring the practice of sanctuary fed into the workshops and performances which, with many colleagues there and elsewhere, we organized in Palermo. The project Stories in Transit is carrying on – though the work was severely interrupted and nearly suspended during the pandemic. The participants, principally young men and a few women who have crossed the Mediterranean to reach Europe, with a few local teenagers who have been lost in the system, met with visiting musicians, artists and writers from London and other places in storytelling workshops. I describe the work they have made and are making and argue that collective stories, mixing experience, memories and traditional tales with freewheeling fantasy, can help tell it true more richly than the personal depositions required by the gatekeepers of Europe's borders, and build a sense of home, of arrival and presence, of being in place.

These stories draw on the experience of the participants, to show

how, inspired by the cultures those fleeing are carrying with them, they can help overcome barriers of language and custom and difference and develop a place of refuge where the narrators feel they belong. I address the question of imagination's role in creating threads which may be woven into the fabric of belonging. If literature and its many vehicles, on stage, screen, airwaves, are to come alive as sites of exchange, where thoughts and ideas and feelings can build a common ground, the material needs to make geographical and linguistic journeys, migrate and cross-pollinate.

As a cultural historian, I've explored the imagery of belief systems and have long been aware of the fluidity and malleability of stories, and of their character as ideological vehicles. Attitudes to newly arrived strangers, ranging from welcomes to rejections, are always rooted in certain social and historical values, and these aren't stable: ideas of who to accept and who to exclude depend above all on a shared sense of place and history. 'Stories are a form of action,' wrote Hannah Arendt, 'the way we insert ourselves into the human world . . . the ability to produce stories is the way we become historical.'

The history of the practice of sanctuary has been lucidly and valuably drawn up by classicists, medievalists and legal scholars, to whom I am indebted. I am setting out instead to explore the principles on which sanctuary was founded, with the aim of finding ways of readopting *xenia*, hospitality for the arrivant, the stranger-guest. The classical and medieval laws were rooted in a common agreement about sacred, inviolable personhood and offered a valuable respite from violence and expulsion.

Works of literature and art are vitally involved in these processes of consecration and desecration of a certain place and establishing cultural memory. Through the vicissitudes in the lives of mythic and dramatic protagonists, the reader/audience can trace the contours of a larger picture about changing common values and the bonds between individuals and society. Words build the common ground, and they are mostly being harnessed to do their worst, but it need not be so.

Offering narrative as a prime resource for resistance to oppression and resilience in adversity and exile inevitably raises the acute problem that stories – literature, fiction, poetry – have been and are used to entrench dominant ideologies. Those of us who are critics of nationalist ideology, instrumentalized heritage and archaeology may feel compunction about opposing regime lies with fantasy and storytelling; false consciousness should be opposed by criticism founded in truth. But there are long-honoured poetic, imagistic, symbolic ways of speaking truth to power, of tapping the inventive energies of imagination as well as disclosing the facts (as the most assiduous disinformers claim). Audre Lorde's aphorism 'The master's tools will never dismantle the master's house' doesn't necessitate an end to making words work for greater empathy and justice, for language to build a different commons of the social imaginary and new 'integrative realities' in the phrase of Edward Said, 'Merely to urge students to insist on one's own identity, history, tradition, uniqueness', he writes,

> may initially get them to name their basic requirements for a democracy and for the right to an assured, decently humane existence, but we need to go on and to situate these in a geography of other identities, peoples, cultures, and then to study how, despite their differences, they have always overlapped one another, through unhierarchical influence, crossing, incorporation, recollection, deliberate forgetfulness, and of course, conflict ... The fact is, we are mixed up with one another in ways that most national systems of education have not dreamed of. To match knowledge in the arts and sciences with these integrative realities is, I believe, the intellectual and cultural challenge of the moment.

A quest for ways in which such integrative realities have been fashioned lies at the heart of understanding sanctuary in its deepest sense, not only as a sacred site, but as a principal building block of a viable, humane society.

The stories that institute sanctuary involve image magic, relics, mementoes and psycho-geographical mappings, topography, literally the writing of place. Some of the symbolic processes that make a sanctuary or regain a home belong to the language of consecration or *hallowing*, as mentioned before and as the root of the word 'sanctuary' reveals, and those processes – which can be secular representations and re-enactments as well as religious rituals – are multifarious in history and different societies' practices. Making literature plays a crucial part in this process of establishing sanctuary: the cartographies of longing across place are as much a part of storytelling as the chronicle through time. Rediscovering history also figures crucially in this process of generating symbols and establishing sanctuary. But mapping common ground does not always draw on history or claim to do so, as religious sites do (and when they are denounced as false the ecclesiastical authorities, both Christian and other, often destroy them). Nor do they need to be old, authenticated by individuals from long tradition. They can be efficacious as sanctuaries also when they are fabricated, which is where the work of imagination – and imaginative artefacts – play such a part in ways of dwelling. And in conditions of dislocation, stories grow more urgently.

The implications of this perspective led me to think of a commons of wonder, filled with stories of possibilities, secondary worlds, speculation, irrealities. Can a memory of literature and the process of making it over and over again build a country of words? Can literature – especially imaginative works of myth, legend, fairy tale and fable – map geographies of home on to surroundings that are not home? Can a story provide shelter? Is there such a thing as a haven of the mind? Is it possible to narrate a place of belonging without a nation? For native citizens and strangers to be united by a story held in common?

Humanism has been much criticized recently, for collusion with colonialism and many other injustices, but the idea that a cultural artefact, such as a fairy tale or animal fable, is available for anyone and everyone to reshape and retell extends humanism beyond its classical antique and European territory; this approach moves it towards embracing a different future, rooted not in past learning but in a desire for ways to use what is there to remake what is to come. Artefacts created by the power of the imagination can communicate, I believe, more deeply and more broadly than the finest scholarly criticism; the main arena of struggle is fantasy, fantasy taken broadly speaking to embrace supernatural narratives, from scripture and hagiography to fairy tales, forms of storytelling that flourish in popular milieux, among less valued elements of society, often subject to condescension and mockery from their own clergy and prelates.

The rise of nationalist cultural propaganda presents a danger to us all, a sclerosis of imagination. Leaders in Europe are asserting ethnic particularity – of Hungarian or Italian art or literature, of Britishness in post-Brexit Britain; they invoke history and religious adherence as the ground of that ethnic culture, and oppose 'strangers' on the grounds of faith differences. Giorgia Meloni stresses the purity of Catholic Italy, for example, where Matteo Salvini rattles his rosary in public. But this is only one perspective, one way of telling the story of that place.

I should perhaps clarify my own relations to belief: I was brought up a Catholic and was a passionate believer till the age of seventeen and have since then used historical and deconstructionist enquiry to understand the mythopolitics which still pervades contemporary experience (think only of the mass response to the death of Queen Elizabeth II); the mysteries of the Christian faith seem to me as non-rational as other, so-called primitive, faiths. But this position no longer leads me to want to demolish them with reason or attempt to strip away illusion through analysis and argument. Human thought processes are necessarily and inextricably bound up with imagination, and this will lead to fantastic products (even Isaac Newton, for all his supreme intelligence, pursued with unappeasable passion studies in astrology and alchemy). Furthermore, rational argument has been used to justify the worst moral catastrophes (enslavement, genocide). So I now want to raise alternative stories – reinscribing old ones and diverting their course. Myths are stories held in common, and as such they exercise a powerful hold on our minds, providing existing structure to experience retrospectively but also generating meanings out of the past which then translate into patterns of action for the future. Is it frivolous, hypocritical, mere conscience-salving and futile to ask what can culture do? If literature, in its broadest sense, can make a difference? History and historiography are key to the work of literature in this area. We can argue perhaps about the interactions of research, verification, interpretation and imagination. But the main endeavour is storytelling: *la storia*, narrative in all its forms.

'Telling a story is deploying an imaginary space for thought experiments', Paul Ricoeur writes (what he says is worth repeating), 'in which moral judgement operates in a hypothetical mode.' Myths and the related corpus of folk and fairy tales are stories held in common, protean and ancient – though there are new variations generated all the time and they pose vital questions about the central aspects of existence and offer different angles of view. Stories are not only records, but also thought experiments, providing vehicles for personal invention and witness.

Human beings respond imaginatively to the perplexities of reality; as a storytelling species we're deprived if the stories are swept away, however much what is called *reason* resists the snares of myth; secondly – and this is more important – the lessons of history, and especially of twentieth- and twenty-first-century history, are that myth is always being made and remade to serve the interests of a group. Stories can also peddle lies alongside truth; they can express the most yearning ideals of the utopian imagination and entrench the most obscurantist righteous bigotry. We live in the stories we pass on and the stories we invent and in the way they report on experience. One of the territories that needs to be reoccupied is narrative.

When the poet Denise Riley in her recent collection *Lurex* looks back in one of the poems at the saints and martyrs of her childhood, she puts the question I have quoted as an epigraph to the book: 'What hope is there of a purely secular grace?' She sounds despairing, but also yearning. I share these mixed feelings, but – if we are ever to find a purely secular grace – borrowing from long-serving ways of hallowing developed by religious practices might help reveal ways of being at home in the world. Ways of telling shape ways of dwelling alongside one another. How stories made sanctuary, how sanctuaries became effective, what purposes they met and how they can be regained and refashioned, these are some of the questions this book sets out to explore.

# Part One:
# A Kind of Freedom

Shall we desire to raze the sanctuary,
And pitch our evils there? O, fie, fie, fie!

Shakespeare

The Frid Stol or 'Peace Seat', Sprotbrough Church, Yorkshire, *c.* 1100.

# I

# Laws:
# A Brief History of Sanctuary

> Mightier than a tower is an altar, an unbreakable shield.
> Aeschylus

## In Ancient Greece

In *Oedipus at Colonus*, Sophocles' third play in the Oedipus cycle, we see the tragic hero enter, an outcast and a fugitive, his empty eye sockets streaming blood; he is leaning on his daughter Antigone, and they arrive in an unknown place, a clearing; she recognizes that it's a sanctuary, from its seclusion and peacefulness, from the laurel, olive trees and vines flourishing there, and from the many songbirds giving voice, and she helps her father to sit down on a ledge of 'unchiselled rock'.

Oedipus has been thrown out of Thebes where he once ruled, after his parricide and incestuous marriage have been revealed; in this play he insists he committed them all unwittingly – contrary to his acknowledgement of his guilt in the conclusion of *Oedipus Rex*. Oedipus is not carrying the ritual signs of a supplicant, such as branches with white wool, and when a local 'Man of Colonus' approaches he orders him to 'get up from this seat': 'you're on a place where it's not pure to tread.' A harsh exchange follows; Oedipus stubbornly stays put. He's warned that the ground is consecrated to 'fearsome goddesses, / the daughters of the Earth and Dark', and he then recognizes the grove as the place where, according to the prophecy of Apollo, his *katabasis* or descent and final end will come about. When the Athenian chorus arrives, they yield to his supplications and declare,

> No one shall remove you
> From this place of refuge,
> Not if you refuse it.

Only after this reprieve does Oedipus reveal who he is, and he is then allowed to stay – given leave to remain, as official permission now puts it – yet he must perform a carefully structured ritual to the dread goddesses of the underworld to expiate his treading on their sacred ground. Then Theseus, the ruler of Athens, arrives to meet the mysterious stranger; Oedipus tells him who he is, and Theseus acknowledges him and grants him sanctuary. In this holy place, Oedipus will be safe from seizure and, ultimately, transfigured and purified of his sins.

This tragedy evokes several features of the law of sanctuary that persist, in spite of the very different circumstances that face refugees in the present day: first, the place of sanctuary does not require defending by visible, fixed boundaries; it may be a special part of a place, a *temenos* consecrated to a deity ('land marked off and set apart as sacred', according to the Homeric dictionary); its boundary will have been instituted by ritual, by libations, to mark it out as divine property. It may also be a clump of trees, a knoll, the source of a river, established by belief, custom and consensus. Secondly, the precincts are holy, forbidden to all; to enter them, as Oedipus does, is to trespass and profane them, yet they possess real power to lift pollution and cleanse a supplicant.

A sanctuary offered protection to irregular elements, to marginal, outcast fugitives and criminals, and to a 'stranger-guest' (*xenos*), as the Chorus calls Oedipus. The Bible offers an analogous process for fugitives who, like Oedipus, have committed a crime unwittingly. In the Book of Numbers (35:11–28), five Cities of Refuge are described, founded to offer safety to perpetrators; in these examples, murderers who have killed someone unintentionally, and were consequently being pursued in a quest for vengeance according to the law of blood feuds that obtained, are the specific subjects of the reprieve. Later mentions in the Bible enlarge the number of cities and modify the terms of eligibility and potential exclusion (Joshua 20: 7; Deuteronomy 4: 41–3, 19:2–13). The emphasis, however, in Judaic law fell on atonement, rather than protection, on cleansing after pollution, and it doesn't match contemporary ethical arguments for extending a welcome to arrivants today, who have not committed a crime except the attempt to move across borders and seek asylum.

Oedipus is looking for a place where he will be freed from the actions that have made him a pariah; in his case this reprieve will coincide, in Sophocles' play, with his numinous disappearance, a kind of vaporizing or assumption into the next world rather than a mortal death that lays him in the earth. Oedipus in fact shows no contrition, whereas in medieval times this was required, while today's asylum seekers also need to present themselves as victims of their circumstances, and they have a stronger case if they can prove they have fled a country which has been declared a failed state. Later in the play, Sophocles puts the scope of sanctuary under strain, dramatizing how Creon acts blasphemously when he moves to seize Oedipus in spite of the divine protection he has sought from the Dark Ones, the goddesses of the underworld – to which the Chorus has agreed. Polynices, Oedipus' son, also later petitions to be treated as a suppliant: 'Look, I'm a beggar and a foreigner, the same as you . . .' he pleads, but his father (who, having the same mother, is also his brother) rejects his pleas and curses him in blazing, unforgiving fury. Oedipus' vengeful rejection of his son, because Polynices had once, with his brother Eteocles, assumed the throne of Thebes and driven Oedipus out of Thebes, reveals an under-recognized aspect of sanctuary that is crucial to its working: its effectiveness depends on the consent of all involved. In Polynices' case, Oedipus' refusal prevents the younger man's immunity:

> And so these curses overbid this suppliancy of yours
> and all your thrones of power,
> if venerable Justice takes her seat
> alongside Zeus according to the ways of old.
> And so to hell with you, spat out by me,
> defathered, lowest of the low.

The pitilessness of this father's curse on his child may seem excessive, or at least may strike the viewer/reader as startlingly contrary to natural feelings and excite in us wistful thoughts of a different, less implacable idea of justice. But in the present book about sanctuary my interest doesn't attach to these specific moral and psychological dilemmas, involving as they are, but focuses rather on the nature of the sacred and the limits of its reach, as the actions of Oedipus in this play reveal. Sanctuary commanded deep, widespread assent, but it remained conditional – higher, supernatural forces haunted it as necessary guarantors because of their power to abrogate or overlook it. In Polynices' case, an immoveable idea of justice overruled the sanctuary he asked for. But the invocation of superior ratifiers clearly depends on human agreement: the Chorus decides that Oedipus may stay in the sacred place, even before they have heard his story and he has revealed his identity, and it is Oedipus himself who turns away Polynices and does not grant him sanctuary.

Suppliants sought sacred territory to preserve themselves; they were defiled by something they had done – unknowingly, as Oedipus protests in this play, or in full consciousness, as in the case of Orestes in Aeschylus' *Oresteia*. Or they are fleeing danger. In *The Suppliants* by Aeschylus, the fifty Danaids who are pleading for sanctuary in Argos are young women who have rejected arranged marriage with their Egyptian cousins and are threatening to kill themselves if their request isn't granted. The play reflects deeply on the quandary in which their supplication places the ruler of Argos, but ultimately their rights as sanctuary seekers are upheld. In this play, the sacred site is a precinct set with statues. By contrast, *Oedipus at Colonus* throws into heightened relief the enchanted character of a sanctuary site, with no evident markers, no cult image to identify the place.

The Acropolis of Athens itself gave shelter to fugitives: in the seventh century BCE, a champion athlete called Cylon led an uprising against the tyrant of Athens, his father-in-law, but fled to the temple of Athena and claimed sanctuary by the statue of the goddess. During the siege that ensued, Cylon escaped, but his men began to suffer from hunger and thirst. They negotiated an agreement and were promised safe conduct to their trial, but were stoned to death, except for two who escaped. One account of this rebellion adds the detail that the rebels tied themselves with a rope to the goddess, but it broke – signifying to their opponents that she had withdrawn her protection. The reprisal violated the law of sanctuary and brought down a curse on the killers, a miasma or stain which would be transmitted down the generations.

## Laws: A Brief History of Sanctuary

Cassandra, a daughter of King Priam and a priestess
of Apollo, tries to escape Ajax the Locrian.

The sense that breaching sanctuary was a greater crime than insurrection also resonates throughout the story of the Trojan war. When the Greek warrior Ajax the Lokrian assaults Cassandra, daughter of Priam, she flees to the statue of the goddess, but he seizes her regardless and rapes her. In the scheme of the Trojan war this crime presents a diptych with Paris' abduction of Helen; it recurs depicted on pots, some showing the Trojan princess naked, one arm flung around the protective body of the goddess's cult statue, the palladium (protector) of Troy. When Ajax the Lokrian attacks her, a suppliant, in the goddess's shrine, he commits a double violation – of her person and of the holiness of sanctuary. The assault, described in Euripides' *Trojan Women* and in Lykophron's poem *Alexandra* (Cassandra's other name), was a sacrilege for which the Greeks were to be punished by many long or abortive homecomings. Cassandra's attacker was to die at sea far from his native land, others would never reach theirs either, and Odysseus, as we know, was to wander through ten more years of shipwreck and other adventures.

The classical historian Robert Garland, in his book *Wandering Greeks*, argues that much evidence shows that the laws of sanctuary were commonly flouted. Yet their very existence, the sanctity and safety they promise, the outrage that followed a breach and the consequent dread of retribution, of divine anger (as seen in the case of the Trojan war), convey an attitude to strangers and to personal integrity that is intrinsically ethical and therefore valuable. Kindness to strangers continued to be enshrined in the ethos of Rome: the first metamorphosis in Ovid's great poem punished Lykaon, after he killed, cooked and served up a prisoner in his care to Zeus disguised as a passing stranger. For this double crime — killing a hostage and defiling a guest — Lykaon is changed into a werewolf.

The Man of Colonus tells Oedipus that the whole area around the grove is sacred to Poseidon and to the Titan Prometheus as well as to their local hero, a man called Colonus. The structure of sanctuary often depends on several superior forces, who must agree to sustain the fugitive's safety. Sophocles will have had in mind Aeschylus' *Oresteia*, in which Orestes, after he has murdered his mother Clytemnestra, goes to Delphi and the oracle of Apollo to seek purification from his crime: in this third play of the trilogy Orestes is an outcast like Oedipus, though in Orestes' case his mother has not killed herself, as Jocasta does after her incestuous marriage to Oedipus has been discovered, but rather has been murdered by her son. Orestes is also a suppliant, polluted and damned, pursued by the Furies. In *Les Mouches*, Jean-Paul Sartre revisited the myth and dramatized the Furies as furious bluebottles stinging like horseflies; for the memorable production at the National Theatre, in which all the actors wore uncanny masks designed in the ancient Greek style by Jocelyn Herbert, the Furies were costumed as monstrous and bloody tatterdemalions, menstrual and feminist nightmares from the bowels of the earth (as in Ted Hughes's image of the goddess in Shakespeare's *Venus and Adonis* as 'a sort of uterus on the loose'). They are bent on harrying Orestes and bringing him to justice for the ultimate crime of matricide. He is seeking refuge from their tormenting in Delphi, where the god Apollo sends him to Athens to face judgement; there, at the close of a prolonged trial, Athena makes the final pronouncement that clears Orestes of his guilt. Such a pyramid of supernatural forces recurs in the operation of sanctuary: the law is always controversial, with different parties struggling over the fate of the miscreant, the fugitive seeking safety.

In *Oedipus at Colonus*, Oedipus invokes 'the sweet daughters of the dark', the divinities of the sacred place. He's echoing the euphemism that characterizes them as the Eumenides, the kindly ones, when these chthonic forces are more properly called the Erinyes, or Furies. There were three of them in Greek myth, causing some blurring with the three Fates, or Parcae, who spin and wind and cut the thread of life, and who, unlike the Furies, have individual names: Clotho, Lachesis and Atropos. An air – a miasma? – of ancientness hangs about both the Furies and the Fates; they figure as primeval, existing before the rise of the Olympians, buried deep in time as they are imagined dwelling in the depths of the earth: the rocky seat 'the bronze-stepped threshold', the stone where Oedipus takes his seat, may indicate an entrance to the underworld.

The right to sanctuary beams out such a connection to antiquity, which can represent a state that has always been and will always be, and the sites themselves consequently tap into the most material symbol of that long reach into time: the heart rock of the earth, the ore deep below the surface, a site of awe and terror, saturated in the ambiguity of the sacred.

The Greek myths' ideas about individual responsibility and free will differ from ours and have done so over a very long period, and religious concepts of pollution no longer command belief. However, it seems to me that certain elements of their vision are exercising a renewed imaginative hold: the audience for Greek tragedy is strong, as shown by the frequency of new productions of the *Oresteia*, *Medea*, *The Trojan Women* and many others; a case could be made that drama, taken at its fullest extent to include installation and performance as well as dance, opera and pantomime – still meets the Greek conditions of a shared ritual and, in consequence, retains that ritual purpose.

Images of drowned bodies on the shores of Italy, Turkey and Spain bring home the actuality of what is happening and stir pity more powerfully than statistics or political discussion because a drowned child is a tragedy. But the many dead in the liquid cemetery of the Mediterranean are also an atrocity, and a reproach to the community to which I belong. Not for an individual act I might have committed – though a chain of my own actions over my lifetime may have contributed to the situation.

But rather these deaths pollute me, as does building high walls and unrolling kilometres of barbed, concertina and razor wire along national frontiers against border crossers and even suggesting that anyone attempting to enter Europe should be met with force (gunboats in the Channel?). Anxieties about national sovereignty have always run through attitudes to race and immigration and have been horrifically amplified in the slogans of Trump and his followers. But rejection is no more effective a remedy than it is for a transplanted heart.

Sanctuary is the balm, acceptance the path to recovery and health. Not only for the seeker but for the host, too. As the suppliant enjoyed his or her indemnity, the community which allows it, safeguards it and continues its efficacy is also strengthened.

## Sacred Spaces

Rocks recur as indices of especially holy places: the Dome of the Rock is one of the most venerated sanctuaries in the world, and centres on a great slab of almost featureless stone, from which the Prophet Muhammad, during his Miraj or miraculous flight to paradise, rode upwards on the mare called Buraq which had, according to some legends, the face of a beautiful woman (see Plate 1a). The Via Crucis in Jerusalem, which tracks the last days of Jesus from his torments to his Crucifixion, burial, to eventual resurrection and ascent into heaven, is marked by many natural rocks of varying sizes: for example, in the centre of the chapel of the Ascension, on the ground, lies a stone with two parallel depressions, identified as the imprints of Jesus' feet before he rose to heaven.

Rock is a natural symbol, in Mary Douglas's terms, expressing human relation to time and space, to origins and, it is imagined, to ultimate destiny, and sanctuaries are confirmed by its presence, sometimes unadorned but sometimes hewn into stone altars in which a precious relic is embedded or beneath which a saint's body or body parts lie buried. Pilgrim ways, often staked out by stone landmarks from one shrine to another, retrace a journey in the past and unfold a distant story as they recreate the geography where the events took place. Relics are portable memories and pilgrim stations a form of mobile storytelling.

Santa Rosalia's grotto on Monte Pellegrino became a site of fervent local devotion ever since her remains were discovered there in 1625.

There are material reasons for this investment of significance in mere stone: it is durable, it is almost impervious to corruption (unlike living things), it signifies deep time – hence too its popular use in official contemporary institutions, in grand hotels and in banks.

After a sacrilege or natural disaster has occurred in a certain place, a temple or shrine may be founded there, to expiate the wrongdoing and purify the community, to appeal to the powers responsible to avert such dangers in the future, to lift a plague or to prevent another polluting catastrophe. A major shrine, such as the white marble basilica of Santa Maria della Salute which dominates the vista of the Grand Canal from San Marco, was built in thanksgiving for the end of the plague in Venice in 1631, as its name conveys: St Mary of Health. But it is also in effect a memorial to that horror, raising symbols of purity – the Virgin Mary, the gleaming and precious fabric of the ostentatious baroque church – against the memory of the disease that ravaged the city, and spending lavishly to secure the divine other's continuing protection. The icon on the high altar was attributed to St Luke and was brought to Venice from the cathedral in Candia (today's Heraklion) in Crete by the Venetian forces' general, Francesco Morosini, when he was forced to surrender to the Ottomans in 1669 after a long and pitiless siege. She is a Black Madonna, a Byzantine work of the twelfth century, and her story corresponds closely with that of the statue of Athena, the palladium of Troy which Odysseus and Diomedes carry out of the besieged city. In Palermo the cult of Santa Rosalia, the city's patron saint since medieval times, intensified sharply when, during the plague that raged through the city in the 1620s, her remains were miraculously located in a grotto on Monte Pellegrino, where she had retired from the world to repent and to pray. The discovery and the subsequent memorials, processions and prayers were credited with lifting the plague; the 25-year-old Anthony van Dyck, in the city to paint a portrait of the Spanish viceroy and other grandees, found himself locked down for several months from 1624 to 1625. He kept busy: his visit coinciding – as if by a miracle – with the providential discovery of her relics, he painted several votive pictures of Santa Rosalia and defined this little-known saint's iconography – long blonde hair and rosy lips and complexion and rose-wreathed forehead (a Flemish beauty), to echo her name. He also worked on a luxuriously coloured and turbulent cycle of religious scenes for the Oratorio del Rosario di San Domenico, one of several such small shrines in the city that are uniquely and richly ornamented by baroque white stucco reliefs framing glowing oil paintings (see Plates 2 and 3). These oratories were usually paid for by confraternities rather than clergy and they belonged to the neighbourhood, which organized feasts, pageants, processions and rituals that, like the recital of the rosary, are not purely sacramental. The Festino della Santuzza (the little feast of the little saint) is still the most popular event in the Palermo calendar, and during the pandemic of Covid-19, Santa Rosalia's relics were again carried through the streets of the city to entreat her to help and to thank her for doing so. Such activities can be performed without a priest (though priests are usually present): the oratories are civic and popular, their celebrations closer to carnival than to the Mass. Many of them are now mostly tourist attractions and have been wonderfully restored. Some still function as intermediate zones between church and home, an aspect that still matters in the contemporary character of sanctuary (see Coda).

The same syzygy of pollution and holiness is found in more modern memorials, such as another basilica, the Sacré Coeur in Montmartre in Paris. Erected by public subscription as a memorial to the disaster of the Franco-Prussian war of 1870–1, it later became identified as an expiatory monument for the impiety of the Commune. Purgation and pleas for protection motivate the making of sanctuary.

A consensus of belief, formed in assembly and accepted by community, is a necessary condition of sanctuary: when consent to the story collapses, the holiness of the sanctuary fades. The line between the outside and the inside of the sanctuary was not necessarily marked by a solid partition, a wall or a fence, though the image of a stout door and the fugitive hanging on to its knocker for dear life is graven in my mind from the film I saw as a child. This image imprinted itself on me, erroneously, it seems, for several of the knockers in question have 'no plate of any kind on which to knock; they are merely ornamental rings ... intended for the prosaic purpose of closing a heavy door', writes the Revd J. Charles Cox, in *The Sanctuaries and Sanctuary Seekers of Medieval England* (1911). But he concedes that fugitives may well have hung on to the great knocker on Durham's cathedral door, a beast's head measuring 22 inches across. All such knockers depict what Thomas Browne called Poetical Animals, imaginary monsters with no connection to Christian symbolism, archaic survivals that acted as monster guardians of the place. In his astonishing, highly wrought, metaphysical epic novel *Cuddy*, Benjamin Myers, who was brought up in Durham and still lives there, pays tribute to the power of the relics of St Cuthbert, on which rose the immense medieval cathedral exploding out of a rocky outcrop (see Plate 1b). He conjures the power of a holy place, not from a Christian believer's point of view but from his sense of deep time still alive in the present, in the stones, the art, the rituals and the astonishing labour of the workers who made the place. He evokes the old pagan magic of the Knocker and the Sanctuary it opened for the fugitive:

> There hangs on the door of Cuddy's cathedral a gimbled face most diabolical. A grimace cast in copper, it has turned a mottled green from the rain ... To some its eyeless sockets are those of the snarling Barghest that stalks the barren uplands beyond the birth of the Wear, while to some he has the mouth of Jack-in-Irons who haunts the lonely rides in chains, and to others still his is the visage of the grisly goblin Redcap or a boggart of the fields, or the troll who fell from the tower or a sin-eater or an evil wyvern trapped forever in molten metal, or the firebird that lives for five hundred years before being reborn in flames, or simply the hideous mask of all the city's sinners condemned to wander the smoking planes of hell for evermore. But to most folk it is the

Sanctuary Knocker, whose stout handle is to be rapped against the sturdy door of the most impressive building in the world while the words *Sanctuary! Sanctuary!* are yelled by those who seek it and often with the hue-and-cry mob baying at their tail.

The sanctuary of a church designates the holiest part of the building, where the altar stands and where, therefore, a saint's body or other sacred relics are often enshrined. The medieval law of sanctuary is founded on religious ideas about space that has been made sacred in this way, by the presence of a thaumaturgical power; these ideas are closely related to the concept of sacred ground in ancient Greece and Rome as well as other parts of the world. A memory of bloodshed guarantees the sacred character of a place – 'sacrifice' means to make holy, and the words for blood and blessing are related. But this profound and troubling bond at the heart of the sacred has been uncoupled – and lightened – by the use of symbolic surrogates rather than the literal killing of victims, as I shall show in discussing alternative ways of establishing sanctuaries.

The medieval law of sanctuary meant that fugitives could take refuge in certain churches and surrounding territory within specified limits, whatever the reason for their flight, as long as they were unarmed since no weapon should defile the holy space. Once sanctuary had been claimed, the felon or suspect could not be touched; it was sacrilege to break sanctuary. Anglo-Saxon and medieval fugitives could be innocent, victims of a blood feud or other interests. But guilt did not invalidate their claim to safety. However, anyone claiming sanctuary had to express remorse. The shelter of the church placed the suppliant in the role of a penitent rather than a defendant.

The offer of indemnity was not unconditional, unlike Greek sanctuary. Besides forgoing all arms, the suppliant enjoyed only a limited reprieve (often forty days) which at least allowed tempers to settle. When this truce had elapsed, the sanctuary man or woman could either choose to turn themselves over to the authorities or 'abjure the realm' and go into exile for the rest of their lives – even the death of the monarch under whose reign they had been sentenced could not set them free to return. After abjuring, they then had to walk, in bare feet with head shaved, in sackcloth and ashes, and carrying a white cross as a sign of their penance, to the port of embarkation specified by the coroner – sometimes this stood a great distance away – and there leave the country. The road to the nearest harbour was often long, and not a few sanctuary men and women may have shed their costume en route and melted into the crowd (it is not impossible that the conditions were unconsciously designed to make such evasion possible). In any case, in exile or living underground, the sanctuary seeker had escaped the thumbscrews, the gallows and the block. Faced with the choice between the law and exile, some sanctuary seekers stayed on; they became 'sanctuary men'. Benjamin Myers imagines their bleak destiny thereafter: living 'where if the locals don't get you, the loneliness shall'.

~

The French sociologist Roger Caillois made understanding the sacred in society his principal quest, and in *Les Jeux et les hommes* (1958) he explores the relationship between games, gambling, play, permission and prohibition. In any game, rules are laid down and the players agree to abide by them: this applies to sports, throwing dice, dancing, chess and other board games – and to ritual. Seeking sanctuary is clearly not play-acting, nor a sport or a pastime: it is performed in all seriousness; it is sacramental, enacted for real, not 'as if' it were real. Sanctuary works because the rules are known and obeyed by all sides taking part, as in a game of pursuit.

A children's game most of us have played when we were in the playground reveals the analogy. A game of He or Tag starts: a tree or a coat thrown over a post of a fence or a corner of the playground becomes a landmark, often called 'Home'; a magic circle drawn on the ground similarly marks out a place of refuge any of the players may run to be safe, by touching the tree or standing inside the chalk circle where the catcher who is chasing them cannot seize them. If the catcher does succeed in touching them before they reach that magic place of safety, they can cry out 'Pax!' or 'Cruces!'

During lockdown in 2020, the artist Francis Alÿs filmed children playing a chasing game on a rooftop in Hong Kong; they dash about pell-mell to escape, and a series of raised tiles offer them refuge: they take up position on one, cross their arms over their chest, and . . . become inviolable. The memory of sanctuary law shadows this child's play: the haunting scene of the medieval runaway grasping the knocker of a great shrine and crying out for sanctuary still survives in the playground (though often the chaser succeeds in taking prisoners, who in some games become catchers in their turn – a move that itself reflects some aspects of reality). Likewise, the ladder chalked on the pavement in a game of hopscotch culminates in a zone called Heaven which the player aims to reach by hopping up the rungs of the ladder without landing on any of the chalked lines. In the version I played, I had to hop all around Heaven three times and pick up the stone thrown there to complete the game and win (get to heaven!).

One category of games, defined by Caillois as 'mimicry', bears on these games of tag and hopscotch, for they might well enclose a memory of the ancient stories of sanctuary seekers and the inviolable area of the heaven or haven they are hoping to reach. It is significant that this category of approach to experience dominates many of the processes of making home and belonging that I explore in this book.

The most remarkable contemporary example of spatial enchantment is the growing Orthodox Judaic practice of an *eruv*, or corridor, to turn two separate sites into one, by drawing connecting lines, suspended in air from poles – in Hebrew *eruv chatzerot* means a merger of (different) domains. A space is pegged out with wire or string to create a permitted arena for activity on the Sabbath; the area itself isn't hallowed but has the power to lift pollution from those passing through it. The custom began in the shtetls of central Europe, when communal living around an inner courtyard meant that the women needed to leave their homes on the Sabbath to draw water or fetch bread from the communal oven; as this kind of work was prohibited, the rabbis devised a way of extending the home. The practice first spread to the US in the twentieth century; there are now extensive *eruvs* in Jerusalem and in London. The artist Sophie Calle has documented, in a series of photographs, the Jerusalem *eruv*: the very inconspicuousness of the cat's cradle of wires which mark out the territory, designating one part of it safe and the other unsafe, renders the custom all the more thought-provoking. The making of these precincts has often caused controversy or worse in places where they have been put up: far lighter than a wall, the strings nevertheless have an effect and seem to annex the space they traverse even for those who do not belong to the belief system which supports them. An *eruv*, like the even less visible boundary of a sacred grove, depends on imaginative consent, as in a children's game, when one place is Heaven and another Hell, where the post by the tree is safe and the chaser can't take you when you reach it. This principle of demarcating special, hallowed ground with very light means relates to the arena of performance, and I shall return to the function of the performance *skene* or scene and its relation to sanctuary today in Part Three. But these examples reveal that the ultimate foundation of sanctuary is magical. It is instituted by a speech act that declares it to be so, and that declaration enters the collective imaginary and is then translated into physical space.

~

Churches were not the only places offering refuge, but they were the most legal and approved; yet pagan ideas can be glimpsed, as if in palimpsest, in some sanctuaries where heroes undergo trials and thereby prove themselves. Quarantine in these cases acts as a test, just as in conditions of plague everyone suffers lockdown on their own to wait and see if symptoms develop. The mysterious Green chapel, for example, in the domain of the Green Knight, where Gawain must undergo the dread trial he has agreed to face, is a hideaway. But it is also a sacred place deep in the forest reached by Gawain only after many days' riding with help from locals who warn him again and again of the dangers he will face. This uncanny other world, deep in a gully in the thick forest, both dreadful and holy, pulsates with pre-Christian beliefs in nature divinities and woodland spirits – the Green Knight is a Green Man who has been Christianized. Such an enchanted grove continues some of the features of the Greek shrine in *Oedipus at Colonus* and other divine *temenoi*. Fugitives from justice and vendettas hid away in inaccessible places; forests and caves in unbuilt environments were the terrifying zones of mystery, the haunts of outlaws, escaped prisoners, evicted peasants, indigent workers from abroad, poachers and runaways. Yet over time, the most common cause of flight was debt.

The legendary history of Robin Hood and his band of Merry Men recalls this type of flight and alternative, quasi-utopian society, as does the court in exile in the Forest of Arden in *As You Like It* supporting Duke Senior and his followers, who later in the play attract Rosalind to join them. But the legend of Robin Hood establishes the fugitives as a society within their society and pictures them defending it by force, while the exiles and runaways in Shakespeare's play are hiding themselves away, waiting for the old order to pass. The place of safety comes to resemble a no-go area rather than a shrine, a part of a city where invisible barriers keep out strangers and mark a border, which may turn into a no man's land, the inverse of sanctuary: a zone of exposure and danger rather than shelter and safety.

While the forest as a refuge shares some features with sanctuary it is not equivalent, because the forest stands outside society, sometimes offering an alternative to its corruption and wickedness and developing a more equal, purer way of life. Not for nothing did Stephen Sondheim call his exhilarating musical *Into the Woods*. Fairy tales from northern Europe stage the woods as the proving ground for any number of protagonists, a place beyond society, a dangerous, pathless site of struggle and survival: Hansel and Gretel are abandoned in a forest where they encounter the witch and overcome her; Rapunzel wanders in another with her twin babies after the sorceress has cut her hair and thrown her out, till she is reunited with the prince, whose blinded eyes she heals with her tears; the ordeals these fairy-tale heroes and heroines undergo may lead to a happy ending but it is not the equivalent of sanctuary. Yet the stories retain the memory that sanctuary is often sought by those suffering persecution – in fairy tales usually unjustly. In life, in history, that innocence often remains debatable. Nevertheless, the forest is a liminal site where many protagonists undergo transformation. It is significant that Shakespeare dramatized such spaces, as theatre itself opens a different space and can function as a form of sanctuary; his return to varieties of refuges and asylums alongside prisons and cells, whether in the wild wood, the bucolic countryside (*The Winter's Tale*), or in isolation on an island (*The Tempest*), mirrored the stage itself where perils and problems could in principle be named, faced, explored and resolved without riot or trouble.

The fugitives in the forest are waiting for a different time, for better times for their party or their interests, when 'the world would againe turne', as the cartographer John Speed said in 1470 of the loyal supporters of Edward IV, who had fled for sanctuary during the Wars of the Roses. A valuable revival of sanctuary rights today would not wait upon change for the freedom and vindication of its inhabitants, but would form part of a society in which they could belong. Escaping danger is not the same as acceptance on equal terms and justice. Two contradictory ideas of sanctuary compete in the general understanding of the term: on the one hand, sanctuary is a transitional process (refuge), even 'a reformatory' or species of boot camp, an interval, pause or fermata, suspending time and activity for the seeker until he or she is readmitted into society; on the other hand it is a permanent state of safety and belonging, of recognition and harmonious acceptance (home). Resolving the tension between these two ways of understanding sanctuary in today's turbulence remains the sharp question; moving from a state of suspension and exclusion to a condition of settled inclusion requires a passage, a bridge, a porous threshold.

~

The law of sanctuary held for more than a thousand years from Anglo-Saxon times throughout the Middle Ages until Henry VIII began to abolish it, as an essential step in his dramatic rebalancing of the power of the state against the church. The right had its origins in times of intense conflict, of civil war and family or clan feuds, when internecine murders were a constant threat and many had to flee for their lives. The king did not reject the concept altogether, however; aware of the glory that had accrued to his predecessors for the magnanimity they showed, he attempted to establish broad zones of sanctuary in several different parts of his realm which had not traditionally offered refuge to fugitives. Henry's intention was of a piece with his general ambition, to extend royal control of the state, and in these new territories he could sharpen surveillance of those elements in society who seek sanctuary. The new provisions did not succeed, mostly because the chosen localities, such as Manchester, jibbed at the task of housing and handling an influx of unruly citizens. But Henry's effort to retain sanctuary rights while modifying and controlling their scope shows how deeply the custom commanded respect. The old rights were briefly restored by his daughter Mary, but James I finally legislated against them in 1623, although pockets of sanctuary lingered on, on former church land where the ghost of medieval law still haunted the customs of the place.

Beverley minster is a magnificent thirteenth-century parish church (one of the largest in the country) in the West Riding of Yorkshire, which preserved the relics of St John of Beverley and became one of the most potent and extensive sites of sanctuary. Scrupulously combing through coroners' reports, Charles Cox was able to set out the great variety of trades and conditions of men and women who, between 1479 and 1539, sought sanctuary at Beverley, in the form of 'perpetual immunity' and 'took the oath of obedience to the canons and town authorities'; the list includes one gentlewoman and sixteen gentlemen, part of a roster of every useful occupation of the era imaginable, like a series of engravings of the Cries of London: two arrow makers, two bakers, three barbers and on through the alphabet, amounting to a hundred names, to conclude at two wheelwrights, one woodmonger, one wool driver, one woolman and twenty yeomen.

More numinous than the knocker of Durham, the frith stool at Beverley promised safety to anyone who sat down and claimed immunity. The large squat stone throne has been subject to many vicissitudes, but now takes pride of place again near the high altar and the relics of the patron saint. 'Frith' comes from Anglo-Saxon English and Old German and means peace, security and freedom from molestation; it survives in the German word for peace, *Friede*, which gives *Friedhof*, meaning churchyard, and the name Frederick, or peace ruler. In Chaucer and elsewhere, it also denotes a wood: this double meaning has perplexed lexicographers, but woods were proverbial and actual places of refuge (see below). Frith seats can still be seen, mainly in the north of England (in Hexham Abbey in Northumberland and St Mary's church in Sprotbrough, Yorkshire), and exude a sense of antiquity and an authority deriving from that antiquity, not least because they have lasted for centuries often *in situ* or have been buried by Reformers and subsequently unearthed. The rugged stone from which they have been roughly carved adds to their numen: like Oedipus' unchiselled ledge, frith stools seem to anchor their occupants to forces below, in the core of the earth. The frith stool at Beverley is austerely plain, but others are carved with grotesque beasts and figures, apotropaic symbols that relate to the protection intrinsic to sanctuary: such monsters act as guardian demons.

Across cultures, sanctuary laws differ in detail but not in substance: a cathedral, a church, a mosque, a temple, a chapel or an area near one of these sacred places was known to all as a holy refuge. The difference between outside the safety zone and inside it was sometimes marked by the stout door and its mighty knocker. Barriers might surround the site of inviolability, but in principle no fortifications were necessary, and many celebrated spaces of sanctuary were not barred by physical means but only marked, as at the great sanctuary site of Beverley minster, by boundary crosses, which have inherited the function of classical *horoi* or stones that demarcated, for example, the precincts of the temple at Corinth. Though nations differed and the conditions of sanctuary altered over time, it is possible to find traces of the tradition all over Europe.

A fugitive from their enemies or from the arm of the law was protected by the prestige of the sacred, which in the past the classical gods or the church guaranteed. It is telling that the word 'prestige', from the Latin *prestigium*, means a spell or a magic turn or trick. Sanctuary seekers were spirited away from their pursuers' assault just as surely as Aneus in the thick of the fighting at Troy was wrapped in a cloud by Aphrodite and lifted out of danger. The protection that sanctuary offered against the secular arm resembled the force field Prospero conjures to freeze Ferdinand to the spot and render him incapable of raising his sword to attack Prospero or defend himself (*The Tempest*, I. ii). The device has become familiar from current magical entertainment in general: in the Harry Potter world, where the spells are in dog Latin, 'Petrificus Totalus', also known as the Full Body-Bind, is the magic spell that immobilizes an antagonist. The pursuers of sanctuary seekers were subject to a similar full body-bind.

The prohibition on eating in churches – defiling the holy place – meant that the clergy, in order to provide for men and women who had fled to them for safety, began to expand the boundaries of sanctuary beyond the church interior. At Beverley, the area of safety spanned several square miles and was demarcated by stone crosses, standing at each of the five roads into the town. Three are still standing, but the bas-reliefs and the arms have disappeared – possibly first damaged through iconoclastic zeal under Elizabeth I and then worn down by wind and weather, showing that even granite is subject to time's fell hand. As lumps of stone or ruinous posts, they nevertheless testify to the enchantment on which sanctuary depended since they did not erect a physical obstacle or barrier but only signalled a significant change of territory. At Beverley, Athelstan created a series of concentric rings around the minster with greater levels of sanctuary the closer people came to the centre. Five degrees of sanction – unfenced but understood – defined precise degrees of sacrilege, with rising level of fines to be levied against anyone violating the law by seizing someone on that tract of territory: in the outer circle, it was £8, but if the attempt were made in the choir the fine went up to £144, while breaking into the sanctuary itself, where the high altar stood and the patron saint lay, exceeded all reparations and the offender forfeited his life.

The boundary stones stand as prohibitions against entry, as warnings to the sacrilegious, the equivalent of a sign saying 'No Trespassing', but without back-up from palisade or ditches or sentries or snipers (the artist Richard Wentworth, in a series of photographs called 'Making Do and Getting By', has documented with acuity and humour how such signs institute frontiers: the flimsiest tape slung across a street effectively prevents someone crossing it).

A sanctuary was made of words: its power was commonly agreed, and its sanctity observed, as a result of shared ideas about the rights and freedom of others, the obligations of *xenia* or hospitality in Ancient Greece and the relations of humans to higher powers, and it therefore contributes to defining the claims of nation and home, of state and citizen. The Greeks' concept was absolute and unconditional, an ethic of total self-abnegation to a suppliant who fulfilled the proper rites; by contrast, over the long centuries of European sanctuary, the practice gradually accepted conditions, exemptions and expectations of the sanctuary seeker.

Breaches of sanctuary were indeed committed – the most infamous being the murder in 1170 of the Archbishop of Canterbury, Thomas Becket, at the altar of his own cathedral, and also, later, after the battle of Tewkesbury. But, as Cox points out, these sacrilegious acts were few and far between and the horror and fear they inspired did not fade; for example, in *Richard III* (III. i), Shakespeare exposes the deep-dyed villainy of the king and his supporters when the Duke of Buckingham urges Richard to go ahead and murder the young prince:

You are too senseless – obstinate, my lord,
Too ceremonious and traditional

> Weigh it but with the grossness of this age,
> *You break not sanctuary in seizing him.*
> *The benefit thereof is always granted*
> *To those whose dealings have deserved the place,*
> *And those who have the wit to claim the place:*
> *This prince hath neither claim'd it nor deserved it;*
> And therefore, in mine opinion, cannot have it:
> Then, taking him from thence that is not there,
> You break no privilege nor charter there.
> Oft have I heard of sanctuary men;
> But sanctuary children ne'er till now. [italics added]

Buckingham is deploying the most blatant casuistry, but it is telling that he stresses that the young prince should have claimed sanctuary and deserved it in order to meet the exact conditions of the law. The courtier is of course speaking in bad faith, but his cavils reveal the transactional nature of the agreements between several parties which are necessary for sanctuary. Buckingham nevertheless shrinks from violating sanctuary himself but Richard has listened and goes ahead and kills – hiring assassins to murder the first of the two Princes in the Tower.

The speech resonates with the grossness of our age, too. The lines 'The benefit thereof is always granted / To those whose dealings have deserved the place' chime with arguments today defining deserving and undeserving sanctuary and attempting to distinguish between degrees of status – economic migrant versus asylum seeker.

The next line 'And those who have the wit to claim the place' also applies to current arrivants who are obliged to tell a convincing story to make their claim to stay – to sanctuary.

Shakespeare was writing this play in the aftermath of Henry VIII's reforms and the Dissolution of the Monasteries, when church authorities no longer enjoyed independence of action, including over sanctuary, and he catches perfectly the change from a near unconditional privilege that took no account of guilt or deserts into a judicial even forensic reckoning of each case according to its merits. In these new circumstances, the story the fugitive told began to count more and more: testimony as in a court of law, with the verdict depending on whether the accused convinced their audience. Not quite a legal tribunal or formal trial but almost.

After the Reformation 'debtors' sanctuaries' declared certain areas havens for fugitives from justice. 'Alsatia' in London, in Farringdon, situated outside the walls of the City of London proper, between Fleet Street, the Temple and St Bride's church, grew over the seventeenth century into an unofficial refuge mostly for fugitives from creditors, as at Beverley in medieval times. The inhabitants of these improvised communities were inspired by various motives – workers' conditions, especially weavers', political disaffection, republican ideals. The longest-lasting sanctuary of this kind took root at the Southwark Mint; it was closed down in 1722. (Nahum Tate, the poet laureate, was among their number and died there in 1715 – we shall meet him again in Chapter 5 as the librettist of Purcell's opera *Dido and Aeneas*.) By then these enclaves had become notorious not only as offering shelter to transgressors against civil law but as dens of thieves, hideouts of dissidents and dangerous no-go areas; they were frequently raided and eventually closed down when the remnants of ecclesiastic exemption from state authority were abolished. The conflicting views of these places of refuge eerily foreshadow attitudes to the squatters' movement in the 1970s in London and to unofficial refugee camps, such as the Jungle in Calais.

The long history of sanctuary is very tangled, and I am not attempting an account of the legal shifts, the practice's vagaries and manifestations during its long formally legal existence (others have done this far more richly than I ever could). With policy on immigration in the more prosperous quarters of the world, the US and in Europe, growing increasingly exclusionary, sanctuary represents a startling, almost inexplicable precedent and a commanding ideal.

## The Safety of Home

Entering one of these sacred places, if permitted – the Dome of the Rock, for instance, or the high altar of a Catholic church – the force of this sacred state feels physical, like an invisible barrier of high pressure. The fourth wall in the theatre offers a revealing comparison:

invisible, yet when an actor breaks it and looks out and addresses the audience, the effect is palpable.

An analogous invisible aura envelopes objects on display in a museum or even in a stately home open to the public. The paintings on the walls, the sculptures and furniture positioned around the rooms, are sometimes cordoned off. But not always. It's understood by visitors that the items they are looking at exist in a separate sphere and must not be touched or used.

Not all shrines lie open to the passing stranger in the same uncanny way as the Furies' sacred wood lay open to Oedipus and Antigone. The refuges which offered sanctuary differ from many different kinds of holy sites, entry to which may indeed be physically barred with strenuous obstacles: the pilgrimage church of Loreto in Le Marche, Italy (see Chapter 4) is one of the few churches to be built as a fort, with ramparts guarding against Turkish raids across the Adriatic. Convents proclaim their separation from the world behind high, windowless walls and solid doors, and continue, as the term 'enclosed orders' implies, this seclusion in the shared spaces – the chapels, the visitors' parlour – of their buildings by keeping the nuns concealed behind grilles. In the convent of Santa Chiara in Palermo, Sicily, the walls of the nave are inset with small, oval, colander-like conches, behind which the Poor Clare used to sit or kneel in her cell as if wearing a visor, to attend to Mass or other offices.

The idea that the refuge is 'home' lays the emphasis on its character as a place of safety, but also implies that home can be set up at will here or there; it is not necessarily identical with birthplace. Sanctuary is mobile; it does not inhere in any particular set of coordinates but can be established with certain provisions and then acceded to by everyone.

Sanctuary opposes retributive justice with a concept of respect, and while it was offered by bishops and other ecclesiastical authorities on precincts they controlled separately from the ruler or the feudal nobility, it is far older than Christianity; legal scholars and historians have explored its relations with Roman law in particular.

It does not derive only from Christianity's principles of forgiveness of sins after due contrition and repentance. The forest refuges where

Robin Hood and the Duke have taken flight and hide out remember these ancient ways of thinking about exiles, outlaws and *xenoi*, which allowed for the possibility that the law might not always be just, that the pursued might be persecuted not criminals.

Justice was a principal motive for ending sanctuary rights at different times in history, and certainly in Henry VIII's reign. That felons of every stripe were eluding the courts and punishment excited indignation against the church authorities for harbouring criminals; conditions were imposed, and murderers and traitors, for example, were denied the right to sanctuary. When sanctuary seekers set up semi-permanent societies, and sanctuary itself became synonymous with lawless impunity, and was even defended by vigilantes like a sectarian quarter of a city in a state of civil war, then the scandal became acute, and the old rights to a hearing and to mercy ceased to command the necessary consensus to make them hold. Prevalent understanding of justice continues to cast suspicion on the kind of immunity sanctuary offers. But the provisions of ancient and medieval sanctuary could be revisited.

There have been many revivals of the practice, especially during times of crisis: during the Vietnam war, for example, several pastors in the United States offered sanctuary to anti-war protesters who were refusing to be drafted, and more recently refugees from wars in Afghanistan, Iraq, Syria and several other zones have inspired a movement to declare cities sanctuaries for those seeking asylum or defying deportation. Stories still intermittently reach the news reporting churches acting as sites of refuge for people who have in one way or another outlawed themselves: in Italy, during the extremely desperate last decade or more of arrivants coming across the straits dividing Sicily from North Africa, some priests have opened the doors of their precincts to the illegals. Their actions achieve something like the medieval quarantine, creating in effect a cooling-off period, a time and space for negotiation. The idea of cities of refuge is being revived in the form of Cities and Universities of Sanctuary and within universities, Colleges of Sanctuary. These institutions can't bypass the immigration laws, but they offer the most they are allowed to do, in the form of bursaries and negotiations with lawyers for visas, and they campaign against expulsion by every means available; above all, their actions change the ethos, revive ancient traditions of hospitality, to the stranger-guest. The organization CARA (Council for At Risk Academics), supports scholars prevented from working by the destruction of their universities or oppressive censorship. The seaside town of Eastbourne, in that part of the south coast where many illegal landings take place, has a flourishing centre called 'The Sanctuary', a place of welcome, conviviality and practical support and information. It is one such organization among many. Scholars and experts who work with refugees today argue that the Geneva Convention of 1951, with its definitions of the required criteria for entry and safety, no longer fits the circumstances of the current migrations. Such endeavours, often led by the local community, are guiding the future shape of concepts of citizenship, rights and mutual obligations.

By contrast, the exclusionary character of some of world religions' holiest places has inspired non-denominational retreats, idealistic, ecumenical spaces, resolutely non-referential to any creed or divinity and open to all regardless of faith or ethnicity. For example, in Helsinki, the Kamppi chapel was built in 2012 and won an international prize for the architects. Like one of Barbara Hepworth's ovoid sculptures, it is curvilinear, without angles or corners; it is built of golden, very lightly corrugated curved wood on the outside, as if a shipwright had made a beautiful carvel piece of joinery, and painted on the inside pristine white over a rough surface, with the light pouring down from apertures concealed under the roof; the space encloses visitors quietly, as if they were nestlings or embryonic chicks inside its egg-like form. It is intended to inspire calm and steadiness during the urban clamour by eliminating a sense of time passing and abolishing other coordinates to the world outside. And this succeeded where I was concerned. It felt to me enfolding, like an ark, but my companion, Rachel Kneebone, herself a sculptor, rebelled against it, feeling trapped, stifled, and I could see the reason. In many ways, our divergent experiences of the Chapel of Silence, as the refuge is also called, catch the ambivalence that surrounds the principle of a sanctuary: such an enclave is a heterotopia, and can be a refuge or an enclosure, a haven or a ghetto.

Sanctuaries are demarcated sites where the rules are distinctive; they can be havens, but the history of the concept reveals disturbing and divisive features that persist, for example in the current conditions of official UN refugee camps and unofficial settlements like the Jungle at Calais, and in the exacerbated debate about legal and illegal immigrants. The precinct of a sanctuary can also often become *ipso facto* a zone of exclusion and exception, sometimes in the interests of equality and tolerance, as in 'safe places' for certain groups who are claiming protection from the prevalent prejudice. When spaces in museums and universities are designated for use by women only, or black, LGBTQ+ and other groups, they become zones of exclusion for those who do not belong to or identify with this or that group. The notice 'sanctuary' may equate to 'Keep Out' and its territory resemble a sectarian stronghold defended by vigilantes, as in Belfast in the worst days of the Troubles. In this light, my nation becomes my sanctuary, and barring it to outsiders sustains this privilege. The ancient principle of hospitality which governed sanctuary has been turned upside down.

~

Home offers another kind of sanctuary, and the word 'home' chimes, as I've mentioned, with refuge and haven, but it is not identical in meaning: a house is not a home, according to the proverb. When Odysseus suffers from *nostos*, he longs for home and all that Ithaca means to him – including, the epic makes clear, his dog. The Ithaca that is his hearth is his home on the one hand, but on the other, the place is also an imaginary mooring for his sense of himself as fashioned over time.

Ways of making holy and keeping a space figuratively clean and safe may seem to call for legal definitions and clear philosophical thinking but shifts in values and attitudes happen through imaginative approaches too, which is where the work of literature and art plays such a part. But this mode of reattaching oneself to a place that is not home but must become one, and of filling it with meaning and hallowing it, does not necessarily depend on transmitting an existing story. Nor on inheriting one through historical or geographical bonds.

Quiet, enclosed spaces, such as multi-denominational chapels in airports, come close to the dominant sense of a sanctuary today, a place of protection, 'a safe space'. A library's reading room can generate a hushed, reverent atmosphere and give its users a numinous sense of stepping into a different social space, where respect for the exhibits and for one another follows. This is also true of some museums and art galleries. The home of artist and filmmaker Derek Jarman, Prospect Cottage near Dungeness, has become a shrine to his memory and also 'a space of queer sanctuary' for many visitors/pilgrims. These are all pre*cincts*, from *cingo* meaning to bind or encircle, set apart as separate and different. Like the sacred 'sanctuary' of a church, such modern enclaves admit only the initiated (often in spite of their avowed desire to be open to all). The ancient idea of sanctuary that sheltered suspects and fugitives is far more capacious, and tilting the emphasis towards inclusiveness rather than privacy is one of the objectives of this study.

Sanctuary develops through shared notions about the rights of others and the obligations of hospitality, and therefore contributes to defining the claims of nation and home; these contradictory elements have been formed historically by a complex mesh of taboos, laws, customs and values that still reverberate today, in times when the numbers of refugees, from war, famine and other causes are rising. Sanctuaries are havens, but they share features with sites of exception, such as sanatoria: for example, Thomas Mann's Magic Mountain is a place where the patients are enrolled to be cured and cleansed, which Hans Castorp, the protagonist experiences as a time out of time, a place out of the ordinary world, a form of enchantment.

# Part Two: Sites of Memory

Legendary history is as important as the history of facts.

Jocelyn Wogan-Browne

Pilgrim tattoos, though forbidden by the church, remember acts of devotion: here, the cult statue of Our Lady of Loreto commemorates a visit to the Holy House.

2

# Traces:
# The Flight into Egypt

> I loved . . . unfashionable literature, church Latin, misspelt erotica, the novels of our forebears, fairy tales, little books from childhood, old operas, naïve refrains, naïve rhythms . . . The ways of old poetry played a good part in my alchemy of the word.
>
> Arthur Rimbaud

One of the most ancient sanctuaries in Egypt lies deep in the rock of Old Cairo, formerly called Babylon. Built in the fourth century, it is the episcopal seat of the Coptic patriarchs, and is dedicated to St Sergius and St Bacchus, military saints who died for the faith in Syria. Its full name used to be the church of the Martyrs Sergius and Bacchus of the Cave, but it is now called the church of the Holy Virgin and is revered because Mary, Joseph and the baby lived there, it is said, at the end of their wanderings in Egypt; Joseph worked on the building of the new city. The crypt, 10 metres down into the bedrock, is narrow, dark and, despite Egypt's climate, damp and cool. When the Nile rises, it may flood, connecting the impressive built environment with the ungainsayable forces of nature. It is another intensely chthonic place, not exactly habitable, but still saturated with the mana of centuries of devotion.

The Flight into Egypt tells a story of exile, and its narration never wavers in its solidarity with the fugitive family who prefigure, in their need, hunger and thirst, and their sheer exposure to danger, the state of forced exiles at any time. The ordeals the Holy Family suffer, as the three of them flee south-west from Bethlehem, unfold across territory that rings in the news today – Gaza, Rafah, the Sinai desert. They

Crossing to safety in a small boat, Joseph, Mary and Jesus take refuge in Egypt from Herod's murderous plans.

reach Egypt and wander there homeless, moving from one place to another. They are sometimes given welcome but mostly not.

Here and there along their aimless route they bring blessings on the place: the sick are cured, freshwater springs and fertile fruit groves miraculously appear. However, at the same time, in a fairy-tale spirit of vindication, they also see their enemies struck down by divine punishments: tyrants are overthrown; false gods fall from their pedestals. The different strands of the story proclaim the destruction of the old order that brought harm to people like themselves. As Susan Stewart writes in *The Ruins Lesson* (2019), ruins paradoxically offer hope of transformation. And in the apocrypha, ruination envelops Mary, Joseph and the baby; ragged and displaced wretches, they are figures of ruin but, the story promises, of ruin averted.

The canonical story appears in the gospel of Matthew, told over a sequence of nine verses (2:13–21). Joseph is warned by an angel that Herod, the ruler of Galilee for the Roman authorities, is seeking the child in order to kill him, and that he, Joseph, should take Mary and the baby and flee to safety in Egypt. Joseph immediately obeys. Herod meanwhile orders the massacre of all male babies under two years old in Bethlehem.

Three years later, Joseph is again visited by an angel in a dream and told that Herod has died. The family can safely return to Nazareth.

The evangelist is intent on showing that Jesus of Nazareth fulfilled the messianic prophecies of the Old Testament. 'Behold a virgin shall conceive,' for example, from Isaiah, is a plain-speaking oracle, but in the case of the family's Flight from Herod the links between the Old and New Covenants can sound strained. Matthew invokes a prophecy: 'When Israel was young, I loved him, and I called my son out of Egypt' (Hosea 11: 1). Matthew 2: 15 reprises it baldly, writing that Mary, Joseph and the child stayed 'until the death of Herod: *that it might be fulfilled which was spoken of the Lord by the prophet*, saying, Out of Egypt have I called my son' (italics added). Matthew also calls on the Bible to corroborate, proleptically, the Massacre of the Innocents, for which he is the only source. He quotes a prophecy of Jeremiah about Rachel weeping for her children in Ramleh, and then states, 'So that what had been spoken through the prophets might be fulfilled.' (2:23).

The story of the Flight into Egypt inspired an imagined itinerary through the territory, a thread of 'privileged, uncommon places, the holy spaces and beings that open channels between the two worlds' – the actual world and the imagined realm. As the gospel story came to be received as a historical account, intersecting with reality, it was mapped on to the geography of Egypt, and early in the history of Christianity several apocryphal gospels elaborated richly on the exile in Egypt. In the early years of Islam, Egypt also figures as place of refuge for Mariam (Mary) when she gives birth to Jesus – Issa in the Muslim tradition. European artists subsequently treated the episode realistically, imagining the plight of the fugitives with intense sympathy.

Typology, oracles, figural patterning: these are ways of storymaking to be kept in mind when reading narratives, beyond the literal meaning of the words. This structure, proleptic in intention, architectural in form, endows imagery with doubled voices, speaking in chords resonating across time: the past becomes prologue. Mythic material demands this way of reading, for what Italo Calvino calls the *filigrana*, the watermark or 'tracery of a pattern', which allows an ethics of hope to flower. 'Only in Marco Polo's accounts,' he writes in *Invisible Cities*, 'was Kublai Khan able to discern, through the walls and towers destined to crumble, the tracery of a pattern so subtle it could escape the termites' gnawing.' Looking beyond the patent, visible surface opens a text to poetical truth-telling distinct from historical veracity or believability.

The story's imprint on topography throughout southern Palestine, the Sinai desert and the Nile valley in Egypt exemplifies how a fantasy narrative can be realized, graven in rock and stone, announcing it happened here. The landscape was closely mapped according to the stories about the infant Jesus' experiences as a refugee from Herod, according to the accounts given in many early versions, Greek, Latin, Syriac, Arabic and Ethiopic. Pilgrimages in the Nile valley continue today, to a cave, a spring, a tree associated with Mary and Jesus' sojourn there.

Since antiquity, Egypt has held a key place in the imaginary of the holy, as a locus of supernatural power with a magical aura: in the Old Testament, it is the site of servitude, a place from which Moses safely delivered the Israelites, and in the New Testament, the place of salvation, where the Saviour, the child Jesus, fled to from the murderous designs of Herod. The figural significance of Egypt is also strongly marked in Qur'anic tradition. The two strands are intertwined especially in the main sources – apocryphal gospels, written in Arabic and Syriac, and pious legends that were composed and circulating during the first centuries of our era, before and during the emergence of Islam. These stories – several found in documents unearthed in the great deposits at Oxyrhynchus on the banks of the Nile north of Luxor in Upper Egypt – form a fabulous corpus in the genre of *aja'ib*. Apocryphal meant 'hidden' rather than false as it does now, and these texts from the earliest era of Christianity, the most ancient repositories of the doings and sayings of Jesus, commanded belief and reverence from their listeners and readers. Their fantastical tale-spinning gives us a glimpse of the way imaginary narratives underpin social and political relations.

The vision of the past and of the order of destiny that this kind of marvellous story expresses shows us the central role that the imaginary plays in the formation of meaning for the communities that receive and circulate its creations. As for Egypt in the childhood of Jesus – Issa – it represents a treasury of magical knowledge, where prodigies and miracles are considered autochthonous, natural. What interests me even more is the hope of coexistence that flickers at their heart. 'Without question', writes Stephen J. Davis, the religious studies scholar at Yale, 'Muslim and Arabic Christian readers still read these infancy tales for their own distinctive theological and social purposes, and [they] occasionally used such stories to mark off religious difference. Nonetheless, their respective interpretations of Jesus's childhood were shaped by – and in turn helped shape – a shared sensibility, a common cultural heritage.' He goes on to identify four specific areas of coexistence and practice: scriptural interpretation, storytelling about prophetic miracles, the production of scientific knowledge and ascetic discipline. 'Through these particular practices,' he writes, 'the Christ child became part of a shared cultural memory among Christians and Muslims in the Islamic Near East.' To these categories of enquiry, I would add the mapping of place and the attempt to fashion a sanctuary, in other words a place of safety, a grounding, a home.

## Mary in the Qur'an

The figure of the Virgin Mary and the multiple narratives in which she figures fashion a common *lieu de mémoire*, a common place, for she also plays an important role in the Muslim imaginary and faith. A sura – Sura 19 – is called 'Mariam' and dedicated to her, granting her more space in the Holy Book of Islam than in the New Testament; other passages also honour her. A much circulated anecdote about the Prophet relates that when he entered Mecca in triumph and gave the order that all the images in the Kaaba be destroyed, he covered up an icon of Mary and Jesus with his cloak, thus sparing it in an act of 'special reverence'.

Mariam is the only woman named in the Qur'an, and she is considered a great saint, even a prophet. A strong theological movement in ecumenical circles searches for a rapprochement between Islam and the Catholic and High Protestant churches through the person and symbol of Mary. Many pilgrimages all over the world are dedicated to her, and sites in Egypt bring Copts and Muslims together: Zeytun in Cairo where Mary manifested herself in a series of apparitions in the 1960s is still attracting devotees. The principle that theologians invoke when discussing the overlaps between Islam and

Christianity is *conviviality*, as proposed by the noted Lebanese (Maronite) Islamologist and Arabist Youakim Moubarac (1924–95), who dedicated a vast corpus of writing, much of it still unpublished, even less translated, to deconstructing the entrenched hostility to Islam in Christianity and vice versa.

Conviviality, which now means warm sociability, still carries a memory trace of *convivencia*, a stronger historical term for coexistence, which has been much invoked in relation to the ideal state of toleration and mutual respect that is thought to have prevailed in Andalusia before 1492 when the Catholic monarchs Ferdinand and Isabella expelled Jews and Muslims or forced their conversion (the facts may not altogether bear out the truth of this picture of an ideal, harmonious Andalusia). Moubarac's thinking is knottily theological and not disseminated, which may be a symptom of the divisions that are fostered on all sides. We need to hear more about mutual interests of the Abrahamic faiths and more about their interactions over time. The fissiparous character of the Christian churches in their original seedbed and the internecine antagonism between the different branches of Islam today do not offer hope. Nevertheless, 'traditional practices of sharing sacra . . . belonged to the historical heritage of Eastern Mediterranean societies, where the coexistence of more than one religious group within one territory, under one authority, represents a legacy of the Byzantine and Ottoman systems . . . religious practices of both Muslims and Oriental Christians are an important part of this common cultural heritage.' With the help of Mouchir Basile Aoun's work on Moubarac, certain strands can be pulled out in relation to 'civic religion' and conviviality in a social and secular sense. Shared saints such as Mary/Mariam, their feast days and pilgrimages figure strongly in this endeavour.

The Qur'anic story of the birth of Jesus is that Mariam receives the message of the angel – the Arabic word is sometimes rendered as 'an immaculate human' – and he tells her she will have a child (Sura 19: 15). As in the gospel of St Luke, Mary protests that it cannot be, 'since no man has ever touched me'. The narrative continues, 'so she conceived him and withdrew with him to a distant place' (Sura 19: 21). There 'labour pains came upon her as she stood by the trunk of a palm tree'. In pain, she cries out that she wishes she could die and disappear from the memories of men before all this was being forced upon her. A voice from above intervenes and tells her, 'Do not grieve.' The unnamed voice tells her that the Lord has caused a stream to flow at her feet, and that if she shakes the trunk of the palm tree 'it will drop down on you dates soft and ripe'. The voice then commands her to rejoice, but not to 'speak a word today to any human being'.

The mysterious injunction of silence foreshadows the curse of mutism laid on many heroines, as in the fairy tale 'The Seven Ravens', in which the sister saves her brothers by staying dumb and knitting them shirts from nettles. It is a recurring magical motif to convey heroic female virtue.

Mary, after giving birth, returns to her relatives with the child and they reproach her bitterly, accusing her of being impure, of committing a 'monstrous act'. She keeps silent, as the voice ordered, and points to the baby to indicate that he will explain. Her relatives doubt that an infant can do so, but the child announces aloud at some length his vocation as a prophet and his total submission to his mother.

Egypt is not given as the desert where Mary retreats, but a tenacious tradition identified it with the Egyptian landscape, and in a later sura, 'The Believers', we read: 'We made the Son of Mary, and his mother a wonder. We caused them to retire to a high place, with level ground and a fountain' (Sura 23:50).

This verse seems to point to a correspondence with the Flight to Egypt and has given rise to pilgrimage sites where, according to tradition, the Holy Family stopped and found shelter during the three years they spent in Egypt. And among these shrines, scattered all over the Nile valley, some are identified in Qur'anic tradition. For example, al-Maqrizi, a fifteenth-century historian, identified a palm tree at Ahnassiah al-Madinat, in the southern Nile valley, as the very tree where Mariam/Mary gave birth, and at Sakha, in the Nile delta, Jesus touched a rock with his foot to indicate a source of fresh water for his thirsty family; his foot imprinted the stone (an eighth-century homily reported). Sakha became a cult site, still on the pilgrim route which includes the Holy Family's last refuge in Egypt, the cave of the church in Old Cairo.

## Apocrypha: Hidden Tales

Significantly, the more unofficial the devotion, the less upper clergy are involved in authorizing it, the less intra-faith hostility arises, as the anthropologist William Christian Jr has explored in relation to popular piety in Spain. His findings apply more widely: the closer to folklore lie tales of miracles and visions, the less division grows between the petitioners: the Marian shrines offer hope to women of various faiths, where they pray for the love of a good man, for a child, for safety giving birth or for respite from further sex and childbearing, and for cures, especially of sick or disabled children, since the Infancy apocrypha tell of Issa/Jesus' miracle-working powers in this regard.

Several apocryphal gospels circulated far and wide from their origins in the early years of Christianity and Islam and embroidered fantastically on the Egyptian period of Jesus' life: the infancy narratives in the gospel of St Matthew influence apocryphal offshoots, the Book of James or Protevangelium, and the so-called Pseudo-Matthew; several more apocrypha, such as the gospel of Thomas and the gospel of Mary, contribute scenes of further miracles performed by the child Jesus. More importantly, the Arabic gospel of the Infancy, which was probably written in the sixth century and also exists in a partial Syriac *History of the Virgin*, reports yet more signs and wonders around the conception, birth and youth of the child Jesus.

Many of the miracles that happen to help the Holy Family on their way inspire scenes in medieval and Renaissance art, revealing how travelling tales from the birthplaces of Christianity and Islam appeal across the centuries and leap boundaries of language and even creed. Some of the artists who spread these wonders far and wide seem to have heard of episodes that the authors of the Arabic gospel of the Infancy were also picking up. It isn't possible, with such heavy traffic of magical tales, to ascertain sources or precedence; rather the surfacing of a scene here and there should draw attention to ideas circulating beyond dogmatic divisions and ethnic definitions.

The dates are disputed, and the apocryphal gospels were composed and written both before and after the Qur'an; the echoes between the texts are numerous – they resonate but with marked differences.

Nevertheless, the parallels are rich and poetic, and we must remember that the documents that have come down to us, that have survived the centuries, are not complete: several important apocrypha were found in the excavations of Qxyrhynchus not so long ago. Nevertheless, it is obvious that from the third to the seventh centuries a profusion of wonders and stories poured forth throughout the region, from Syria to Egypt, that the Qur'an and the miraculous events told after the revelation to the Prophet grew in this same territory, and that an exchange of ideas, motives, images enriched the legacy of the two religions. The Pseudo-Matthew, for example, was composed during the eighth century, therefore after the vision of the Prophet, so the currents of influence run in both directions; the signs and wonders in both traditions were inspired by and respond to one another.

The Pseudo-Matthew, so called because of the parallels with the evangelist's canonical gospel, follows the conventional story but adds fabulous episodes with a strong echo of the Qur'anic narrative. Of these, the most familiar is the rest, on the third day of their Flight, when the Holy Family pauses on the road, and Mary, tired, thirsty and hungry, asks Joseph if they can 'stop in the shade of a palm tree'. He leads her and the child on the donkey, and she sits down. Seeing the fruit on the tree above, she wishes she could pick it, and Joseph replies that the tree is much too high and that above all they need fresh water. Immediately, the child Jesus begs the tree to bend down: no sooner said than done. After they have eaten, the child commands the tree to stand again and to open its roots and reveal the stream of fresh water flowing under its trunk.

In a further variation of this episode, angels intervene, bending the date tree so that Mary can pick the fruit and at the same time reveal a spring at the base of the tree. The German goldsmith and master engraver Martin Schongauer had learned of the episode and illustrated it, with scientific attention to species *c.* 1470–4 – the dragon tree he includes growing beside the inclining date palm swarming with angels makes a full-colour appearance in the scene of the Fall on the left-hand wing of Hieronymus Bosch's *Garden of Earthly Delights*. There must have been a specimen growing in a northern European botanical garden. Schongauer's engraving itself was portable, a perfect medium for a travelling tale wandering far beyond its desert origins.

The biblical episode inspires a varied and rich tradition of magical tales and, for some, seductive fantasies. For example, according to one legend, the stone of every date is marked with a small O to honour the Virgin Mary, because, after tasting the miraculous fruit, she exclaimed at its deliciousness. This is an example of a small aetiological myth, a tiny sliver in the mass of stories about the origins of things, a detail I myself had never noticed but have since found to be the case: a little O is inscribed on each pit as if it were the navel of the fruit's body.

Further portents accompany the family's Flight into Egypt and are remembered in the visual record, especially manuscript illuminations in Books of Hours: statues of pagan gods tumble from their pedestals as Mary, Joseph and the baby pass by; a large cornfield miraculously grows up overnight so that when Herod's soldiers, in hot and murderous pursuit of the Holy Family, ask the locals if they have been sighted, they are able to answer, quite truthfully, that nobody has passed that way since the corn was sown. This miracle echoes a story from the Muslim tradition, which relates that when the Prophet, fleeing his persecutors, hid in a cave, a spider wove a web over the entrance; his pursuers took this as evidence that nobody could have entered there recently.

In all the Infancy apocrypha, the child has powers: dragons, lions and wild beasts bow down and adore him; he heals the sick and raises the dead; he slides down rainbows; when Joseph makes mistakes in his carpentry, Jesus corrects the planks he has cut. He is not entirely saintly: when his schoolfriends don't show him proper respect, he kills them. Then to make amends, he raises them from the dead.

The prodigious child also brings inanimate matter to life: he models birds from clay, claps his hands and they fly away – a miracle which he performs in the Qur'an (3:49 and 5:110), though in the Qur'an, he breathes/blows into the clay figures, like God creating Adam, to bring them to life.

Needless to say, these narratives of miracles and prodigies hardly resemble fiction as understood in relation to the constitution of the human subject; like fairy tales they are characterized by syncopated handling of time, non sequiturs, cryptic epiphanies and startling prodigies – from exceptional natural portents to supernatural healings and resurrections. They are, above all, inauthentic by the standards of canonicity or historical accuracy. In their syncretism, they do not demarcate strong borders; they

Prodigies performed by the boy Jesus are reported in New Testament Apocrypha and the Qur'an. Winifred Gill (d. 1981), Jesus creates living birds from clay.

offer an antidote to the edicts handed down by authorities, secular as well as religious, to define true culture, proper literature.

Such miracles seemed far too close to pagan magic for comfort among Christian theologians and these apocrypha were discounted, in some cases condemned as heretical. This did not prevent their becoming popular; and, as we have seen, manuscript illumination and prints and other visual materials testify that they travelled far from the stories' birthplace. Tiles made in 1310–30 for a local church in Tring, in the Chiltern hills in England, show many of the child Jesus' exploits, including an episode when he frees a playmate who has been locked up by his father in a tower to prevent him associating with Jesus – his parents frown on the child Jesus, finding him weird. But Jesus pulls his playmate out through the keyhole.

The tiles are unique, their makers unknown, but they exemplify the way tales travel and, in this case, baked into clay, may survive.

Of the apocryphal material so far unearthed, the Arabic gospel is the most packed with wonders, several of these occurring only in this narrative. At the approach of Jesus, a possessed child, the son of a priest, is cured; he is the first of a series of miracles. Soon afterwards, a possessed woman is healed, then another, followed by the cure of a little girl who is suffering from leprosy, after she has bathed in water in which the baby Jesus has been washed. Many of the reported miracles across the apocrypha are wrought by means of a garment worn by the child, or by the water in which Mary bathes him. The Holy Family are then waylaid by robbers – Titus and Dumachus, whom the infant Jesus prophesies will hang beside him in thirty years' time. Titus will be saved, Jesus continues, because he recognized that the baby is the Saviour and bribed Dumachus not to molest the family.

Scenes not occurring in any other apocryphal source except the Arabic gospel were known in Italy, as a series of bas-relief bronzes reveal. They show the robbers attacking the holy party and the baby cured by Jesus' bath water (they are attributed to Ferdinando Tacca (1619–86), a monumental sculptor who worked for the Medici as a stage designer and engineer).

The presence of the two thieves highlights a fundamental principle of these texts, which we saw governing Matthew's gospel: the authors work with prophetic figuration, not historical records. Variations of these stories resonate: in the uses of holy water in both Catholic and Muslim ritual, and in the flourishing cult of the Good Thief – known as St Dismas – in the Catholic world, especially in Spain and Latin America.

The Syriac version of this Arabic Infancy gospel is packed with further startling anecdotes. In the long – and, it must be admitted, tedious – catalogue of miracles a fantastic story of metamorphosisis is told; it later appears, with some variations, in *The Thousand and One Nights*. A young woman employed by the Holy Family meets three sisters coming from a cemetery, accompanied by a mule covered in splendid silks which they caress while weeping loudly. They confide in Mary's servant – someone not previously mentioned – that they were visiting the tomb of their parents who had left them an immense fortune, and that the animal they are tearfully caressing is none other than their brother, transformed into a mule by an enchantress whom he had married.

Here we find ourselves in the pure terrain of *aja'ib*.

But the narrative is also spiritual, so the fable turns into a miracle, a sign of divine power: the maid takes the sisters and their metamorphosed brother to Mary, who implores Jesus to help them; and so the mule is changed back into a man, and, with a return to the world of the fairies, he takes the young maid for his (second) wife).

The repertoire of miracles in the Syriac variant is long and repetitive, but it demonstrates the effectiveness of Mary's mediation with her son, the belief in second-order relics such as swaddling bands, and the fundamental link between miracle and purification (demons are driven out of madmen, lepers are healed as their skin is washed clean of evil). The shrines on the route are primarily places where pilgrims pray for healing.

Given the centuries of conflict in Jerusalem between different Christian sects and between Muslims and Jews today at the Dome of the Rock and the al-Aqsa mosque, it seems hopeless wishful thinking to propose that there could be sacred spaces enjoyed in common, that fighting for exclusive access to them and possession of them might cease, that territory can be hallowed as common ground rather than as forbidden property fenced off by signs. Can a sacred event be imprinted on to territory without sectarian consequences? In ways that bring people together rather than provoke claims and counterclaims? In the apocryphal gospel written in Arabic (but not included in the Syriac version), a scene of wonder takes place during the Holy Family's stay in Egypt at a place called Matariyya (Mataria, Matarea), where Mary washes the linen of the infant Jesus, and from his sweat and tears and no doubt other bodily fluids – which she 'scattered with the water she throws away' – she creates balm (or balsam) trees. An alternative version of the legend describes Jesus breaking Joseph's staff into little pieces and planting them, digging into the ground to uncover a spring with an 'exceedingly sweet odour' which he uses to water his plants, which then grow into the valuable, perfume-producing trees.

The fact that the village is named in the document reveals that a place of pilgrimage already existed by the sixth century, one of many stations on a very long itinerary up the Nile from the coast and on both sides of the river, and that it was a garden where balsam was cultivated. Later references testify to its continued existence: in 1285–95, a travelling monk, Burchard of Mount Zion, tells us that during a tour of the East, he bathed in the stream where Mary had washed the infant Jesus and that he took away as much balsam wood as he could. And in 1549, Matarea appears on the *Veduta* or panorama of Cairo made by the Venetian Matteo Pagano. Among the many vignettes is a group of buildings on the outskirts of the city, which bear the legend: 'In questo orto se cava el vero balsamo' (In this garden the true balsam is gathered).

Not far from the garden of the true balsam, the map indicates the 'Lodgings where Our Lady stayed when she fled to Egypt for fear of Herod'. The picture shows a similar precinct behind high walls. Below this scene, the artist has included the tree ('Pharaoh's fig') and labelled it as follows: 'Here the holy family rested in the shade.'

The balsam garden lay on the pilgrimage route of the Flight into Egypt as elaborated in the apocrypha and developed as a sanctuary, revered not only by Christians. In Matarea today the balsam trees have long gone, but 'Pharaoh's fig' still stands. On the day I visited Matarea in 2009, the sacred precinct was arid and empty, but it nevertheless provided a quiet refuge from the very noisy city and radiated the memory of very remote events, as if they were still active in the present. In this sense, the garden of Matarea is a heterotopia, where different time zones are compressed, bringing the past to fold into the present.

Matareya, near Cairo, where Mary and her child stayed, developed into a garden of precious balm, the basic ingredient of Holy chrism.

A grand tourist, M. de Maillet, visited Matarea in the 1700s and reported on it in his memoirs. This 'gentleman of Lorraine' was consul-general of the French king Louis XV in Egypt and ambassador to the court of the 'king of Ethiopia'. M. de Maillet recounts that the spring was considered sacred by Christians and Turks, and that a mosque stood next to the Coptic church in the garden.

The balsam produced by the guardians of the garden had a special place in Christian cult – it was sent from Egypt all over Christendom to be used for the chrism with which babies are anointed at their baptism. Christians also recommended it as an antidote to snake bites and other poisons, and as a remedy for toothache, while Muslims prescribed the balm for nasal problems, lumbago or knee pain. The apothecary monks of the sanctuary benefited from the trade.

Thus the place where Mary and the child rested becomes, over time, a material sanctuary offering not only fresh water, ripe fruit and precious balm, but also a metaphysical site of ease, of healing and blessing. Tussles broke out as rivals sought to control the production of the precious balm, and occasional bans were issued forbidding non-Christians to handle it, but over the centuries the treasured substance superseded sectarian claims. Matarea exemplified how a natural resource – a spring, a substance that, like water, is pristine, uncooked, like honey and scented resin – can draw people together, to overlook their differences when it is shared, because of course scarcity will cause competition and often enmity.

The sanctuary was restored in 2000 as part of a large heritage project, but the miraculous spring was looking dried up on the day of our visit, and the Pharaoh's fig tree struggles; the main branch rests on a crutch and its withered limbs and split seams are protected from further damage by bandages. One of the early travellers states authoritatively that the tree is, in fact, a sycamore of a local fruit-bearing species planted in 1672 – in which case, though ancient, it is not quite as old as Jesus.

I am not praising the Coptic church – its priests do not speak out against the military regime of General El-Sisi any more than the Russian Orthodox church protests against Putin's regime. Nor do I want to belittle the very deep divisions along religious lines throughout the region. But I am interested in how ritual assemblies on the ground might relate to narratives of shared ownership and belonging, how the storied map orients its denizens and may shape their expectations of one another.

Catholic artists were inspired by the apocryphal accounts, and by the topos, the Rest on the Flight into Egypt, following both apocryphal and Qur'anic lore about the miraculous spring and the generous date palm. How the transmission took place remains to be explored further, especially as the devout would have shuddered at the thought that anything they venerated in paint might agree with beliefs of the infidel. However, belief in the magical properties of holy water is held in common, and paintings of the Rest frequently feature Mary scooping up water from the miraculous spring in a copper or brass bowl to bathe the baby. Correggio's tender, al fresco domestic scene, painted in 1529, now in the Galleria Nazionale di Parma, refers to the bowl in the title – *Madonna della Scodella*. The painting circulated in an engraving by Simon François Ravenet II (1778). Nearly half a century later, Federico Barocci recaptured the sweetness of mood in Correggio and echoed the Virgin's almost sacramental gesture of pouring the water with her right hand, but he heightened the interactions of the three figures, his Jesus being very much no longer an infant as he joyfully accepts a fruit from Joseph. Paolo Veronese tackled the subject in a magnificent canvas in which angels swirl in the palm tree above a lovingly observed scene of family life: Jesus' small clothes have been stretched out on a frond to dry. In this tumultuous and gorgeous-coloured composition, Joseph is handling the bowl. The treasury at Loreto claimed that it possessed bowls used by the baby Jesus, although it sounds as if they were made of earthenware rather than copper or other metal, as imagined by artists. But magic bowls, used for healing or purification, are a prominent and common feature of Islamic piety. Of all the scores of artists who have rendered the scene of the Flight, Rembrandt captures for me the depths of sympathy it can stir and speaks most directly to the current predicament of so many displaced peoples. In a small painting of 1620, a halo glows around the head of the baby, but otherwise Rembrandt's realism strips away supernatural or miraculous elements to concentrate on the everyday ordinariness of the couple and their child; unlike some of his Italian predecessors, the Dutch artist does not include a pyramid or other element of Egyptian set-dressing (although in many of his paintings he costumes himself or his models).

Rembrandt was inspired to make many images of the Flight into Egypt, which resonate with his sympathetic studies of paupers, beggars and vagrants; his intense, involved observation of a homeless family has the effect of conjuring away the scriptural references to allow a documentary effect to take over. Yet these drawings and engravings powerfully represent the effects of exile.

Slashing downward strokes and frantic hatchings of the burin on the plate sharpen the urgency of their predicament: Mary looks out at us, her face lopsided, her eyes apprehensive, hunted; a hard rain falls – components that add an apocalyptic accent to the scene.

The artist returned to the story again and again, and his pen-and-ink drawings and prints exude intense fellow feeling for his subjects. His portrayal of the Holy Family as a homely group on the road, such as he might have seen among his neighbours, the recent mother worn down by her experience, draws on the many sketches he made of the urban

The flight into Egypt recurs in Rembrandt's work: this early etching captures the harried vulnerability of the Holy Family as they flee Herod.

poor of Amsterdam. Darkness gathers around the fugitives as they make their way, the donkey weary too. Rembrandt retains some specificities of the traditional story: Joseph is older than his wife as he visibly trudges along leading the donkey. The artist imagines them setting up camp for the night, building a fire, their figures very small and vulnerable in the roiling empty darkness around them.

Rembrandt read scripture carefully and he keeps close to the canonical story, without miraculous date palms or overnight cornfields. His gift for emotional drama, his tenderness and compassion, rooted in personal observation, exemplify the commonality of the sacred story. The message about the exhausted and downtrodden conveys the command to care and shelter issued in both Islam and Christianity, especially towards the poor: the seven works of mercy in the latter, the duty of almsgiving and mutual support according to the former.

## Cultural Nettles

The story of the Flight has offered a meeting point for different faiths; could it present a model of the way a story held in common can work to build conviviality? Moulids, or saints'-day festivals in Egypt, were frequent and highly popular, both local and countrywide; they still flourish in spite of official disapproval, filled with a spirit of conviviality, fostered because – just as in more restrictive times in Europe – girls and boys, men and women, can meet there and mingle freely and enjoy themselves.

In a pioneering and invaluable first-hand study published in 1941, *The Moulids of Egypt*, J. W. McPherson describes his enthusiastic participation in the festivals. He sometimes visited them with his friend the anthropologist E. E. Evans Pritchard, and wrote his book as an urgent plea for the preservation of the customs, the dancing and singing, the recitations, processions and other entertainments that took place and the fellowship and mutual enjoyment they inspired. McPherson was an old Egyptian hand: he lived for over thirty years in the country, working in the Ministries of Education and Agriculture in Cairo in

1914–18 and later in the Ministry of the Interior. His book maps and inventories hundreds of festivals, from 'microscopic', 'very small' and 'very unpretentious' to the fully fledged, splendid examples of which the moulid at Matarea is one. He is a high-spirited guide, relishing the joyous and often anarchic atmosphere and lamenting official clampdowns on exuberance and the disappearance of rides, swings and sideshows, such as the Egyptian puppets: 'Has it suddenly become a sin to watch a shadow show or a *hawi* or a snake charmer, or a conjuror, *balawani* or fire-eater? And poor Qara Goz, the Punch of the East who has been a good Moslem here and in Turkey and elsewhere for hundreds of years! Has he turned heretic in his old age?' He sees a killjoy reductionism in separating sacred and profane activities and reminds readers that *profanum* simply meant in front of the temple (rather than inside it). McPherson, who had for a period rented a 'chalet' in Matarea as a refuge from the city, describes the custom of hanging handkerchiefs on holy trees – he notes three such shrines in the area, two being sacred to Muslim saints. He adds, 'Many Moslems come to the Coptic relics of Mar Tadros in the hope of cures or blessings, and hundreds of non-Catholics, largely Moslems, to the Catholic shrine of St Teresa of Shoubra, bearing their votive gifts. Numerous similar cases could be cited, where Christians have sought cures and blessings at Muslim shrines.' These customs were already under threat when he was writing, and the majority of the moulids he attended gathered in groups along religious lines.

In a thoughtful article, 'What Do Egypt's Copts and Muslims Share? The Issue of Shrines', the scholar Catherine Mayeur-Jaouen records that by 2009, when she published her observations, interfaith conflict had reached a level of serious and violent hostility. She regrets the waning of mutual entertainment, regardless of denomination, which had existed before, when the traditional festivals celebrating a local saint coincided with significant dates in the agricultural cycle. These moulids drew together neighbours whatever their creed, to eat, sing, dance, pray and make offerings to shared holy figures, such as Mary/Mariam. The public recitations by a *raawi* or storyteller on such occasions were inspired by ancient *siras*, or epics, featuring St George and the Dragon or St Theodore overcoming another fiend.

Mayeur-Jaouen relates the friendly eclecticism that had prevailed in the common work of agriculture and the seasonal cycle on which the inhabitants of Upper Egypt depended. She states that societies which need the harvest to succeed, which pay equal attention to rainfall, dew and the rising waters of the Nile, develop easier relations with one other on account of their necessary common interest, whatever their religious allegiance. The agricultural calendar regulates their lives, and binds them to a shared destiny, whichever god or prophets and holy figures they address in their praises and prayers. Agrarian communities are more likely to make common cause than urban ones – a very important insight, garnered mainly from anthropological research. She points out that the fundamentalist side of contemporary Islam is growing ever more severe, and that the Copts, through an effect of mimicry, had already also begun, in the early 2000s when she was doing her research, to purify the cults and erect barriers between the belief systems. This trend has hardened in recent decades, recalling Puritan iconoclasm, when similar official opposition to popular forms of religious expression, led to the razing of Walsingham (see Chapter 4). In Saudi Arabia, popular shrines around Mecca have been demolished, on the grounds that they are rooted in pure legend and are therefore superstitious, false, apocryphal. For example, the site of the tomb of Amina, the Prophet's mother, where pilgrims to Mecca have visited and prayed for centuries, was destroyed in 1998. In Middle Egypt, the funeral songs of local inhabitants, sung by professional female mourners, are beginning to disappear; the Islamic authorities disapprove of the tradition, a survival of pre-Islamic ritual, some of the laments even reprising the ancient *Egyptian Book of the Dead*.

Omar-Hussein Radjy, a journalist living in Cairo and an admirer of McPherson's fieldwork, is himself a keen participant in moulids, and reports that many are still thriving as ebullient social gatherings, combining pilgrimage and partying, though the *rawis*, fortune-tellers, snake charmers and fire eaters have retreated. But he casts doubts on their current ecumenical openness.

What can be concluded from these inconsistent glimpses at different periods is that popular folk practices, especially when followed by women, tend to be less doctrinally pure than official rites, and have consistently been censured and stifled by authorities, clerical and other, who invoke principles of authenticity and canonicity. As Virginia Woolf remarks, only half-ironically, about Betty Flanders in her novel *Jacob's Room*, 'who shall deny that this blankness of mind when combined with profusion, mother wit, old wives' tales, haphazard ways, moments of astonishing daring, humour, and sentimentality – who shall deny that in these respects every woman is nicer than any man?' Woolf was always split between patrician disdain and emancipatory sympathy with women's lot, and there is a clear edge to her portrait of Betty and the rhetorical question she asks, but it raises a persistent unease about country customs.

There are traces of a Pascalian wager in the plurality of some gatherings: any saint or all saints, whichever faith reveres them, however apocryphal, might help. But in relation to creating sanctuary now, syncretism is intrinsically more tolerant than purism and offers a basis for dissolving binaries of exclusion/inclusion, purity/impurity, belief/unbelief, naivety/sophistication, true/apocryphal, high/low.

Sanctuary figures in a double sense on these occasions: as a holy site hallowed by the body of a loved and revered saint, and as a form of freedom – to mingle, to move, to assemble (with strangers), to have fun. A moulid can be seen as a carnival, and in the United States, the UK, Latin America and all over Europe, Catholic and Protestant, Mardi Gras celebrations have long forged communities from disparate elements, with far-reaching strengthening effects. Amid the mounting racism – and violence – of postwar Britain, Claudia Jones, a Trinidad-born editor and journalist, helped found the Notting Hill Carnival as a conscious act of repair: 'she understood the power of culture as a tool of political resistance', commented one of her colleagues. This three-day annual summer festival has grown, unimpeded by periods of difficulty, into a crucial fixture of the city's calendar and a defiant statement of its identity, plural, multi-ethnic, tolerant and joyous. 'It's sanctuary and it's acceptance,' Matthew Phillip, the carnival CEO from 2020, has said.

Attitudes to the carnivalesque are changing and the festival's role in fostering common bonds has been widely recognized. It is no longer seen as dissident and disruptive, conducive to disorder and violence, a mere interlude of licensed topsy-turvy before society sets itself back to rights; instead, regarded as a tool of unity, it has entered mainstream and official culture. No less an institution than the National Gallery in London commissioned the artist Jeremy Deller, who is politically radical and committed to folklore and folk practices, to celebrate the gallery's bicentenary in 2024–5; he is organizing nationwide popular expressions of joy and activism, to be called 'The Triumph of Art', with processions, pageants, manifestations – in effect, a series of moulids. The conjoining of date and place with a mass assembly in a public space that is free to enter and move around in, united in a common cause for celebration – or supplication or placation – can act as a powerful catalyst to the making of sanctuary.

~

The apocrypha of the Infancy gospels have returned in two very divergent milieux: in the fiction of J. M. Coetzee, the Nobel Prize-winner and acerbic observer, and in the Gipsy ballads performed by Sam Lee, one of the most remarkable folk singers working today.

To the bafflement of many critics, Coetzee consciously revisited the apocryphal tradition in a trilogy of novels (2013–19) which invoke the New Testament in their titles – *The Childhood of Jesus*, *The Schooldays of Jesus* and *The Death of Jesus*. The story centres on an uncanny, prodigious orphan boy in a strange place at an unspecified time, with a feel of the present or perhaps the near future. The child is never named Jesus as such but is known as David. He is adopted by an older man, Simon, who feels compelled to take charge of him, and a woman, Inez, who's inexplicably recognized by Simon as destined to become David's mother. This summons to an unforeseen destiny, somewhat resembling the numinous calling of Matthew in the New Testament, replaces the annunciation to Mary, and represents Coetzee's off-kilter yet flat approach to his perturbing narratives. The boy and his mismatched and perplexed parents are also migrants, fleeing one place for another, called Novilla, or new town. They will be displaced again and will remember only fragments of their lives before and who they were. When David is noticed and labelled strange by the authorities, the makeshift family must move again.

While resisting interpretation, the three novels palpably align themselves with uncanonical literature and the tradition of apocrypha, for the young protagonist of Coetzee's fable is likewise unique, prodigious and unintelligible. He is a charismatic figure, a child magus with a peculiar aura who ineluctably draws those around him into caring for him, following him. In the last book, he falls mysteriously ill and dies.

It is hard to catch Coetzee's tone. He is clearly not a subaltern writing back to empire, as in Salman Rushdie's phrase, but has chosen to leave his native South Africa for Adelaide in Australia, and his public identity is now hybrid, partly Australian. The novels are heterodox as works of contemporary fiction, as well as reinventions of the figure of the young Messiah/Jesus. Are they seriously intended, or are they parodies? Deep reflections on displacement, charisma and providence, or mocking fables? Are they oblique attacks on trust in charismatic figures? The inscrutability is the point. The writer is unquestionably engaged with an alternative tradition distinct from both the analytical novel of mores and the magical realist fiction of dream and fantasy. Coetzee destabilizes psychological and social norms of mimesis, creates a strange young prodigy as his unfathomable young hero, and follows him into made-up countries of exile, a contemporary dystopia, as he exercises a powerful, mysterious effect on his surroundings and on all those who come into contact with him. If Coetzee were not a Nobel Prize-winning writer, no publisher would have taken the risk of bringing out such works, which resist comprehension and conventional storytelling so truculently. However, Coetzee's double iconoclastic move against pieties, literary and religious, intensifies the trilogy's enigmatic hold on the reader, while the books' disorientating effect is oddly pleasurable, like seeing a familiar place as if for the first time. But it would be clumsy to read Coetzee as a contemporary Voltaire, for his social critique shows no sign of Voltairean levity. The Jesus trilogy is funny peculiar, written in Coetzee's characteristic formal monotone, as if he were struggling with a foreign language, and the phrasing is stiff and lustreless, which intensifies the bizarre effect of the scenes evoked. However, this simplicity and lack of ornament picks up on the genre of the apocrypha, whose authors also tend to declare the prodigies bluntly, blocking out the narrative in paratactic sentences following one after the other.

At midpoint in the first book, *The Childhood of Jesus*, Coetzee stages a discussion between Simon and others about 'the concept of the real'. One of the interlocutors argues that 'climate' is real because you can feel the wind and the rain. But history cannot be felt in the same way. 'He looks around. "Which of us has ever had his cap blown off by history?" There is silence. "No one. Because history has no manifestations. Because history is not real. Because history is just a made-up story."' Here, Coetzee is addressing the question of writing the past, and letting the reader into his confidence, admitting to the unreliability of his literary art. He's not a historian but has written fictions that are intricately bound up with history. In his Jesus trilogy, he almost declares the writer's work akin to marvellous tales spun to excite allegiance and belief. The exchange admits that stories are also effective when they are fabricated, as they frequently are.

Another surprise resurfacing of Middle Eastern Christian apocrypha came to my attention when I heard Sam Lee sing in London, in the Foundling Museum. For a decade Lee travelled the archipelago of the British Isles to learn songs from traveller communities, and he now has a vast repertoire of ballads which would otherwise almost inevitably have been lost. His voice has an eerie, otherworldly beauty, and he floats it in its shimmering purity in astonishing vibrating sheets of sound, with thrilling trills, slides and grace notes. He often sings unaccompanied, standing up straight and tall as if the music were descending into him from the sky, just as the men and women from whom he learned this music do when singing for one another in family groups or larger gatherings. One of his chief teachers was Stanley Robertson, who knew hundreds of ballads from his aunt, the legendary Scottish folk singer Jeannie Robertson; Stanley adopted Lee as a keeper of their traditions and songs by giving him a ring and a talismanic stone. Lee also tracked down many other balladeers – including a shepherd called Enos White, and a woman, Freda Black, who was born a Romany in Somerset and married into a traveller family. In her eighties when Lee met her, Freda remembered an old ballad about the child Jesus. Just as in the apocryphal gospels he pleads with 'Mary mild' to let him go out and play with other boys and, when she does, the boys reject him crying out, 'we are lords' and ladies' sons', so in the ballad Jesus magics a bridge from sunbeams and lures his playmates on to it and they drown. The lyrics then part with the ancient sources and describe how Mary 'laid our Saviour across her knee / And with a handful of bitter withy / She gave him lashes three'. Black also passed on to Lee songs about curses and metamorphoses from a fusion of Ovid and Christian piety: a woman who refuses to give alms to a beggar is turned into an owl.

'The Gypsies are our Native Americans,' Lee told the *Observer* journalist Ed Vulliamy. 'They practise a kind of shamanism mixed with Christianity and the old beliefs.' He also remarked, speaking directly to ways of making sanctuary today, that culture is made by working with what is to hand. 'What is wilderness in this country,' he asked, 'where there is no real unspoilt land? I see wilderness in Britain as stinging nettles submerging a disused rubbish tip. Or a Gypsy camp, washing hanging between the caravans. Gypsies and nettles fit into any landscape, and Gypsy folk song is *made-up cultural nettles*' (italics added). Is it possible to foster nettles, to make them up, to sow and plant them?

Cultural nettles! Seeded by chance, growing untended, nutritious, self-defended.

'Leisure worlds, or worlds for pleasure,' writes Thomas Pavel '[often] derive from older discarded models' such as feudal society, fairy tales, stars of the silver screen. 'Each culture has its ontological ruins, its historical parks where members of the community relax and contemplate their ontological relics. Greek and Roman gods performed this function till late in the history of European culture' (and, one might add, world culture has not done with them yet). The memorial enterprise honours the departed by preserving their things, their habitat, but it also writes and rewrites history to include figures who represent the excluded and marginalized. The dwellings are consecrated as *lieux de mémoire*, while the methods used to summon the dead are adapted to realize figures of fantasy, the Sleeping Beauty or the mermaids in *Peter Pan*. The two worlds overlap and the distinction between history and imagination dissolves in the tableaux, such as Disneyland's *Pirates of the Caribbean*, which draw on history to include fantastic and thrilling personae alongside remembered heroes, and to generate fresh ones on the screen. Since impresarios like Walt Disney conceived this modern form of commemoration, the hunger to re-enact the past and make contact with the aura of the dead has been on the increase: a form of secular sanctity, a variation on the tradition of shrines and sanctuaries, and a stage for generating ontological moorings or compass bearings, for activating dwelling places of the mind.

In his fantasy castle, Neuschwanstein, near Munich (left), King Ludwig of Bavaria's lived a dream past; his vision inspired Disneyland's Sleeping Beauty Castle (1955) and its many progeny.

Many of the principles that form the state of sanctuary are also operating in theme parks: pilgrimage, relics, assembly, re-enactment and sales of souvenirs (often miniature models of the sacred edifice), all characterize the infinitely popular outings to Disneyworld or Alton Towers. These are present-day heterotopias, established within their boundaries, sometimes with their own currency, and filled with simulacra and models of other places that share their iconic aura. Ludwig of Bavaria obsessively recreated German legends of Siegfried and enchanted swan maidens in his pleasure gardens and palaces, and sought to reproduce faraway wonders, such as Capri's Blue Grotto. His follies translate once sacred myths into secular vehicles of individual pleasure. His scene-setting depended on a linked chain of images – his Siegfried idyll was transmitted through Wagner; in turn the Wagnerian motifs generated a fugue of more travelling dreams. Ludwig wasn't altogether de-hallowing the territory – these stories were in many ways holy to him. His fairy-tale castle of Neuschwanstein (New Swan Stone) inspired Walt Disney to construct the first of the signature centrepieces of his theme parks. He invoked a fairy tale – *Cinderella* – rather than the *Ring* cycle. This first steepling castle, which rises in Anaheim, a dreary, flat, dusty part of Greater Los Angeles, has podded many more fantasy castles – reaching as far as China and Japan – which enshrine different

'Disney princesses'. These edifices, dwellings of fantasy beings, fold back on reality and change it in their own image, until the local inhabitants, as well as travellers or literary pilgrims, revel in those places in the light of the narratives that have been made up and take place in them.

The marvellous does not remain in the mouths of storytellers or in the pages of print or manuscript but can be inscribed on the territory, conferring precise coordinates on prodigious events, and thus embodied material landmarks – buildings where such and such took place, trees which witnessed the miracle, stones which retained the imprint of the events. It is less a literature than a form of land art, often audible rather than visible, less intelligible than cryptic, inscribed in signs that only the community of the story can discern.

In *Figuring the Sacred*, Paul Ricoeur provides a generous response to this process; referring to the many divergent legends of Mary Magdalene, he writes, 'new possibilities of being in the world are opened up within everyday reality . . . and in this way everyday reality is metamorphosed by means of what we would call the imaginative variations that literature works on the real'. The slippage between the imaginary and the actual can be seen in pilgrimages, ancient and more recent, that identify a place as belonging to a sacred time and seek to make it present and real.

# 3
# Relics:
# Helena Dreams of the Cross

*'But we have other lives, I think, I hope,' she murmured. 'We live in others ... We live in things.'*
Virginia Woolf

The story of the discovery of the True Cross by the Roman empress Helena was known across Christendom: in a sermon given in Milan in 395, St Ambrose described Helena praying to the Virgin Mary and identifying herself with her role in salvation: 'As the holy one bore the Lord, I shall search for His cross ... she showed God to be seen among men; I shall raise from the ruins the divine standard as a remedy for our sins ...' The miraculous achievement of St Helena was commemorated in the calendar on several different feast days: the Invention – or Finding – of the Holy Cross on 3 May, the Exaltation on 14 September (which Anglicans call Holy Cross Day) as well as the Feast of St Helena herself on 18 August, while other saints, for example the pope St Sylvester, who was associated with miracles worked by the cross and its relics, is remembered on 31 December. Other Christian churches keep various feast days – for example, the Armenians celebrate the Finding on the Sunday nearest to 26 October.

These feasts of the cross are exceptional in the calendar, in that they memorialize and honour not a person, an individual, but a thing – a relic that was the most precious trace of the Saviour. As he had resurrected and ascended into heaven, there could be no bodily remains; his blood was preserved, his tears, his foreskin (in several examples) and in some churches his hair (but relics of hair are rather too witchy for most Christian believers).

Relics of the Passion: the finger with which St Thomas probed the wound in his side, spines from the Crown of Thorns, and the sign which proclaimed him, 'Jesus of Nazareth, King of the Jews' (bottom right). S. Croce in Gerusalemme, Rome.

In the case of Mary, her analogous, bodily assumption into heaven was widely believed, though it would not be affirmed until the papal bull of 1950, and there were no bones and few other physical remains, except for her milk and a sandal, sometimes a footprint (such physical traces are known as must-be relics, because they must exist). Both Jesus' and Mary's essence was consequently infused into material objects, technically secondary relics, things with which they were in contact: the holy lance; the pillar to which Jesus was tied when he was scourged. These played a vital part in keeping the gap of time closed between the moment of salvation and the present; among the most precious and revered relics were her shift, worn at the Annunciation and kept at Chartres where it drew thousands to pray to conceive, and her girdle, which possessed similar fruitful powers. The Sainte-Chapelle in Paris was built, in all its exquisite, luminous, jewel-like luxury, as a reliquary for a spine from the crown of thorns, which St Louis had acquired at fabulous expense. Baby Jesus' swaddling bands are kept in a strongbox in Aachen, also richly enshrined.

The Veil of Veronica, to which Jesus' features were miraculously transferred, was venerated in Lucca as the cult of the Volto Santo, or Holy Face; the Holy Shroud, similarly imprinted with Jesus' body, became the object of mass devotion in Turin. The wood of the manger, the robe that was torn at the crucifixion, and so on; and in their cult sites local feast days would celebrate the arrival, or translation, of these relics. But it would be fair to say that these cults follow the pattern set by the relics of the True Cross, which according to legend becomes the hero of a salvation epic in itself, generating a parallel scripture and martyrology in which actual historical events and characters interact with fantastical narrative, structured according to the exegetical pattern of prophetic sign, compounded of prefigurement, recapitulation and fulfilment.

In Christian cult the cross takes on the qualities of an autonomous saint, an actor in the drama of salvation, with a dynamic part to play as the hero of an elaborate, circumstantial and ambiguous legend that

Verses from the Anglo-Saxon poem *The Dream of the Rood* are carved in runes on the stone cross (eighth century?). Ruthwell Church, Scotland.

intersects with human history at numerous points and communicates on complex levels of allegorical meaning. *The Dream of the Rood*, written perhaps as early as the seventh or eighth century, stages the cross as it addresses the poet directly, speaking in the first person as if the wood from which the voice issues were imbued with consciousness:

> I was reared as a cross: I raised up the mighty King,
> the Lord of heaven; I dared not lie down.
> They drove dark nails through me; the scars are still visible,
> open wounds of hate; I dared not harm any of them.
> They mocked us both together . . .

The cross continues to suffer with Jesus and indeed merges with the Saviour. In this way, in the Old English poem, attributed to Caedmon (seventh century) or Cynewulf (eighth to tenth century), the supernatural is allowed full presence. The story of the cross as it unfolds in Christian culture loses this unapologetically magical, personified character, and identifying and enshrining actual pieces of material wood takes over. (Traces of this ancient use of personification linger however in the idea of St Cross, as in the names of the feast days and certain places such as St Cross College, Oxford.) The wood has been sanctified by its role in the sacrifice of Jesus, but actual spilling of blood does not, as far as I can tell, play a part in the cult of the many fragments. Veneration of the cross, moving away from bodily literalism towards a condition of pure symbolism, became the focus of new sanctuaries or sacred sites. According to her multi-branching legend, St Helena, the mother of Constantine, the first Christian emperor, saw the True Cross in a vision and set about building churches to house the relics she then sought out and found.

The long poem *Elene*, about Helena, survives in the same tenth-century manuscripts as *The Dream of the Rood*. In it, the Anglo-Saxon poet modifies the anthropomorphic, even animist concept of the cross in the *Dream* poem and moves towards a quasi-positivist quest for actual evidence and historical proof. In this shift from dream to fact the fantasy of the cross's vitality, the speaking wood, is replaced by relics formally certified to be the real thing. It's a decisive change of perspective, from confidence in fantasy and the supernatural to a need for proof of authenticity.

*Elene* was written in Old English after a lost Latin version sometime between 750 and the tenth century; some scholars have identified the signature – in runes – of Cynewulf. If this is so it would be his longest extant poem. It relates how St Helena, the mother of the emperor Constantine, set out to find the True Cross on which Jesus had been crucified and succeeded in discovering where it had been buried in Jerusalem; she then had it cut up and distributed the fragments throughout Christendom where these inestimably valued relics were enshrined in reliquaries and displayed on or enclosed in altars to hallow the ground. Through the power of connection to the original sacrifice of Jesus, the humble splinters – it is a central paradox that the most precious relics are the paltriest bits of stuff – created sanctuaries.

Helena's vision and activity provided Rome, Constantinople and many other cities with a backstory. The arrival of a new relic served to transform the site of a temple into a Christian sanctuary, erasing the memory of the pagan divinity worshipped there before. But the historical connection the relic established was above all a future plan, directed at leading the imagination of worshippers; it drip-fed into the unconscious the symbols of Christianity; these then continued to pulse through the bodies – and the minds – of the people, shaping the community and furnishing it with a history.

By looking for bones and other mementoes and material traces of the founding centuries of Christianity, Helena closed the gap of three centuries that separated the origins of the faith from its recognition by Constantine. Above all, her legend credits her with the coup of excavating the very cross on which Jesus died, and identifying the nails used to hang him on it. This most famous episode in her story is probably the most apocryphal, in a history that is largely imaginary already. However, it remains the case historically that the True Cross, dispersed in tiny shards and splinters, founded sanctuaries the length and breadth of the empire. A relic of the True Cross hallowed a place, incorporated it into the community of the faithful, Christianized it.

Helena's deeds are well recorded elsewhere, including in the eulogizing biography of Constantine written by Eusebius, Bishop of Caesarea; he rhapsodizes about Helena's virtues, recounting what a force the empress mother became in establishing a Christian cult, especially when she identified 'two mystic caves' in Bethlehem and

Jerusalem, one as the birthplace of Jesus and the other as the Holy Sepulchre. There she founded churches, and 'continually making personal visits to the church of God, she adorned the place of worship with shining treasures ... One might see the wonderful woman in dignified and modest attire joining the throng and manifesting reverence towards the divinity by every kind of practice dear to God.'

Eusebius, the leading contemporary witness to Helena's life and character, doesn't mention her finding the True Cross. Early chroniclers tend to be partisan, and embroider their material in order to magnify their subjects. History becomes a form of panegyric – or diatribe – written for maximum drama, packed with supernatural interventions and fairy-tale coincidences and epiphanies.

According to her legend, Helena is credited with creating a network of churches in a structure parallel to the far-flung Roman empire, sowing relics across the map of the empire in order to establish new places of worship. Her political effect in joining disparate communities across the turbulent later empire in the unity of the faith, as exemplified by its temples and shrines, raised her to a prime place in Christian myths of origin. The warranties were stratified: first the gospels, then the blood of the early martyrs, and, when the church was no longer persecuted, relics. Relics, introduced into a building, transformed it, raising a place of public assembly or private devotion to the status of a holy precinct. In this sacred economy, the cross and its relics were the paramount bearers of value, and the saint who had found them in the first place became subject to competing stories and claims of identity by artists and writers as well as the faithful, who find in Helena the person a stimulus to the recreative imagination stronger than the inanimate wood of the relic.

This was a central strategy of the church; the liturgy and related storytelling planted material evidence all over the territory of the faithful and potential believers, mobilizing the power of a story by inscribing it in the fabric of buildings in the form of fragmentary relics and images: sacred icons and also storytelling cycles. Jacques Le Goff, in his book *In Search of Sacred Time*, discusses the most influential anthology of saints' lives, the *Golden Legend*, by Jacobus de Voragine. 'Within Jacobus sacralized time', he writes, 'there are feasts commemorating the discovery or translation dates of saints' relics, and there is no more sacred relic in Christendom than the cross of Christ.' He adds,

'The sacralization of time can only be accomplished by a complementary and sometimes synchronic sacralization of space.' Relics changed the meaning of a place: they made it the tomb/home of a certain holy power, through the narratives that located them in historical time and enfleshed them. They do not age, the power of their originals lasts: copies are filled with numen.

The *Legenda Aurea* or *Golden Legend*, written in the second half of the thirteenth century by Jacobus de Voragine, the Dominican Bishop of Genoa, presents the most widely circulated source for Helena's rich legend, compiled by the garrulous prelate from older sources. His popular, widely disseminated book follows the calendar of the year, with all the feast days narrated in colourful and even lurid scenes, unfurling the immense historical panorama of salvation from Adam and Eve onwards. It served as one of the richest primers for artists to draw on and, through the paintings on walls of churches above all, the stories spread. As Jacques Le Goff writes, 'The sacred time of the *Golden Legend* is a profoundly imagistic time.' Jacobus' entries for the feasts of St Helena, of the Invention of the Holy Cross and of its Exaltation combine to relate an extraordinarily elaborate and circumstantial story of prophecy and fulfilment as the tree which will become the cross suffers the vicissitudes of history. For centuries it served as an alternative canonical sourcebook, a fabulous, often gruesome gallimaufry of traditional lore, miracle stories and chroniclers' evidence, not found in the gospels or the Acts of the Apostles; its author conveys irrepressible excitement about the incidents, miracles and anecdotes recounted.

One would expect that the Feast of the Exaltation of the Holy Cross would count as a most solemn occasion, but the learned bishop repeats a story from Gregory of Tours: a nun sees a fine plump lettuce in the convent garden and can't resist it; she takes a bite out of it without making a sign of the cross beforehand, and a devil jumps out at her and, taking possession of her, throws her down. A saintly bishop has to be called in, and the devil protests: 'What have I done? I was sitting on the lettuce and she came and bit me!'

Until the Counter-Reformation, the *Golden Legend* remained the most influential handbook for artists in every medium – hymn writers, poets and liturgists. The stories accruing around the True Cross exhibit the far-fetched fantasy, the liking for prefiguration and allegory, and the taste for the outlandish and the marvellous that so disgusted the Reformers about Catholic cult that they attacked relics, scorning them as false, and destroyed many images that reproduced the legend. So many pieces of the cross were claimed to be authentic that Calvin, an indignant critic of Catholic superstition, scoffed: 'if all the pieces that could be found were collected together, they would make a big shipload. Yet the Gospel testifies that a single man was able to carry it.' In the nineteenth century, the devout architect Charles Rohault de Fleury calculated, by carefully adding up all the known fragments of the cross (from Aix-la-Chapelle to Wambach) that they would amount to only a small part of the necessary size of the crucifix (178 million cubic centimetres).

Such a defence would have provoked the fine mirth of Voltaire; both Calvin's attack and Rohault's scrupulous sums offend rational thought and lead to wastes of absurdity. The insistence on the wood as the actual cross misses the significance of symbolism and the experience of such fantastic stories for their receivers.

The *Golden Legend* presents providential history, the past as wonder tale made up by God. Jacobus is a blithe, rambling storyteller and, like many a gleeful gossip, loves to pass on hearsay and innuendo and speculation with a stream of evasions, protestations and disclaimers. Towards the beginning of his very full and lively entry for the Feast of the Finding of the Holy Cross, he says, 'Whether any of this is true we leave to the reader's judgement, because none of it is found in any authentic chronicle or history.' Yet he cannot stop himself relating that, quite apart from the True Cross and the nails, Helena also brought back hay from the manger at Bethlehem and the bodies of the three kings, which are still enshrined in Cologne cathedral in a magnificent silver-gilt casket, created *c.*1225 and sculpted in high relief with numerous figures of saints.

The *Golden Legend* plunders sources in Greek, Latin and Syriac, but it overtook them, imprinted the legend of the True Cross on the Christian world, and triumphantly entered orthodoxy, exercising a huge appeal to many artists whose works travelled. Illustrations to manuscripts of the *Legenda*, and paintings on the walls of churches provided the congregation with the backstory, with especial vividness when one of the precious pieces of wood from the cross was enshrined in that place.

The elaborate story cycle begins with the Death of Adam who, as he lies dying, sends his son Seth to the angel barring the gates of Eden to ask for the oil of mercy. But instead the angel tells Seth to plant a slip from the tree of knowledge (in other versions, a pip of one of the apples) on Adam's grave. The seedling that sprouts from it is destined to grow into the tree that will be the instrument of human salvation, the very wood from which the cross will be made.

This story appears in the entry for the Feast of the Exaltation of the Holy Cross because 'on this day the faith and the holy cross were raised to the heights'. The frescoes Piero della Francesca painted around 1452–66 on the walls of the sanctuary chapel in the basilica of San Francesco in Arezzo, remain the most celebrated and consummate pictorial rendering of the whole narrative cycle. It closes with a lunette fresco showing the cross held on high before a group of worshippers in exotic attire, to emphasize the worldwide reach of the faith in the present and in the future.

Piero's complex series is among the greatest achievements of the early Renaissance. It unfolds the legend of the True Cross in an elaborate

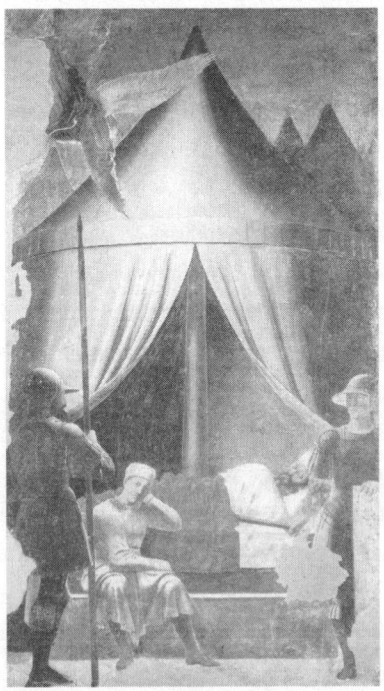

The Roman Emperor Constantine dreamed he would triumph under the 'sign of the Cross' over Maxentius, his rival. Piero della Francesca, S. Francesco, Arezzo.

sequence of scenes, which follows closely the story as it is told by Jacobus; indeed the narrative remains opaque without knowledge of the *Golden Legend*. Although Piero draws from those picaresque adventures a lucid analysis, his storytelling also reproduces the prejudices of medieval Christianity, especially its deep anti-Semitism. Such religious images pose an acute dilemma: the works' visual grace, inventiveness, harmony and supreme aesthetic qualities clash with the contents of the narrative and the values that it presumes to share with its receivers.

Piero organizes the story in an intellectual and harmonious counterpoint from one side of the chapel to the other, establishing the play of diachronic correspondences between historical characters and events: the Queen of Sheba prefigures the empress Helena; the emperor Constantine's victory over his rival Maxentius foreshadows the triumph of Heraclius over the Persian emperor Chosroes II in 628.

One of the most memorable compositions shows Constantine tucked up in his bivouac, with one of his attendants keeping watch. Piero's sense of drama in this scene brings out the recurring function of prophetic dreams in the story of the True Cross, the crucial connection between visions and relics, and the role that dreams play in the making of sanctuary. They frequently give instructions to the dreamer/visionary as to where a holy trace can be found and where a holy site should therefore be built.

Before the battle that will seal his position as Roman emperor, East and West, Constantine has a dream of a flaming cross and hears the words, 'In hoc signo vinces' (By this sign you shall conquer). A seated youth in the centre of the composition looks out at us, watchful and enigmatic, but seemingly unaware of the dramatic irruption of the angel above, who flies down towards Constantine with his back to us, in an early baroque, virtuoso flourish of *sotto in sù*. The silence of the emperor's sleep and the unconcerned guards on either side of the wakeful young man accentuate the private mystery of the dream message; they exemplify Piero's artistry, which uses the *Golden Legend* only as a structural scaffold. A comparison would be Shakespeare's perceptive choices when he develops his source material. Similarly, there are pillars and groins and fastenings which make up the basic scaffolding that are intrinsically problematic ethically: Jacobus' material belongs to its era, and he shares the attitude to unbelievers of his order, the order that founded the Inquisition. Again this resembles the way that the premises and arguments of the sources for *The Taming of the Shrew* and *The Merchant of Venice* — and indeed Marlowe's *The Jew of Malta* — continue to make those plays profoundly troubling for contemporary audiences.

According to this sacred history, his dream fulfilled prophecy and inspired the victorious Constantine to declare Christianity the official faith of the Roman Empire.

When Helena questions the Jews in Jerusalem about the whereabouts of the cross on which the Saviour died, they refuse to divulge it because they realize, Jacobus tells us, that their religion will be superseded if they do. But one Judas vacillates and Helena has him lowered into a dry well and deprived of food and water until he confesses and agrees to take her to the burial place of the three crosses — including the ones on which the two thieves were crucified on either side of Jesus. (Later in the *Golden Legend*, Judas converts and eventually is martyred and becomes St Cyriacus, and Jacobus adds that one of his sources claims that he was the

St Helena identifies the True Cross. Copy made 1804–7 from original frescoes. Guild Chapel, Stratford-upon-Avon.

brother of St Stephen the proto-martyr who was stoned to death (Acts 7: 54–8). In a typical aside, the Dominican author comments that he doesn't credit this story, because the time gap is too great, but he can't resist adding that perhaps people lived much longer in those days.

Helena has the three crosses dug up, but nobody can tell which one is the True Cross on which Jesus died. The scene was illustrated in a woodcut in Caxton's edition of the book in 1430. She therefore has each of the crosses tested in turn, held over the corpse of a dead youth or, in some versions, of a young woman. The True Cross instantly resuscitates him or her: it is charged with supernatural power (see Plate 5b). This episode from the *Golden Legend* that is most often depicted down the years and this continuum – dream–relic–healing – will characterize the origin and function of many sanctuaries. We saw in the last chapter how Joseph receives his divine messages in his dreams. Helena, clairvoyant dreamer, becomes the protagonist of another sacred story.

Helena doesn't dream in the *Golden Legend*, but in an echo of her son's clairvoyance, later narratives endow her with prophetic powers. She is called to her mission of finding the cross in a dream. Several artists show her as a seer: in a restrained, meditative, austere painting (1570) by Veronese in London's National Gallery she is daydreaming while the cross, full-size and massive, appears in the window beside her, airily aloft in the arms of cherubim (see Plate 4). Ten years later the same artist painted her again in sumptuous colour; this scene (in the Vatican Museum) is far more sensuous and unrestrained as it shows Helena enthroned, her head resting on her hand, opulently arrayed in a rich brocade dress and velvet cloak with a splendid diadem on her head. She inclines in a reverie, while a cherub, his naked back to us, manoeuvres the cross on the ground towards her; it seems too hefty for him to handle, as if Veronese became anxious that the flying *angioletti* of his earlier painting did not give an adequate sense of the materiality of the relic Helena would discover and identify.

## Helena Augusta

The *Golden Legend* mingles verifiable events from the past with symbolic narrative and supernatural fantasy in a form of proto-magical realism. But

Helena herself is a historical figure of great interest, a powerful innovator of what Leslie Brubaker has called 'matronage' in Byzantium.

Helena was born around 250 CE in Drepanum in Bithynia (now Hersek, a small town in Turkish Asia Minor); she was said to be a *stabularia*, which might mean a stable girl or even a tapster and carry worrying overtones of easy virtue (one source glosses this as 'a common woman not different from strumpets'). She met the future emperor Constantius when he was an officer in the Roman army; he was known as Chlorus (Livid), probably after his complexion. Around 272, they had a son, the future emperor Constantine. But when the boy was about sixteen Constantius repudiated Helena to marry Theodora, emperor Maximian's daughter; in 305, he rose to become the senior deputy Emperor of the West; his death the following year ended his ambitious ascent and precipitated his son into the role of emperor-in-waiting and Helena into the role of dowager empress.

In 306 Constantine was proclaimed Augustus by the army, in York. In 323, with the Edict of Milan, Constantine famously declared religious tolerance across the empire, including the newish religion from the East, Christianity, thus ending decades of bloody persecution. In 323, he had the momentous dream of future victory under the sign of a flaming cross; he went on to defeat his co-emperor Maxentius for the supreme position in the Roman empire at the battle of the Milvian bridge over the Danube. He began restoring church property, and convoked and was present at the Council of Nicaea which defined, in the Nicene creed, the tenets of the faith. The year before, he had proclaimed his mother empress: 'Augusta Imperatrix'.

As an act of homage to the instrument of Jesus' death, he ended the Roman penalty of crucifixion, it is recorded. His mother Helena converted before her son, as early as 312 CE, though it is not known when or how she travelled to the Holy Land. She is reputed to have strongly influenced her son's merciful attitude to Christianity and Christians, although Constantine himself probably didn't become a professed Christian until he was dying in 337, when he was baptized. He too became a saint and often shares cult rituals with his mother – in the Orthodox church they are venerated together on 21 May (along with Mary and Jesus, they make a rare mother–son appearance in the calendar).

Constantine seems to have held his mother in great honour, not only proclaiming her 'Nobilissma Femina' and empress, but renaming her birthplace Helenopolis and burying her in the magnificent mausoleum in Rome he had originally planned for himself. Gold coins were issued in her name during her lifetime – without Christian symbols. Her porphyry sarcophagus – imperial, pagan and classical – had also probably been intended for Constantine. In the eleventh century it was moved from the mausoleum to the Lateran and is now on display in the Vatican. The ruins of the vast spherical tomb itself, which stands on the ancient Via Labicana (now the Via Casilino) near the entrance to the catacombs of SS Marcellino e Pietro ad Duas Lauros, have been restored and reopened.

This Helena figures as a builder of churches, and an effective Christian activist. However, it is likely that her legend grew up to validate existing cult sites, and that her journey to the Eastern empire was motivated by diplomatic and political needs rather than piety, though the two are intertwined. But the stories of her heroic role effloresced, putting down deep roots; they can be compared to a cutting taken from history, as it were, and planted in a rich loam of dreams and political ambition, well fed on fantasy and watered in hopes, until it grows tall, becomes an object of passionate veneration and overshadows whatever really happened.

## The Essex Girl

Constantius' military campaign in Britain, and their son Constantine's proclamation as emperor in York gave a British complexion to Helena's family, and a parallel and contradictory story of her birth and upbringing began to flourish. When I was researching the legend of the cross in the Warburg Institute, I came across an inscription written in a neat scholarly hand on a photograph of a Lucas Cranach painting: 'St Helena. Empress. d. circa 328, Aug. 18, Rome. *b. Colchester*' (italics added). According to this tradition, vigorously upheld in the town to this day, Helen was the daughter of King Coel, the *dux Britannicorum*, or leader of the Britons, in the mid-third century CE; Coel (pronounced Coil) derives either from Latin Colonia, which may have given the name to the local river, the Colne, or from *ceol*, music or melody in Gaelic. Hence, perhaps, his character in the nursery rhyme: 'Old King Cole was a merry old soul, / And a merry old soul was he; / He called for his pipe, and he called for his drum, / And he called for his fiddlers three.' The sense has melted into mood, sound and pattern, forming a song that's part of the memory fabric of English childhood.

Old King Cole has been long identified with the Col in Colchester (Coel's castle) and with the historic personage, the Coel who reigned over territory from the Wash to Hadrian's Wall. Born in Wales, Coel made an accommodation with the Romans and their general Constantius; he remained in power – a kind of satrap within the Roman empire. The agreement with the Roman colonialists was sealed in 270 when Coel married his daughter Helena to Constantius. At least that is how the history lives on as told in Essex.

Rumour that Helena wasn't a Greek from Bithynia but an Essex girl began with Henry of Huntingdon's *Historia Anglorum*, first published *c.*1129, an account of the history of England from its beginnings up to the year 1154 when the *Historia* stops. (It's assumed Henry died.) Henry had a knack for colourful anecdote: he is the source for the story of King Canute holding back the waves, for example. It seems that he mixed up a daughter of King Coel who was indeed called Helen with the Helena who married Constantius. That the empress mother was an ancient Briton then passed into the highly readable and popular *History of the Kings of Britain* by Geoffrey of Monmouth, written *c.*1136, which maps a mythological vision of his own times linked to ancient Rome through King Arthur and his ancestor Brutus who, according to this legend, was a Trojan who landed in Totnes.

Geoffrey's *History* is lively and colourful and went into many editions; translated into Anglo-Norman, it stimulated the growth of Arthurian legends in English and French. It also gives the story of King Lear and Cordilla (Cordelia), which inspired the opening scene of Shakespeare's play, and of King Bladud, the father of King Lear, who was cured of leprosy and died while attempting to fly. Geoffrey's heroine is a paragon: 'The dead man has only a single daughter, the most devout Helen [sic], endowed above all the girls of the Western regions with beauty of face, wise, eloquent, noted for the liberal arts and stamped with the mark of Christ.'

The city of Colchester is dedicated to St Helen, and she is remembered on its coat of arms, on the crowned turret of the town hall and in several street names. The town is by no means the only site in the British Isles where, in spite of the Reformation, the empress whose son recognized Christianity across the Roman empire is commemorated. Over a hundred parish churches are dedicated to her, including St Helen's, Bishopsgate, which was Shakespeare's local place of worship for a while when he was in London working in that area. The legend took root across the world, in Byzantium as well as Western Christendom. The medieval church of Saint-Leu-Saint-Gilles, in the Rue Saint-Denis in the 1st arrondissement in Paris, includes a crypt where the Greek Orthodox rites are observed beside a resplendent Gothic Revival ark-like reliquary containing another relic of St Helena, rescued from the Revolutionary iconoclasts and enshrined in Saint-Leu-Saint-Gilles in 1820. The Moscow Patriarchate hold weekly ceremonies here. The island of St Helena was so called because the Portuguese admiral, João da Nova, anchored in a bay of the then uninhabited rock on one of her feast days (21 May) on his way home after his victory over the ruler of Calicut. His anchorage was marked by a wooden chapel, and grew into the island's chief settlement, Jamestown.

In the ruins of the Roman theatre in Colchester, situated against the former city walls, stands St Helen's chapel, a very small, simple and ancient casket-shaped building of ashlar and brick; local claims describe Helen founding it herself, and even being buried in it; it has been used for a variety of purposes, for example as a chantry and as the original grammar school. It was restored by the Victorian Gothic Revivalist William Butterfield no less, and in 1995–6 consecrated as a Greek Orthodox parish church in the Patriarchate of Antioch. The congregation had previously 'worshipped in the Coop funerary chapel', I was informed by Father Alexander Haig, the parish priest of St Helen's chapel.

Around twenty years ago, he received a parcel from Wichita, Kansas; inside was a round silver box – like a napkin ring if the apertures were glazed. In this pyx Father Alexander found a tiny piece of bone, about the size of a splinter that you might come across in a sausage or a hamburger and feel a little worried by the live contact the fragment gives you to the flesh you are eating: bone brings back the animal. This reaction wouldn't be disrespectful, as the cult of relics aims to pin time back against itself and raise the heroes of the faith vividly before one's eyes, within reach again – sometimes a pilgrim will be invited to touch, kiss and wear a relic, establishing material contact with the body of the saint.

The bone was gifted to the parish in Colchester by Bishop Basil, who had been visiting the monastery at Tiptree for a prayer retreat. There he had met Father Alexander, and on parting from him promised to send him the relic in his possession, because he thought it far more fitting for the patron saint to be enshrined in Colchester than in Wichita, Texas. Bishop Basil passed on that it had been certified authentic in the eighteenth century by the Archbishop of Malines, Belgium, who had taken it from the empress mother's body in its burial place in Rome.

When he had described the relic's history, Father Haig retired behind the iconostasis – the screen which separates the inner sanctum where the altar stands from the body of the chapel where the congregation gathers – put on his vestments of gold damask and returned bearing the bone of St Helena in its silver reliquary. Every year, it is carried in procession around the chapel and the old town. By means of these rituals from the Eastern branch of Christendom, Bithynian Helena and Essex Helen fused.

∼

The British Saint Helen makes a sparkling appearance in Evelyn Waugh's historical novel *Helena* (1950), which, unexpectedly, he considered his best book. His heroine is the daughter of Coel, but Waugh has taken his cue from the *stabularia* from Bithynia, for his Helena is also pony-mad and spends her time mucking out stables and galloping across the fields of East Anglia. The Catholic writer combines an affectionate cartoon picture of upper-class young Englishwomen and their horsey pursuits with a fervent manifesto of Christian historicity, drawing a marvellously comic and engaging portrait of a teenage Amazon, red-haired, intelligent, vivacious and expert in the saddle – and in the stable yard. Waugh opens his novel with his heroine reading Homer with her tutor and wondering at her resonant name and its implications for her own role in the history of the world. When she first meets her husband-to-be – Constantius 'the Green', as Waugh keeps calling him – she sees through his claim that he has travelled from Rome because she recognizes the breed of his horse and knows that it comes from further east. The future Roman empress talks in a mixture of debutante excitement, schoolgirl slang and no-nonsense frankness: her spiritedness shows in everything she says and does, with great good humour and a sense of female potential heroism that comes unexpectedly from this writer.

Waugh also has fun with insider know-how thanks to the book's dedicatee, Penelope Chetwode. She was a very keen horsewoman and the wife of the poet John Betjeman, chief chronicler of the parish churches of England and champion of antiquarian admiration for medievalizing Victoriana. During the interminable banquet in Helena's father's hall when he welcomes Constantius and hands Britain over to him by treaty, we see Waugh at his most virtuoso. He interweaves a hilarious dramatization of the nursery rhyme about Old King Cole and his pipers and fiddlers three, with a comic account of the Greek, Trojan and Arthurian history of the British Isles taken from Geoffrey of Monmouth, and intercuts it all with a wild, adolescent fantasy of freedom on horseback in the mind of Helena as she half-listens to the proceedings. His characteristically diamond-sharp prose produces marvellously mischievous effects, tending to be salacious:

> His need was simple; not today, not tomorrow, but soon, sometime before he grew too old to make proper use of it: Constantius wanted the World.
> 'They are singing of the flagellation of Boadicea,' said Coel; 'rather a delicate subject to us Romans, but very dear to my simple people.'
> The subject was scarcely less familiar to Helena than to her father; she withdrew from the catalogue of mortality and, eupeptically, withdrew into a fantasy she had cherished since childhood . . . Helena was playing horses . . .
> [She] galloped while through the hypocaustic air the death-song of her ancestors rumbled and wailed.

Waugh's Helena is recognizably a sister of Miss Joan Hunter Dunn, 'Furnish'd and burnish'd by Aldershot sun', and the jolly-hockey-sticks tone of Helena's general approach to matters of love and matters of state also echoes Betjeman's whimsical parodies of sporty gels from the middle or very top drawer (the best known is 'The Subaltern's Love Song', 1941).

The vicissitudes of Constantius Chlorus' career unfold clearly, Waugh having researched the period, and he spares no detail of his treachery, violence, machinations; nor, later, does he paint a more appealing portrait of his son the Emperor Constantine. The novelist is also fully in charge of the complex, shifting contours of the Roman empire in the fourth century, a time of unceasing civil turmoil as well as resistance to invaders: the book traverses little-known areas of the Balkans and the Near East where Constantine held power and where Helena was installed by her son in various palaces. What does not succeed for many of the book's first readers – and later ones, including myself – is the shift from the levity and sparkle of the beginning to the author's earnest profession of faith towards the end. Channelled through Helena, Waugh's curious, positivist version of belief is grounded in what he chooses to see as historical fact:

> The Holy Places have been alternately honoured and desecrated, lost and won, bought and bargained for, throughout the centuries.
> But the wood has endured. In splinters and shaving, gorgeously encased, it has travelled the world over and found a joyous welcome among every race.
> For it states a fact.
> Hounds are checked, hunting wild. A horn calls clear through the covert. Helena casts them back on the scent.
> Above all the babble of her age and ours, she makes one blunt assertion. And there alone lies Hope.

This earnest assertion of the 'fact' of the cross confirms how widely felt is the need for material evidence to support ideas and beliefs, how the imaginary or spiritual landscape requires bodily traces.

After reading the novel, John Betjeman wrote to Waugh to congratulate him but added: 'Helena doesn't seem like a saint.' Waugh, who had tried for years to entice the devoutly Anglican Betjeman into the Catholic Church, replied with a brief catechesis on the Catholic understanding of saints:

Saints are simply souls in heaven. Some people have been so sensationally holy in life that we know they went straight to heaven and so put them in the [liturgical] calendar. We all have to become saints before we get to heaven . . . And each individual has his own peculiar form of sanctity which he must achieve or perish. It is no good saying, 'I wish I were like Joan of Arc or St. John of the Cross.' I can only be St. Evelyn Waugh – after God knows what experiences in purgatory. I liked Helena's sanctity because it is in contrast to all that moderns think of as sanctity. She wasn't thrown to the lions, she wasn't a contemplative, she wasn't poor and hungry, she didn't look like an El Greco. She just discovered what it was God had chosen for her to do and did it.

Waugh ultimately places his trust in faith, underpinned by relics.

## And Was Jerusalem Builded Here . . . ?

One shard of the True Cross was sent to Rome and presented to the church of Santa Croce in Gerusalemme in Rome, which Helena founded on the imperial Sessorian estate, near the palace of her son. It is an imposing basilica, much adorned in the High Renaissance and since, standing in a complex of monastery buildings with flowering gardens enclosed within ancient burnt-umber walls. The relic of the True Cross is still enshrined in the crypt, where Helena herself is venerated, in the form of an adapted Roman statue of a matron, now holding a large wooden cross. Earth from the Holy Land is also preserved there, underfoot and protected by a glass floor, confirming the dedication of the basilica, whose very name declares that Jerusalem has been brought to Rome. Earth/dust makes no claim to the status of a relic, but pilgrims bring back phials filled with earth or sand from the sanctuaries they visit, and indeed secular tourists also do so from different places, without imputing any sacred meaning to these residues, but valuing contact with the literal presence of specific soil (see Chapter 4 for more on the aura of dust and earth). But the earth scattered near the statue of St Helena in the foundations of the church in Rome conveys the way centres of worship superimpose one place on another by various means, including the migration of soil.

Replicas of special sacred sites – of shrines and sanctuaries – rose on foundations that often incorporate material from the site of origin, the ur-model, the template. But imitation does not always need the guarantee of an actual, grounded connection: an indexical link may be replaced by the exactitude of a simulacrum (again see Chapter 4). At the size of a pillbox, as pocket reliquaries, models of holy places also become mementoes, used to contain a pinch of dust from the sacred origin.

Christian cult practices are founded on the principle that a story can be reproduced again and again in different locations: the layout of a church reproduces Calvary, the high altar being Golgotha, while the ritual of the Mass re-enacts the death of Jesus on the cross; round churches all over the world reproduce the Temple in Jerusalem.

Islam offers a different cartography, by orienting its churches towards Mecca and requiring Muslims to face that holy, originary place of their faith when they pray. (In Abu Dhabi, in the United Arab Emirates, mosques are sited diagonally to the grid of the city streets and, viewed from above, from one of the tall hotels for example, they look like aircraft lined up for take-off.)

But the most effective intervention, the basilica Helena herself founded, rendered the journey to Jerusalem itself unnecessary because Jerusalem could be regained – built here, as much later William Blake would hymn in his poem, actually called 'Jerusalem', which has become an alternative English national anthem.

The church of Santa Croce in Gerusalemme maps out the Passion of Jesus in an elaborate Stations of the Cross, incorporating several relics of Christ's Passion: a spine from the crown of thorns, a bone from Doubting Thomas's finger, a scraping from the column where Jesus was scourged.

I was brought up taking part in rituals which also conjured one place in another. The Stations of the Cross, a devotion that grew in intensity during the Counter-Reformation, transposes events in far distant time and place. Fourteen episodes in the Passion of Jesus were drawn up by St Alphonsus Liguori in 1761 and still appear on the walls of every Catholic church – and now sometimes of Anglican churches as well. Alphonsus composed graphic accompanying meditations, which act as prompts to empathy, inviting the faithful to reimagine Jesus' sufferings. This devotional practice, part of the Counter-Reformation's spur to a revival of the faith, grew out of earlier, dramatic installations of the Via Crucis. In Varallo, Lombardy, for example, towards the end of the fifteenth century, a local aristocrat who had been a patriarch of the Holy Land, laid out New Jerusalem on a *mons sacer* or holy mountain, to reprise the story of salvation. The series of forty-eight chapels, each a small theatre, contain *tableaux vivants*, beginning with Adam and Eve in Eden and continuing to Christ's Ascension into heaven, including vivid re-enactments of Christ's entry into Jerusalem and his crucifixion; the crowded, histrionic sculptures are dramatized with ferocious naturalism and feature throngs of life-size figures, fully costumed, with glass eyes, porcelain teeth and real hair. Proto-cinematic, precursors of waxworks and theme parks, these effigies map the Christian story on to the Italian landscape.

In the basilica of Santa Croce in Gerusalemme, in Rome, besides the original splinter of the True Cross which Helena donated (now encased in a nineteenth-century reliquary), another major link with the past was found, miraculously, in 1429, during restoration works: the *Titulus Crucis*, or the notice nailed to the cross was hidden in the wall. One of the most precious relics in Christian history it proclaims in Greek, Hebrew and Aramaic, in clumsy lettering, 'Jesus the Nazarene King of the Jews'.

The chapel of the relics beneath the basilica shows how the practice has by no means lost momentum – rather the contrary. It was redesigned and rebuilt in 1925 to receive the huge numbers of pilgrims expected in Rome that Holy Year, was inaugurated in 1930 and was completed in 1950; all the relics have been reset in valuable modern (and ugly) reliquaries after the original settings were destroyed in 1798 by Napoleon's soldiers. The reigning pope still makes the all-important Good Friday Stations of the Cross in this basilica, re-enacting the death of Jesus in an eternal and present Jerusalem.

The historian Peter Brown once wrote, in a startling image that has clung on in my mind, that the saints in the early church were like generators: their bodies in their holiness emitted energy from which others took light and strength. Similarly, in the fourth century, the project of distributing fragments of the cross hooked up the new faith on to a grid – reaching the far-flung outposts of Christendom (electricity substations if you like) and connecting them to Jerusalem and to Rome through a network of relics, some of them corporeal, some of them not, but made sacred by contact, like the pieces of the cross. Helena was a *matron* – a female patron – and an indefatigable builder of monuments that entrenched the new religion in the empire. An equivalent in modern times would be the nineteenth-century cult of Joan of Arc, which raised statues to *la Pucelle* (the Maid) throughout France and its colonies – Algeria and Vietnam and elsewhere – or the raising of the Union Jack in outposts far and wide during the heyday of the British empire, or the planting of the Stars and Stripes on the moon by the Apollo astronauts. Except that in early Christianity the relics of the True Cross were not symbols but were believed to be the thing itself; their scattering across the map of the faithful, like the dismemberment of saints' bodies for display in reliquaries, acted to symbolize the unity in diaspora of the faithful.

Relics supported a pre-nationalist imagination of belonging, establishing a network of affinities across geographical and ethnic boundaries. This community – universal, as the word 'catholic' proclaims – was bonded together by heroes, by martyrs, but also by great figures, sometimes saintly but not always. And beneath the individuals and the relics, beneath Helena and the fragments of the True Cross, lie stories, historical memories freely mixed with fantasy building a secondary world, an imaginary landscape of affinities.

A live current runs from relics down through time and across space and connects the viewer/pilgrim directly with a narrative in the past. This practice, which is widespread in world religions, is growing very strongly today in culture quite separately from acts of faith, and largely through the capacity of new media to archive living memories. Relic hunting and relic worship arise from structures in the mind that lie very deep and have inspired and continue to inspire imaginative stratagems for remembering, for bonding, for taking bearings from common compass points. They can draw pilgrims to a specific place, but they themselves are portable and signify the place – and the bodies – from which they came. The part would sanctify the whole; like a stem cell, the splinter could grow a complete organ of the church, another building where its work would continue.

This transmission of power was among the principal spurs to the Reformers' scorn, not only the far-fetched plausibility of the relic itself. An incisor tooth of Mary Magdalene, hay of the manger, a feather of the angel Gabriel. These claims provoked Chaucer's taunt, that the relics inside the Pardoners wallet were 'pigges bones'. During successive waves of iconoclasm, the Protestant revolution set about crushing all practices to do with relics, icons, statues and pilgrimage. Elizabeth I in her decree of 1559 ordered that 'they shall take away, utterly extinct, and destroy all shrines, coverings of shrines, all tables, candlesticks, trindals and rolls of wax, pictures, paintings, and all other monuments of feigned miracles, pilgrimages, idolatry, and superstition, so that there remains no memory of the same'. In the half-millennium since then, resistance has weakened, and relics and pilgrimage are again popular, in secular as well as religious settings. A bone of St Thérèse of Lisieux, 'the Little Flower', who died in 1897, began a world tour in 1994 and has been visiting countries ever since, above all, those at war, including Ukraine. Her relics also entered Protestant places of worship, such as York minster, where Reformers would have suppressed relic worship a few centuries ago; the dean now throws open his doors in welcome.

His action wasn't backward-looking but exactly in step with the contemporary trend, which sees relics as depth charges into memories. The trend is drifting away from fleshly remains, with all their grisly origins (after Teresa of Avila's thumb was stolen from her body, her coffin was walled up to prevent further relic harvesting). Sensitivity to 'human remains' has risen sharply, and the British Museum, in its pioneering exhibition, *Treasures of Heaven: Saints, Relics and Devotion in Medieval Europe* in 2012, displayed many magnificent reliquaries, but refrained when possible from including any bodily tissue, blood or bone. (However, the right eye of the Blessed Edward Oldcorne, SJ, who was martyred in 1606, had been rescued by a bystander and subsequently encased in a jewelled medallion, by far the goriest and most disturbing item on display.) Pieces of the True Cross remained in place, though. Curators now prefer clothing and other association items. The treasury of Notre-Dame de Paris, for example, which I visited before the fire of April 2019, used to exhibit the gloves of the archbishop who was shot on the barricades during the revolution of 1848 and died the following year, as well as the skull cap of Pope Pius X, canonized in 1954. In Naples, a shrine to the doctor St Giuseppe Moscati (1880–1927) inside the baroque Jesuit church, the Chiesa del Gesù Nuovo, recreates the beloved local hero's study, complete with bookcase, lace-covered couch, a suit and the armchair in which he died. He is still the subject of many prayers, and ex-votos in the chapel thank him for many cures, several of them recent.

The poet Susan Stewart, in her inspired study *On Longing*, looks at souvenirs among other things. Souvenirs are not invested with numen in a religious sense, but they act like secular relics. In contemporary customs and culture, a new kind of belief in things, as not altogether inert but imbued with memory and consciousness, is flourishing in the work of writers and thinkers and artists who incorporate things – archival deposits, possessions, clothing and even bodily traces – into their work, annexing religious modes into secular works of mourning and counter-mourning, critique and celebration.

In the 1980s, the poet Seamus Heaney made a pilgrimage to Lough Derg, one of the most sacred and popular shrines in Ireland, and composed a magnificent poetic sequence, *Station Island*. In the tenth canto he describes the sounds and smells in the pilgrims' hostel, how they took him back to his childhood home:

> . . . I saw the mug
> Beyond my reach on its high shelf . . .

It was sprigged with cornflowers, 'old and glazed and / haircracked'. He continues:

> It had stood for years
> In its patient sheen and turbulent atoms,
> Unchallenging, unremembered *lars*
> I seemed to waken to and waken from.

*Lars*: as in 'Lares et Penates', the household gods of ancient Rome, who were tended and worshipped at home and in local shrines, keeping the neighbourhood and the home safe, watching over the inhabitants, as long as their statues were properly respected, propitiated with offerings, remembered by daily prayers. Neglecting them was dangerous, losing them a terrible thing – a loss of connection, a separation from the protective powers of the house. These mysterious minor divinities were portrayed as two curly-haired youths accompanied by large, undulating snakes; they originated in ancient, local and popular belief, expressing the connection to down below so often established in sanctuaries.

But a china mug? How could Heaney imagine such benevolent potency in something pretty but humdrum?

That is precisely what is meant by a live artefact, consecrated or not. The hair-cracked mug sparks memory and awakens forgotten emotions; stirred up again they leap across the interval of time that has elapsed. The mug is a lesser god, a cord attaching the older man to the universe of glowing hyper-real experience that is childhood for each of us; it acts on him as an animate thing, imbued with active energy radiating and reaching out to touch him. And not only across time, but across space-time, for mute yet speaking things reverberate with the place they came from, in this case the kitchen of the young Heaney's home.

The mug is only one of many such symbols in *Station Island*, for a pilgrim's path proceeds from one such sign to another: they mark the way on the ground and linger in the mind like mnemonic prompts, laying out the pattern of a story the pilgrim can then hold lastingly in mind and replay in solitary thought.

Artefacts today that prompt devotion and recollection unfold narratives of another kind. Orhan Pamuk tells a tale of lost love in a museum he has created in a nineteenth-century house in Istanbul. It celebrates Füsun, the heroine of one of his novels, *The Museum of Innocence*, through a multifarious, deeply nostalgic assemblage of period items, displayed as her personal belongings – more than a thousand items of clothing, furnishings, books and implements. But Füsun is imaginary, and the museum conjures an illusion based on a fiction; its elegiac displays serve to realize a figment. This young woman and the doomed romance in his book are fabrications by Pamuk (which may or may not be inspired by his own experience, transmuted by the art of fiction), but they have acquired substance, a material presence, through the objects that are on display. The writer is planting signs in a sanctuary that creates a monument to his yearning for a bygone Turkish society – and obliquely to his own creative powers.

The museum has been hugely popular with tourists and the art-loving public (parts of the exhibition have toured Europe). The assemblage also evokes an Istanbul of the past and protests against the vanishing of a certain liberal, secular urbanity and sophistication. Like many sacred sites, Pamuk's conceit is not simple, but freighted with political argument, and his act of sweet, even sentimental nostalgia draws on age-old methods of instilling history, retrospectively, into inanimate things. He has adapted methods that can be seen in action most clearly in religious storytelling and its rituals.

Since the early austerity of Protestant practices and aesthetics, and the fierce rejection of religious ceremony in Revolutionary France, where saints' days were replaced by the Fête de la Liberté, or the Fête de la Raison, there has been a largely unremarked return to public ritual – largely unremarked, that is, until today, when the photo-opportunities offered by social media have encouraged its reinvigoration. This trend is evident in state rituals everywhere, the official portraits of rulers standing in the place of icons, the military parades, the new processions proclaiming power and unity (these often combine forces with the ecclesiastic hierarchy).

The Catalan philosopher Eugenio Trías has argued that symbolic communal events, rather than inward prayer or private acts of faith, have become the dominant means of reaching the sacred today. His perceptions about the transformations of religious and public uses of symbolism allude to currently thriving forms of assembly and manifestation; these range widely in form, but his thinking, first formulated in the 1980s, anticipates developments such as the worldwide political demonstrations of the Occupy movement from 2011, the mass sit-ins of the Arab Spring and other protests in Cairo's Tahrir Square and elsewhere starting the previous year. Commemorative acts – including nationwide recitals of the names of the dead after recent massacres and disasters are solemn but not strictly religious occasions. The cascade of poppies down the wall and into the moat of the Tower of London in 2014 to remember those who died in the First World War, was a commissioned artwork, and delivered an unprecedented ceremony that adapted religious requiems to a secular context; its aesthetic value was questionable but its emotional pull undeniable as crowds flocked to take part, planting the ceramic poppies until the huge castle evoked, as the title expressed it, *Blood Swept Lands and Seas of Red*.

Alongside public displays of state power which adapt religious ritual, a vigorous form of non-aligned, secular metaphysics has been developing in social interactions and personal expression at least since the beginning of the last century, but the vital role that questions of the sacred have played in modernist aesthetics has been sidestepped – for reasons that include a certain embarrassment. In contemporary customs and culture, a new kind of belief in such aids to memory has arisen: the burial places of stars and singers – Rudolf Valentino, Jim Morrison – became and still are pilgrimage destinations for fans, while Madame Tussaud's, which began with memorabilia (the blade of the guillotine; a half-eaten toffee from the pram of a murdered baby; Napoleon's bed), surpasses year on year all other tourist attractions in the UK. Current celebrities, when modelling for their wax effigy, are asked to donate an outfit, preferably worn, to dress the statue.

Charity auctions are sustained by such items – Princess Diana's gowns, footballers' T-shirts and rock stars' jeans – secular memorabilia which remember relics in their bodily stains. The rise of such entanglements with things and 'thing theory' which accompanies them has added poignancy – for non-believers as well as believers – to the destruction of works of art by the Reformers as they set out expurgating the spurious storytelling, far-fetched miracle stories and inauthentic claims to direct connection with the past through relics, such as splinters of the Holy Cross (see Plate 5a).

In the prosperous town of Stratford-upon-Avon in Warwickshire, the substantial, castellated and high-windowed Gothic chapel of the Guild of the Holy Cross was dedicated to the Holy Cross, and a fair was held in the town on the feast days of the cross, 3 May and 14 September. The chancel was gaudily frescoed in the last quarter of the fifteenth century, unfolding the story of Helena's pilgrimage to the Holy Land and her discovery of the relics as well as several other scenes from scripture and medieval hagiography – St George and the Dragon, the martyrdom of Thomas Becket. Here, in full colour, were pictured the curious adventures of the cross from the arrival of the Queen of Sheba to visit Solomon, when she refrained from stepping on the bridge made from the future wood of the cross, to the mission of Helena's old age: her journey to the Holy Land, the interrogation of the possible witnesses, the miracle that proves which is the True Cross, the conversion of Judas Cyriacus and the victory of Heraclius over Chosroes, followed by the raising of the cross itself as the sign of salvation. The images are directly taken from the woodcuts circulating in books at the time, such as Caxton's illustrated edition of the *Golden Legend* and the Dutch edition by John Valdener of *The Legendary History of the True Cross*; these handbooks provided a journeyman painter or painters with the models for the images frescoed on the chancel walls a few years after the books first appeared in 1483.

What is most intriguing, however, about the destruction of these frescoes by the Reformers is that the signature authorizing the payment of two shillings for the work of the lime pails and brushes is that of William Shakespeare's father John Shakespeare, who was alderman of the town in that period.

The Shakespeares' relationship to the old religion has excited much scholarly discussion. William was born around the time his father began the work of painting over the chapel's papist pictures, and the destruction continued during William's childhood, with his father presiding over the dismantling of the rood loft and the removal of the stained glass. In some way, the iconoclasts of the second intense wave of the Reformation, which began when Elizabeth issued her decree, were cultural patriots. Caxton successfully presented Chaucer as a new Ovid or a new Virgil in order to stake a claim that English literature could hold its own. The defacers of old Catholic stories and images were asking for history to start again; they were radicals reshaping the landscape of imagination. In former hallowed ground they were hollowing a new space in which to plant another form of life.

Catholic memories haunt Shakespeare's plays – sometimes literally, when Hamlet's father's ghost rises in agony out of purgatory. The family's entanglement with the old religion leaves its mark on William's dramatic imagination: it surfaces in his many spectres and sinners, goddesses and virgins, and the several subjects of hallucinations and prophetic dreams. In *The Winter's Tale* (its very title signals that it is a traditional story), the virtuous wronged queen Hermione appears to

Antigonus in a dream, a vision that foreshadows her later materialization as a living statue who comes to life ('Oh, she's warm!' must be one of the happiest and most awesome lines in Shakespeare). The Bard is combining dream visions with other Marian echoes, of miracle stories, as depicted in the frescoes of Eton College chapel (whitewashed over in 1560 and now partially restored). Ophelia, crazed and handing out flowers to Gertrude and others, sings snatches of the 'Walsingham Ballad'. In *Pericles*, Shakespeare stages a virgin martyr's triumph in the brothel against would-be violators; they find themselves magically incapable of assaulting Marina, just like numerous villains of the *Golden Legend* when confronted with a heroic virgin. Marina, eloquently defending her virtue, wields a form of enchantment, as does St Catherine of Alexandria when she confounds her attackers – her unassailable holiness shatters the wheel on which her torturers want to bind her and deflects all other missiles they use to assault her. Another virgin martyr, St Cristina, has her tongue cut out by her pagan father, but it continues quivering on the ground and rails against him, then flies up and pierces him through the eye. Shakespeare took the image of the severed tongue from Ovid's tale of Philomel, but his mutilated Lavinia in *Titus Andronicus* also echoes the dreadful torments of young women martyrs in the *Golden Legend*.

The decoration of the Guild church is known only from copies made by the antiquary Thomas Fisher in 1804–7, during the short period when they were uncovered before being painted over again. He didn't finish the work, but his illustrated account was published in 1836 in a lavish limited facsimile edition. In an interesting coda to this history, which gives evidence of the strong return of stories, cult practices and even belief in relics, the imagery has been reprised in a series of embroidered tapestries, made around 2003–5 by a group of local needlewomen. These highly wrought contemporary embroideries have been made at a time when artists at the highest end of the current art establishment, such as Louise Bourgeois (d. 2010), Tracey Emin and Grayson Perry, are embroidering, stitching and making tapestries – though in Perry's case he doesn't weave or sew them himself. They are consciously reclaiming a tradition with lower status than painting or sculpture, for handicrafts are coded female and less valued for that reason.

Meanwhile the social historian Richard Sennett has also re-evaluated, in Ruskinian terms, the importance of craftsmanship not only in aesthetics, but also for social wellbeing and community. The embroideries in the Guild chapel at Stratford have translated pattern books surviving from a fifteenth-century English publication, one of the first printed books in these islands, and they interpret a story told four centuries before. They introduce their own colour palette, far softer and more gently blended than the paintings reproduced in the facsimile from 1804–5. The figures are naively pretty, childlike in effect rather like playing cards, also an example of folk memory returning to old designs. The needlewomen show a lively pleasure in fashions, textiles and animals and have indeed enlivened their models, introducing three delightful creatures – deer? – pricking their ears as Chosroes is slain by Heraclius (a detail not found in Piero della Francesca).

They have concentrated on Helena's role in the legend, partly because, one may conjecture, they sensed a sympathetic link with her place in the scheme of providence. In an unassuming, easily overlooked series of images, small in scale and close to pew cushions in form, they have kept alive an ancient and fantastic story, rooted in events that were inspired by intense dreaming of possible connections across time and space, and a symbolic arrangement of human history. The legend of the True Cross and St Helena's driving role in it embodies a form of storytelling that obeys a principle of myth, as pithily defined by Roland Barthes: myth turns history into nature. The narrator puts the story forward as history, not as report but as prophecy, in the optative mood of providential literature rather than the indicative mood of historical chronicle, of wishful thinking and prognostication rather than mimesis and documentary record. The Invention of the True Cross may be well named, but *inventio* is a prime function of imagination.

These acts of time travelling and communion with ghosts involve displacements: the past brings with it the geography which the people inhabited, and that scenery had different compass points – our forebears were held in networks that connected them across distances as we are now linked together in our revolutionary communications systems. But theirs were differently imagined, not only different technologically.

Home can be made by imagination's connection across wide terrain; our imaginary homelands and kin are often tied to compass points somewhere else, far away. When they are invoked and rekindled, they may afford comfort, deepen a sense of belonging and identity. But they can also sometimes bump up against strongly held conventions, disturb the sense of security and inspire anxieties about severed ties and betrayed allegiances.

When this happens, figures in the past turn into ghosts that haunt us disquietingly. This isn't the uncanny of the familiar, once repressed, according to Freud's analysis of the feeling of being there before, déjà vu. It's another field of experience that is communal, not only individual . . . that the past has been betrayed and that it wants revenge. Retribution *or* propitiation.

It would be wrong to present a picture of stable continuity across millennia, and to pass over radical changes in consciousness and values, or to argue for archetypal strands in the imagination. There are deep fissures, bitter struggles towards historical truth-telling and recurring iconoclastic fervour. Islamic devotions also focus on relics and relics *in situ*, and the temperature of Muslim ardour in this matter rises and falls as in Christian history. Popular practices and beliefs in holy sites are often censured by contemporary religious authorities; zealous assaults on shrines and artefacts, revered and loved by faithful Muslims, have been taking place in Iraq, in Syria, in Saudi Arabia around Mecca, and in Mali and Yemen, following Wahabi and Alaawite interpretations of scripture and the law. I mentioned in the Introduction that the tomb of Amina, the Prophet's mother, was destroyed in 1998; since then the house of Khadijah, the Prophet's first wife, 'has been turned into a block of toilets'. The urge to destroy popular sanctuaries is tightly correlated with the desire, on the part of official or aspiring authorities, to assert full control and prevent the free play of popular imagination.

But the hold of relics continues at a deep level across a surprisingly large community, not only Christian. The lineage of magical thinking is live, or perhaps live again, under the influence of sword and sorcery medievalizing fantasy (as in *The Lord of the Rings*, *His Dark Materials*, *The Hunger Games*, *Dungeons and Dragons*) and can't be consigned to the past altogether: at the coronation of King Charles III in 2023 Pope Francis gave Charles two splinters of the True Cross; they are set in the 'Cross of Wales', made of Welsh slate, wood and silver, embossed in a Celtic interlace pattern; the cross was carried into Westminster abbey at the head of the royal procession. The ceremonial display of an ancient relic gave a public sign of exceptional ecumenism on the part of both the Vatican and the church of England, of which the British monarch has been the official head since Henry VIII's split from Rome. King Charles has never concealed his eclectic and holistic ideals; his acceptance of fragments of the True Cross, a hugely contentious relic in the history of Christendom, conveyed his personal commitment to healing religious rifts, through a claim of sacred provenance dating back before the conflicts and separation.

The character of credence has changed, and the relic's authenticity may be tacitly allowed to be metaphorical rather than factual, to belong in the irrealis zone of hope and dream. The wood of the True Cross still offers a potent medium that reaches back into antiquity to strengthen adherence to a collective story.

# 4

# Dust:
# The Flying House of Loreto

> Oh, we have a home, just we haven't yet found where to put it.
> A refugee child (anonymous)

In 1657, the Franciscan friar Joseph of Cupertino, whose propensity to ecstasy and uncanny foresight had led to popular adulation and official suspicion, was being conducted at the orders of the pope to a new friary at Osimo; Assisi had wanted him to return there, but the pope had deemed that they already had St Francis, and two saints were an excess. Joseph, staying overnight in a local farm, glimpsed from his window the dome of Loreto on the horizon and saw, swirling above it in the sky a multitude of angels; he asked what place it was. And when told it was the sanctuary where the house of the Holy Family in Nazareth was enshrined, he exclaimed, 'No wonder then that so many angels come down from Paradise . . . Oh happy place, oh blessed place!' He then rose into the air in ecstasy, floated 'off the balcony and perched for a while in a nearby almond tree about twelve feet off the ground'.

From the fifteenth century until Napoleon sacked it in 1796, the sanctuary of Loreto, a magnificent hilltop basilica enclosing the relic of the Santa Casa, became the most frequented pilgrimage destination in Christendom, alongside Rome and, in England before the Reformation, Canterbury and Walsingham, and eclipsing them in popularity afterwards.

Alongside bodily relics and traces of former presence, affirming a connection across time, sanctuaries can become surrogate homes, private sites of freedom and autonomy, by reproducing a shelter, rebuilding a lost dwelling, translating it to a new environment and repossessing it,

St Joseph of Cupertino (1603–63) a Franciscan friar famous for his ecstatic flights, took off when he glimpsed from his window the basilica of Loreto.

as can be seen in the case of Loreto's Santa Casa. This devotion constitutes another form of mimicry, of the house itself and by extension the presence of Mary. The Holy House represented Mary in bricks and mortar, and the Holy Family at home with her; by extension it also represented – represents – the homeland of salvation, the Holy Land, Palestine. In the absence of her physical body, which had been assumed into heaven, the category of sacred mortal remains that inspired veneration underwent a profound change: the attempt to assert a story and give structure to the providential past took a different direction, away from the individual personal house of the soul in the body to a claim for more general ground, for the home of the community. By imagining that a home could be transported whole from Nazareth itself to offer a new Nazareth in Italy, the legend of the Santa Casa proposes a symbolic point of attachment for Christian believers. It also shows how the Christian cycle of wonder tales are themselves migratory, travelling to Europe from the Middle East along the narrative pathways – not only scripture, commentaries, hagiography, sermons and prayers, but also by means of far less formal networks, mercantile traffic by sea and land, the voices and the repertory of storytellers – priests and nuns, Crusaders and their ladies, pilgrims, adventure seekers, prostitutes – Chaucer's pilgrims to Canterbury.

The fall of Acre in 1291 set the seal on the failure of Crusader ambitions in Outremer, as the territory they had conquered was called. There would be many more crusades and many further attempts to regain the Holy Land and wrest authority from the Turks. One of the consequences of the exodus from Muslim-controlled Palestine was a vigorous traffic in relics, and an efflorescence of pilgrimages within Europe to shrines where relics from figures and sites central to Christian faith maintained the connection with lost holy places; at the same time, many liturgical practices, such as telling the rosary, setting out a crib at Christmas, performing the Stations of the Cross, rituals which evoked Christ's life and death, were either enthusiastically adopted or developed, and are still of course much loved seasonal customs. Both pilgrimages and prayers were making a passage from the home territory of Christianity in the eastern Mediterranean, and they imprinted the cultural landscape of western Europe with travelling and translated stories, adhering to specific transplanted objects and to imported verbal formulae. The essence of both Jesus and Mary was infused across centuries and millennia into material objects (as discussed in the previous chapter), items which had been touched, used or worn by them and thereby hallowed.

Bethlehem and Jerusalem, the sites of the birth and death of Jesus, mark on the map his beginning and his end, but scripture, legends and lore also featured Nazareth: it was the town where Mary received the news that she was to bear the Saviour, and which provided Jesus with his name, Jesus of Nazareth, as inscribed on the *Titulus Crucis*, discovered as we have seen in the church of Santa Croce in Gerusalemme in Rome.

As with building Jerusalem here, so with Nazareth. The places associated with the story of Jesus became more and more difficult to reach under the Ottomans, and the supply lines more and more stretched until they failed altogether, so attempts were made to reproduce the holy places in Europe. And not only reproduce them. If the claim to authenticity were to be made convincingly, attempts needed to be made to transplant them, move them, import them.

Among these relics stimulating intense devotion, by far the largest and most surprising is the Santa Casa, the Holy House, the tiny home where Mary had lived in Nazareth, where the Annunciation took place, when Gabriel told Mary that she was to have a child and the Virgin accepted that she would become the future mother of God, when she spoke her fiat, 'Let it be done unto me according to thy word' (Luke 1: 38). The Santa Casa embodies an instance of space-time, the all-important historical juncture when the Virgin's acceptance of her role begins the merciful era of the new covenant. The dwelling, according to the legend that grew up around it, had also seen the childhood of Jesus, and perhaps his youth as well, though those years remain hidden from the record, until he set out on his mission when he was in his thirties. It was also the house where, according to another strand of the story, Mary died (there are contradictory accounts, with Ephesus being the strongest contender, claiming another version of the Holy House).

This home inspired, at a certain period of history, a most remarkable mythical and imaginary response to the experience of exclusion and

A monumental marble revetment encloses the Holy House as if it were the relic of a living body, and this monument a tomb.

displacement, involving a literal translocation of a dwelling, from Palestine to Italy. At first it seems an absurd tale, but on closer inspection (and after a visit to the sanctuary itself) it represents a very thoughtful expression of the deep longing to take your home with you, carrying it like a snail wherever you are made to go. It presents an exceptionally fertile test case for understanding sanctuary.

The legend goes that the Holy House flew, carried by angels from Nazareth to Italy in a 'wondrous flitting', the splendid Scots account preserved in the church still proclaims. Humble, dilapidated and cramped, the whole edifice stands concealed in the middle of an immense baroque church, encased in a sumptuous sculpted carapace, like a rare fossil set in a precious jewelled vessel for a prince's cabinet of curiosities.

This miracle displays the principle of the irrealis mood in narrative, when a wish is realized as fact and a metaphor becomes act: the angels who liberate the Holy House from the infidel recall the jinn who carry Solomon and his vast retinue on the flying carpet or, in any number of stories from *The Thousand and One Nights*, whisk off the heroes and their loves on various kinds of furniture or in different dwellings (Aladdin's airy palace). A literal cast of mind has shaped many fantastic

Santa Polvere (Holy dust), scraped from the walls of the Holy House, was mixed into paints used to decorate souvenirs from the shrine.

tales, and in the case of Loreto a home has settled in a new place, making a home from home.

The flying Holy House of Loreto claims to be the real thing, but it obeys the principle of replication that governs secondary relics, and, like Christ's tomb in Jerusalem, it engendered many copies, full-scale and miniature models. Loreto also illustrates the investment in homeland as earth, as stone, as dust, an analogue of our humanity (dust to dust); in exile, the need for home ground grows stronger and the yearning to regain it more acute. Keeping pieces of earth or stone from home is an impulse which runs very deep among forced exiles and displaced peoples, and pilgrims to the shrine would scrape the walls of the Holy House and have themselves tattooed in ink blended from the dust and grease they had taken – or, a less penitential process, buy a souvenir relic of a pot or dish decorated with paint blended with the same *santa polvere*, holy dust.

For The Seeds of Hope, a project with the United Nations Refugee Agency, the conceptual artist Kate Daudy is working with refugees to grow plants from seeds carried in soil from home, brought with them among their few possessions, to add familiarity to their new surroundings. The Chinese-American poet Wang Ping, also acknowledging the widespread psychological reflex to identify earth with home, segues from soil with memories, and then following the logic of imagination, to mortal remains. Her poem 'Things We Carry on the Sea' opens:

> We carry tears in our eyes: good-bye father, good-bye mother
> We carry soil in small bags: may home never fade in our hearts
> We carry names, stories; memories of our villages, fields, boats
> We carry scars from proxy wars of greed
> We carry carnage of mining, droughts, floods, genocides
> We carry dust of our families and neighbors incinerated in
>   mushroom clouds.

Pilgrimage and prayers involve many forms of storytelling, relating events that took place in the past, for example in the Holy Land during the lifetime of Christ, and projecting them on to local surroundings, a palimpsestic act of imagining a cycle of stories into a new setting, amounting at times to a re-enactment. Each bead on a rosary similarly acts as a prompt to bring up in the mind's eye a scene from the life of

Mary: first the Joyful mysteries, then the Sorrowful, then the Glorious. Telling one's beads is just that, a persevering act of narrative imagination. In Islam, strings of beads – *misbahah* – also have a devotional use, a mnemonic device for counting off the ninety-nine names of God (they are rather more familiar as worry beads flicked and fingered all over the Middle East without any pious – or storytelling – connection). The rosary's popularity spread through Christendom rapidly during the same period as the pilgrimage grew to Loreto, where pilgrims saying the rosary together could imagine scenes of Mary's life transposed to the church in which they were kneeling.

Like other relics, the Holy House is material, and while its materiality – stone, brick, dust – differs in species from the blood, bones and flesh of an individual's mortal remains as well as from their garments or effects, it offers instead a crucial instance of symbolic embodiment. A house is a special kind of secondary relic, not a body part or an article of dress. Crucially, it is not linked to a site of death; it does not testify to sacrifice of a bloody kind; the cult ascribes power to a dwelling, to this *specific* dwelling, because for pilgrims it is imbued with the presence of the Virgin as a child and young woman and a mother, and sanctified by the events that took place in its precincts. The Holy House was identified specifically with the chamber where Mary was praying when the angel Gabriel appeared to her.

The house is a home, and this house manifests the Holy Family at home: Loreto's popularity also coincides with the promotion of the cult of St Joseph and an idealization of Jesus' childhood. According to the economy of remembrance in which relics play a supreme part, the house stands in for the body or bodies which cannot be present. And overarching the two disparate elements – house and body – is the unifying imagery of dust, dust which is also ash, recalling pilgrims to their mortality and inviting them to repent their sinfulness, as in the liturgy of Ash Wednesday: 'Remember, man, dust thou art and to dust thou shalt return.'

The story goes that in a rare form of divine intervention – a wonderful, miraculous stratagem – the house was picked up bodily by angels and carried through the air, first to Trsat (Tersatto) in Illyria (Rijeka in present-day Croatia, known in Italian as Fiume), and rested there for three years, until 10 December 1294. These precise timings, coinciding exactly with the fall of Acre and the end of Christian power in the

Holy Land, act to verify the events. The 'disappearance' of the Holy House left the local population 'disconsolate' and a sanctuary grew up to remember its brief sojourn.

The angelic bearers of the Holy House did not linger in Illyria, for reasons not recorded, but picked up the salvaged relic and transported it across the sea, past the ports of Recanati and Ancona on the Adriatic coast, intending it to travel to Rome.

A more practical and persuasive record of the house's origins lists it as part of the dowry of Thamar, the daughter of Nicephorus (degli) Angeli, together with an icon painted by St Luke. After the fall of Acre, a dynastic alliance was struck with the Angevin house ruling in Naples, and Thamar was married to Filippo, Prince of Taranto, the son of Carlo II (1254–1309), King of Naples. According to this account, the ruler of Epirus arranged for the transport of the stones of the Santa Casa, and the house may have later been presented by Carlo II to the pope.

Another, alternative history of the house's origins gives added background: that the local ruler in Trsat, Prince Nikola Frankopan of Krk, had had the house measured, the stones brought from Nazareth and the house reassembled on his lands, but then decided to send it to the pope as a present. The Vatican at the time was in a state of turbulence, and so when the Holy House arrived in Italy the pope, Celestine V, was absent: he had renounced the Holy See and is indicted in Dante's *Inferno* (III: 6) as he 'Che fece per viltade il gran rifiuto' (Who made through cowardice the great refusal). The church was effectively in schism, so the Bishop of Recanati decided to keep the Santa Casa in his diocese, particularly as the region of Le Marche belonged to the Papal States – thus pursuing a form of early regional regeneration through art and its powers of attraction. The pilgrimage began and was so successful that the three brothers who owned the land where the house had settled fought over the profits. Early traces of the devotion include prints and paintings of the several halts the Holy House made en route to its permanent resting place where traces of the pilgrimage go back to the fourteenth century.

The flying house's story reproduces the dislocations of exiles and castaways before it puts into safe harbour. In this respect its adventures reprise the ordeals of scattering and desecration that many martyrs' and saints' shrines suffered not only in the earliest era of Christianity but also during the purging of superstition by the Reformers' coinciding with the first traces of the Holy House's appearance in Europe. When the iconoclasts cleared a pilgrimage site, such as St Frideswide's tomb in Christ Church cathedral in Oxford in 1538, the saint's remains were scattered. In her case as in other Catholic saints' sanctuaries, fragments were eventually sifted from a jumbled burial, identified and then reburied; sometimes the return of their relics and the revival of veneration at the shrine restores the saints' powers to heal and bless and save (St Frideswide's shrine was splendidly restored in 1985 and now attracts votaries again).

The angels removed the Santa Casa from the land of the quarrelsome brothers and deposited it in a laurel grove on an inland summit overlooking the sea – hence the shrine's name, Loreto. The word 'Loreto' and its derivatives 'Loretan', 'Loredana', travelled far and wide with the order of nuns founded in honour of the shrine, and in girls' names in the Catholic world. Pilgrims endowed the shrine with fabulous treasures. After years of infertility, on the birth of the future King Louis XIV, in thanksgiving to Our Lady of Loreto, Anne of Austria presented the shrine with a baby Jesus whose weight in gold matched that of the dauphin at his birth. This royal votive offering was looted in 1797, along with the entire contents of the treasury, by Napoleon on his Italian campaign, when he needed funds to pay the army.

The magnificent edifice in Loreto that was erected over and around the Holy House is an unusual example of a church fortress; its proximity to the coast made it vulnerable to attack from the sea, not least by pirates. The Ottomans occupied the Illyrian and Dalmatian coast from the sixteenth century and, from this dangerously neighbouring territory, harassed the cities of the Adriatic south of Venice, their great rival and enemy. For this reason, images of the Holy House's peregrinations also show Recanati and Ancona heavily fortified.

## Walsingham: England's Nazareth

As every church in some sense replicates Calvary, so Mary's house in Nazareth multiplied – in replicas or simulacra– here and there. The popular pilgrimage to Walsingham in Norfolk promised contact with the Holy House, as it had been constructed at Mary's specific request in a vision. She appeared to a wealthy local noblewoman called Richeldis de Faverches and specified the location; a miraculous fall of dew later demarcated the dimensions of the house and where it should stand.

According to this origin myth of the shrine, the vision took place in 1061, and when Richeldis' son, Geoffrey, set out for Jerusalem, he transferred a lavish benefaction of buildings, land and tithes to the new chapel his mother had founded. Further gifts came thick and fast from landowners in the area, and the shrine grew in size and fortune.

Walsingham was to become the most popular pilgrimage in England, overtaking the shrine of St Thomas Becket in Canterbury. Its replica of Mary's home claimed status as a true relic on the principle, as we have seen that a copy can be infused with the power of the original: a corporeal relic lights a fuse and the fire passes from one point of contact to another, undimmed. Walsingham also enshrined other relics: of the Virgin's milk, a stool from the Holy House and oddments such as the porringer baby Jesus used (the shrine at Loreto also possessed La Santa Scodella, the holy bowl – in fragments).

The shrine and its extensive buildings were razed in 1538 by order of Henry VIII. Two anonymous ballads, composed soon after the event, remember the devastation. The 'Arundel Ballad' laments:

> Levell, levell with the ground
> The Towres doe lye
> Which with their golden, glitt'ring tops
> Pearsed oute to the skye.

And ends:

> Sinne is where our Ladye sate,
> Heaven turned is to helle;
> Sathan sitte where our Lord did swaye,
> Walsingham, oh, farewell!

The heyday of the sanctuary was brief; the earliest description dates from 1479, from a certain William Botoner, known as William of Worcester. Erasmus visited the flourishing cult site in 1512: by this time the foundation ascribed to Richeldis had become a sprawling, fabulously prosperous establishment. Still, Erasmus tried to explore it, and he made enquiries into the original relics and raison d'être of the shrine. He wrote up his findings in a Dialogue, giving a valuable if conflicting account. While his tone remains caustic, he nevertheless took notice of what he found. The description he gives of the House of Mary tallies with the scale and the layout at Loreto.

A single Gothic arch remains standing from the vast opulent establishment, and rises in the picturesque gardens, carpeted with snowdrops in spring, next to the eighteenth-century house known as the 'Priory'. Like Tintern abbey and other ruins from the Dissolution of the Monasteries, the vestiges of Walsingham reverberate in Shakespeare's line 'bare ruin'd choirs where late the sweet birds sang' (Sonnet 73); in Angelo's brooding self-questioning in *Measure for Measure*, as he plans to seduce Isabella – 'Shall we desire to raze the sanctuary / And pitch our evils there?' (*Measure for Measure*, II. ii); in Ophelia's lament, 'How should I your true love know? / From another one? / "By his cockle hat and staff / And his sandal shoon"' (*Hamlet*, V. v). Walsingham's ruins also became a source of inspiration in the Romantic era, in the watercolours of Thomas Girtin, for example. Detailed historical research was carried out, especially in the context of the Oxford Movement and the Anglo-Catholic revival of the nineteenth century, and two popular sanctuaries, one Anglican, the other Catholic, grew up near the ruins; they both attract throngs of pilgrims, the Anglican church feeling more Catholic than its more austere Catholic counterpart. It includes a Way of the Cross in the adjacent gardens, a Holy Well and an edifice at the centre of the church which is an approximate model of the Holy House. Significantly, into the exterior walls of this replica has been stuck rubble of the medieval shrine, gleaned from the ruins.

Which shrine came first? Walsingham or Loreto? On the face of it, Walsingham has priority, because Richeldis de Faverches' vision occurred, according to the sources, at a precise, early date, 1061, and the pilgrimage flourished thereafter, attracting gifts from kings: Henry VIII and Catherine of Aragon made the pilgrimage, and in 1511 the king, before his repudiation of Rome, offered a collar of rubies to the shrine. The account of Richeldis' vision was written in 1465, just before the earliest written evidence for Loreto. But the first traces of both are very close in date. The material presence of the house itself would seem a bold claim to greater value, made in a spirit of emulation – rivalry? But this speculation must remain just that.

In 1582, when Michel de Montaigne stopped at Loreto during his travels in Italy, it was crowded day in day out by pilgrims. Montaigne's account is surprisingly reverent for a writer famed for his questioning and sceptical mind; he is impressed by the miraculous cure of a friend's long-painful knee, and by the clergy's modesty in accepting the rich offerings lavished on them by pilgrims. He reports that the walls were so densely covered in icons that he could hardly find a gap where he could hang his own votive offering, an image showing the Virgin, himself, his wife and daughter, made of silver. He also writes that he couldn't resist the goods on offer in the boutiques around the shrine: 'For my part I left there nigh on 50 good écus' – a huge sum. Montaigne shows no signs of anything but belief in the Santa Casa, though he does sound surprised at the wretchedness of the house: 'The site of the devotion is a little cottage, very old and tumbledown.'

The poverty of the Holy House figures strongly in the cult of Loreto. Caravaggio's painting *La Madonna dei Pellegrini* (The Madonna of the Pilgrims, or The Madonna di Loreto) still hangs in the Cavalletti side chapel of Sant'Agostino in the Piazza del Popolo, Rome, for which it was painted in 1604–5. It shows two pilgrims from behind, lifting their joined hands imploringly as they kneel at the feet of Mary, who holds out the baby towards them. One of the pilgrims, with a full beard (which he may have grown as a sign of penitence on his pilgrimage), is wearing good-quality clothes but no shoes; the soles of his feet are facing us, bare and grimy: he has made the penitential journey barefoot. Next to him, an old woman with a peasant's kerchief wound around her head also kneels and raises her joined hands in entreaty. Both have pilgrims' staffs they have set down (See Plate 7).

The painter's conception is striking for the proximity of the Madonna: this is no lofty celestial being or bejewelled icon, but a flesh-and-blood young Roman mother standing on the threshold of her home – the marble jamb and brickwork wall recall the Santa Casa. She bends strongly towards them as her large, naked toddler blesses them; they belong in the same earthly dimension as the suppliants before her, almost on the same ground (Madonna and Child are standing on a doorstep); the pilgrims might have passed her in the street any day. Caravaggio is celebrated for casting friends and neighbours in his pictures – the model for Mary has been identified as a famous courtesan of the time. Caravaggio conveys, tenderly, intimately, the trust and hope not only of these two devotees but of many like them. His intense, sensual realism succeeds in dissolving the distance between lived experience and illusory artefact, in embodying distant religious mysteries in palpable immediacy.

In a startling but logical consequence, pilgrims to this church used to dedicate the dirt from their feet to the Madonna.

∼

Documentary traces that might provide context to the miracle are late, by the standards of Christian narrative. No evidence for the prodigious flight is extant for the time — the thirteenth century — when the miracle is meant to have happened. A small and not very distinguished bas-relief made around 1470 has the distinction of being the earliest visual representation of the flying house. It now hangs in the gallery leading to the treasury of the basilica in Loreto, metope-like in form, and most likely northern Italian; the artist remains unknown.

A chapbook appeared around the same time, written by Pietro di Giorgio Tolomei, known as 'Il Teramano', from the province bordering the Adriatic south of Loreto. It is tiny (15cm high) and displays a woodcut on the cover showing the cottage held aloft by angels, with a half-length Mary and the child Jesus floating above — or perhaps even sitting on the roof as in the bas-relief. This iconography, which does not resolve the pictorial problems of the story very satisfactorily, would become traditional in scores of later devotional images. Puffs of cloud are often added by the artist to serve as a cushion under mother and baby and effect a transition between them and the roof.

This highly circumstantial account of the house's arrival in Loreto opens with the words 'The church of Holy Mary of Loreto was the chamber in the house of the Blessed Virgin Mary, mother of our lord Jesus Christ,' and adds that 'this house was in a city of Galilee whose name was Nazareth'. 'It was', it continues, 'the house where the Virgin Mary was born and brought up ['educata'], where she was greeted by the angel and where she nourished her beloved son our lord Jesus Christ until he reached the age of twelve.' After the Ascension, the story continues, 'the blessed VM remained on earth with the Apostles and other disciples of Christ, who, seeing the many divine mysteries which had been made in the said chamber, decided by common consent of all that they should make the said chamber into a church in honour and memory of the BVM; and so it was done.' The Apostles and disciples subsequently consecrated the chamber as a church; St Luke painted the image of Mary that was enshrined there, and worship was held, 'until the people abandoned the faith of Christ and received the faith of Mohammed'. Then angels removed this chosen church and carried it off to safety, but more reversals lay ahead before the house came to rest on the pinnacle of the hill with the laurel grove.

The picaresque account includes agonistic episodes: the relic suffers, its ordeals resembling a martyr's. For example, after the house is set down near Ancona, 'the greatest quarrels and fights broke out' between the brothers who owned the land, over the takings ('lucrum') from the pilgrimage. So the angels picked up the house again and set it down on the public way. Although the success of the pilgrimage at the house's first resting places, such as Trsat (Rijeka), suggests otherwise, nobody knew where the house had come from originally, the report continues; its identity only became known in 1396 when the Virgin Mary appeared in a vision to a hermit, Paul de Silva (Paul of the Wood), who lived in the laurel grove. Sixteen men were then despatched to the Holy Land to verify its provenance, and they took measurements in Nazareth and found 'traces of the foundations' which then matched the miraculously transported remains.

Teramano's publication is surprisingly lively and reads more like a newspaper account than conventional hagiography; the stress he lays on the vicissitudes of the house's journey serves to magnify the importance of Loreto as the final settlement, a new, happy, final homecoming. As a resting place, the basilica implies the corporeality of the relic and turns the whole edifice around it into a container, a sarcophagus. The house where Mary lived became the surrogate mortal integument of her soul, and pilgrims making their way to Loreto prayed at her house in the same way they would have prayed at her tomb.

In the basilica, the story is inscribed on huge calligraphic tablets hanging from the pillars of the nave; browned and gluey with cracked varnish, they show their years. Commissioned by Cardinal Moroni, they were written in 1634 by an Irish Jesuit Robert Corbington, and, reflecting the learning and the cosmopolitanism of the Counter-Reformation, they proclaim the miracle in Welsh, English and Scots versions – it is the last that is called 'the Wondrous Flittinge of the Kirk of the Blest Lady of Loreto'.

Seamus Heaney drew on the legend in a poem called 'Remembered Columns'. His immediate inspiration may have been the ceiling painting by Tiepolo in the church of S. Maria of Nazareth (known as I Scalzi, after the order of Barefoot Carmelites for whom it was built) in Venice, completed in 1774, in which the artist created a soaring illusion that the building was open to the empyrean. The original was destroyed in a bombing attack on 28 October 1915, but the artist's glorious vision of the house's flight survives in a monochrome photograph. In a small but sumptuous preparatory panel, now in the Getty Museum, the *sotto in sù* perspective is even more dramatic, the sightlines more vertiginous, as the tremendous vortex of angels, clouds and house spirals upwards towards Mary, who is looking down from the apex of the ascending mass and bathing all with her smile (See Plate 6). Heaney captures the airborne energy of the work in the poem:

> The solid letters of the world grew airy.
> The marble serifs, the clearly blocked uprights
> Built upon rocks and set upon the heights
> Rose like remembered columns in a story
>
> About the Virgin's house that rose and flew
> And landed on the hilltop of Loreto.
> I lift my eyes in a light headed credo,
> Discovering what survives translation true.

Heaney figures a visual epiphany as a page of a book, and plays on the metaphors' shared elements, moving from typography and mise-en-page to sacred architecture, blocks and columns. He is conveying the action of the mind as we read, the materiality of the text turning 'airy' as it forms phantasmata, mind images. The movement of the first verse keeps ascending – airy, uprights, heights – and the stress on 'rose' keeps the mind picture aloft and helps to realize the impossibility of the story in the next verse: 'the Virgin's house that rose and flew'.

He is here declaring his belief not only in miracles but in acts of language, in translation. The term *translatio* properly describes the transportation of a body between one place and another, as in the 'translation' of St Mark's relics to Venice, or it can be used of the passage of a body – of an embodied person – from one form to another: 'Bless thee, Bottom, bless thee, thou art translated,' as Peter Quince cries out when Bottom the weaver re-enters the stage wearing his ass's head (*A Midsummer Night's Dream*, III. i).

Himself an eloquent translator, Heaney takes up the pun, and the translation he invokes here is first the miracle of the house's flight, and secondly a play on words: on the power of language to forge realities in the mind's eye and his own ability to move across borders from one culture to another. 'What survives translation true' sets up a paradox between the literary work of cultural exchange on the one hand and, on the other, the unverifiable metaphysical objects of faith.

Supreme Baroque masters worked on the opulent revetment
and sculpted narratives that encase the relic of the Holy House.

## Home Regained

At the heart of Loreto's grand High Renaissance basilica, a baroque architectural complex designed by Bramante to replace the medieval church, the Holy House stands at the centre of the crossing, the usual location of the high altar. A magnificent, sculpted marble monument, a *rivestimento*, or revetment of the relic, was first commissioned in 1509 by Pope Julius II (Michelangelo's patron); he was only the first of a succession of popes to give the shrine of Loreto his full support. The surface is carved all over with reliefs, sculptures and ornaments in a pictorial scheme devised by Andrea Sansovino and worked on by numerous artists and assistants for over twenty years. The wraps were not lifted on this marvel of High Renaissance art till 1538. Sansovino carved the dramatic scene of the Annunciation over the entrance to the house itself, a low door into the sanctuary: a beam of divine light pierces the composition aslant like a blade, on which the Holy Ghost perches in the form of a dove. Several others contributed to the complex assemblage of statues (sibyls, cherubim) and busy narrative scenes that makes up this monument of Renaissance art.

The architect Bramante, who also worked on the *rivestimento*, took his inspiration from triumphal arches of Rome or from classical sarcophagi, such as the monumental Mausoleum of Halicarnassus and Augustus' Ara Pacis (Altar of Peace) in Rome, and from actual tombs, such as Helena's, now in the Vatican. Like these monuments, the central structure enclosing the Holy House is a princely casket, densely sculpted with dynamic scenes, making a Counter-Reformation statement about ornament and images. With Giuliano da Sangallo and many others, Bramante revisioned the tumultuous Dionysian scenes found from Greece and Rome funerary marbles and replaced them with narratives: one unfolds the life of Mary and another pictures the vicissitudes of the house on its journey and the many ordeals of its devotees. One of the bas-reliefs, for example, by Niccolò Tribolo and Francesco da Sangallo, depicts a band of pilgrims assaulted by bandits; the composition echoes the tradition of a virgin martyrdom – a young woman is about to have her throat cut by a ruffian.

This sculptural edifice dominates the view down the nave of the spacious and beautiful interior of the church, a sanctuary over a sanctuary, an ordinary house for worship inside an ark or temple of infinite preciousness. It underlines the story as it is told in the historical record: Loreto isn't a famous and popular medieval sanctuary, like Canterbury or Chartres or Conques, but a Renaissance phenomenon, an apogee of Counter-Reformation piety and an emphatic act of retaliation against Reformers' scepticism.

Inside this elaborate encrustation stands the humble shack of stones, laid higgledy-piggledy. The interior measures only 31 by 13 feet; the walls are uneven, made up of different sizes of brick and stone; the only window, in the rear wall, is square, barred with a grille and set a little off-centre. The chamber is lit by sanctuary lamps and the sparkle of gold, silver and jewels from the high altar where the cult statue of Our Lady of Loreto glows in a gilded niche. Its shape, size and closeness intensify the feeling of a treasury.

Entering the hushed, glittering space through the narrow door in the side and leaving it through the even narrower passage behind the altar suggested to me swimming through a shipwreck – passing through a cabin door into its mysterious obscure interior where everything has suffered a sea change and the humdrum becomes transfigured by the concentration of belief, the accumulated hopes and wishes of centuries. Visitors kneel on the stone floor and shuffle round the outer edge, where their penitential progress over time has worn a shallow trench.

The relic of the house itself has not changed since 1582 when Montaigne observed his Easter duties here, except that the silver and gold offerings no longer cover the walls edge to edge as he described. The walls are now bare and uneven, made up of different sizes of brick and stone. On the altar opposite the single window, the cult statue of the shrine stands impassively on high; she is one of numerous Black Madonnas, as is also Our Lady of Walsingham. Marian pilgrimages all over the world centre on such cult images, spanning early medieval times (Altötting, Einsiedeln, Le Puy, Rocamadour, Clermont Ferrand, Zaragoza, Cádiz, Montserrat and many, many others) onward to more recent devotions, especially in the Americas (Our Lady of Guadalupe in Mexico being a leading example), where the connection with the local people is intended. Often crowned, enthroned and bejewelled and, on her special feast days, arrayed in precious embroidered vestments, these effigies are, like Loreto's cult statue, replaced with a fresh copy when pillage or other accident necessitates. Such sacred

The interior of the Holy House of Loreto is cramped and dim, emphasizing Mary and Jesus's humble circumstances.

objects are treated not as unique works of art but as contact relics, conserving and transmitting power reproducibly. The original statue at Loreto disappeared in the sixteenth century; the current copy, made from the wood of a cedar of Lebanon growing in the Vatican gardens, has in turn replaced many predecessors lost to fire or looting.

On feast days the Virgin's limbs are entirely cocooned in a gem-studded tunic, like a priest's vestment or dalmatic, blazoned down the front with crescent moons in silver and gold set with diamonds; this precious, papoose-like sheath often swaddles the baby too, but occasionally the arrangement of the drapery allows him to extend one hand in blessing and in the other hold the orb of his kingship. The vestments and regalia are changed as to colour and ornament according to the liturgical calendar and sometimes the Virgin wears a papal tiara. Stiff and inexpressive, this votive statue nevertheless provides a numinous focus for devotion to the sacred personage whose relics we are privileged to witness. As Jacques Le Goff points out, the imagination needs someone to focus on. However potent a symbol of hearth and home the Santa Casa may be, it is hard to direct prayers to a heap of stones.

Loreto is unusual in offering these two major focal points for pilgrims, the house *and* the statue, but together they fulfil the function of the classical palladium of Greek civic worship and the household gods of Rome. When Odysseus and Diomedes stole the cult statue of Athena from the doomed city of Troy, their act symbolized their achievement in tearing the heart out of the Trojan identity and annexing the goddess's power.

The small, latticed window of the Holy House appears in a painting of the Annunciation by Lorenzo Lotto. This artist, startling in his original and sometimes arcane iconography, came from the nearby town of Iesi and was devoted to Our Lady of Loreto; he became a Franciscan lay brother, serving the shrine of Loreto, and he died in the town in 1556. His characteristically quirky scene-setting of the crucial moment in the history of the Incarnation includes a cat leaping in alarm. Was the artist imagining an animal's instinctive response to the irruption of the angel? Or does the cat represent a diabolical familiar fleeing its enemy?

The axial position of the Santa Casa recalls the siting of Christ's tomb in the church of the Holy Sepulchre in Jerusalem, and, encased in its

The angel Gabriel startles the cat when he salutes Mary in her house in Nazareth: the room reproduces the single window of the Santa Casa. Lorenzo Lotto, *Recanati Annunciation*, c. 1530s.

marble monument, it does look like a huge sarcophagus, a tomb for a colossus. The position of the Santa Casa also brings to mind the Kaaba, the massive opaque cube standing at the centre of the complex of Mecca. The architectural echo might be far-fetched, but narrative links them: the Kaaba marks the place where the angel Gabriel appeared and announced to Muhammad that he was God's prophet and would inaugurate the new era of revelation. There is a spot called Gabriel's Station just beside the Kaaba, and its name in Arabic, *Baytu l-Ḥarām*, means Sacred House. The word 'baetyl', rare in English, is derived from Greek, where it means a meteorite or stone of heavenly origin, with certain powers, often considered sacred; this most holy sanctuary of Islam enshrines just such a sacred stone, set in its outer wall. In Mecca, circumambulating the Kaaba is a required part of the ritual but, unlike the penance at Loreto, it is not performed on the knees – the crowds and the crush are too great.

These correspondences might depend on structural axioms – of mythological stories and ways of worshipping; they may also reflect the intertwined histories of the faiths. Sacred places in antiquity often centre on a stone, as we have seen regarding *Oedipus at Colonus* and the Dome of the Rock in Jerusalem. But the transmutation of the fount of holy power from the usual bodily remains of a saint into the fabric of a building does make Loreto peculiar in Christian cult practice, edging Mary the person into a manifestation of territory. The cult of Loreto conveys a story that gives the providential past a different direction, away from the individual personal house of the soul in the body to a claim for more general ground, for the home of the community.

The symbolism of Mary's body focuses on her as a container, the special vessel of the incarnation – for example, in the litany of Loreto, a long, hypnotic, richly metaphorical prayer. Its images show the strong influence of Near Eastern mystical poetry, the voluptuous riches of the lyric biblical tradition and the rhapsodes of early Christianity such as Ephrem of Syria and Gregory of Nyssa. The litany lists symbols and cult objects, several prefiguring the wonder of Mary's virginity: the *hortus conclusus* or enclosed garden, 'the spring shut up' and 'fountain sealed' of the Song of Songs. She is invoked again and again as a house and a vessel: House of Gold, Tower of David, Tower of Ivory, Temple of God. Several receptacles also feature: Spiritual Vessel, Singular Vessel of Devotion and Ark of the

Covenant. The Holy House in Loreto taps sacred associations along a continuum that runs from a tomb to an ark, from a mausoleum to a reliquary.

The Holy House is an extreme and blatant instance of literal-mindedness, a fabulous story actualized, transported and relocated, fossilized in its own stones. But attachment to place can be appeased through symbolic imagination, and models, simulacra and copies may act to manifest – at different scales, in various media and materials – the site of memory and the beloved homeland. The ancient Egyptians were buried with miniaturized scenes of everyday life as it was conducted on earth while they were alive, alongside all kinds of furnishings and instruments they might need after death. Their soul houses were miniature simulacra of their own dwellings, where the departed could be soothed and nourished after their death, by symbolized food, shelter and charming gardens. The custom continues in Buddhist funeral ceremonies in Asia; in Vietnam and Malaysia, for example, the dead take with them beautiful paper and cardboard reproductions of necessary and useful things so that they can refashion familiar surroundings in the afterlife – television sets, electric fans, cooking pots. Susan Stewart discusses the crucial role of mementoes in our lives: in contemporary experience, many of these are replicas in little of the *lieux de mémoire* that have meaning for us. Tiny charms of the pyramids, the Sphinx, the Statue of Liberty. Visitors to Paris will have seen the vendors with their huge hoops, on which thousands of miniature Eiffel towers are strung, glinting and flashing in the sun to seduce tourists into buying a souvenir.

Replicas of numinous places at full scale also exist: the Parthenon in Nashville, Tennessee, aims to be just as good as the real thing. As we saw in the last chapter, the Temple, the Holy Sepulchre and other sanctuaries have been replicated here and there. In many ways exile intensifies the symbolism of specific places identified as home, but whereas the stories of Loreto and Walsingham tell of methods to compensate for loss by locating replacements elsewhere, the contemporary trend doubts simulacra and prefers a literal occupation of geographical territory: no symbolism, no duplication.

There are other remembrances of Nazareth in the grounds of ecclesiastical establishments. The most ambiguous development was an institution called 'La Solitude de Nazareth', which offered refuge to young women out of prison, to battered and abused girls, to delinquents, to sex workers, to those suffering from alcohol, drugs and other harms. These asylums reveal, as do hospitals like Bedlam, the double meaning of such enclosed safe places. La Solitude de Nazareth set up reformatories, first founded in Montpellier in 1841 by the Abbé Pierre Coural, who had taken orders in the aftershock of the French Revolution; the *Solitudes* were run by nuns. After the revelations about the 'rescued' girls in the Magdalene Laundries in Ireland, such benevolence inspires doubt – and dread. No wonder Patrick Modiano's narrator in *Dora Bruder*, his 1997 novel about Paris under the Occupation, shudders when he passes under the walls of one such establishment in Paris and wonders at the name 'La Solitude-de-Nazareth'. Then, sensitive to the implications, he repeats the word 'Solitude'. As for Loreto, churches and convents and schools named after its Madonna spread globally – the clergy and nuns and missionaries working, not always consciously, as part of the networks of empire and trade.

Neither theologians nor many of the votaries still insist that angels carried the house from Nazareth. However, the claim that the house may truly have come from the region of Nazareth is still made. Some Crusader crosses on cloth and coins from the right period were allegedly found in the foundations, and analysis of the structure and the stones, according to scientific investigators, shows a possible origin in the eastern Mediterranean. Yet official ecclesiastical accounts today no longer demand that we believe in the wondrous flitting of the Holy House from Nazareth to Loreto. If the official line no longer insists

This commemorative medal, one of many, was issued by Pope Innocent XI in thanksgiving for the Christian forces' victory in Hungary 1683.

that angels carried the house from Galilee, it does claim the house is authentic. That it was Mary's does not seem to be asserted, but the heap of stones may well be some kind of shelter that originated in the eastern Mediterranean and was transported to Italy by sea.

At the beginning of the twentieth century, the eminent Catholic scholar Ulysse Chevalier, set out arguments against the house's authenticity, on the basis of the archaeological history. His book, *Notre Dame de Lorette* (1906), caused much controversy and heartache. For example, he could discover no early references to a cult of such a relic in Nazareth itself, nor any report that one day it had vanished. Though many rebuttals ensued, Chevalier's arguments struck home, and a certain air of embarrassment shadows the miracle.

Yet the Madonna of Loreto's associations with marvellous flight have only grown stronger as modernity has seen new machines take to the air. A tabernacle in the basilica of Loreto invokes her protection for air balloons and all who embark in them, and a plaque on a pillar expresses the thanks of a band of parachutists for a miraculous escape. She was declared the patron saint of the Italian air force in 1922, and of pilots, airports and passengers everywhere – she is the St Christopher of the airways. Fiumicino airport in Rome displays her statue; ex-votos from survivors of plane crashes hang in the treasury, with some model planes. She presides over space flight as well: at the time of the first moon landing, the pope declared Our Lady of Loreto the special patron of astronauts.

A booklet for young readers that I bought in the shrine bookshop sets out the new interpretation that the house was transported by sea in a ship, not by angels. Its cover interestingly conflates the *Santa Maria* of Columbus' voyages to the New World with the ship that brought the relic. But this children's illustration does reveal very clearly something that has been politely effaced at the basilica today. Its ingenuous blazoning of the Crusaders' red cross discloses the shrine's history: the basilica itself stands inland on a height; it is a redoubt, the only church in Italy to be built like a castle, with steep perpendicular outer walls, battlements and bastions to withstand attack from the sea.

The cult of Our Lady of Loreto played a prominent part in resistance to the Ottoman empire. Numerous medals were struck by one pope after another, while offerings made to the shrine commemorate several battles won against the Turk over the long period of conflict. In the treasury at

Historic sanctuaries, visible repositories of divine power:
1a. (*Above*) The Dome of the Rock (*Al-Haram al-Sharif*) in Jerusalem, seventh century, houses the stone from which the Prophet Muhammad ascended to Paradise. 1b. (*Below*) Durham Cathedral, founded in 1093 on the remains of Saint Cuthbert, offered a beacon of hope to fugitives.

2. The cherub in the foreground is holding his nose in this votive altarpiece painted during an outbreak of plague in Palermo to entreat protection from the Madonna and Santa Rosalia, the city's patron saint. Anthony Van Dyck, *Madonna del Rosario*.

3. Angels come to the rescue of the exhausted travellers: one bends down a branch and tosses dates into the cloth held out by another, and a miraculous spring appears at the feet of the holy family. Paolo Cagliari (Veronese), *Rest on the Flight into Egypt*.

4. *Opposite:* The cross on which the saviour was crucified is carried by angels into the reverie of the Empress of Rome, inspiring her journey to Jerusalem. Paolo Cagliari (Veronese), *The Dream of Saint Helena*.

5a. Splinters from the Holy Cross, most precious of relics, were disseminated throughout the Christian world.

5b. Having unearthed three crosses, Helena identifies the True Cross when it resuscitates a dead youth. Piero della Francesca, *The Legend of the True Cross*.

6. The house where Mary received the news of her destiny and where she brought up Jesus is transported to safe keeping in Italy. Giambattista Tiepolo, *The Flight of the Holy House of Loreto*.

7. The Madonna of Loreto, portrayed here as a young mother contemporary with the painter's time, receives two pilgrims who have made the journey barefoot to plead for her protection. Caravaggio, *The Madonna of the Pilgrims.*

8. A footprint presents a trace of a holy presence, to be venerated in their absence. Footprints of Imam Riza, much venerated in Shia Islam, were imprinted on a rock when a spring miraculously appeared so he could perform his ablutions. From the dispersed *Falnama*.

Loreto today the sultan's pavilion from the siege laid to the church fortress in 1518 is still on display, and some battle standards captured in the fighting (the trophies had no monetary value for Napoleon's purposes). Our Lady of Loreto's intercession, it was widely acknowledged, secured victory in the battle of Lepanto in 1571, of the Christians over the Turkish fleet. After the battle of Párkány in 1683, which began the recovery of Hungary from the Ottomans, Innocent XI (1678–89) issued a silver medal which, under the inscription 'Sub tuum praesidium' (Under your protection), depicts the Madonna and child riding on the flying house. Beneath them, in the position of the serpent under the feet of the Immaculate Conception, a vast Turkish war banner fills the image, emblazoned with the double-bladed sword of Ali and Ottoman insignia; beneath it, a company of knights face Turkish troops, against a skyline of onion domes. The banner was taken in the battle and presented to the treasury of Our Lady of Loreto. On the reverse, the pope appears in profile, with heavy-lidded eyes and a prominent chin, looking somewhat like the *commedia dell'arte* character Pulcinella, except that he wears the high papal tiara; Mary and the infant Christ are embroidered in an aureole in the border of his cope. An unusual painting of the period, called *Pius V Gives the Earth of Rome to the Polish Ambassador*, picks up the belligerence of the Papal States. It is a stiff, rather repellent picture, attributed to Domenico Valeri, a native son of Iesi, on the coast near Loreto. Under the eyes of Pius V (1566–72), earth is being sprinkled into a cloth and dripping through it to fall on to the ground in drops of blood. The portent echoes libations to the gods in Greek rituals, as well as the miraculous transformations of Christian cult: the bread and wine into the body and blood of Jesus, the liquefaction of relics on saints' feast day, the reanimation of an icon when Mary weeps or bleeds. But the miracle of the Holy House precisely sidesteps the concept of blood sacrifice, substituting her house for her body, a dream of home for martyrdom, in what is, as suggested before, a crucial symbolic move.

Pius V was pontiff when the crucial victory over the Turks at Lepanto was won, and he showed crusading zeal as well as his devotion to the Virgin Mary, especially in her local aspect as the Madonna of Loreto, in numerous acts during his papacy: he condemned Elizabeth I of England as a schismatic and confirmed the privileges of the Society of Crusaders. He was also a local boy from one of the ruling noble families of Iesi, the

Ghislieri, and the painting therefore constitutes an act of local piety and commemorates the pope's famous zeal – he was rousing the warrior spirit in the defenders of one of the many kingdoms whose borders were under threat from the Turks. In the painting he has a halo, as he was canonized in 1712, the year when the picture was painted.

In Croatia, which since the break-up of communist Yugoslavia has been a bastion of conservative Catholicism, the sanctuary of Our Lady of Trsat has been reinvigorated as 'Nazareth in Croatia'. A Franciscan monastery, founded in 1453 by the ruling Prince Frankopan invoked the thirteenth-century legend of the sojourn of the Holy House in Rijeka on its way to Italy; the whole cult site has grown impressively in size. John Paul II, the Polish pope and former Cardinal Archbishop of Kraków, who fervently supported the church in eastern Europe, made a pilgrimage to Rijeka in 2003; an ample outdoor plaza welcomes the masses who come on special feast days, and an immense modern chapel exhibits an impressive accumulation of ex-votos and model ships. Most dating from the nineteenth century but some going back to the seventeenth, they record miraculous escapes from shipwreck and storms, for the sanctuary, sitting

The Temple Church in London reproduces the Church of the Holy Sepulchre to give visitors a surrogate experience of visiting Jerusalem.

above the Adriatic, especially attracted sailors; other accidents are pictured in these immediate, moving images made by what might now be called outsider artists, or organic intellectuals. Miraculous reprieves from falls, fires and violence hang side by side with memories of many wondrous cures and the heartfelt thanks of the *miracolati*. In various media – watercolour, oils, paintings on glass, embroidery, straw-work – they cover the walls, frame to frame, while clusters of crutches, sticks, trusses and chains testify to more healing and deliverance.

In eastern Europe, replicas made of different materials and carved by very different hands, are numerous: in Prague, the sculptures on the revetment are finely reproduced; there are other facsimiles, too, in Kraków, and in Rumburk, in the northern part of the Czech Republic near the German border, and elsewhere. Contrary to Walter Benjamin's celebrated warning about fading aura in the era of reproduction, copies of this relic, simulacra of the Holy Houses, even when approximate, retain their sacredness and their efficacy.

The multiplication of the Temple in Jerusalem and of the Holy Sepulchre presents forerunners of the many copies of the Santa Casa. In Cambridge, England, the church of the Holy Sepulchre, known as the 'Round Church', is a reduced version, dating from $c.1130$, while in London the Knights Templar established a far grander homage. In Italy, in the Rucellai chapel of San Pancrazio, Florence, the exquisite *opus sectile* and marble Sacello or Tempietto, was built according to the exact measurements of Jesus' tomb. The visitor can enter this chamber tomb through a low door; the Rucellai family are buried within, in pious yearning to be close to their Saviour. The chapel of St Helena below the church of Saint-Leu-Saint-Gilles in Paris (described in Chapter 3), reproduces her shrine beneath Jesus' tomb in Jerusalem. A few years ago, while looking at Coptic churches in Abu Dhabi, I came across – to my surprise – a perfect reproduction of the Dome of the Rock, including the standing arches of the Al-Aqsa enclave. The gilded dome and gorgeous tiling in azure and green have every appearance of being perfectly imitated, only at a much smaller scale. These surrogate shrines are only a few of many such sites. But the desire to replicate can be satisfied with much less ambitious warrants of contact with the source of divine grace. Pilgrim souvenirs were issued in the form of large or small models of the holy sites.

The principle of replication has increased its purchase in an era of infinite media of copying. A startling recent popular phenomenon involves another house that a community of faithful holds sacred, which has likewise generated a chain of doppelgängers far and wide. These quasi-replicas provide anchor holds for a religious group, the Chabad Lubavitchers, who follow belief in an esoteric branch of Hassidic Judaism as interpreted by Menachem Mendel Schneerson (1902–94), known reverently as 'the Rebbe'. His home in Brooklyn, New York, at 770 Eastern Parkway, where the sect has its headquarters, is a Victorian Gothic double-fronted and gabled brick building. Replicas of this urban, domestic, bourgeois American home have sprung up in Los Angeles, Ukraine, São Paulo and Jerusalem, with only slight architectural differences, their multiplication borne along by the contemporary rise in Orthodox Judaism and interest in Kabbala (see Plate 12). As of 2005, there were five in Israel. In its various unfamiliar environments, this travelling holy house is often incongruously wedged between soaring towers of glass and steel, like a child's toy lost in a giant's car park.

Over the years since the loss of their leader, the house itself has acquired numinous powers, a symbol of his lost presence in the same way that the Santa Casa embodies the absent Mary. In a thought-provoking essay, George Prochnik chronicles how the house number itself – 770 – has gained mystical and occult meanings, as have several other features of the dwelling. As Hillel Schwartz writes at the close of his study of copies, likenesses and 'unreasonable facsimiles': 'Telling true spirit from false has never been simple . . . The more we attempt to tell things apart, the more we end up defending our skills at replication.'

Nazareth is not only a lost holy place for Western Christianity but continues to radiate potent symbolic meaning for Arab Christians, especially Palestinians. For example, the Palestinian poet Mourid Barghouti, who lived in exile – in Hungary, in Egypt, in Jordan – for most of his life, describes an emotional return he made to Palestine. He wanted to show the family village to his son Tamim, who had never set foot there. Although Mourid himself was a Muslim by birth, Nazareth was 'the cradle of our people'. 'At the Church of the Annunciation in Nazareth,' he writes, 'we found ourselves at the heart of our history.' Later, he rails at how 'our history' has been treated: 'The worst thing about wars is that they reduce the enemy to a single characteristic. The country ceases to be history, language, architecture, theatre, gardens and legends: a heritage of love stories, philosophy and science; shared ancestral dreams and uncountable versions of human striving along the road of the universe. Instead, every country becomes a mere label, blot, field of battle . . . The whole of history is now "today" and today has become a reduction of every "yesterday" that has passed over the face of the earth, a reduction of all history.' The richness of religious coexistence is one of the historical realities that was and is being destroyed by the conflicts and violence of the region.

The Barghoutis are not Christians, nor even observant Muslims, but the cultural resonances of religious motifs remain live in secular contexts, as reflected in the poetry of Mahmoud Darwish and others (see Chapter 9). Edward Said, probably the most celebrated Arab intellectual in Europe and America, was brought up a Protestant Christian. He himself was an exceptional individual, but the complicated mosaic of family coordinates in his life is unexceptional among Palestinians before 1948. His mother, Hilda Musa, was born in Nazareth. I don't intend to make a strong claim that the lost town of Edward Said's mother's childhood was consciously moulding Said's polemical criticism, or that he had any attachment to that particular place. He argued against nativism and nationalism, but he also passionately advocated historical and cultural recognition of Palestine. Nazareth didn't appeal to him, and Hilda herself found the town 'old and dour'. But recent violent confrontations have erased the enmeshed histories of the eastern Mediterranean (or Western Asia, as the UN has renamed the contested region) and simplified them in compliance with ethnic and religious ideological divisions. The history of Nazareth, the ravelled family connections to it and its mythic accretions throw light on different forms of attachment and attitudes to home.

Enough affinities can be glimpsed between Edward Said's methods of figural interpretation to linger a moment on the vicissitudes of Nazareth as a symbol, which, by analogy with Jerusalem, was superimposed on to the sacred and imaginary cartography of Europe.

That plural world of the eastern Mediterranean was disrupted, and secularism was a crucial catalyst to the progressive, emancipatory spirit of modernity and nationalism. The presence of Arab Christianity should still not be overlooked. In *Out of Place*, Said describes the work of his aunt with Palestinian refugees; he shows her active at the heart of the Protestant community in Cairo – Anglicans, Presbyterians, Baptists. 'It was through

Aunt Nabiha', he wrote, 'that I first experienced Palestine as history and cause in the anger and consternation I felt over the suffering of the refugees, those Others, whom she brought into my life. It was she who communicated to me the desolations of being without a country or a place to return to . . .' He is scornful of another aunt, Ida, 'an avatar of today's Jesus freaks', who would regale her captive audience in the doctor's waiting room where she helped out with slide shows about the Holy Family.

At the risk of turning into another Ida, I think it is worth remembering this substratum in Edward Said's consciousness: Nazareth stands for the lost homeland more precisely for Palestinians than it did for fifteenth-century and later would-be pilgrims from Europe.

## The Golden Stain of Time

Anxiety that this major relic might be spurious, and the accompanying quest for authenticity distract attention from the imaginative engagement involved in these processes and the reasons for their vitality: to touch base with Mary's surroundings by telling a story in bricks and mortar, by remaking her habitation far from its locale, putting down a bit of Nazareth in Loreto, where it can be re-entered and touched. When the cult of the Holy House was truly flourishing, pilgrims used to take home with them something of its fabric: as mentioned above, dust from the house, created by dander and candle grease and time, would be scraped off the walls and mixed to make ink. The practice was strictly forbidden, Montaigne reports, explaining that 'if it was permitted to carry some off, it wouldn't last three days'. Loreto wasn't the only shrine where pilgrims sought to record their penitence on their body: the crucified, resurrected and ascending Jesus provides a tattoo sleeve to the inner arm of a pilgrim to the Holy Land in 1669. (The practice was forbidden by the church at Loreto in 1860, but continued until the 1940s.) To create more mementoes for pilgrims, the *santa polvere* was not only mixed into the glazes of pottery and china, but also wiped onto cloths which were then torn into tiny pieces and attached to holy pictures, as certificates for pilgrims. They were assured the fragments had been in contact with the cult statue of the Madonna, and granted them, if they performed the stations around the sanctuary, remission from punishment in hell.

In this way, the Santa Casa was treated as if it were not merely a substitute mausoleum of the Virgin but an organic body itself, exuding and shedding, just as some saints such as St Nicholas in Bari continued to yield a miracle-working manna from their tomb. The holy dust carried an indexical trace of the Holy Family's home in Nazareth and its power could then be transported in turn from Loreto to radiate the contact with origins, work miracles and guarantee salvation, short-circuiting time and space to unite the pilgrim with the object of cult and its powers.

The potency of dust is not intrinsically a religious belief, except as a mark of penitence, as in the Ash Wednesday rite alluded to earlier (p. 117). Its symbolism arises from an instinctual sense that dust is itself a witness, a repository over time of what happened where it lies or sticks and accumulates. It is an index that holds within it the record of people and their doings in that place. John Ruskin praised the ingrained dirt that accrued on the doge's palace or other architectural marvels and campaigned against restoration that stripped grime from ancient buildings. 'It is in that golden stain of time,' he wrote, 'that we are to look for the real light, and colour, and preciousness of architecture; and it is not until a building has assumed this character, till it has been entrusted with the fame, and hallowed by the deeds of men, till its walls have been witnesses of suffering, and its pillars rise out of the shadows of death, that its existence, more lasting as it is than that of the natural objects of the world around it, can be gifted with even so much as these possess, of language and of life.' In *Ethics of the Dust*, a series of imagined lessons in crystallography for young girls, Ruskin hymns the wonders of rocks and, in the spirit of Blake and Wordsworth, urges his circle of young pupils to see divinity in the least forms of matter. He closes with a paean to dust, in readiness 'for the time when Dust of the generations of men shall be confirmed for foundations of the gates of the city of God'.

In Ruskin's vision, the beauty of crystals and marbles reveals the transformation of primeval ooze, mud and slime as wrought over time; this process provides him with an analogy for the resurrection of the body and its future transfiguration, as promised in the Christian credo. Dust here conjoins mortal remains to the enduring dwelling in eternity, the happy home of heaven. The eschatological body of the seeker and the permanent place that is sought become fused. To accept this deep symbolic investment in the dust of the person and their home, it need not lead us to the bloodthirsty nativist worship of soil as in the Nazi ideology of *Blut und Erde*. These associations have been resisted most imaginatively by Philip Pullman in his trilogy *His Dark Materials* (1995–2000), where he follows Ruskin's line of thought in raising dust to metaphysical heights, though as a 'religious atheist' he rejects Christian interpretation in favour of a scientific cosmological theory. Dust is the life force in the novels, but it is polysemous; the novels stage an apocalyptic struggle to possess it and control it, and the forces of evil are resisted throughout with varying success. But the dust itself is not contaminated and keeps its character as energy, vitality and personhood.

At a less ambitious level, the artist-photographer Duane Michals, celebrated for his elliptical sequences of images, created in 2003 a book called *The House I Once Called Home: A Photographic Memoir with Verse*. Michals likes to tap his medium's affinity with the uncanny, and his works are often tinged with bittersweet wistfulness, as here; he tells this story with spidery, faux-naïf scratched-in captions almost like spirit writing of mediums in trance. He revisits his childhood home in McKeesport, Pennsylvania, the house in which he was born and which he had left seventy years earlier, and finds it abandoned, overgrown with vegetation, the once familiar rooms crumbling and peeling. Industrial decline has ruined the town; as a young man, Michals had wanted to leave and was free to do so. His elegy to the lost home does not speak for the refugee who cannot do otherwise than flee, yet it expresses piercingly the pain of separation and loss of home. Across a double-page spread, Michals shows his palm – an old, lined, working hand – with a handful of 'plaster dust from the house' and ends with the lines: 'It seems a peculiar irony to learn / that most of us must cease to be / to know the real of our reality.' Here the chain of association – home–dust–destiny – carries no religious meaning, but strikes powerful emotions nonetheless. The attachment can and does take humbler and more innocent forms: the hacked-off fragments of the Berlin Wall, the jars of sand tourists bring back from a summer holiday, the stone picked up from the ground while strolling with a friend or lover. Comparable instances of the most ordinary stuff of the material world acting as a point of attachment across time and space could be multiplied.

Raja Shehadeh, the civil rights lawyer and writer from Ramallah, Palestine, remembers how a cobbler he knew in Hebron would sprinkle inside the shoes he made a bit of local dust, so that the wearer, no matter how far away they found themselves, would always be treading on some Palestinian earth.

The artist Donald Rodney's photographic work *In the House of My Father* crystallizes the conjunction of home, attachment, loss, mortality and belonging: it shows the artist's open hand, with a tiny house sitting on the palm. This dwelling, existing as an image, expresses the poignant ephemerality of self, house and home. The miniature home is made from the artist's own skin, shed during treatment for sickle cell anaemia, an illness that is passed on in families and particularly afflicts individuals of Caribbean ancestry. Another version of this work is called *My Mother. My Father. My Sister. My Brother*. But the Father in the title is also, in a patriarchal system, the representative of the household: home is the artist's body, and also the ancestral line to which he belongs. This bodily relic seems to me to touch that same state of anguished yearning for home as the ramshackle disrepair of the Holy House.

The longing for material contact has spurred on the preservation of secular sites which are perceived to carry in their fabric some trace of the person who once lived there. The homes where a poet, singer, artist,

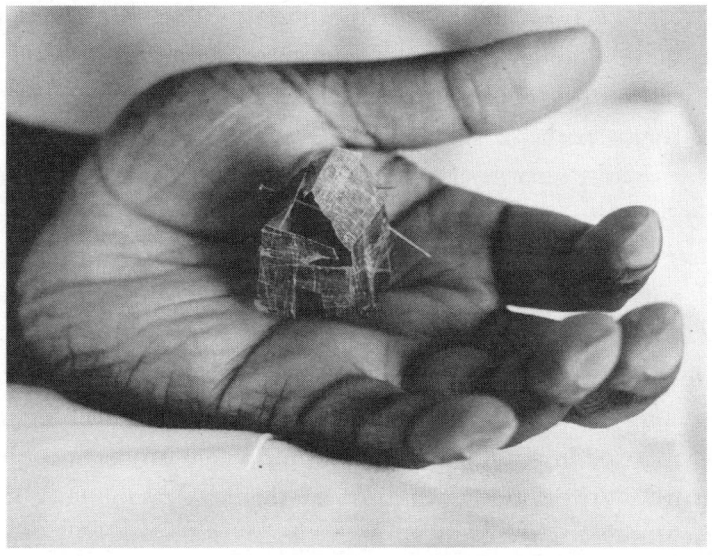

Artist Donald Rodney created a fragile dwelling made of his own skin, remembering his history and lineage. *In the House of My Father* (1996–7).

national hero/ine or other respected or often beloved figure was born or lived at the height of their fame have becomes shrines to their memory. Captain Cook's cottage, the family home in North Yorkshire, was moved bodily to Australia in 1934, during a time when he was still a revered founding father, the 'discoverer' of the continent. Ellisland Farm in Minecraft, Scotland, Robert Burns's house, which he built for his family and where he wrote some of his most famous poems, 'has changed little since the 18th century', declares the website, 'and remains the most authentic of all his homes'. Graceland, the home of Elvis Presley in Memphis, has attracted millions of visitors since it was opened to the public in 1982. The Harlem home of the poet and musician Langston Hughes has just become another site of black history, of enacted resistance to forgetting. The childhood house of Nina Simone in Tryon, North Carolina has also been saved and opened to the public. A small dwelling, it uncannily echoes the modesty of the Santa Casa.

These are contemporary, secular *lieux de mémoire*, brimming with value for the communities that form around a star, hero or heroine. As long as there is a trace – a spoor – the aura is transmissible, as with a saint's relics, and the traces and their potency distributed. The classicist Helen Morales journeyed through the American south on the trail of the singer and star Dolly Parton and discusses in her book *Pilgrimage to Dollywood* how such heritage monuments of vernacular celebrity have developed along a continuum from the quests of the faithful in the world religions to the spectacular entertainments of the gigantic theme parks of Disneyworld and Disneyland.

Secular shrines also exist that are founded in stories, the products of writers' imagination. On Prince Edward Island in Canada, where the writer Lucy Maud Montgomery was born and lived and set her beloved novel *Anne of Green Gables* (1908), a theme park has been built *in situ*, which reproduces sites and scenes from the book; meanwhile, in Hokkaido in Japan, a duplicate has been created, so that Japanese fans – of whom there are many – need not travel far and can even get married in a replica of the parlour where Montgomery herself was married. Writers' houses become lay shrines, crucibles of collective memory however fictive and, often, of local and national identity.

But the links can be less direct, mere associations through the charismatic figure's works. In France, a chain of Literary Hotels has sprung up, not in the actual homes of the writers whom they commemorate but in their *quartier*. The Hôtel Littéraire Gustave Flaubert is in the centre of Rouen, where *Madame Bovary* unfolds, and the hotel has a fine collection of parrots. Also on exhibition in the foyer are a majestic life-size sculpture of the author, engravings, portraits, as well as much ephemera and memorabilia. Each bedroom evokes a friend of Flaubert's with images and apt quotations from his letters (I was given the George Sand room). Are the hotels sanctuaries? Yes, in a secular, non-denominational key. The writer is an object of veneration, and the surroundings give visitors a flattering sense of being an insider, of belonging to a group of initiates.

## Postscript

In 1993 the artist Rachel Whiteread created a powerful monument, *Untitled (House)*, it became overnight a famous work, a lasting contemporary memorial – in spite of being pulled down after only eleven weeks. The sculpture condensed into a single monumental form the concept of home as sanctuary: Whiteread cast the entire interior of a house in London that was due to be demolished by the local council against the wishes of its occupants. It was the last dwelling in the street block to remain.

Whiteread thus created a cenotaph – an empty tomb – which also issued a profound and tragic protest. She drew attention to the void its destruction would leave by literally filling the emptiness, entombing in cement the hollow of what had been a habitation. She raised a memorial that even resembles a sarcophagus to the condemned dwelling. The huge sculpture, with its ghostly imprints of the fireplaces, chimney stacks, doors, windows, alcoves, stood like the negative of a photograph of a once living and beloved face. It memorialized loss and the ruin of a home. It also epitomizes an all-important stratagem, of appropriating sacred languages for secular social purposes. *House* acts as a tombstone without religious associations, a ritual act of blessing, propitiation and consolation that depends on no higher cosmology. Ways of dwelling in times of loss need to annex these long-tried languages of symbolic action.

Whiteread's *House* was itself torn down, but the artwork lives on in its story and its images. This vanished monument lives an afterlife in the records, a testament to the unhoused everywhere.

# 5

# Bonds:
# The Migrant Queen

'Poetry is a violence from within that protects us from a violence without.
It is the imagination pressing back against the pressure of reality.'
Seamus Heaney, after Wallace Stevens

In the *Aeneid*, Virgil's hero Aeneas flees his native land of Troy. The Roman poet has Homer's Odysseus in mind, but with the major difference that Aeneas has no Ithaca to return to: Odysseus is going home whereas Aeneas is a refugee, whose situation foreshadows the circumstances of many today. He loses his wife Creusa as he leaves the burning city but manages to rescue his father Anchises by carrying him on his back and to keep hold of his young son Ascanius by the hand. As they drift westwards across the Mediterranean, Anchises dies, and the Trojan fleet is driven, by a violent, divinely raised storm, on to the shores of Dido's kingdom of Carthage. There the queen receives the shipwrecked Trojans generously and offers them shelter – gives them refuge (see Plate 10).

Later, when Dido meets their leader Aeneas face to face, she offers him even more generous terms, because she knows, she tells him, what the fugitives are experiencing, the loss of home:

*Me quoque per multos similis fortuna labores*
*iactatam hac demum voluit consistere terra.*
*Non ignara mali miseris succurrere disco.*
(My destiny, harrying me with trials hard as yours, / led me as well,
at last, to anchor in this land. / Schooled in suffering, now I learn
to comfort / those who suffer too.)

Dido speaks in sympathy because she is herself a refugee, who has been forced to flee her home in Tyre in Phoenicia after the ruler, her brother Pygmalion, murdered her husband Sychaeus. Warned in a dream by Sychaeus' ghost, Dido hastily takes his treasure from its hiding place and takes flight by sea, making across the Mediterranean for the coast of North Africa. There she is welcomed by the local ruler and with his support (love interest is implied) she founds a city which she peoples with incomers – with arrivants. (Dido's Middle Eastern origins make her, in biblical genealogies, a great-niece of Jezebel – a startling connection.)

In this way, in Virgil's story of Dido and Aeneas, one forced migration intersects with another. The unforgettable love story he dreamed up revolves around acts of settlement and displacement: Aeneas arrives as a defeated refugee from a battle zone, and leaves as an empire builder called upon to expel or destroy the inhabitants of the land of his destination which he will occupy before becoming its ruler.

No special sacred ritual marks Dido's open-hearted act of political welcome to the Trojan fugitives, though the queen receives them in a temple where she holds her court, the poet tells us. Nevertheless, she insists, throughout Book IV of the epic, that there has been a contract with Aeneas. Virgil throws the emphasis on the tryst in the cave where Dido and Aeneas, out hunting, take shelter from a sudden ferocious storm, and he has Dido insisting that what happened there between them constituted marriage (we are not made privy to what took place). Significantly, the original sequence that brought the Trojans to Carthage – storm–refuge–contract–change of status – is reprised, placing Dido's belief in their formal union in the same position in the narrative as the bond that Aeneas accepts as her guest. Underlying the personal betrayal is another; a social transgression can be glimpsed, a disregard of sanctuary and the relations that sanctuary establishes between host and guest.

The love story, famous from Virgil's imaginative and dramatic telling, is bound up with ideas of duty and *pietas* – Aeneas is repeatedly called 'pius Aeneas'. The conflict is framed primarily as a clash between private desires and the obligations of society and nation – and destiny. Yet the contract between refugee and host runs implicitly through the towering, tragic story of passion: Aeneas leaves Dido to found Rome because the gods call him to this high task, and Dido is undone when Aeneas, flouting the laws of hospitality, tries to leave without telling her and then, in spite of her grief and curses, departs without her.

The scenes of Dido and Aeneas' passion and of her raging suicide have overshadowed this theme of another duty because it runs counter to Virgil's design, which is to exalt the future of Rome; Dido's destruction through love – and shame – has fascinated posterity to the exclusion of much else. Virgil's powerful dramatic imagination refashioned his sources and exceeded them in order to realign her story to fit a less emotional, more civic portrait of female authority and conduct. His desperate lover has struck so many readers and inspired so many memorable renderings, especially on the stage, that his creation has eclipsed all others, and concealed from view. Beneath the tragic passion, some underlying structural elements of his vision reverberate in later reworkings of the legend and throw light on today's urgent issues of xenophobia, concentrations of power, migration and settlement. Aeneas' mission to build Rome and Virgil's relation with his patron the emperor Augustus lead to the poem sympathizing with Aeneas, casting him as the emperor's forerunner and showing the greater imperative that impels him to leave Dido, breaking sanctuary obligations in order to obey the higher calls of nation building and the future of empire. Aeneas is torn and is acting against his own desires, he tells Dido when she confronts him, in a famous farewell speech that ends in the half hexameter, catching his split, broken state:

*Italiam non sponte sequor*
(I make for Italy but not of my own free will.)

Their desperate love story serves to mask wrongdoing on the part of the Trojans, who are breaking the reciprocity of a pact – of the unspoken laws of sanctuary by which the host and the refugee are interdependent and have mutual responsibilities. The balance towards passion – and female passion at that – away from concepts of mutual agreement and reciprocity camouflages the future Romans' moral character and was necessary to uphold the hero's *pietas*; but the way the story is told has ethical consequences which have gained sharper significance for readers and audiences today. The call of duty, the gods' commands to found Rome, Aeneas' sense that he must obey them and bend to his fate, exalt the imperial mission in the poem and also establish moral guidelines in which the woman – the weeping, lovesick woman – stands for something lesser.

Dido's story is usually presented as historical, though it is a case where the boundaries between fact and fiction are very blurred. It was told rather differently by writers before Virgil whose work he knew or might have known of, and his far more famous scenario vividly reveals that the way a story is told, how we see strangers and their behaviour, reflects desiderata of the story's audience; a classic epic of this order also acts to instil moral values. In earlier sources Dido, Queen of Carthage, has another name by which she is still known in the North African and Arab worlds: Elissa. This alternative, Phoenician name is used by Virgil now and then interchangeably with Dido. It has been interpreted to mean 'mighty' while the name Dido has been associated with words for wandering. The verb *errare*, to wander and also to err, recurs in many variations in the original Latin, striking notes again and again in relation to the circumstances of both Dido and Aeneas; they are political wanderers, fugitives from wars and violence, as well as figuratively in error for what they do. Dido/Elissa the mighty, the wanderer, founds a Punic or Phoenician home from home, a colony in Africa. But Virgil does not characterize the new city (Carthage means New City) as a Phoenician outpost, since in his story the queen's connections to her native land have been violently severed. The alternative chronicles of Dido's story, written before Virgil's epic, do not foreground the love story with Aeneas, nor even mention him. But these accounts haven't commanded the attention of readers down the centuries, as they lack the dazzling poetic ferocity and musicality of the *Aeneid*. They do, however, bring out themes that Virgil, in the interest of epic and tragic passion, sidelines; they illuminate the implicit contract between arrivant and host, and the all-important place of loyalty and good faith in belonging and hospitality. The unconditional generosity of ancient Greek xenia was developing into a reciprocal social bond.

Virgil was composing the *Aeneid* between 29 and 19 BCE (he left the poem, it seems, incomplete at his death, though scholars differ on this point). The story of Dido and Aeneas fills Books II, III and IV, while in Book VI, when Aeneas glimpses her wraith in Hades, accompanied by Sychaeus, she turns away from him without a word; these passages have long stood as the most memorable, heartbreaking sections of the poem.

Dido's sorrows and wanderings unfold in flashbacks, at the beginning of Book II, when the goddess Venus, the mother of Aeneas, accosts him after he is shipwrecked. He is in despair; harried by the goddess Juno who has pursued the Trojans vengefully ever since the Judgement of Paris, when Paris the Trojan prince awarded the apple 'for the most beautiful' to Venus, Aeneas' ships have been destroyed, many of his compatriots lost to the waves' fury in the storm the angry goddess has raised against him. Venus is in disguise as a local girl, and speaks to her son alluringly of the queen who rules the region where he has washed up, enticing him with a stirring portrait of a magnificent woman who, incidentally, has amassed huge wealth as well as securing a kingdom for herself. The goddess is acting here in character, intent on safeguarding her son from further harassment by her arch-rival Juno and inflaming his desire, but her account may also contain a mother's reproach to Aeneas for his faint-heartedness and despair, as Venus enlarges on how Dido collected together the gold of her native Tyre and loaded it on board before she took flight. She crowns her account with the ringing phrase 'dux femina facti' (I:364), a woman becomes leader.

During this encounter Venus is dressed as a huntress, and indeed when Aeneas realizes she is no ordinary mortal he takes her, understandably, for Diana or one of her nymphs of the hunt. But in her flippant way, caught well in Robert Fagles's translation, Venus explains,

> It's just the style for Tyrian girls to sport
> a quiver and high-laced hunting boots in crimson.

In this way, Aeneas' first encounter with a woman in the place where he finds himself off course and lost sets up a sense of female independence, mobility and unsubordinated authority. With an implication of gender inversion, Venus has slid into the persona of her sister Olympian Artemis, goddess of the moon and of the hunt, associated with wild places, forest pools and their inhabitants, bears.

Venus continues,

> What you see is a Punic kingdom, a people of Tyre
> and Agenor's town, but the border's held by Libyans
> hard to break in war. Phoenician Dido is in command,

she sailed from Tyre, in flight from her own brother.
Oh it's a long tale of crime, long, twisting, dark . . .

She then regales her son with a dramatic, fast-moving account of Dido's life story so far: how Sychaeus, Dido's husband, was also her uncle, a priest, and the richest man in Tyre, coveted Sychaeus' great wealth and broke into the temple while Sychaeus was sacrificing at the altar and murdered him – a grave sacrilege, a breach of the laws of sanctuary. He then concealed his crime, leaving the dead man unburied, until one night Sychaeus appeared to Dido in a dream, all bloody from his wounds. It was then he revealed to her where he kept his treasure hidden and urged her to gather it all and take flight. Dido did as he instructed and, calling together many of her fellow citizens, set out across the Mediterranean; when they reached the coast of Libya she bought land to found Carthage. Virgil gives one line to this purchase, and indeed Venus' story leaves out many episodes of the adventures of this African queen as told in other sources, in which the strength of mind and cunning of the young widow are emphasized. The stratagem which Virgil alludes to in passing shows Dido to be a trickster in mythology as well as an independent female ruler: she asks the local king for as much land as can be enclosed by an ox hide, and once he has agreed, she has the oxhide cut into as narrow a strip as possible and then laid out to mark the perimeter of a large expanse of territory. (Technically the problem is called 'iso-perimetric inequality'; in mathematics it is known as 'Dido's theorem' – how to determine the largest possible area of a plane with a boundary of a specified length.)

Soon after this fast-paced and indeed alluring introduction to Dido, designed to ignite her son's interest and keep him in Carthage, sheltered from Juno's spite, Venus reveals herself in her full radiance to her son. She then wraps him and his companion Achates in a mist so that they can approach Dido's new city, undetected and unobserved. A magnificent spectacle unfolds before them: the new city rising, the Tyrians building an ideal and splendid citadel abutting the sea, with a harbour, bridges, a theatre and a huge temple . . . Virgil unspools one of his extended pastoral similes, comparing their work voluptuously to bees in summer, the rising city a honeycomb of busyness and plenty and promised sweetness.

The memory of Dido the builder of Carthage was honoured by posterity – in Phoenicia, for example, her image appears on coins issued in the third century CE during the reign of the Roman emperor Heliogabalus. They reveal that Carthage was still primarily seen as a Phoenician colony.

In the epic, as soon as the invisible Aeneas enters the new city, he finds himself confronted by a great temple where the stones have been carved with scenes from the fall of Troy: Virgil here is setting another vivid narrative-within-a-narrative, one epic framing another, offering a series of imbricated stories, first a flashback to Dido's journey, then, through the sculptures, a flashback to Aeneas'. Through Virgil's highly dramatic, animated ekphrasis, Aeneas revisits the harrowing deaths he witnessed in the war which he fled seven years before, and then comes face to face with himself, depicted in the mêlée of the battle.

At this point, the two trajectories of the main protagonists converge, and Dido, with her splendid court assembled about her, arrives at the temple and takes her throne. Virgil here compares Dido with Diana: the Amazonian vigour and independence of the Tyrian girls and their new realm in Africa envelopes her. Virgil tells us that Latona, the Titaness who gave birth to Diana and her twin, Phoebus Apollo, 'thrills with joy too deep for words' at the sight of Dido striding through her people and her possessions. Aeneas and Achates are both still invisible, privily watching Dido as she exercises full command of the busy scene, dispensing justice, making laws and then greeting their shipwrecked companions, who have found her there and are pleading for mercy and shelter – for sanctuary.

Virgil's preludes to the meeting of Dido and Aeneas moves the plot along axes of flight and settlement. Home is the place left behind for both Aeneas and Dido, but she has succeeded in making a new home and he has been called by Destiny to found another, in Rome, and has been blown off course. The struggle between them will turn on where they settle and who can be permitted to be in charge. Dido makes her appearance *in propria persona*, heralded by Venus' intentionally exciting backstory, and is above all presented as a widow who holds sovereignty and property in her own right, a force of civilization and order – what used to be called in medieval law a *feme sole*, a lone female in full possession in more ways than one.

Virgil may have come across the interweaving of Aeneas' story with Dido's in the surviving fragments of a lost source, Gnaeus Naevius' epic about the first Punic war, and lost text by Varro, a contemporary of Virgil, in which it is Anna, Dido's sister, who kills herself for love of Aeneas. But whatever the anterior sources may have reported, the immense and unforgettable conflagration of Dido's passion owes its lingering power to Virgil's imagination and dramatic skill. He plucked out of the *Iliad* a minor and not entirely illustrious Greek warrior who nevertheless possesses a special aura because he is Venus' son, one of the very few beings born of a goddess's love for an ordinary mortal – Anchises, a Trojan who was looking after his sheep when he caught Venus' eye (by contrast, male gods rape mortal women all too routinely, and, as Homer tells us, 'a god's embrace is never fruitless' (*Odyssey*, XI:235)). In the *Iliad*, Aphrodite protects her son with a mother's care, and with the help of Poseidon saves him from Achilles on one of his rampages (Book XX) by dropping a magic mist over the Greek hero's eyes – the episode inspires the scene in Virgil when Venus hides Aeneas and Achates.

In various other early sources of the story, Elissa's adventures after the death of her husband focus on local African suitors' attempts to win the hand of the wealthy widow, and do not connect her with the story of a Trojan at all. In Timaeus' lost history, the author proposed that Rome and Carthage were founded at the same time, in 813 BCE; it also contains the earliest mention of Dido, under the additional name Theiosso; Virgil departs from the chronology but picks up on certain narrative elements. In Timaeus' account, the local Libyan ruler wants to marry Elissa; her fellow exiles persuade her she must consent, but, pretending that she needs to perform a ritual in order to be released from her marriage vows, she builds a huge pyre, and then throws herself on to it out of the window of her palace to immolate herself.

The fullest history of Dido before Virgil's poem was written by Pompeius Trogus, and survives in a later epitome by Justin, composed in the first century BCE. In this account, which the author presents as a factual chronicle, Dido inherits the throne of Tyre jointly with her younger brother. She is also portrayed as a strong woman and a cunning one, a trickster of shrewd foresight and calculation: on the way to Libya, for example, she and her companions stop off at Cyprus, Aphrodite's island, and pick up eighty young girls – temple prostitutes according to the custom of the goddess's birthplace; she marries them off to the Tyrians who have fled into exile with her, in order to help stock her future settlement. Once in Libya, she rejects the local ruler, the bellicose potentate Hiarbas, King of the Maxitani – Mauritani in some editions; she claims she needs to sacrifice to the gods in order to be freed of her vows to her dead husband, and then runs herself through with a sword.

Virgil clearly borrowed from both the lost Timaeus and Justin's version of Pompeius Trogus, and bent the sources to his purposes, to create the searing tragedy he achieved. He was also providing a convincing, glorious backstory for his patron, the emperor Augustus, for whom he was composing his epic of imperial destiny. Virgil retains the figure of a sacrificial widow committing a form of suttee but alters its emotional weight, by infusing rage and vengeance into her personal despair. But he also transforms the regal figure of Dido into a darker, unruly force practising magical arts in her desperation and bringing down fatal curses on her betrayers, as she sees them.

## Dido's Curse

The story of the founding of Rome by Aeneas, as powerfully propelled by Virgil's mission to aggrandize the empire in his own time and its emperor Augustus and his lineage, retrospectively and prospectively, turns on this opposition to the other new city, Carthage. Again, it is not known whether the linked origins of the two cities, which had clashed in bitter struggles during the Punic wars, were widely discussed or accepted, or whether this doubling and dividing are essential pillars of Virgil's architecture, providing narrative shapeliness in the opening books of the epic. Virgil's Dido takes pride of place within the sphere of culture: the wild lies beyond that oxhide perimeter and the barbaric locals do their worst in uncharted territory on the edge of her great city, and it is she who offers sanctuary to the Trojans, demonstrating her justice and her alliance with civilization. When Aeneas' companions are entreating Dido to help them, they complain about the locals who have prevented them landing:

> What land is this
> that you can tolerate such barbaric ways?

They are denouncing the tribes beyond the walls: Massylians, otherwise called Numidians, whose name might associate them with *nomadi*, nomads, and Gaetulians; Iarbas, the local ruler who wants to marry Dido, is identified as a Gaetulian in Virgil, the King of the Maxitani in other works (he is even sometimes called *Ira*bas to emphasize anagrammatically, his barbarous rage). Like Aeneas, Iarbas is the child of a god – Jupiter Hammon – and his rape of a local nymph, Garamantis. When Iarbas hears, from Rumour, about the queen's passion for the Trojan fugitive, he's ablaze with fury and rails against the Trojans as a band of eunuchs, while Aeneas himself is a second Paris, effeminate, dissolute, his hair oiled under his bonnet, wining and dining at the expense of the queen, herself a mere vagrant (*Aeneid*, IV:255–74). But through contamination, by the end of Book IV, Dido herself has mutated and lost the regal authority of her first appearances, her dignity and self-possession. Virgil wraps her in scenes of foreign magic; he pushes her – through allusion, imagery and dramatized scenes – across the barrier of decorum into wildness, and that wildness belongs to his Africa, pictured as distinct from Phoenicia-in-Libya. The madness of love that comes upon her explains her metamorphosis. Dido is utterly overborne by her love for Aeneas because, in the ontology of the narrative, she has stepped out of the frame of variable contingent narrative into the unchanging dimension of an eternal myth: she is a pre-eminent figure of the lovelorn woman, *sedotta e abbandonata*, who kills herself for love – for revenge, for hurt. But the woman whom Aeneas clandestinely observes dispensing justice, making laws and building her city, does not tally with the woman who organizes her own death, deceiving her sister Anna in the process. In order to accomplish the transformation, Virgil surrounds her with traditional imagery of witchcraft and barbarism; he expands on the torments of love but communicates them in a lexicon that shifts them to the edges of the world map.

With the death of Dido, Virgil mounts one of the fullest scenes of magical conjuring from classical literature (see Plate 11). He relates how Dido persuades her sister Anna to help her build her funeral pyre and load it with mementoes of Aeneas while assuring her that she is performing a love spell according to the instruction of the priestess who guards the orchard of the Hesperides and watches over the dragon at the golden apple tree. This sibylline, witch-like figure, keeping vigil at the westernmost ends of the known world, is described as a Massylian, a word generically meaning African. So Virgil too casts his mind into the furthest reaches of classical geography when Dido invokes the mind-altering drugs and songs that the priestess commands, and describes her powers over natural forces. The poet recalls the sorceresses Circe and her niece Medea in Greek myth, for this priestess can also:

> release the hearts
> of those she likes, to inflict raw pain on others –
> to stop the rivers in midstream, reverse the stars
> in their courses, raise the souls of the dead at night
> and make earth shudder and tremble underfoot – you'll see . . .

The speech ends with Dido promising her sister, her words echoing Aeneas' own sense of a controlling destiny:

> I arm myself with magic arts against my will.

The magic to which Dido has recourse here includes power over darkness, though it is not entirely clear from the text whether she is simply making up the enchantment as she goes about arranging her own spectacular death, in order to deceive Anna into helping her build the pyre. Later, the priestess appears in person and officiates, calling on the gods of darkness, and the Goddess of the underworld, the Triple Hecate, and performs elaborate and rather queasy love magic around Dido's pyre. She offers herbs, reaped with sickles by moonlight, and bursting with black poisonous milk, and with them, the love charm, the *hippomanes*, bitten from the forehead of a newborn foal before the mare could gnaw it off. With her hair unbound, calling in a voice of thunder, sprinkling that pretended water from the underworld, this priestess is a fraud, and in this respect doubles Dido herself, as she is deceiving Anna and the rest of her entourage into thinking she is

The priestess officiates at the burning of all mementoes of Aeneas.
Anna, Dido's sister, is unaware Dido is planning her own death.

exorcising Aeneas rather than immolating herself. With this startling transformation and auto-destruction of the wise and generous queen, Virgil is operating a stratagem highly adopted in the political discourse against opponents – be they strangers or other perceived danger, including women.

The priestess's malign magic has a vivid afterlife, haunting us through Ovid's *Medea* and her sorcery, then Seneca's reprise of that tragedy, and once more in Prospero's rough magic in Shakespeare.

As Dido prepares to die, her last words move through love song to lament to climax with that terrible curse on Aeneas and his posterity. Virgil uses his knowledge of Roman history and the long enmity between Carthage and Rome to give Dido a thrilling and terrifying prophecy that is also an order. She addresses her people, 'my Tyrians', and commands them to 'harry with hatred all his line, his race to come' in memory of her death. 'No love between our peoples, ever, no pacts of peace!' she cries and then calls on an 'avenger still unknown' to pursue 'those Trojan settlers' and:

> Shore clash with shore, sea against sea and sword
> Against sword – this is my curse – war between all
> Our peoples, all their children, endless war!

This ferocious imprecation, to which Virgil gave his most potent oratorical skills and passion – those caesuras have the effect of hammering the curses, very like the nails driven into votive dolls in late antiquity and the bristling metal spikes of *nkisi* figures from the Congo, each verbal blow striking home – has rung in the ears of readers and audiences beyond Virgil's pages and elite classicists.

The speech was so admired – and possibly so well known – that in his play *Dido, Queen of Carthage* (1587–93), Christopher Marlowe's heroine quotes the curse *in Latin* just as she is about to throw herself on the pyre. The resounding lines follow a swerve in Dido's farewell, Marlowe rising to the occasion to dramatize her troubled, volatile and contradictory inward workings. At first she imagines Aeneas on the sea and prays for his safe return to her, in vivid word pictures of shipwreck. But after her sister Anna reports that the fleet has sailed, Aeneas on board and, in cowardly fashion, 'clapped under hatches', Dido's mood shifts to despair and revenge: her death will blacken his name for a traitor and a murderer – 'for perjury and slaughter of a queen'. She prepares to consign to the flames all mementoes of him – Marlowe leaves out the bridal bed itself (which Virgil has listed), perhaps because the playwright doubted that stagecraft could manage such a scene without bathos. At this point in her speech, Dido's dream of redress in the remembrance of posterity turns political and Marlowe reprises Virgil's prophecy:

> Grant, though the traitors land in Italy,
> They may still be tormented with unrest,
> And from mine ashes let a conqueror rise,
> That may revenge this treason to a queen
> By ploughing up his countries with the sword!
> Betwixt this land and that be never league . . .

During the period Marlowe was writing, the tensions in the Mediterranean arose chiefly from the rival ambitions of Spain and England, and they competed to bring the rulers of North Africa to their side, Elizabeth I negotiating many alliances, as Jerry Brotton has described in his fascinating book *This Orient Isle*. The character of Marlowe's Iarbas, King of Gaetulia, reflects this history, and the prominent and romantic part he plays in the plot, as the ardent suitor of the queen, and the object of fatal love in Anna, her sister, reflects the contacts made through the complex diplomatic ballet taking place at the time, and the resulting, unexpected respect – perhaps tinged with fear and expediency – with which the Elizabethans viewed the power of the Barbary Coast, the Maghreb, and its rulers.

Marlowe blended into his vision of Dido the accents of Ovid's heroine, from her 'Letter to Aeneas' in the *Heroides*, the seventh of the passionate complaints by mythic women that Ovid imagines. Dido speaks of the double death that Aeneas, abandoning her, will bring about: she might be having his child, she says. Later in the poem, as she tacks this way and that in her attempt to sway him, this possible future baby has become a lost child they might have had together.

The soliloquies of the abandoned women have been generally disparaged as sexist, repetitive, cynical and even kitsch. The poet Clare Pollard disagrees, finding Ovid's ventriloquy an extraordinary tour de force of empathy, corresponding to the androgynous mind that Virginia Woolf proclaimed. In her deliberately updated version, Ovid's Dido, from a defiant beginning, then spills a great vortex of words as she twists and turns, trying one argument after another, one emotional approach after another, appealing to Aeneas to stay in Carthage with her. She is a suppliant who makes quasi-maternal overtures to the man who once besought her for shelter:

> Choose me!
> choose my dowry, people, wealth.
> Remake Troy in Carthage –
> you'll be happy here as king.
> If you're zealous for war, if Iulus needs
> a field to prove prowess and earn glory,

> I can find enemies.
> You won't lack anything: peace or conflict . . .
> May that inhuman war be your last loss.

Here enemies are cast as toys to placate a martial lover as Dido laments the war in Troy and hopes it may be the last Aeneas suffers. Her passionate pleas twist and turn over lines until she pronounces her own epitaph. Clare Pollard renders these lines with an internal rhyme on two heavy monosyllables:

> Aeneas gave cause and sword,
> But Dido destroyed herself.

In the *Fasti*, his unfinished calendar poem, Ovid returned once more to interpellate Virgil's history when he relates the origins of the Roman cult of Anna Perenna, kept on the Ides of March. The narrative poem, written with the poet's witty, mischievous insouciance, can be read as a riposte to the whole intrinsic grandiosity of Augustus' imperial project and in particular to his reform of the calendar and institution of new gods and cults. The fanciful story Ovid tells about Anna Perenna identifies – with no evidence at all except the coincidence of the names – a local river nymph with Dido's sister Anna, and offers a mini-epic which mirrors the grand tragedy of his compatriot; it reprises Virgil's themes, including the holiness of sanctuary, in the entry for this feast day. Anna, fleeing Iarbas, who after Dido's death has sacked Carthage, and escaping from Pygmalion, who is pursuing them to regain Tyre's treasure, lands in Melite, Malta. There, the king, Battus, would like to take her in, but he is too scared of Pygmalion's might, he says, and his kingdom is too small to offer Anna his 'customary long-standing hospitality'. She takes flight again, and is shipwrecked on the coast of Italy near the future site of Rome; then, walking on the seashore, disconsolate and dispossessed, she meets Aeneas. He is strolling there with Achates by his side – in an inverted repetition of the original encounter with Dido in Carthage when the victims of shipwreck were Aeneas and Achates. Aeneas immediately offers Anna sanctuary – in the kingdom he has received through his current wife Lavinia, as Ovid does not let us forget. Aeneas recognizes Anna's plight as his own, speaks remorsefully of Dido, whom he had seen, he says, in Tartary – Ovid is recalling Book VI of the *Aeneid*, and the poignant, silent sighting Aeneas has of his former love.

Ovid's Aeneas explicitly invokes the law of hospitality and instructs his wife Lavinia, 'I have a reason of duty, Lavinia my wife, for entrusting this lady to you: when I was shipwrecked I lived on her resources. She was born in Tyre and possessed a kingdom on the coast of Libya. I pray that you may love her like a dear sister.'

The *Fasti* often offers revisions – sometimes irreverent – to the received narrative, and in this case Ovid's Aeneas seems to conflate Anna with Dido herself and tries to make amends for the chilliness of Virgil's hero; he portrays him owning up to his broken faith, not primarily as a lover/husband but as a fugitive and a guest.

However, Lavinia is jealous, and Dido's ghost appears to warn Anna and, against a backdrop of lurid, horror-story effects, urges her: 'Flee this gloomy house! At her word a breeze struck the creaking door.' Anna obeys, and throws herself into the River Numicius where, in an Ovidian metamorphosis, she is transformed into the nymph Anna Perenna of the sacred spring.

The spring was excavated between 1999 and 2000 and a large cache of late antique votive lamps was unearthed. In a belated, uncanny coda, these objects were found to contain curled-up scrolls and lead lamellae, inscribed with a variety of curses – *defixiones*. They invoke the name of the destined victim or victims, with lines such as:

> Light versus darkness
> Warm versus cold
> Fire versus water.

The cult in classical times had been primarily kept by young girls disappointed in love, and in late antiquity the lamps had been thrown into the water to conjure death for the target. As the scholar Attilio Mastrocinque writes, 'A lamp represented a person and the ritual was a symbolic homicide.'

Can there linger here a distant memory of Aeneas, Virgil's pious hero?

## Persuasions of the Storyteller's Craft

Storytelling as a means of persuasion in the tragedy of Dido and Aeneas gives the *Aeneid* unforgettable momentum and texture; it also embodies Virgil's self-reflexive deployment of his powers as a supreme narrative wordsmith, who uses words to play the audience as skilfully as any orator. Rhetoric is not ornamental in the *Aeneid* but inaugural. Rome is a city of words, and Virgil intentionally laid them down, just as Dido laid down the walls of Carthage. Virgil returns again and again to the profound effect that the telling of a tale in words and in images can have on the receiver – the listener or the viewer; he also mines the power of repetition, elaboration and re-enactment. The passion of Dido for Aeneas and her loss of self that it brings about in Virgil has an ultimate cause in narrative itself, it could be said, rather than in Aeneas' character as he interacts with her *in propria persona*. Of course, the capricious and tyrannical gods drive on the tragedy, but the immediate catalyst is story, told and retold by one voice after another through one medium and another, adding to the lustre and seduction of both protagonists. First Venus, as I described, evokes Dido's magnificence and autonomy, then Aeneas relives his own ordeals in the last days of Troy in the frieze on Dido's temple – in that extended ekphrasis. These recountings lead, in the same way as an overture prepares the audience for the full development of the motifs and melodies, to Dido's invitation to Aeneas. 'Wait, come, my guest,' she urges, 'tell us your own story, start to finish . . .' And he does so, in Books II and III: in Virgil's version, Aeneas tells his own *Odyssey* unlike his prefiguring Greek hero, Odysseus, who finds himself listening to his own story recited by the blind bard Demodocus and weeps when he recognizes his own misfortunes. The shift from third-person bardic memory as in Book VIII of Homer's *Odyssey* to first-person lived experience in Virgil's *Aeneid* is itself inaugural of the long-lasting turn towards testimony as the strongest form of truth-telling, one which has played a part in sanctuary seeking since the ancient and medieval past and has grown in modern forensic settings, such as asylum tribunals, into the central prerequisite for granting rights to remain and belong.

And when Aeneas reaches the close of his tale, after nearly 2,000 lines of carnage, fire, ruin and loss, 'he fell silent now, his tale complete, at rest'.

The spent catharsis of this cadence, almost sexual in its sense of plenitude, immediately comes up against seething turmoil in the queen. Book IV opens with the lines:

But the queen – too long she has suffered the pain of love,
hour by hour nursing the wound with her lifeblood,
consumed by the fires buried in her heart.

Virgil, and Venus, have introduced and will introduce other catalysts to kindle her fiery love for Aeneas and keep it aflame; most heartlessly, Cupid, at his mother's suggestion, impersonates Ascanius, Aeneas' son, whom he has brought out of Troy, and in this role plays on Dido's affections, using his gifts to fire the queen to madness, in order to stir up her most intense feelings, 'weaving a lover's ardour through her bones'.

The child playing in her lap is not however Aeneas' son as Dido thinks. This is a magic semblance of Ascanius, conjured by Cupid at Venus' command. The adorable playfellow is a pure phantom of desire and, though Virgil does not say so in as many words, the scene of her cruel deception by the little boy god, who sits in her lap and kisses her, hints at the maternal longings of a childless widow.

Destiny, swerved to its fatal course by the power of narrative, especially spoken by a witness who was there, figures so vividly in Virgil's dramatic technique that it inspired stories and revisionings which recognize the overwhelming effects of a work of literature, recited or performed, and this acknowledgement of the power of words to mould minds and sway feelings has more importance than a simple affirmation of literary creation. It can alert us to the way fictions interact with experience, leading responses that in themselves then shape cognitive understanding, and consequently moulding values.

An anecdote from a *Life of Virgil*, written as part of a commentary on his works by the third-century scholar Donatus, tells us that the emperor Augustus was eager to read the *Aeneid*: 'Indeed, Augustus (for, as it happened, he was away on an expedition in Cantabria) jokingly entreated him [Virgil] in his letters, with threats as well as prayers, "that you send me" (to employ his own words) "your first sketch of the *Aeneid*, or the first *colon*, it does not matter which".'

Later, he relates that Virgil was reading to the emperor and his sister,

Octavia, from Books II, IV and VI. In Book VI, when Aeneas descends into the underworld, accompanied by the Sibyl, he meets the ghost of his father Anchises; his father and the Sibyl then unfurl for him a vast vision of the future, with the lineage of their family stretching all the way to a young boy, Marcellus. There the prophetic vision breaks off with a cry of grief:

> Oh, child of heartbreak! If only you could burst
> the stern decrees of Fate! You will be Marcellus.
> Fill my arms with lilies, let me scatter flowers,
> lustrous roses – piling high these gifts, at least,
> on our descendants' shade – and perform a futile rite.

Marcellus was Augustus' nephew, the son of his sister Octavia, and his adopted heir, in the dynasty that according to the heroic mythology that Virgil consecrated in his epic traced itself back to Iulus (Ascanius), Aeneas' son. But this future descendant, Marcellus, had died young, in 23 BCE, and had been the first Augustan to be buried in the enormous mausoleum Augustus had built for himself in the Campus Martianus. Donatus tells us that when Virgil read the words 'Tu eris Marcellus' (You shall be Marcellus), Octavia, the mother who had lost this child of destiny, was said to have fainted away. A later interpolation into Donatus' account then informs us that Octavia 'ordered ten-thousand sesterces to be granted to Virgil for each of the verses'.

The scene creates a kind of emotional diptych with the scene in the epic where Cupid plays the part of Ascanius/Iulus; both use a child to ignite a potent access of emotion, in the protagonists as well as in us, the audience. The prolepsis of Marcellus' doom echoes the simultaneous apparition and vanishing of a fantasized child of the future in Dido's longing.

The story that Donatus tells about Octavia resonates, in its many vivid reprises in art, with the way Virgil's poem touches on the love of children and the threats to them, revealing how a passing anecdote in a recondite source can gain considerable substance from the activity of human sympathy, as it is stirred by the phantasmic summonses of imaginative literature. More importantly, with hindsight, Virgil is able to place a prophecy on the lips of a character in the afterlife: this casts the scene of storytelling as an oracle for those inside the frame of the narrative, but for us, listening to it, in the same relation as Augustus and Octavia, the story produces a piercing anagnorisis – recognition of something that has happened, one of the central properties of myths, because they are intrinsically stories already known to the audience/readers. Prolepsis becomes the stance of a story when it comes from a shared myth, like the story of Troy and its branches, as Greek survivors and Trojan fugitives leave the city.

The scene became a favourite trope in painting, especially for the neo-classical artists during Napoleon's reign and afterwards when classicism was invoked to glorify and characterize the new regime. Significantly, the scene of storytelling renders participants deeply susceptible – strips them of their defences, makes them subjects of a form of imaginative hypnosis.

The Matter of Troy, or the whole wheeling cycle of stories that spin outwards from the *Iliad*, enacts the power of storytelling as a means of persuasion, wrought by the poet deploying words as

The power of literature: when Virgil read from the *Aeneid*, the emperor's sister, Octavia, fainted; the epic seemed to predict her son's death. Jean-Auguste-Dominique, *Virgil Reading Aeneid to Augustus, Livia and Octavia*, 1812.

instruments – descriptions of suffering, blandishments and imprecations. Stories interact with experience, the poet shows us, but the ethics of their power are not simple. We are all aware of the dangers of foundational myths, of the conflicts that turn on competing claims rooted in ancient stories of belonging to particular places – Jerusalem is the heart of the matter. So the prominence of narrative as the motivational force of individuals' behaviour raises crucial questions about myth and its interrelations with propaganda.

The power of storytelling, both inside the epic itself and outside it, blazes in the response of the earliest audiences, the poem's patron, the emperor Augustus and his family, and continues to reverberate in the effects on readers now. The motif returns in full force in *Othello*, when Desdemona in the listener role of Dido is smitten by the warrior's story of his stirring deeds told from his own lips – Shakespeare may have Virgil in mind but more obviously is responding to Marlowe, who opens his play with Aeneas recounting his travails and exploits to Dido, setting her afire with pity, admiration and love. Shakespeare gives the same motif a specifically theatrical spin in *Hamlet* when the Player King recites a scene, in a distinctly Marlovian, high-flown key, about the fall of Troy and the death of Priam at the hands of Pyrrhus, and weeps with emotion at his own performance, provoking Hamlet to rail against his own inability to move or be moved – 'What's Hecuba to him or he to Hecuba that he should weep for her?' We are all aware of Hamlet's problem, that he cannot move or be moved by what really matters, whereas circumstances as distant as Troy can bring quick tears.

The Player King's emotions bear on Hamlet's state of mind but they aren't the crux of the plot whereas in *Othello*, which Shakespeare wrote after *Hamlet*, the playwright sets the power of imagination to kindle passion at the very centre of the tragedy; he stages Othello's account of his exploits to Desdemona in what is an echo of Marlowe's Aeneas and, hovering above them both, of Virgil's hero. With Iago's fatal persuasions, the play also grasps their roles as erotic stimuli, and goads to hatred, the devastating consequences of disinformation, and the sway of falsehood and imputation. As the poet Jason Allen-Paisant writes in the title poem of his recent collection *Self-Portrait as Othello*, the play perceives 'a real structure of feeling taking shape' against Othello, 'an extravagant and wheeling stranger' (*Othello*, I. i. 131). In Act I, scene iii, Othello has been summoned to the presence of the duke and grandees of the Republic to explain himself after Brabantio, Desdemona's father, has been roused from his bed with the news that Othello has married his daughter – stolen her away. Brabantio rails against the witchcraft, magic and drugs – 'practices of cunning hell' (I. i. 103) – the Moor must have used to make her 'fall in love with what she feared to look on' (line 99), an echo of the sorcery imputed to another African, Dido.

Othello sets out to clear himself and promises he will tell a 'round unvarnished tale' (1. i. 91). Yet his oratory strikes up a grandiloquent, symphonic sound, which chimes with Iago's loathing, expressed in the play's opening scene, for Othello's tone: 'bombast circumstance / Horribly stuff'd with epithets of war' (I. i. 12–13). This note of suspect rodomontade continues thereafter to reverberate through a play which uncovers how rumour and slurs lead to fateful actions.

Othello's first eloquent appearance includes the self-deprecatory line

The power of storytelling: Othello sparks the love of Desdemona as he describes his travels and exploits. Carl Ludwig Becker, *Othello Relating his Adventures to Desdemona*, 1880.

'Rude am I in speech' (I. iii. 76–94). He is introducing himself to us in the audience as a plain soldier, a Moor lacking in the refinements and graces and flourishes of the senators who have summoned him to face them. But an ironical gesture to his audience's bias can be heard in these words, and the quasi-apology also issues a claim to plain speaking, that is truth-telling – his tale will be 'plain' and 'unvarnished'. What follows from Othello's protestations of plainness does indeed belie this modesty. When the Duke tells him to respond to Brabantio's furious accusations, ordering him, 'Say it, Othello,' Othello rises to the occasion with forty-two lines about his heroic sufferings in highly wrought, orotund blank verse, reminiscent of the Player King from *Hamlet*. Brabantio encouraged him, Othello explains, to describe his life, his ordeals and exploits, and spurred him on – 'It was my hint to speak' – to enlarge on his adventures and travel beyond familiar geography into the fantastic, relating how he met:

> the Cannibals that each other eat,
> The Anthropophagi, and men whose heads
> Do grow beneath their shoulders.
> (I. iii. 143–5)

Drawing on popular legends circulating in Shakespeare's day, and led on by Brabantio's attention, he's embroidering his experiences. Meanwhile, he tells the company, his stories attracted Desdemona, who urged him on: 'she'd come again . . . and with a greedy ear devour up my discourse'. She was 'pliant', and 'These things to hear / Would Desdemona seriously incline . . .' Her hunger for more encouraged Othello to 'dilate on my pilgrimage' (I. iii. 128–70). He remembers:

> My story being done,
> She gave me for my pains a world of kisses [sighs].
> She swore, in faith, 'twas strange, 'twas passing strange,
> 'Twas pitiful, 'twas wondrous pitiful.
> She wished she had not heard it, yet she wished
> That heaven had made her such a man. She thanked me,
> And bade me, if I had a friend that loved her,
> I should but teach him how to tell my story,

And that would woo her. Upon this hint I spake.
She loved me for the dangers I had passed,
And I loved her that she did pity them.
This only is the witchcraft I have used.
Here comes the lady. Let her witness it.
(I. iii. 158–70)

After this, Desdemona testifies to Othello's honesty, and professes him her freely chosen husband; her father admits, bitterly, that she was 'half the wooer' (I. iii. 175).

Shakespeare is reflecting in this tragedy on the ways imagination makes things. Othello's noble rhetoric gives this tragedy its power to hold us, as it holds Desdemona and her father. Just as Aeneas' account of the horrors he experienced at Troy leapt up in Dido's mind's eye and spoke straight to her heart, Othello's oratory winds us in the magic of its web: the magnificence of its word pictures and the fraught emotional tension of his language enthral us too – command our belief.

The speech also throws light on the reciprocal projections that are exchanged between the tale-teller and the audience of the tale, the pressure that listeners, pursuing their own pleasure, exert on the speaker. More broadly, when the relationship involves an ethnic Other, as it does in the case of most strangers and refugees, the speech conveys how the expectations of an audience exercise an influence on the storyteller's self-presentation and narrative. 'He is striving', Allen-Paisant writes, 'against / badmind.'

At the same time, you can hear in the speech how Othello is playing up to his reputation (the 'extravagant and wheeling stranger' of Act I. i. 135), how he rises to meet his listeners' appetite for more exciting, exotic Moorishness. His self-irony will ultimately fail; his audience and his enemies' ideas of him will prevail. In the case of asylum seekers asked to report on their trials and reasons for fleeing, it worth remembering this Shakespearean insight into the way expectations exert an influence on the story.

Desdemona likes the ambiguity of her feelings – through Othello she's experiencing the allure of strangeness, in strong contrast with Iago, who revolts against Othello for his very foreignness. 'She wanted in I mean / she wanted in- / to an outside world' is how Allen-Paisant puts it. Othello's status as a black man, a former slave and a convert to Christianity, makes him an outsider who has transitioned to an insider role. Tensions remain taut. Twice Desdemona exclaims how strange his story is: "twas strange, 'twas passing strange, / 'Twas pitiful, 'twas wondrous pitiful' (I. iii. 160–1).

Imputation takes varied forms in Iago's procedure: innuendo, slander, smear. Othello is as susceptible to Iago's words as he has shown himself to be in relation to Desdemona's longing for excitement, storytelling, adventures. As Iago works on Othello's mind, Othello begins to mirror Iago's view of him. Such interactions are familiarly known today as the cruel process of 'gaslighting'.

The tragedy unfolds a struggle – to the death – that is very recognizable today, between two kinds of stories, between the wonders words can conjure and the violence they can arouse. It is a duel between different modes of speech in which the victory goes, as so often now happens, to the shoutiest detractor, to calumny and insult. The persuasiveness of Iago gives a model lesson, worth discussing in every schoolroom, in the rhetorical feints and tricks that can be deployed, showing that the way the story is told can mask its deceit and fraudulence.

In many different circumstances – in families, love, schools, law courts and immigration tribunals – expectations mould the character of individuals involved and consequently their self-image and self-presentation. The personal story has become more and more a passport to acceptance and those who cannot tell it well are unfairly discounted.

Desdemona brings out the extravagance of the stranger in all innocence and joy, showing the youthful curiosity of a young woman sequestered in the home. Iago, who first talks of Othello and Desdemona in startlingly gross language ('an old black ram / Is tupping your white ewe' (I. i. 87–8)), succeeds in smearing that filth on all he touches, most of all on Othello. The play enacts the principle of labelling that criminologists have defined since the 1960s in relation to young people in trouble and other deviant and marginal individuals, who may then accept and internalize the labels and become more deeply entangled in the attitudes and behaviour which made them suspect in the first place.

The pity Othello inspires in Desdemona we would now call empathy and we value the emotion very highly, as Othello himself does – he loves her for the pity she feels for him. Empathy opens the door to mutual understanding and social bonding, tolerance and harmony. But Shakespeare also gives us a sharp insight into the way social media and broadcasters today stoke emotions. The craving for sensation and the willingness of journalists to supply it, the insistent template of victim stories and the slippage within narratives between reportage, conjecture and fantasy govern the presentation of news reports – especially about strangers. Asylum seekers, forced migrants, foreign workers and other arrivants seeking survival far from home attract labels that estrange them; they are constantly pressed, as Brabantio and Desdemona press Othello, to tell the stories of their mischance and travails. The hope, among those who wish to create a just and equal society, is that the tale of these heroic struggles may inspire pity and thereby win over their opponents. But the problem is, as Othello's tragedy reveals, that the testimony to their sufferings pins labels on them that can box them into a stereotype; similarly the prohibition on taking jobs and working for money forces them into the despised roles of claimant, dependant and even beggar and keeps them in the position of an outsider, a stranger. And to pity someone may also imply, even claim, superiority (see Chapter 7).

Shakespeare, with his exceptional psychological incisiveness and subtlety, dramatizes the instability of our identities under any kind of pressure, and the strong effects of other people's projections upon us, the intimate dance between ascription and behaviour, expectations and outcomes.

## The Matter of Troy

Virgil's lurid colouring of Dido's last hours powerfully underlies the afterlife of North Africa in the many retellings and responses to the *Aeneid*, and its particular relation to Virgil can be set against a much lesser-known legacy, carried by different sources, in which Dido marries the African king and lives in this world prosperous and happy, while in death becomes assimilated to a goddess. Less stirring, of course, but interestingly confident.

For example, *La Didone*, by Francesco Cavalli, first performed in 1641 at San Cassiano, Venice, rejects Virgil's plot and gives Iarbas the role of knight errant. *La Didone* is one of those scores of operas inspired by the story of Dido and Aeneas, as mentioned before, and it shares with several of them the desire to resist tragedy and imagine instead a happy ending for the queen: in this work, the librettist, Giovanni Francesco Busenello, finally marries Dido to Iarbas, who has been patiently courting her and rescues her from her despair after Aeneas takes flight.

Three years later, the same composer created *L'Ormindo*, with another comic and insouciant libretto by a different writer, Giovanni Faustini; this was produced at the Wanamaker Playhouse, at the Globe, in London, in 2015. The opera strongly reflects the concurrent traffic in the Mediterranean – the wars, piracy, trade and shifting alliances – between Venice and other Italian ports and the rulers and marauders of the Barbary coast. The amusing, knotty plot involves such baroque staples as multiple disguises, cross-dressed maidens, foundlings, mock deaths and mistaken identities. But the two main characters, both of them oriental lovers and warriors, are unexpectedly simpatico. The opera is set in Anfa, now Casablanca in Morocco, where the hero Ormindo has arrived with his friend Amidas to help the local ruler Ariadenus and fight off a Spanish attempt to seize power and land. In the witty 2015 production by Kasper Holten, both soldier-adventurers were dressed in full Moorish costume. Historically, their lending their sword arms to help the King of Morocco would correspond to Othello's service to Venice.

Like *L'Ormindo*, *La Didone* assumes an easy familiarity with the Maghreb; their baroque orientalism points to shared geography and political encounters that have since faded from view. At the Edinburgh Festival in 2007 *La Didone* was directed by Elizabeth LeCompte of the experimental Wooster Group. Always daring, even outrageous, she spliced Cavalli with a Cold War space-race Italian pulp-fiction cult movie *Terrore nello Spazio* (*The Planet of the Vampires*, 1965), directed by Mario Bava, in which spacemen land on an unknown planet and encounter terrifying aliens who deflect them from their empire-building purpose. In this way, in their unwieldy spacesuits, sci-fi astronauts bent on conquering space became contemporary counterparts of the Trojan heroes searching for a new home and building a new Troy. Lucy Hughes-Hallett, reviewing the show, pointed out: 'Queen Dido . . . may not, on the face of it, have much in common with the hideous papier-mâché-headed zombie which results when an astronaut's corpse is reanimated by an extra-terrestrial, but the two narratives being laid out simultaneously on stage are close enough to generate a sequence of excellent ironic jokes, as well as a shimmer of mutually transferred meaning which greatly enriches both.' Roused by her Trojan lover from her extreme state of bereavement, Dido puts both husband and lover behind her and accepts the boy next door, King Iarbas.

When Nahum Tate revisited Virgil's tragic story, and adapted it – very freely – for the libretto of *Dido and Aeneas*, Purcell's lyric masterpiece, first performed in 1689 by a group of schoolgirls, his dying queen's magnificent lament, 'Remember me . . . but forget my fate . . .' reverses the thrust of Virgil's epic and asks, ironically, for her suicide to be consigned to oblivion; she pleads instead for her achievements as founder of Carthage not to be forgotten.

The ruins of Carthage now stand in Tunisia near the border with Libya, but in Virgil's poem, and in other accounts in which Dido figures as the founder of the city, Libya and the deserts around stretching east and west along the North African shore are the geographical location, while in the imaginary realm, shaped by Virgil, Carthage stands for the life of ease and love that Aeneas forgoes in order to fulfil his god-given destiny and found Rome. When he relinquishes Dido for the higher purpose of empire building, the choice of Rome over Carthage signals his transformation from a Trojan into a Roman. Carthage in Africa, ruled by a woman who is expert at witchcraft, is the testing ground for a crucial myth about the exigencies of civilization; by passing through it, and rejecting Dido, an African queen, the oriental fugitive is changed into an occidental hero, forefather of Western civilization. The founder of Carthage, dispenser of its laws and steward of its great wealth, curses the hero with bloodshed and vengeance, not only personal but also geopolitical. Dido's ringing prophecies corroborate the division between the northern Mediterranean and its southern littoral.

This implicit fault line between barbarity and civilization in Virgil's cultural map, and the location of this line in North Africa reproduces historical antagonisms that have continued since the Punic wars, wars which were uppermost in Virgil's memory. Later, in *Les Troyens*, the opera that Hector Berlioz composed in the mid-nineteenth century to his own libretto after Virgil, these themes are ferociously refracted. The character ascribed to the indigenous peoples of North Africa by Virgil's drama, its imagery and language reverberates in the work of his admirers and has continued to resonate today in the very tissue of thinking about the region.

Opera may be perceived as a very restricted and elite medium, with its interpretations of stories reaching only a well-heeled minority and so remaining of little consequence to the shaping of ideas over time. On the contrary, I believe that music intensifies the telling of stories and enhances the texts, especially when interpreted in dramatic colour and intensity by the human voice, and contributes significantly to their mobility. Music is migratory, and it sustains the movement of stories. Its travels across barriers of time and local language make it an exceptionally powerful conduit of myth – we need remember only Dido's lament from Purcell to recognize this. The digital age of downloading has intensified this potential of music as a carrier of narrative. Indeed the relationship is symbiotic, since composers and librettists continue to be attracted by myth and fairy tale, allowing the very qualities of opera – and ballet – to expand meaningfulness beyond and above linguistic boundaries and semantic referents. With the help of designers and directors, they can approach contemporary themes through mythic material, costuming, locating and visually projecting a work into another time and place beyond its setting or its own moment of coming into being; performance happens live in the time when it is taking place, and *ipso facto* takes up occupation of the here and now, radiating meanings – conscious and unconscious – into the audience's moment in time. This significant feature of theatrical experience exemplifies that human purpose, as argued by Arendt, of using stories to 'insert ourselves into the human world' and of refreshing history through retellings because, as quoted before, 'the ability to produce stories is the way we become historical'. Opera is also a medium of passionate feeling. As W. H. Auden, himself an inspired librettist, pointed out: 'singing is a form of public outcry: it is on the voluntary level what an *ouch* of pain or the howl of a hungry baby is on the involuntary'.

*Les Troyens* was composed and written by Berlioz in 1856–8 but not performed in its entirety until very much later – astonishingly not in full anywhere until 1957 when it was staged at Covent Garden, London.

Since then it has received hugely ambitious productions, and its performance history has made it a more recent work than it is. Its overwhelming attempt to encompass war, empire, virtue and heroism, carried on a vast, symphonic fusion of inventive melody and orchestration, makes it speak to audiences today – for acute historical reasons which we, they, recognize.

Although Berlioz follows Virgil closely, he does not set one story inside another, but unravels the Roman epic's coiled chronology in present-tense dramatic, filmic narrative: he opens with the fall of Troy, then shows Aeneas' flight with his father and his son; his landing in Carthage and the love affair with Dido unfold consecutively. It's a towering work of tragic grandeur and intensity of feeling, and bears on the theme of sanctuary on a few points. The opera does not follow the *Aeneid* very closely: there is no priestess at the pyre, for example, and Dido's autonomy in the opera adds to her unappeasable passion and her stature. But the emphasis falls even more strongly on her ravings and her sorcery as she summons up the deities of the underworld.

Certain Virgilian strands are much strengthened by the context of the opera's times, during the aftermath of France's own empire-building ventures in North Africa. The French had taken over Algeria after violent fighting around twenty-five years before Berlioz was creating the opera, and the work recognizably belongs in the same highly coloured, fierce orientalism as French paintings inspired by the campaigns in North Africa and the shifting alliances of the local clans. In the opera, after the Trojans have landed and been magnanimously given sanctuary by Dido, Berlioz's libretto describes the new city coming under attack almost immediately from Iarbas and his army. Aeneas rallies the Trojans and, in an unfettered language of martial, imperial glory, accompanied by suitable marching music, offers them to Dido as warriors to repel the attackers:

> Against this filthy horde of Africans,
> Let's march, men of Troy and Tyre,
> Let's fly to victory together!
> Let's drive back to their burning desert,
> Like sand carried on the wind,
> The doomed Numidians. Let them quake!

Victory over the *horde immonde* follows without much struggle. In the opera, unlike the epic, Aeneas meets the barbarian king and proves himself against him, his eagerness and courage and manliness demonstrated in a trial of strength that Virgil does not accord his hero. In later scenes, the opera does however shift the boundaries around barbarism with some sensitivity. For example, Aeneas avows his love for Dido repeatedly, but is called to his destiny, the Trojans' rousing cries of *'Italie! Italie!'* ringing all around; he castigates himself bitterly and convincingly for his faithlessness, and Dido echoes this, crying out that he must have been suckled by a she-wolf rather than the goddess of love. By showing Aeneas and the Trojans to be superior to Iarbas and his hordes of Numidians and clearly discriminating against the latter, Berlioz can then dwell on Aeneas' savagery without aligning him with the local wild Africans. The two poles of Carthage and Rome strike the listener as equally matched; in the 1985 production at the Metropolitan in New York, the designs recalled Napoleonic neo-classicism and the Egyptomania that swept Europe after Napoleon's expedition to Egypt: Dido is another Cleopatra, a great oriental queen keeping a general from his duties, and the Maghreb another Egypt, endangering the state. In her rage Berlioz's Dido invokes the sceptre of Libya which she had offered to Aeneas. Her majesty remains in the foreground, and few listeners would not shiver at the resounding last anthem, promising enmity for ever between Carthage and Rome.

The words echo her curse in Virgil, but the rippling soprano voice with the full orchestra in crescendo beneath her aria winds the passions still more tightly. These are the final words of the opera:

*Chorus:*
Endless hatred for the Trojan race!
May a pitiless war forever throw our sons against them,
May their ships, attacked by ours,
Founder, wrecked, in the depths of the sea.

May our last descendants on land and sea, still armed against them,
Shock the world one day by their destruction.

The ambitions of modern empires in the Mediterranean reinvigorated the matter of Dido's curse and repositioned her vision of the future in relation to current politics and changing attitudes to Africa and Africans. It is disillusioning to find that it was in the eighteenth century with the Enlightenment and the rise of Romanticism and its dreams of Liberty, Reason and knowledge that present-day hostilities and prejudice were fostered, to flourish thereafter, growing ever more virulent. Today, Dido's curses seem to possess fresh prophetic power.

For every generation that hears them, in Virgil's poem, or, as happens now far more frequently, ferociously voiced by Didos on the screen or the stage, the ringing words seem to foresee contemporaneous conflicts: when Berlioz was composing the full-throated climax of his magnum opus, Carthage swearing vengeance against Rome for her humiliation seemed to express the rage of the defeated Maghrebins at French colonization. In the decade before Berlioz was creating *Les Troyens*, thousands of Frenchmen and women were expatriated to Algeria to settle the colony as the government's policy, their dreams stoked by false promises of unoccupied territory and future riches, only to find themselves planted among hostile inhabitants and forced to endure all the troubles that followed. In *Le Premier Homme*, Albert Camus' unfinished and posthumously published autobiography, the Algerian-born writer described his grandparents' emigration from France in 1848: they were towed downriver to Marseilles where they embarked for their new world. Camus' voice is bitter and his memories of the poverty and illiteracy of the women of his family are harrowing; the questions the colonial enterprise raised run through his writing and his contentious political thinking about Algerian independence.

Representations of Africa and specifically of North Africa or the Maghreb, are no more monolingual or monolithic than representations of other countries and their cultures, but Virgil's mythic creation has overshadowed the counter-narratives and created an imaginary map that only partially reflects the territory, its history and its culture. One does not expect more from a single writer, of course, but mythic works tend, as Barthes pointed out, to turn history into nature and fix their subjects in an eternal set of meanings.

The literature and culture created by locals from the region remains underexplored. It is important to recast the formulaic perspectives of the past and discover what could be called, in parallel to Paul Gilroy's *The*

*Black Atlantic*, 'the Black Mediterranean'. The poet Erri De Luca keeps the legacy of the classics in mind when, in a poem of 2005 called *Solo Andata (One-Way Ticket)*, he speaks of the migrants coming to Italy from Africa. He was born in Naples, another old place with a name that, like Carthage, means New City, and his first name, Erri, a diminutive of Enrico, oddly chimes with his chosen recent concerns, as in Italian it means you wander/you do/are wrong. In *Solo Andata* the subtitle *Righe che vanno troppo spesso a capo* (Lines that too often go back to the beginning) refers to the failed crossings made by the refugees, and also to the verses he is writing which go to and fro around his subjects, unable to settle, incapable of ending the suffering. Single voices tell their stories, interspersed with choruses that recall classical tragedy, echoing images from Virgil while also specifying particular causes of the migrations:

> The soldiers burn the villages while we are grazing our herds
> They throw into the flames people and animals, wool and white beards.
> They kill the well with dynamite, trample plants,
> Roll around children's heads with the points of their boots
>
> You have never seen nations migrate? We who come from Africa have,
> They rise with the smoke of fires, they are spread like manure.

De Luca also touches on, unsparingly, social conditions peculiar to Italy today:

> We are the numberless ones, doubling on every square of the chessboard,
> We are paving your sea with skeletons to walk across on it . . .
>
> No police force can overcome us with their strength
> so greatly have we been injured already.
>
> We shall be your servants, the children you don't make,
> Our lives shall be your books of adventures.
> We bring Homer and Dante, the blind man and the pilgrim,
> the smell you have lost, the equality you have suppressed.

De Luca's verses reprise, with savage irony, European fears about Africa, in which the echoes of ancient prejudice and antagonisms sound; but the effect of the whole is elegiac, unspooling lines of language to ease and soften the bleak and cruel content of the sufferings he is reporting. His poems face up to the reality of contemporary fugitives who, like Aeneas in the myth of Rome, are seeking to settle in Italy; they make a kind of apology, a peace offering and an act of expiation in the form of words. Isaac Julien's video installation *Western Union: Small Boats*, which made such an impression on me (see Introduction), was shown in 2007, two years after De Luca's collection was first published – both artists were prescient in their fellow-feeling.

Virgil set out consciously to inscribe his emperor and the Roman empire into an ancient myth and he succeeded all too splendidly, with lasting effects on Mussolini's fascist vision; but Virgil could not have known how his epic would also institute a potent imaginary cultural split between the West and the non-West in the future, or that the historical connections between the cultures of the Maghreb and Asia Minor continuing long after Virgil died would still fall under the shadow of the curse his Dido pronounced.

Many cultural currents meet and combine in the prevailing hostility towards foreigners, especially those with black and brown skin. The influence of that central human activity, of telling and retelling stories, should not be underestimated. Stories are the way we approach memory, present conditions of existence and the future, and they can rearrange the scene, closing some doors, opening others. In 2014, four years before her death in 2018, Ursula Le Guin showed her characteristic prescience when she warned, 'Hard times are coming, when we will be wanting the voices of writers who can see alternatives to how we live now and can see through our fear-stricken society and its obsessive technologies to other ways of being, and even imagine some real grounds for hope. We will need writers who can remember freedom. Poets, visionaries – the realists of a larger reality . . . Any human power can be resisted and changed by human beings . . . Resistance and change often begin in art. Very often in *our* art, the art of words.' Herself a brilliant deviser of alternative worlds in speculative fictions such as *The Left Hand of Darkness* and *The Dispossessed*, she presents a beacon of storytelling imagination in action over decades of work.

Her last novel, *Lavinia* (2008), represents a departure from her usual territory of speculative sci-fi, as she travelled back in history and, in her seventies, learned Latin in order to read the *Aeneid* in the original Latin and recast its vision of the founding of Western civilization. Lavinia her heroine is silent in Virgil; Le Guin, writing in the first person as Lavinia, is giving her consciousness and voice – and a moving, subtle story. Aeneas marries her in a dynastic match, for she is the daughter of Latinus, the local King of Laurentum, the original ruler in the territory where the Trojans will settle and Rome will rise in future. Le Guin unfolds the point of view Virgil neglected in the poem; she also reintroduces Virgil as a spirit communicating with Lavinia, now engaged in acknowledging her role and her personal significance. Through her eyes we see Aeneas in the final years of his life, a man haunted by his past, burdened by destiny, prone to hallucinatory visions: 'Aeneas always speaks out of silence,' Lavinia tells us, 'seldom at length, usually in a low voice. He is never sullen, but he is quiet' (the inverse of the hero who tells the tale of his trials in the *Aeneid*!). His end is mysterious, and eerie, recalling Oedipus' disappearance in the sanctuary at Colonus: he visits the shrine of the old gods of Rome, where he often goes to commune silently with himself, and does not return.

The novel consequently continues many of Le Guin's themes, the demands of masculinity, the inequalities between rich and poor, men and women, the powerful and powerless. Lavinia knows an Aeneas broken by the violence that attended the foundation of Rome, from the fall of Troy to his abandonment of Dido and the bloodshed of his victory over the local inhabitants, including his wife Lavinia's family. Dido is not present except as a spectre, overshadowing all that subsequently takes place, unseen and unheard but insistent, giving warning of the costs of empire. The novel is a very fine example of historical reimagining. With sensitivity and perceptiveness, it nuances the rather stiff and frankly offputting personality of *pius* Aeneas and the poem's limited and lurid portraiture of women.

Le Guin's historical fiction is one of the sources the British composer Errollyn Wallen and her librettist the novelist Wesley Stace drew on for *Dido's Ghost*, their sparkling reworking of Purcell's *Dido and Aeneas*, which premiered in London at the Barbican in June 2021 during the first faint gleams of opening up after lockdown.

The opera extends the emotional emphasis to Aeneas, deepening his character along Le Guin's lines. Errollyn Wallen and Wesley Stace address the Virgilian tradition with verve, wit and sympathy and redraw the love story in the light of Aeneas' deep depression after leaving Dido for worldly power in Rome. The opera's melancholic and disturbed hero suffers from bleak despair and remorse over his treatment of Dido, his flouting of the bonds between host and guest, and the ethical choice of glory over personal fulfilment that his actions represent. 'Remember me', the sublime threnody Dido sings on her funeral pyre in Purcell, is transposed to the bass-baritone voice and given to Aeneas, its regrets now encompassing his whole life, and the compromises and brutality his piety led him to. It is his turn to die. Wallen revisits the whole of Purcell's score in all its vivacity and tunefulness, but intercuts it with her own composition, producing a sonorous, inventive and complex mash-up: she introduces a large percussion section to capture the ambience of North Africa and adds jazz and pop elements to ironize the romance and satirize Roman pomp. The libretto interweaves several sources: besides Virgil, Nahum Tate's libretto and LeGuin's novel, he adapts Ovid (the episode in *I Fasti* featuring Anna, Dido's sister, and Aeneas on the shore at Rome (see p. 162).

The classic story about a queen in Africa rejected by the founding hero of civilization has richly effloresced; it offers a major *lieu de mémoire*, a common ground where traditions can be turned this way and that and ideas probed. It is not incidental that Wallen, who has now been appointed Master of the King's Music, was born in Belize in Central America, on the Caribbean Sea, a former Crown Colony and now a member of the Commonwealth. Empire, its assumptions and exactions underlie the epic Virgil invented, and he threw all his dramatic and intellectual and moral gifts into upholding nation building over the bonds of love and high destiny to found Rome over his obligations as a suppliant, the pre-eminence of military power and imperium over the contract on which sanctuary and hospitality are based. The deadly passion he dramatized has occupied the foreground and cast a very long shadow, which has to be lifted, as Le Guin, Wallen and Stace have done.

Troy matters to a concept of sanctuary: it is a blazing symbol of the lost home – blazing in more ways than one. The ancient city in Asia

Minor is a potent example of a home of the mind: most of us are not Trojans, at least no longer, and even if we have visited Pergamon, the postulated archaeological site of the ancient city, that is not the place that burns in our minds when we hear the word Troy. The story of a city in flames, Troy resonates far wider that a Bronze Age conflict in the eastern Mediterranean (see Chapter 8). Troy has been established as a *lieu de mémoire*, a common place fashioned and refashioned by collective imagination working in cross-correspondence with the story's creative interpreters and disseminators – and with us, their audience.

# 6

# Tales:
# The Riddle Princess

> Can you make me a cambrick shirt,
> Parsley, sage, rosemary and thyme,
> Without any seam or needle work?
> And you shall be a true love of mine.
> Anon.

The opera house in Kyiv is bulbous, expansive, magnificent and vast like a redbrick Suleimanye mosque without the minarets but with plenty of domes and half domes that seemed to mimic arpeggios and bursts of music. It was 2005, and Ukraine was confident: the Orange Revolution had just happened, and the packed auditorium gave every indication that opera really mattered then to the citizens of Kyiv. I asked at a ticket kiosk, which was a custom-made booth set inside the outer fabric, and the young woman serving pointed to a poster, in which a towering Chinese headdress with flowering pendants rose above a lacquered face; the writing was in Cyrillic, but I recognized Puccini's spectacular orientalist melodrama. I asked if there were any seats and the receptionist offered me two in the stalls – the only ones remaining and the best in the house. How much? I asked apprehensively. Her answer came; the cost was about the same as the highest and most distant perch in the gods at Covent Garden.

I found myself in the middle of the first row of the central block of the stalls, and all around me, I was to discover, members of the audience were doing serious business on their phones. Now and then they would cease their dealings and cheer the singers, but they would soon return to the work in hand. The astonishing thing was that their chatter didn't matter: the sound – from the orchestra, the chorus, even the individual singers during their duets and arias – was so huge it completed muffled the buzzing and tinkling of mobiles, the cast so numerous they had to stand cheek by jowl in serried ranks on the stage (it is a very large stage, one of the largest in the world). Many of the singers appeared giants with voices to match. Similarly, the playing from the pit rose with Puccini's swelling tunes to fever pitch, and soaring crescendos were met from the packed hall with thunderous applause again and again and bursts of acclamation.

I had expected an opera by Mikhail Glinka or Nikolai Rimsky-Korsakov, or a Russian or Ukrainian work unknown to me. The opera house is home to the National Opera of Ukraine, and since the nineteenth century its history has been closely interwoven with Ukrainian cultural identity and independence. For a long period, according to a decree of 1926, operas had to be sung in Ukrainian. But with touring companies this became impractical and by the 1990s, the prescription had fallen away. That night *Turandot* was being performed in Italian and it was clear from the audience reaction that the language didn't matter. *Turandot* was well known to the Kyivians, well loved, a familiar attraction to the crowd who filled to capacity the enormous building and gave every sign of complete satisfaction as they streamed out into the night.

I was visiting the city for a conference called Writing Europe, organized by the British Council at a time when Ukrainians were jubilant about the democratic success of the Orange Revolution. We participants in the conference were shown, with immense pride, the parliament building which was now cleansed of corruption (and pro-Russian elements); we were proudly told Ukraine was making moves to join the EU – to which Britain still then belonged, and which in those days in some quarters was supporting enlargement, to include countries like Turkey and Ukraine. This feels now a long time ago and a world away.

There were some signs of unhealed tension: for example, the conference was not well attended by local people, and those of us who had come from the UK were worried by this lack of interest. When we asked one participant for the possible reasons, he replied, 'You invited Andrei Kurkov as the keynote speaker and he writes in Russian.'

So much has happened to change perceptions of Ukraine and throw light on the Ukrainians' complex and terrible history in connection with the 'Russian Federation' that this remark, which may or may not have been an accurate assessment, makes little sense. Kurkov himself has been one of the most lucid and courageous commentators on the 2022 invasion and war and, needless to say, an outspoken supporter of the resistance to Putin's imperialism. At the time of writing, he is reporting on the situation in his country, having moved from Kyiv to Lviv on the border with Poland, and has announced that he is now writing only in Ukrainian. In the case of Ukraine, as in the case of many other formerly subjugated countries, it has become clear that sharing a language and a literature does not entail, to those who speak the language and live in the culture, obeisance to or unity with a nation that ruled them in the past. Yevgenia Belorusets, a journalist, photographer and powerful short-story writer, has captured, in melancholy, angry and revelatory pieces, the experience of living under Russian aggression in eastern Ukraine since at least 2014; she writes only in the Russian language and mourns the alienation she is suffering in her own country in consequence.

The evening in Kyiv all those years ago seemed at the time free of political dissension, at least to an outsider, like me. Yet it might be possible to argue that *Turandot* struck a chord with the Kyiv audience because a brave, unbowed young prince emerges from a terrible trial and overcomes a tyrant – in this case a female – subdues her and triumphs.

The historic bonds between opera and politics are tight; Giuseppe Verdi's engagement with Italian national unity has since the nineteenth century tightened them, and enhanced the potential for opera to voice popular yearnings: *Nabucco*, broadly inspired by the story of Nebuchadnezzar from the Old Testament, provoked intense identification among Italian audiences when the Chorus of Hebrew Slaves sang of their longing for freedom. 'Va, pensiero', one of Verdi's loveliest tunes, swells to a chorus of longing laced with despair; as a result this chorale was considered for the new nation's national anthem, and still has the power, in times when Italy feels afflicted by corruption and other ills (which is often), to bring an audience to its feet in tears singing along with the chorus on stage.

Libretti which feature uprisings and plots, evil commanders and kings, all lend themselves to interpretation in the light of current affairs, and the fashion for updating costumes and sets (often to evoke totalitarian or fascist regimes) has intensified this approach to interpreting what an opera might mean. A contemporary production bringing out this or that figural meaning of a work, independently of the intention of the makers and anachronistically in relation to the time when the work was made, encourages the building of common ground for disparate and distant groups.

Puccini's grandiose spectacular is the most popular expression of the tale of *Turandot*, but, premiered in 1926, a latecomer in its history. It does not seem a very likely candidate for supporting the hope of modern sanctuary: a ruthless woman has her suitors executed one by one when each of them fails to answer a riddle she has set. Yet this ancient story, *Turandot*, becomes my fifth and final case study in the possible scope of sanctuary. The protagonist is a stock character in fairy tale, a riddle princess who on pain of death sets her prince harsh and impossible tasks – the traditional adynata of folk and fairy tale. Such figures, living embodiments of verbal trickery, have long exercised fascination for playwrights and librettists, and Puccini's treatment has become a worldwide hit. *Turandot* is a travelling tale: it has migrated across many borders of languages and cultures, shape-shifting as to its meanings all the way. It is a story in diaspora, one of many *spories* – story pods, story seeds, story burrs – in world literature. Its heroine begins life as a cultural fantasy in twelfth-century Persia, where she features already as a foreign princess; she then transmigrates from the page to the stage and climaxes with Puccini's opera. Then, in a sudden, unexpected move of the zeitgeist, the recording of the hero Calaf's aria 'Nessun dorma' by the tenor Luciano Pavarotti became the 1990 FIFA World Cup's anthem, and again at the World Cup Final in Los Angeles in 1994, in Paris in 1998 and in Yokohama in 2002. The aria's climax takes the tenor to a thrilling top B. It has been adopted as a battle cry for all endangered heroes (and heroines, too), not only for the players on the pitch:

*All'alba vincerò*
*Vincerò*
*Vincerò!*
(At dawn I shall overcome/ I shall overcome/ I shall overcome!)

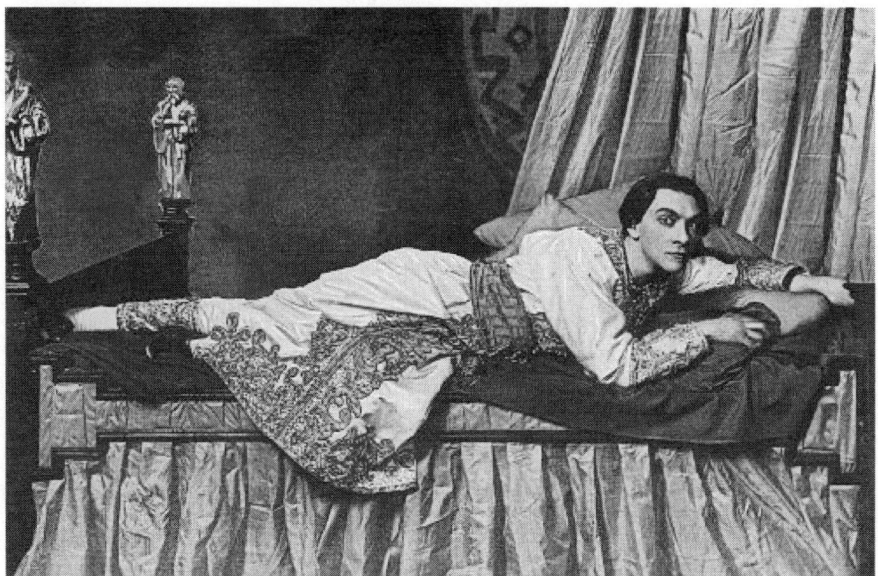

Many suitors die after failing the tests of Princess Turandot. Prince Calaf, played here in New York in 1912 by Pedro de Cordoba, puts himself forward – and succeeds.

It's a mark of the unearthly, otherworldly quality of the operatic wonder tale that, from the Romantic period onwards, the tenor part inherits the castrato role (in Handel's *Giulio Cesare*, the hero's part is sung by a counter-tenor) and this high voice softens the distinction between the male and female personae. Such freedom, permitted by performance and masquerade, can help in the making of sanctuary; a boldly imagined scenario can enact a hitherto unimaginable hope.

Puccini died while he was still working on the opera, and it was subsequently completed, to greater and lesser degrees of satisfaction, by Franco Alfano for the premiere at La Scala, Milan, in 1926, where it was conducted by Toscanini. Productions of the opera since 1927 outdo one another in spectacular Chinoiserie: there was even a staging in China, where performances had previously been prohibited as anti-Chinese. The action in *Turandot* takes place in the orient's own orient, East of East, and stages the conquest of a princess in Peking by a prince of Central Asia. In 1998, in the Forbidden City itself, against that historical backdrop, fantasy replaced history in a move that is emblematic of memory's workings and the part that imagination plays in shaping knowledge of the past.

In what ways does this tale relate to sanctuary, and more particularly to sanctuary in our time?

The legends accruing around Dido, Mary, St Helena and the Virgin of Loreto posit in their different ways a point in the past from which the present and the future fate of a certain community has grown and will continue to grow. They are foundation or origin myths, for the classical Roman empire and for Christendom. The idea of a sanctuary occupies the heart of their stories, very literally in the case of Loreto. Shrines enclose and communicate the essence of their votaries' creeds; temples, churches summon certain divinities and, beyond these particular holy beings, the principles they represent. In each case, the meaning of the place has been conferred by a complex and well-known story, which commands the belief and consent – the faith – of supplicants and pilgrims.

Why does *Turandot* offer a case study of sanctuary? For several reasons: first, the tale has migrated across languages and media for centuries. Certain basic narrative elements compose the DNA of the plot which has been classified among 'Realistic Tales' (!) as number 851A in a scholarly catalogue of folktales, types and motifs worldwide, the Aarne-Thompson-Uther Index: a fiery princess sets her lovers riddles and has all her suitors executed, but still they keep coming. Eventually one of them succeeds, often by outdoing her in riddling trickery. The story has inspired variations across continents, but has not defined a party or group (unless opera lovers could be classified as a community) and it therefore shows its malleability; it makes an early appearance in the Persian poet El Nizami's *Haft Peykar*, translated as *The Pavilion of the Seven Princesses*. Such tales of wonder, purportedly oral in their origins, are returning to the voice with the formidable success of acoustic digital media; they are gaining the art form new, broader audiences, though not reaching quite the breadth of popularity that opera enjoyed in Italy: Verdi knew to keep the catchy, boisterous tune of '*La donna è mobile*' under wraps until the premiere of *Rigoletto*, but the day after, as he had expected, it was being sung in the streets of Milan. Nevertheless, with live streaming, video recordings and film versions, audiences are becoming more various and smaller opera companies are growing in number, even while budgets of the major touring companies are being cut.

The exotic locations of *Turandot* gave designers scope for fantastic costumes and settings: they outdo one another in spectacular Chinoiserie.

In its earliest literary form, *Turandot* unfolds a poetic vision of spiritual initiation, and includes no magic or supernatural interventions from jinn or demons, unlike many of its counterparts in this genre of narrative. In its present operatic form it has become an entirely secular artefact in contrast to the religious and nationalist stories I have explored so far. *Turandot* is however secular only insofar as it no longer conveys belief in a particular faith or creed, unlike the original mystical source, El Nizami's *Pavilion of the Seven Princesses*. The opera's story makes no claim to authenticity in relation to some guarantor in the past, divine or historical, and can't be identified with any particular social group or interest. But magic and enchantment dominate the story it unfolds. It exemplifies the literature of astonishment and wonder, *aja'ib*, displaying total insouciance about plausibility and relishing the marvellous in plot development and characters' destinies. The tale that inspired the opera of *Turandot* is a free-floating fantasy which stirs excitement and interest in its audiences, with no need for verification against an outside referent.

The enthusiasm that greeted oriental tales and *aja'ib* in general during the age of Enlightenment and the subsequent Romantic era points to a potential for thought and entertainment recognized then which might well be valuable again today. Carl Maria von Weber wrote incidental music for Friedrich Schiller's play *Turandot, Prinzessin von China* (including an overture that is still popular), and set a Chinese tune – the first use of an Asian melody by a European composer 'that was not of the pseudo-Turkish kind popularized by Mozart and others'. A work of this kind establishes its own terms of interpretation, and in this sense looks to the present and to the future rather than harking back to a traditional past. This should not sound like unqualified praise, for reasons that will become clear, but *Turandot* is the kind of imaginative artefact that can be held in common by disparate individuals and groups and give rise to variations across time and place. The tale's cousins are many – fairy tales like *Cinderella* and *Snow White*, and myths like those about Oedipus and Orestes. Some of Shakespeare's plays have also attained the polymorphousness of mythemes – *Hamlet* and *Macbeth*, *Romeo and Juliet*. A riddle princess appears in many stories, including Shakespeare's *Pericles* and *The Merchant of Venice*. In 2004, in South Korea, the series of graphic novels called *One Thousand and One Nights* included a stirring version of *Turandot*: both artist and author relish the fierce oriental heroine – with flashing made-up eyes, now scowling, now shrieking, Turandot defends herself against male entitlement: 'You people are all the same,' she cries. 'You take what you want by force!'

*Frozen*, one of the biggest box-office successes of all time, carries traces of the *Turandot* theme: its protagonist is a Disney princess, but in this case icy not docile; she has renounced a future with men on account of something that happened in the past. Alongside *Ali Baba* and *Aladdin*, both of which were translated later, *Turandot* is probably the widest known oriental tale in circulation since the early eighteenth-century vogue for such narratives (as we shall see, it does not appear, as it happens, in the *Nights*). The story presents a test case for a site of memory across barriers, an unexpected common place of enjoyment, excitement and mutual pleasure for a variety of audiences, beyond ethnicity and nation. It is a travelling tale in the sense that Edward Said defined. It offers an imaginary space, a place of refuge, a borderless, open territory which has the potential to become common ground, a commons of wonder.

Such tales also feature travellers, fugitives and exiles as their heroes, the motives for their travels being extremely various. They tell of voyages to places near and far; the plots are peripatetic over wide expanses of territory both on the map and in the far-distant realms of faerie. Travelling is a characteristic topic of the stories themselves, reproducing the conditions that brought them into existence.

The fierce princess's name means daughter of Turan, a region of Central Asia when it was part of the Persian empire; and her story shares features with the history of a thirteenth-century Mongol princess, Khutulun, who rode into battle at her father's side and proclaimed that she would only marry a man who could round up a hundred horses . . . and even then she would see if she agreed and decide for herself. Khutulun's historicity serves to tether the story of *Turandot* to reality, but she is unlikely to be the source of the florid legend.

Gertrud Eysoldt, famous for her fiery sensuality, took the lead in Max Reinhardt's 1911 production, with music by Ferruccio Busoni.

El Nizami (1140–?1217), is also the author of the now classic romances *Khosrow and Shirin*, *Layla and Majnun* as well as a version of the popular mythical biography of Alexander the Great, *Iskander Nama*, in which he retells legends that gathered around the figure of the hero soon after his death. *The Pavilion of the Seven Princesses*, El Nizami's last work, unfolds a passionate and elaborate sequence of seven elaborate *masnavis* – epic tales composed like its predecessors in the flexible form of pairs of distichs. It is a work of rapturous erotic intensity, composed for recitation in courtly and sophisticated circles.

The hero Bahram, who is a historical personage, here figures as a dream voyager, pilgrim and quester after spiritual enlightenment and knowledge, a cult hero; in the course of a week, he visits seven princesses to enjoy blissful nights with each one. Each of their pavilions is a different colour, symbolizing different states and passions according to the signs of the zodiac and astrological correlations between birth signs, bodily organs and temperament. The sequence begins on Saturday (black, Saturn, melancholia) and moves on through to Friday (white, Venus, love). Like many other Persian writers, El Nizami can be read at different levels, and many see in his enraptured love poetry allegories of Sufi mysticism, which suffuses Arabic literature as well as Persian. Illustrators of the poem depict the princesses with wings, like archangels, each of them an Intelligence presiding over a heavenly sphere that itself rules earthly passions. 'Poetry is the mirror of what is visible and what is invisible,' El Nizami wrote, '. . . the curtain of mystery, the shadow of the prophetic veil.' When the orientalist Peter Chelkowski rendered El Nizami's tales into English, he called the book *Mirror of the Invisible World*.

In spite of its metaphysical symbolism, the cycle of love stories is grounded in an altogether worldly source: the seven princesses were inspired by the favourites of the Sassanian king Bahramgur and the story was commissioned by Nuruddin Arslan of Mosul, the son and heir of the book's dedicatee, the ruler of Mosul, Izzuddin Masud. Each of the heroines is a figure of valour and ingenuity, accomplishment and independent-mindedness; El Nizami is distinguished for his treatment of his female protagonists and his egalitarian approach. He describes boys and girls studying together in *Layla and Majnun*, and often invokes the heroines' skills, in such activities as archery and horsemanship. The

Red Princess – who will tell the story of *Turandot* – is an artist who has studied watercolour in China and is so skilled that in her paintings 'she twisted knots in water to seem pearls from her quill, black as the black curl of a houri, and threw on to her painting what seemed a shadow of light'.

This paragon is the fourth of the princesses and is found in the story of the Red Pavilion, the domain of the Princess of the Slavs whom Bahram visits on Tuesday, the day of Mars. The pervasive red of the presiding planet conveys a warlike, ferocious and independent spirit; Bahram is dressed entirely in red (see Plate 9). One tale is imbricated inside another, and narrator and protagonist double each other. The Princess of the Slavs tells Bahram the story of the defiant heroine, the character who will become known as Turandot. In this, her earliest written appearance, the implacable heroine is Russian, and she shuts herself up, rejecting all suitors, in a stronghold cunningly defended by numerous mechanical devices, including automata which behead any suitor who fails the test of her riddles. The motif of these lethal guards recurs in the *Arabian Nights*, most memorably in 'The City of Brass', where they protect the body of the dead queen.

El Nizami's oeuvre predates the first manuscripts of the *Nights* by over two hundred years and indeed a dominant strand in that much more widely read compendium stems from Persian romance as a genre, including the proud heroines, paragons of beauty and skill, intellect and athleticism. Shahrazad (Scheherazade) has a Persian name and she is foreshadowed by El Nizami's protagonist; though Shahrazad doesn't set specific riddles in the manner of Turandot, her wiliness as a storyteller is itself riddling in a broader sense. Her secret plan, for which she recruits her sister, involves cunning and seduction. But the whole pattern of the *Nights* leads the murderous Sultan Shahryar, who has vowed to take a virgin every night and kill her in the morning, to see how mistaken he is in his bloodthirsty misogyny. Shahrazad is a deliverer, an Esther who saves her people. Casting Shahrazad in the role of the Sultan's preceptor, the *Nights* transforms one vigorous tradition of oriental stories – warnings against women – into another – the mirror for princes, or moral education in justice and magnanimity. It understands and uses the craft of storytelling, as it consciously sets up a counter-argument about women in dialogue with circulating beliefs and fantasies embedded in popular imagination in such stories as

*Turandot*. The undoing of Turandot's savage misandry mirrors the transformation of the Sultan.

Just as a riddle hides one thing inside another set of things and trips the normal wires of understanding to move someone to see things differently, so the oriental tale set out to pattern words in one sense while delivering another meaning, not exactly a solution, but the possibility of the narrative taking an alternative direction.

The Persian tale was picked up and recast in French as 'La Princesse Tourandocte' in *Les Mille et un jours* (*The Thousand and One Days*, 1710–12), by François Pétis de la Croix, a baggy story collection published in Paris to trail the success of the first volumes of Antoine Galland's translation of *Les Mille et une nuits* (*The Thousand and One Nights*, 1704–17). Galland's work detonated a craze for oriental tales, fashions and thought – from philosophical treatises such as Montesquieu's *Lettres persanes* (1721) to Voltaire's *Contes philosophiques*, beginning with *Zadig* (1747). In the Age of Reason, fabulism and fairy tale had become, most unexpectedly, a favoured means of passing on knowledge: in 1712, Joseph Addison declared in the *Spectator* that, 'among all the different Ways of giving Counsel, I think the finest, and that which pleases the most universally, is Fable'.

Pétis de la Croix (1653–1713), was an orientalist and man of letters – and, as it turns out, an extravagant fantasist – who worked as an interpreter from Arabic and Farsi for the French in the Middle East and eventually, in 1692, took up the chair in Arabic in Paris. He brought out a vast anthology of 'Persian Tales', which he compiled and translated. The indeterminacy of such an approach provokes scholarly alarm, understandably. But it has a bearing on the theme of sanctuary and belonging, because it presents a model for the free, hybrid development of popular source material and fictive performances.

In 1711, Pétis managed, with the connivance of the publisher, to interpolate two Turkish tales into the eighth volume of Galland's translation of the *Nights*. Both Galland and Pétis frequented the salon culture that Molière satirizes with such malicious bravura in *Les Précieuses ridicules* (1659) and *Les Femmes savantes* (1672). The two orientalists were guests at the soirées called *Mercuriales*, presided over by Gilles Ménage, one of the specific targets of Molière's wit.

When Galland discovered the cuckoos in his book, he was not happy, and when the interference was justified by Pétis and their publisher on the grounds that the most recent volume of *Les Mille et une nuits* needed to be filled out, Galland, who had been distracted from oriental romances by his (lost) translation of the Qur'an, set about gathering more stories for *Les nuits* and collected material for four more volumes.

In an autobiographical note, Pétis describes how he spent two years, from the age of seventeen to nineteen, travelling in the orient to train as a translator for the French foreign service, first in Arabic, then in Farsi; he fell ill, he tells us, and despaired of learning the languages until he found the dervish Moclès, who taught him and gave him the stories that became *Les jours*: the manuscript he is rendering, he writes, had come into his hands in 1675. 'The celebrated Dervish Moclès (which means faithful), whom Persia counts among its greatest personages . . . was head of the Sufis of Isfahan . . . and they feared him because he passed for a learned Cabbalist.' Pétis was aware of the possible seditiousness of the holy man's following and rather disingenuously affirms that he only went to see him to study the language. But his later comments betray his attraction to the more esoteric and ecstatic aspects of the literature he was immersing himself in; the stories that he conveyed in his elevated style take colour from this love of Sufi mystical erotica.

His recent editors now believe that this entire report is made up, and the stories are in fact Turkish in origin, from a collection called *Farraj ba'd al-shidda* ( *Joy after Distress*), comprising variations on several sources including El Nizami, and were retold, slanted and augmented by Pétis.

The putative source, the dervish Moclès, adds authenticity to Pétis' work, according to a pattern of impersonation and disguise that runs through the history of transmitting fantastic stories – Cervantes invokes a manuscript by an Arabic writer, Cide Hamete Benengeli, as the source of his *Don Quixote*, and Marie Catherine d'Aulnoy, the most prolific writer of fairy tales in the vogue that swept through Europe, attributes her *Contes des fées* (1697) to 'an old Enslaved Arab woman who knew a thousand Tales'. She does not name her. This collection of d'Aulnoy's appeared before Galland reworked the stories he had heard from Hannah Diyab, a Maronite Christian from Syria living in Paris, into a further set of *Arabian Nights*. Claiming a dervish source also adds spiritual heft to Pétis' work, the Frenchman showing impish Enlightenment scepticism about the status of his material. Or is Pétis sincerely seeking to elevate his prolix tales of prolonged trials and high emotions on to a mystical plane? Might he be attempting to do both? Pétis was clearly capitalizing opportunistically on Galland's success when he gave his collection the title *Les Mille et un jours*, presenting it in effect as a companion volume to *Les nuits*; as we have seen, it rode the wave that Galland's work had started. Pétis' irrepressible tale-spinning was also well represented in *Le Cabinet des fées*, published in 1785–6 in forty-one volumes, which collected together scores of tales in the fashionable, now mostly unread, rococo 'Fairy Way of Writing', including many oriental variations.

Reading Pétis' versions today is a pastime for a long lazy afternoon or perhaps a lengthy convalescence: his prose is flowery, packed with hyperbole, periphrasis and repetition in the scrolling arabesque tradition, blithely disregarding realist plausibility and psychological enquiry. But it arrests a contemporary reader's attention. The geography is adventurous, the action taking place across the khanates of Central Asia, while the dramatis personae come from Basra to Samarkand and Peking. Violent attempts at usurpation and the wholesale slaughter that ensues are too intricate to list here, but the dreadful carnage in the wars between these peoples gives uneasy glimpses of recent historical bloodshed.

The settings of the oriental stories in volumes published in the eighteenth century, including *Les nuits* and *Les jours*, mirror the methods of their making: they tell of peregrinations and displacements; evoking a far-flung geography, from the straits of Gibraltar to the China sea. The great ports that feature in such tales – Venice, Basra – are also the crossroads where the stories met and mingled, carried by merchants, priests and missionaries of all denominations, pilgrims, diplomats, scholars, explorers, soldiers, sailors, pirates, doctors and their entourages. And here the often unnoticed members of a family or a household also matter crucially – servants, nursemaids, captives, slaves and children.

The structure of *Les jours* echoes that of *Les nuits*, in that tales are set within tales in a narrative hall of mirrors. 'Princess Turandot' appears as the second part or 'continuation' of 'the Story of Prince Calaf and the Princess of China', which is embedded in the larger narrative frame about another beautiful and implacable princess, called Farrukhnaz. In this frame narrative Farrukhnaz also does not wish to marry but prefers to live independently or in chaste seclusion. Her nurse, Sutlumemé, is trying to cajole her charge to change her mind and drop her resolve by telling her of romantic adventures – a score of them – which throw a sunny light on love and marriage. She passes on the narrative baton to one narrator and then another and he – mostly a he in the enchained tales – on to another, giving the whole cycle a feeling of perpetual motion as it moves through romantic exempla. The story of the cruel, proud princess of China, who changes her mind after all and succumbs to love for Prince Calaf is intended to convert Farrukhnaz to thinking more kindly about men and to accepting union with one, just as we saw Shahrazad's tales are intended to cure the Sultan of his misogyny.

The story Sutlumemé tells is a tangled rigmarole, which aims to pin down and delight listeners and readers through its peripatetic complications, improbable mishaps and triumphs. It is another good example of *aja'ib*. Readers today, less accustomed to *aja'ib* and trained to deplore the irrational, find such literature tedious and foggy; it works better performed or recited. Furthermore, *Les jours* lacks the potent ransom motive that spurs Shahrazad in the first place and gives a guiding thread through the cycle of stories in *Les nuits*, that telling a story will save her life. Eleanor Cook, in a fine study of riddles, calls this the 'neck riddle', because the head of the storyteller lies on the block. The story she – or he – tells poses an enigma which defers execution to another time, when the enigma will no longer tantalize and the answer will be known. The need to persuade a stubborn princess to consider marriage does not move the narrative along with the same urgency.

The nurse describes how Calaf, his father the Sultan and his mother have been forced into exile by the victory of the Tartars over their people, the Nogais. They have been wandering eastwards from Central Asia, through Russia and Mongolia, to China where they are set upon by bandits and stripped of all their remaining goods. But they escape, alive. In this beggared state, they meet Fadlallah, the son of the King of Mosul. (The topography of the stories, rich in evocative actual names, plays fast and loose with the map.) Fadlallah takes them in and in turn tells them his story, a wild concatenation of marvellous adventures and metamorphoses. He was changed, he tells them, into a nightingale but has been restored to human form. The story then returns to the fate of Calaf and his parents: after only one night with their rescuers, the family become fugitives once again, and after several days' walking reach the tribe of the Berlas. Calaf rescues the splendidly bejewelled falcon of the King, which had gone astray, and as a reward, is equipped with magnificent armour and supplies of gold and other gifts. Inevitably, he attracts attention and is assaulted and stripped en route to Peking. In this wretched state, he finds a kind widow to take him in, and she tells him about the princess Tourandocte, an incomparable beauty who has vowed not to marry unless her suitor can solve three riddles. The Prince of Samarkand has become, she reports, the most recent victim of her cruelty. Calaf is shown her portrait; he is instantly smitten and determines that he too must make the attempt to possess her. This motif recurs in romances and in *Les nuits*, underlining not only the practice of making portraits but a fervent belief in – or fear of? – the irresistible power of images to spark sincere and irrepressible passion.

The ramparts of the city are decorated with the heads of his many predecessors, who failed; he is not deterred, and when it comes to his turn Calaf answers all three tests easily. Turandot is furious and demands another trial, but her father refuses to hold one. Pétis' plot then braids in another familiar motif: Calaf promises to surrender his prize and go to his death if the princess can find out his name.

Much intrigue follows as Turandot struggles to find out and suborns Adelmulk, a captive princess who has been enslaved in the court. Adelmulk has overheard Calaf crying his own name in the night and she betrays him. When Calaf hears Turandot triumphantly give the correct answer, he faints and Adelmulk, who had hoped to win him and save him, stabs herself. At the sight of such passion – and self-immolation – Tourandocte relents and yields to overpowering love.

Sutlumemé finishes telling the story of the splendid wedding and the wise rule of Calaf and Turandocte, her listeners express their pleasure, and trust, as the narrative tradition I have been exploring maintains, in its potential to change the future. But the nurse's principal target, the young woman Farrukhnaz, remains unconvinced, persisting in her caustic view of male vanity, stupidity and undependability: 'I find him more vain than loving, a bit stupid, in other words what one calls a young man ... My dear Sutlumemé, you may paint men in the most gorgeous colours you like, their faults will always pierce through your painting.' Her dissent gives the nurse a reason for more stories, and so the cycle can carry on.

In English, *Les jours* enjoyed a popularity which now seems surprising. It was immediately translated by the Scottish satirist Dr William King in 1714, only two years after its French publication; his title, *The Persian and Turkish Tales*, identified the cultural origins of the stories. It went through three more editions. In 1722, the poet Ambrose Philips revisited the collection, and he was followed, in 1892, by Justin Huntly McCarthy, who comments in his foreword that all students of folklore will meet familiar figures and plotlines in these stories.

The Moroccan scholar Abdelfattah Kilito has posed the question, is *The Thousand and One Nights* a boring book? The same can certainly be asked of *Les jours*, as recounted by Pétis. Yet the story of Turandot has lasted, perhaps because the ransom motive that spurs Shahrazad drives a hero, a noble prince down on his luck: Calif invites strong, wishful identification from the reader/audience, especially the male elements.

The role of stories in appealing and entertaining across borders and consequently bonding disparate communities continues as *Turandot* travels from the page to the stage: in 1761, fifty years after the first printed appearance of the story in *Les Mille et un jours*, the playwright and writer of fairy tales Carlo Gozzi (1720–1806) dramatized the tale for a production at the small theatre of San Samuele in Venice, a city which had been and still was a point of vital exchange between the East and the West, between Christendom, Islam and Judaism. Gozzi was an outspoken advocate of rococo fantasy and an embattled defender of *commedia dell'arte*, which he adapted freely, adding satirical comments on current affairs, from the elaborate plots and fantastic motifs he found in such collections as Basile's *Pentamerone* and *Le Cabinet des fées*, where he encountered the oriental tale and the work of Pétis. Gozzi called his plays '*Capricci scenici o fiabe dramatiche*' (Theatrical capriccios or dramatic fables) and his *Turandot* is subtitled *Fiaba chinese teatrale tragicomica* (a tragicomic Chinese fairy play).

In a very heated and very public quarrel Gozzi challenged his fellow playwright Carlo Goldoni, the leading exponent of the new theatrical realism, claiming that he, Gozzi, could still fill a theatre with fairy extravaganzas, masks and mime. He was as good as his boast, and the struggle between the two men culminated in Goldoni's departure from Venice.

Gozzi was perceived as the hoary conservative stubbornly stuck in the old ways, and Goldoni as the angry young man, keen to break with the past and become truly modern. (When I was studying for Italian A-level in the early 1960s, Goldoni was prominent on the syllabus but Gozzi unheard of.) The difference between the two dramatists is however more complicated, partly because they didn't belong to different generations – Goldoni was actually older (Gozzi was born in 1720 and Goldoni in 1707), but more importantly Gozzi's approach to the *commedia* was highly innovatory; he did not give the actors *scenari*, or sketches, from which to improvise, but wrote them complete speeches, for which he developed a mixed tone, bizarre and unstable, preposterous and absurd, yet at the same time magical and sublime. Gozzi's work epitomizes the profane spirit of the eighteenth century as found in Diderot's *Les Bijoux indiscrets*, for example. Zany is the *mot juste* to describe the overall mood of this theatre – the word derives from the *zanni* or performers in the *commedia* and their capering, slapstick and clownish tricks. The Chinese ministers Ping, Pong and Pang in Puccini's opera are clear survivors from the *commedia*, adaptations of the masks Tartaglia, Brighella and Truffaldino, while, in strong contrast, Goldoni's progeny on the opera stage would include the social and psychological masterpieces of Mozart and Rossini, *The Marriage of Figaro* and *The Barber of Seville*.

In Gozzi's five-act play *Turandot* (1762) the plot turns above all on the magical effects of language and naming: he expands the plot into a drama about filiation and family. Calaf offers to die if Turandot discovers not only his own name but his father's identity.

This standoff between the fantastic and the realistic that the disagreement between Gozzi and Goldoni exemplifies relates to the theme of making sanctuary, because Gozzi's often outlandish inventiveness and his uses of ancient *commedia* tragicomic traditions leapt borders and has proved an enduring treasure trove for interpreters in all media almost anywhere. His rejection of naturalist representation has long memories, going back to the theatre of Greece and Rome, and it had the effect of lifting the performances across ethnolinguistic boundaries.

Goldoni himself did not altogether strip his plays of these long memories, but as a general rule the drama and fiction of realistic mimesis and psychological plausibility that became established as the generic forms in nineteenth-century literature are tied to the modern nation state, whereas fantastic material and *commedia*-style artifice, circulating often on informal networks, predate the consolidation of those political entities. It is telling that, although Gozzi saw himself as keeping alive a native Italian style, even a local Venetian art, and wrote specifically to give work to the threatened *commedia* company of his friend Antonio Sacchi (a celebrated Truffaldino), his work met with more success abroad, especially in Germany. The Romantics were rediscovering medieval fairy lore and folk traditions and performance methods; Goethe directed the production in Weimar in 1802 of Schiller's version of Gozzi — and it was in the Italian translation of Schiller's play, not in Pétis, that Puccini encountered the tale.

In 1782, Carlo Gozzi, Venetian playwright and champion of traditional Commedia dell' Arte, adapted *Turandot* for the European stage.

Gozzi is not much celebrated today; his presence is felt mostly through the composers and librettists who have been inspired by his writing. Prokofiev adapted *The Love for Three Oranges*, a story Gozzi took from Basile, which has kindled more interest recently, and the German composer Hans Werner Henze recently adapted *Il Re cervo* (*The King Stag*), which was written by Gozzi for performance in the same season as *Turandot*.

The tradition Gozzi fostered with such tenacity lives on in *The Magic Flute* by Mozart and in many more operas: unexpectedly, Wagner's earliest opera, *Die Feen* (*The Fairies*, 1833), was based on Gozzi's *La Donna serpente* (1763). It's a grandiose machine of oriental splendour, evil sorcery, divine women, vacillating heroes, mysterious love tests, all unfolding in a mêlée of supernatural stage effects and interrupted by *commedia dell'arte* clowning. Only later did Wagner nativize his fairy material in a Teutonic key.

The Venetian composer Ferruccio Busoni wrote incidental music, *The Turandot Suite*, for Gozzi's play; it was first performed in 1905, and Busoni then expanded it into a full-scale opera which Max Reinhardt produced in Berlin in 1911. Puccini reported Turandot's grand entrance to Renato Simoni, one of his librettists: Turandot was 'a tiny woman surrounded by tall men specifically chosen for their height; huge chairs, huge furnishings, and this viper of a woman with the strange heart of an hysteric'.

Yevgeny Vakhtangov's production, staging Busoni's music, followed in 1922 in Soviet Russia in what appears, from the surviving photographs and reports, an exuberant and dramatic expressionist interpretation – Vakhtangov was dying while it was in rehearsal. And there were more variations on the story created for the stage. This peculiar, not especially likeable or meaningful story commanded interest and admiration from many quarters, including an audience in the harsh conditions just after the Russian Revolution. Its very limitations, arbitrariness and detachment from life as it is lived offered opportunities for high-spirited treatment. As Marina Volok writes, 'In the midst of cold, hungry and dangerous times, Vakhtangov was able to bring a holiday of theatricality to the audience, conveying to them that one can be happy despite traumatizing conditions, by releasing the power of one's imagination.'

Literary nomadism mirrors actual diaspora, and calls to mind the truth that many voices and languages and approaches are involved in the transmission and metamorphoses of such material. By far the most famous interpretation of the *Turandot* story, surpassing all others in popularity, is Puccini's opera, in many ways a belated work for the twentieth century, and the last he composed.

*Turandot* does not obviously present a metaphor for abuses near to hand now or in the 1920s. As in Pétis and Gozzi, the heroine is a princess who, to her father's despair, has refused to marry unless her suitor can solve three riddles; the opera introduces further love interest through the character of Liù, one of her maids, who is smitten with the stranger and warns him that Turandot, enraged by his success in her contest, is going to have him murdered. Then Prince Calaf imprudently cries, 'Oh, unhappy son of Timurtas, oh Calaf worthy of pity!' In this way, Turandot learns who he is, and Liù, when she realizes she has led him to betray his identity, kills herself.

The opera revels in fairy tale's far-fetched extremism and implausible psychology: one prince after another have lined up to be slaughtered, undeterred by their predecessors' heads displayed on the walls of her palace. The Chinese milieu is fanciful, to put it politely, and makes no concession to recognizable history, although Puccini adapted several Chinese tunes he had heard on a musical box, which the Italian consul had brought back from Peking, possibly among the loot from the Boxer rebellion. Thus a story which has travelled originally in the luggage of a colonial interpreter (Pétis) was set to music that formed a part of colonial booty.

The Chineseyness of the opera is still highlighted in contemporary productions, especially as China ceases to be a region of dreams and becomes entangled in the contests for imperial power in the nineteenth and twentieth centuries. Puccini had directly explored the East–West encounter in *Madama Butterfly* (1904–7) and created a heroine, Cio Cio San or Butterfly, who kills herself for love after a foreigner, the American naval officer B. F. Pinkerton, abandons her. *Turandot* reverberates to this earlier plot but inverts it by providing a happy ending – except that, for Liù, the incoming stranger also brings death.

In 2023 the second opera company of Kyiv (not the main one I had heard performing *Turandot*) came on tour to the UK with a production of *Madama Butterfly*; this opera's libretto is by Puccini's frequent collaborators Luigi Illica and Giuseppe Giacosa, who based it on a short story by an American, John Luther Long, a play by David Belasco, and the reminiscences of an orientalizing French writer, Pierre Loti. The closing scene, high tragedy at any time, was especially lacerating when performed by a Ukrainian company at that stage of the violent war in their country. Butterfly blindfolds the child she has had with Pinkerton and sits him down with his back to their home in front of her domestic shrine; she puts a small Stars and Stripes flag in his hand and tells him to continue waving it. It is as if he is about to be executed, but it is she who, going back into the house, commits hara-kiri out of his sight. Pinkerton and his new – American – wife enter and adopt the child, as it seems Butterfly trusted they would. He will be brought up an American.

After the curtain fell on this queasy tableau, the full company gathered on stage, sang the Ukrainian national anthem and unfurled the national flag; we in the audience rose to our feet and those of us who could sang with them. At that time, March 2023, the tragedy unfolded before us on stage the hopes that Butterfly places in the Western officer, however inconstant he has shown himself all along. The grinding irony of hope in American might, as portrayed in the libretto, started up difficult vibrations with the current war in Ukraine, even before the new Trumpian regime.

Puccini always composed urgent, passionate, tumultuous music, which sweeps up the audience in its strains, especially during a live performance in a packed theatre. But *Turandot* is a very peculiar grand opera, with antithetical elements clashing throughout: the passionate romance of love-in-death with the *commedia* buffoons, three cartoon characters, the Chinese ministers Ping, Pong and Pang. The libretto, by Giuseppe Adami and Renato Simoni, adapted Gozzi's play and also drew on Schiller's version in the Italian translation. They took decisions about the story that exacerbate the intensity of the sex war as its theme, and stoke up the romance into a vast spectacular which relishes its excesses. It retains the generic instability of its forerunners and veers between absurdity and high tragedy: the gorefest of dead princes who haunt the scene revels in fairy-tale excesses of improbability, and the passions of all the main protagonists hit irrational extremes. But this tumult is the point, and for the opera's admirers the music dissolves these strains in the fabric. Adami and Simoni add tragic sincerity to the role of Liù. But, above all, they give the heroine a personal reason for her vendetta, one that strikes very powerful resonances with contemporary audiences, showing the remarkable porousness of these wonder tales to timely reinterpretation.

At her grand entrance in Act II, Turandot sings her first major aria, an *aria di sortita*, 'In questa reggia' ('In this palace'). She conjures the shade of her ancestress Princess Lo-u-Ling, who was wronged by an invader, a stranger, a Tartar conqueror who raped and killed her – in other words, a man like the princes who have wooed her, and now like Calaf. Lo-u-Ling's cry – her *grido disperato*, her desperate scream – reverberates down the millennia and has taken possession, Turandot sings, of her very soul. The violated woman still lives inside her. The high trilling notes of the soprano express the anguish she feels at her ancestor's wrongs at full throttle as she addresses her suitor:

*Turandot*
In this palace . . . Still in the time all can recall,
there was alarm, terror, the rumble of arms!
The Kingdom defeated! defeated!
And Lo-u-Ling, my ancestress,
dragged off by a man,
like you, like you, stranger,
there in the horrid night,
where her sweet voice was stilled!

*The Crowd*
She's slept for centuries
in her huge tomb!

*Turandot*
O you princes,
with your long caravans
from every part of the world,
who come here to try your fate,
in you I avenge

> that purity, that cry,
> and that death!
> No one will ever possess me!
> The horror of her assassin
> is still vivid in my heart!
> No, no one will ever possess me!
> Ah, in me is reborn the pride
> of such purity!
> Stranger, do not tempt Fate!
> The enigmas are three,
> but death is one!

Turandot's implacable rage against the race of men springs from her thirst to avenge her forerunner and appease her ghost; as she sings, she reprises the curse of Dido on Aeneas and Rome from Virgil and his interpreters. With this romantic backstory, Turandot's cruelty is given an intense personal motive, in strong contrast with her precursors in Pétis and Gozzi, who have only heard tales of men and their deeds and have decided to shun them and remain single – and free. At the patent level, the triumph of love over her resolve is a victory against celibacy, but at the latent level, the happy ending promises a broader thaw of relations, the conquest of despair and the ending of violence – which is perhaps why the tale could play in post-Revolutionary Russia and in Ukraine almost twenty years ago.

The cold-hearted princess dominates much folklore: the common ground that enabled the story to travel may have been laid by this figure, a femme fatale who says no until ... the archetype flatters both male and female psyches, and the story of her ultimate conquest presents hope, in the tradition of fairy-tale heroic optimism (however unlikely). The binary opposition that governs religious sanctuary (a sanctuary can be premised on privileging one group over another, as we have seen) operates here as war between the sexes. The conflict in this story arises between a man and a woman, rather than between a national or social or ethnic group. Indeed the multiple regions of medieval Central and East Asia that figure in the opera blur the contours of racial or religious antagonisms, instead crystallizing passion around the couple. The erotic as a theme can be a powerful unifier: audiences identify with both sides.

The misogynist tendency is often matched in the tales by the equal reluctance of a male hero, as in 'The Tale of Camar al-Zaman and Princess Badoura [Budur]' from *The Thousand and One Nights* in which Badoura has vowed never to relinquish her sovereignty to any male. Her father, believing she is mad, imprisons her in a high tower. Meanwhile Camar al-Zaman likewise refuses to marry on account of all he has heard about women. A pair of jinn conspire to fly the two young people in an enchanted sleep to meet each other. On waking, they are each in turn utterly smitten.

Not all such protagonists insist on preserving their chastity on pain of death, like Turandot. Turandot is a monster, unlike Badoura, especially in the peculiarly bloodthirsty variation Pétis passed on. She presents an exact counterpart of the dragons that heroes – Beowulf, Perseus, Frodo – must face and slay, or that heroines – Finette in *The Discreet Princess*, or Gerda in *The Snow Queen* – overcome with steadfastness or guile. Her reasons for rejecting marriage do not command the same degree of support in the tradition. She's fatale, heartless and predatory, like the sirens, Scylla and Grendel's mother, who are all fated to bring death on those who come near them. When survival depends on solving riddles, as it often does, the answers are frequently self-reflexive: to the Sphinx's famous enigma the solution is 'man', as if she were compelling her would-be conquerors to recognize themselves. In the various versions of *Turandot*, the riddles change from one author to another. In the Pétis tale, the answers bear on life and eternity – they are the sun, the sea and the year. In Gozzi, 'the lion of Adria' (the symbol of Venice) is the answer to the third; this specific reference to the city needed to be changed in Puccini's opera in the interests of broader appeal.

The Sphinx's name means strangler, and she is female in Greek mythology. A riddle princess who deals death to all who approach her to end her isolation is another kind of sphinx, and the figure recurs over and over again in fairy tales: she's a stock character, an embodied pun on the knot of virginity, the maiden's knot, and a self-reflexive activation of narrative perplexity and pleasure. The opening of Shakespeare's *Pericles* dramatizes it, linked in this case to the incest between the father and his daughter; in *The Merchant of Venice*, Portia's father's will has tied up her availability in the riddle of the caskets. One of the tales of the Brothers Grimm, 'The Sea-Hare', takes up the motif of a ruthless princess who repels her suitors by setting them impossible enigmas, but in this variation, as the hero makes his way to woo the princess, he meets a raven, a fish and a fox, three magic animal helpers: the raven hides him in an egg, but the princess, who lives in a high tower with twelve windows, discovers him there; the fish swallows him, but she can see through the fish; then the fox – cunning creature – turns him into a sea-hare. This creature does actually exist: it's a marine snail, with tentacles that look like ears and an internal shell. But for the purposes of the fairy tale, it is a riddle in itself, an enigma beyond solution, a gryllus in the margin of a medieval manuscript. The three animal helpers are magical agents and the hiding places they propose are forms of encryption. In the strange shape of a sea-hare, the boy hides himself in the princess's hair. Even she can't see the back of her head, but she feels his presence and furiously pulls him out and throws him down from one of her twelve windows. He has, however, passed the test, the spell is broken and he can claim her.

In the English folk tale 'Tom Tit Tot', the heroine can only free herself from a pact she made by guessing the name of the imp who has come to claim her.

The anagnorisis or recognition at the core of fairy tales takes place when the foundling is discovered or the ragamuffin revealed in his or her true self; in the cluster of stories to which *Turandot* belongs, the resolution follows a magical act of naming, as the philosopher Ludwig Wittgenstein noticed in 'Rumpelstiltskin', which also turns on a pact, but a pact of a different kind: in the story, as written down by the Brothers Grimm, and in the English variant known as 'Tom Tit Tot', the princess is saved by the magical arts of a hobgoblin in return for a promise to marry him – unless she can find out his name. She does so with the help of a friend or by means of a subterfuge – and cries out:

Nimmy nimmy not
Your name's Tom Tit Tot.

In this nursery rhyme Tom isn't a he, but an it, a malevolent thing:

Well, when *that* heard her, that gave an awful shriek and away that flew into the dark, and she never saw it any more [italics added].

Certain features of this history of *Turandot* define migrating motifs in narrative and modify the concept of a travelling *text* in cross-cultural encounters: its peregrinations show that the fairy orient is not simply literature but a form that melds the oral and the written, the sounded and the silent, drama and art and, above all, music. The nearest genre that captures its character is *mime*; in its classical incarnation, the theatre that the *commedia dell'arte* developed and contemporary pantomime partly remembers. The story is also infinitely mobile and changeable, it moves from the page to the stage and continues to tack back and forth. The more startling the passions involved and the situation described, the more exciting and pleasurable the narrative becomes. Finally, the thinness of the story's psychology, plotting and literary craftsmanship is counterbalanced by the thickness of the emotional intensity, of the scene-setting and, above all, of the singing and the orchestral score.

It is not easy to know how a story becomes mobile, or indeed to locate the moment when its life as an autonomous travelling text began, but this mobility and polymorphousness are distinguishing features of traditional literature, which is often anonymous and diasporic: myths and fairy tales, legends, jokes, riddles, proverbs – 'simple forms' in the phrase of André Jolles. The stories about Joseph in Egypt, or Abraham, or Salome, or the Virgin Mary appear in sacred scriptures, the Bible and the Qur'an; the cruel princess or the Cinderella figure has some well-known homes in the collections of Charles Perrault and the Grimm Brothers; Hamlet is most famous from Shakespeare's tragedy. But in all these cases the story has antecedents and doppelgängers and deep affinities with other stories. Hamlet, whose tragedy echoes Orestes' predicament in many respects, has become a 'book runner', a character or protagonist who leaves the text to slip into others. Strong examples of such mythic runners – actually more like a whole caravan of travelling texts – are the cycle of stories, discussed before, about the Trojan war and its aftershocks (including the Virgilian tale of Dido and Aeneas) and *The Thousand and One Nights*.

Stories such as *Turandot* consequently give glimpses of familiar faces in a crowd, as the Esperanto of fairy-tale motifs gets jumbled up and reshuffled. A different term besides 'text' would be useful, because although the tales are woven from many elements (remembering Latin *texuere*, to weave) 'text' suggests a potential definitive version and therefore an author or authors. But the kind of story that is *Turandot* is not really literature according to these criteria. Nor is it orature, unwritten. It could be called a myth, though that does not fit the secular and fairy-tale qualities of this tale and its counterparts. 'Meme' can do good service in this respect. But regarding sanctuary as a form of hospitality, I prefer adopting imagery from botany, because the biodiversity of narrative is evident. Think of a plant such as *Wisteria sinensis*: it travelled from China to Europe in the early nineteenth century, and there also exists a Japanese variety, called *Wisteria floribunda*, which is wonderfully scented; the two species cross-fertilize happily. This beautiful climber, now familiar in urban gardens in London, was named after a late eighteenth-century American anatomist, Caspar Wistar, by a colleague who as it happens misspelt the name, just as in transmission losses and gains alter the tale being told and it doesn't matter. But wisteria is representative in another way: although the plant is identified with Wistar, as if he were responsible for its existence as discoverer or even inventor – in other words, as author of its coming into wider consciousness – he played no part in its discovery.

The many 'authors' of *Turandot* show that a story seeds itself here and there. Think again of wisteria: its dangling tresses of blue-mauve flowers develop into seedpods which, when they open, scatter on the ground and may be carried elsewhere, as other plants are, wafted by the wind or stuck in the fur of passing animals or clinging to their paws or to our human footwear to take root elsewhere. Or the flower can be propagated most securely by taking cuttings, as did the English chief inspector of tea at Canton, John Reeves, when he came upon the magnificent blossom, hitherto unknown to him, growing in a local merchant's garden. A tale like *Turandot* is a narrative stem cell, a story cell or story stem. A professional storyteller's book of scripts, which could be leafed through for inspiration when called on to perform for a sleepless tyrant, resembles a packed seedpod before ripening and bursting, releasing its spores, as mentioned earlier (p. 187). Spore comes from ancient Greek σπόρος, *sporos*, sowing, and σπείρειν, *speirein*, to sow, from which derives the word *diaspora*, a scattering across. Animals are propagators; they carry spores and seeds in their coats, on their hooves and in their droppings: this is how, botanists have shown, the common apple travelled from the woods of Kazakhstan in Central Asia. Many miscellanies like seedpods survive: Greek mythological handbooks, gazetteers of material, Hyginus' *Fabulae* and *The Library* of Apollodorus, and the *Metamorphoses* of Antoninus Liberalis, rather than the structured, complex narrative cycle by Ovid or Apuleius.

These story cells – these *spories* – are active and generative and have the potential to form ties and sympathy across barriers now as such tales have done in the past, spontaneously.

# Part Three:
# The Shelter of Stories

The outer world is only one of the worlds we live in.

Ted Hughes

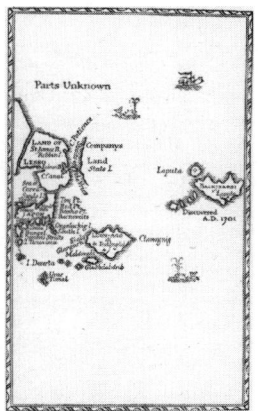

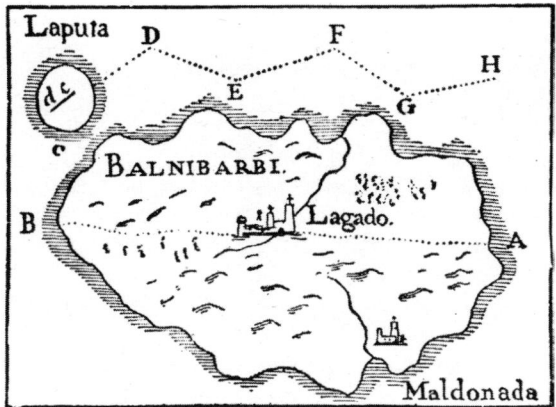

Fictive mapping: Jonathan Swift included precise coordinates for the places his hero visits; many early readers believed his stories and hunted for Lilliput and Laputa on their globes. Jonathan Swift, *Gulliver's Travels*, 1726.

# 7

# In No Man's Land

> the ordinary you and me
> make great efforts to become a You
> in advance of the supposed arrival
> at the Great Me
> who does not exist . . .
>                 Philippe Beck

No man's land has grown and is growing strongly in extent. The erection of walls and fences, the roll-out of miles of barbed and razor wire and electrified and even sonic barriers, define a country's frontiers, but they do not lie contiguous to each other. They enclose 'a zone of abandonment' – a long, wide corridor of no man's land. The Berlin Wall made plain the distance between the double barriers snaking through the city, and cut a wide, featureless swathe of bare scrub where anyone trying to cross could not hide. In 2015 in Hungary, a double fence, alarmed and equipped with sensors and cameras, delineated its southern frontiers with Serbia and Croatia. And as I write, Israeli forces have cleared a kilometre-wide swathe along the whole length of the Gaza Strip's land border and built a road which cuts the north of the Strip from the south; these measures have taken 16 per cent of Gaza's territory and effectively carved out a new, unofficial no man's land. The nomenclature for these barricaded enclaves is euphemistic: buffer zone, DMZ (demilitarized zone), 'depth barrier', 'sterile security zone'.

    A Royal Geographical Society exploratory expedition set out in 2015 to chart no man's lands all over the globe: they travelled 6,000 miles.

'If you look for them, you can detect No Man's Lands in lots of places,' declared the leader of the expedition, Alasdair Pinkerton. 'There are abandoned places and abandoned people within cities, between countries, between different districts of countries, along disputed borders all over the world. No Man's Lands are historic. They're also contemporary, and they take a whole host of different forms depending on the legislation or the boundary-making processes that are underway. That's the kind of thing that we really want to try and unpick with this expedition.' The artist Ursula Schulz-Dornburg has been photographing these contemporary wastelands, often battlegrounds and killing fields, where stand a few remaining edifices, industrial ruins, memorials to past trouble that have cleared away the people for whom these places may have been home. She called the book of these silent yet speaking images *The Land in Between*.

In a more light-hearted vein, here and there in the world a brave spirit — a heroic anarchist, an adventurer or a prankster — will claim a tract of this no man's land as a new nation, free from the jurisdiction of other powers. These endeavours are mostly *jeux d'esprit*, though some Robinson Crusoes may intend their occupation seriously. But beneath the larkiness of some past exploits runs a serious and unsettling similarity between such personal redoubts and sanctuary. The comparison also shows, as mentioned in the Introduction, that the general understanding of the term 'sanctuary' does not distinguish between a refuge and a stronghold, that enclosure can point both to protection and to imprisonment. A refuge is a retreat and way station, not enclosed, but secure, like the forest where Robin Hood hid from the law, and in different manifestations it affords a period of truce and reprieve, while the second, the stronghold, aspires to permanence and keeps out the uninvited. The first would meet the circumstances of asylum seekers today, and governments might argue that detention in a hotel or even on a barge provides such shelter — with conditions. The second interpretation by contrast will tend towards excluding others who do not belong — to the faith, the ethnicity, the language — and will be hedged about by shibboleths barring entry to the ineligible.

On old maps the label *Terra nullius* — the land of nobody — identified unattributed territory, often in ignorance and colonial arrogance since in North America and Australia the inhabitants were simply invisible to the mapmakers and their patrons. In the Middle Ages, no man's land began as a place to be shunned: the waste ground under the ramparts of a fortress, the fosse where the bodies of executed prisoners were left to rot, exposed to carrion birds and animals (Antigone wanted to stop this happening to her brother Polynices). In 1348, the Bishop of London enclosed land under the London Wall and walled it in, to serve as a burial ground for the plague-stricken. The best-known usage is modern and reflects the savagery of modern warfare: no man's land described the battlefield between the opposing armies in Flanders during the First World War, where famously the enemies played football together at Christmas 1914. DMZs (Demilitarized Zones) clear space between warring armies in a civil war or during an invasion, for example between North and South Vietnam during the Vietnam war, between North and South Korea today, and in the fighting in Ukraine between the Russians and the Ukrainian front lines, in an ominous return to trench warfare. DMZs may be substantial tracts of land, desolate and abandoned, like wastelands contaminated by chemicals or radioactivity. They are anti-sanctuaries, killing grounds.

The new, heavily fortified borders rise, glinting, spiked: from the Eurostar train, as it approaches the Channel tunnel on the French side, concentric rings rise across the fields, three to four deep. Were it not so ferocious and menacing, the razor wire might be tinsel, so gaily do its brand-new coils sparkle. These new borders inflict a scar sometimes as much as 12 metres wide on the body of the landscape – indeed, in 1992 and again in 2001, the French photographer Sophie Ristelhueber emphasized this potent metaphorical association with her aerial images of Iraq, treating the earth as if it were flesh, and the war damage as bodily scarification. Figuratively, no man's land is also growing, in the camps and places of detention in Jordan, Kenya, Greece and all the other countries where sanctuary seekers are packed together, often legally stateless, mostly in transit.

There was a time when it could seem amusing that antiquarian collectors in the United States paid good money for varieties of historic barbed wire, used in the staking out of property in the west, parcelling out the prairies to the new landowners, each one identifiable from his design of barb and hook, just as his herds were known to belong to him from the brand burned into their hide. But these curiosities of

No man's land. The bleak correlative of non-personhood grows worldwide as fortified borders proliferate.

a particular connoisseurship now feel ominous when bales of silver concertina wire unfurl for miles and miles to demarcate frontiers of the rich world, keeping out the poor, leaving between the high, thorny fences a wild forbidden territory. In no man's land official armies of one side or the other, or random snipers working for traffickers, or vigilantes working for their own purposes will pick off those attempting to cross. They can try to tunnel their way through. Burrows are one place where they might survive. On the surface concealment is necessary.

The fences demarcate a site of unwelcome, where no man or woman or child lives or can claim ownership, a neutral place, an interzone. Untended, *terrain vague*, as the French call a wasteland. We see these spaces on the map, sometimes narrow, sometimes wider, a gap between two lines inscribed on to desert, meadow, mountains, streets, buildings: occasionally a gap that is not quite an alley has been left between two houses which have not been terraced but remain detached; this gap then acquires a dishevelled, orphan look. Sometimes such a border will slice right through the middle of a house or apartment block, bisecting it, as was threatened when the two mothers in the Old Testament asked Solomon to judge their claims to a baby. A place that was once a home can be left stranded on two sides of a border with a hiatus in between. Passages and holes leave a tailor's offcuts of territory and, if these plots were patched and pieced next to the other for a coat of many colours, it would hang loose on a colossus, and provide enough land for a planetary moon where all those who have nowhere to stay and call their own could make a home. Or would that be an exile, to be in orbit elsewhere far from this world?

In the past, before Schengen lifted barriers between some countries in the EU, I remember how we used to walk through these nowheres, at Ventimiglia between France and Italy, for example, and it used to inspire a strange and exciting feeling, as one left one border post behind with its national guards and stepped into the perimeter that did not belong to anyone, and met the different country's policemen or soldiers and took stock of the way they handled themselves. Did they twitch for their pistols, did they lounge about smoking? What about the cut of their uniforms (the bulk of their boots, the white of their spats, the swirl of their cock feathers)? Why are they taking so long to scrutinise the photo in my passport?

Once, soon after the Prague Spring of 1968, I was with my future husband, William Shawcross, trying to enter Czechoslovakia, and he was ordered to shave off his beard to match his passport picture. But we had no razor except a very small one of mine and it took a long time, with cold water in the lavatory of the obscure frontier post (chosen deliberately, in the hope that we would pass through). Once the beard was off, we were held and questioned. Eventually we were turned back but at least let go. And since those comparatively less dangerous times, we have seen on the news so many undone by war and plague and famine, so many making their way across bridges, across frontiers, across bodies of water like the Channel, moving from one place where others belong, to another place where different others belong.

While the territorial extent of no man's land is growing, its figurative meanings are also deepening their hold: the proper inhabitant of Nowhere is Nobody and the measures put in place on so many borders are designed to bring out this negation of persons, often fugitives who are seeking a better life, establish their personhood and fulfil themselves in ways they cannot in their home country. When Theresa May, the then prime minister of the UK, notoriously declared, 'A citizen of the world is a citizen of nowhere,' she was expressing the underlying principle of 'the hostile environment'. She at least recognized that those who have left their country and, often, their papers, because they are in flight, do not under the UK's present immigration regime have a home. They are marooned in no man's (woman's) land. The deportation that threatens the person who is already dislocated and on the move, who has arrived without papers and is under interrogation and often in detention, corresponds to no man's land – they are living in a state of exception, to use Giorgio Agamben's term. The inhabitants of no man's land – and no woman's land – are deprived of the moorings that I enjoy, and that perhaps you do too. Unlike them, I know that I belong where I am: I not only have an address but also above all rights to freedom from violence, freedom to move, to work, to earn, to assemble, to speak, in short to belong to a hospitable society.

The unbelonging in their flight for sanctuary have been stalled in spaces of nowhere. But those who find themselves relegated in these nowheres do not accept their nullification and begin affirming their presence and, in the process, transforming their no man's lands into places where they can dwell.

Forms of narrative such as memoir and first-person confession relate to and interact with the rise of borders and populist antagonism to incomers and strangers. At one manifest practical level they do so because anyone who crosses a border and claims asylum needs to give a personal witness statement about their own reasons for seeking sanctuary away from their homeland and their country of citizenship. Testimony, a prime form of first-person story, is a prerequisite of legal entry across a border and a claim of asylum. The press, not excluding papers friendly to refugees, as well as thousands of well-wishers also encourage the retelling of the tale, the originary tale of that individual's circumstances: epic odysseys, documents that reproduce and communicate cruelty and terrible suffering; we listen helplessly, trying to feel – to *empathize* – and sometimes feeling that the emotions the stories stir are helping us to do something.

Taking up occupation through narrative has become the necessary strategy to arrive and establish the start of belonging somewhere, of ending the state of uprootedness and non-personhood. Displaced and unhomed existences are major catalysts of certain modes of storymaking, especially the uses of the first person, now so very dominant in the rising popularity of autofiction.

For example, in 1995, Anna Pincus, who lives near Gatwick

detention centre, began a campaign to help the many hundreds of arrivants who are held here. They form a shifting community of individuals whose status is being legally examined prior to asylum – or deportation. Anna joined forces with the poet and author David Herd, who was then working at the University of Kent, the county where many of the arrivants landed. Together they started Refugee Tales.

The campaign organizes walks to raise awareness of the detainees' plight. They modelled them on pilgrimages: participants include many former detainees who walk with the demonstrators. In the first year, Canterbury was the destination, and in homage to Chaucer the pilgrims began telling stories on the way, stopping here and there to tell the tale to one another and to audiences who gathered to hear them. These stories were inspired by the detainees' lives, and were sometimes told by those involved, but more often by others – for many reasons: the individual whose story was being told was still in detention, and access to communication is made extremely difficult. Also, many did not yet have a full command of English.

The first collection of the stories came out in 2016; four more anthologies have followed. I was invited to visit a young couple from Nigeria with two lively little girls; they were waiting desperately to hear if their petition to stay would be granted. Their claim of asylum was based on the dangers of returning to their different provinces of Nigeria, where, as Catholics, they faced persecution. The father, C., had overstayed his student visa (he had studied for a degree in electrical engineering) and his wife, E., who was visiting relations in the UK, exceeded the limits of her tourist visa once the pair had met, in a Catholic church, and fallen in love. C. had been held at Gatwick several times already: the authorities release detainees for a short spell and then incarcerate them again (a revival of the Cat and Mouse tactics used on the suffragettes). E. struck me as dangerously depressed by terror that the next time the police came C. would be deported. She comes from one part of Nigeria, he from another, so because they speak different African languages English is their common tongue. At the time we met, they were living in one room in a rundown rented house, sharing a lavatory and bathroom with troublesome neighbours (one of their little girls told me her mother was upset because these neighbours would leave it in a mess for her to clean). The husband/father was not allowed to work;

above all, they were distressed because, as asylum seekers, they could not marry. This upset them for many reasons, legal and confessional. E. wanted to train as a nurse, but that was closed to her too.

In the 'Refugee Tale' I wrote about them, I changed their names, to avoid putting at risk their claim to sanctuary. An allusion I had made to their local priest about giving the father odd-jobs around the church had to be taken out as it would have jeopardized his petition and, if followed up, also made trouble for the church. I did not reproduce verbatim what they told me; besides, the mother was almost silent from low spirits and worry. I was not setting out to capture an oral history like John Washington's powerful book about migrants from Latin America. Instead, I took imaginative liberties and recounted the couple meeting and falling in love during Mass as if it were a scene in a novel.

Their wretchedness made me angry, indignant and very sad. What a waste. Why subject this young, capable family to this daily vacuum, to the misery of empty days, and to the persistent fear of the knock at the door, deportation and even separation, as the father's repeated detentions took him away from the children and their mother? Why blunt their energy and reject their talents?

Happily, this story has turned out well: the family were granted leave to remain in 2019, after eight anxious years. As I write, the little girls are thirteen and eleven and have known only England, the country where they were born.

Refugee Tales is a closely focused, persevering pressure group and was successfully winning round many MPs to support its aim of abolishing indefinite detention when Brexit swept such progress aside, and the Conservative government, under two home secretaries whose parents had been welcomed as refugees, struggled to implement their exclusionary policy.

Some excellent and much-loved writers have written a 'Tale' for the campaign – Kamila Shamsie, Neel Mukherjee, Ali Smith. The writers who contribute to the later collections are now mostly formerly displaced individuals themselves who have published accounts of their experiences in a variety of literary forms, as plays, poems, novels and memoir. Testimony is the form of narrative favoured by readers and publishers, for good reason. The stories collected in *A Country of Refuge* (2016) edited by Lucy Popescu and in *The Displaced* (2018) edited by Viet

Thanh Nguyen, to give only a few examples from a rich range, bring the sanctuary seeker alive before us as a person; they provide invaluable insider knowledge of the seekers' hardships, but also reveal their unimaginable feats of tenacity and courage; they stir us with their closeness to loss and tragedy. They also wake us up to our own good fortune, as Aristotle remarked about tragedy. 'There but for the grace of God go I . . .' is a strong catalyst to empathy, and empathy deepens the sense of outrage and urgency and helps prevent worse breaches of common humanity, not to mention the occasions when the UN Refugee Charter and the law of the sea are overlooked.

However, calling on imagination to communicate another's experiences sets its own pitfalls. Writing the 'Refugee Tale', for example, stirred some anxiety in my mind – mild but still awkward – that taking someone's story and writing it under my name wasn't right. Other contributors shared this uneasiness about ghostwriting, adopting the subjects' voices and ventriloquizing their story. The 'Tale', told in the first person, acted to position the subject as a person rather than a nameless nobody in no man's land – this was positive. By making their voice heard, by passing on their story, they achieved definition as individuals. Recognition is crucial to visibility and, one hopes, agency. In resistance to the cleared ground of no man's land, someone becomes present, clad in a story that acts as individualizing and protective – or that is the hope and the intention. The stories bring news of what is going on to the public and to readers' consciousness and are aimed at raising awareness of an ongoing illegal practice in British society – the disappearing of many into a no man's land, according to the workings of an inaccessible and unreported and largely unexamined system of incarceration; many detainees have not been formally charged with any crime – because they have not committed one (that is, until 2024, when attempting to enter the UK by irregular means – small boats – was declared a crime).

But to ghost the story under their real names, would that be better? My solution was to invent characters who spoke to me about the family – in effect, to slant what I had learned by visiting them and trying to listen to their ordeal without prying or increasing their worries, through the frame of a made-up set of people who knew them. This approach resembles, in a minor way, the creation of a drama like

*The Jungle*, which grew out of the Good Chance Theatre's work in the refugee camp in Calais. The two founders, the playwrights Joe Murphy and Joe Robertson, shaped the drama from numerous personal stories, and it was staged as an 'immersive' experience, with the audience seated in the Afghan café, as if in the camp itself – we became participants rather than spectators (though needless to say uncomfortably aware of our own good fortune in having a home to go back to).

'The Jungle' was the nickname – and example of ironic self-labelling – given by the inhabitants to the sprawling camp near the French coast where hundreds of migrants were living in provisional shelters. The play dramatizes with compassion and sharp humour their attempts again and again to jump on to a lorry crossing the Channel, the failures and fatalities that met their struggle, and the eventual razing of the camp by the French police. The play was a worldwide success and raised money. Filled with vigorous portraits, sparkling high spirits, bravura music and intense, moving accounts of personal stories, it gives the arrivants a place and a role that transcends propaganda images of the pitiful victim or cynical criminal. *The Jungle* brought them before us as distinctive individuals.

The characters were dramatic composites, and one little girl, a Syrian called Amal (which means hope), who figures in the play as the subject of a harrowing tale, sprang from the confines of the Jungle and took on an independent life as a gigantic puppet (12 foot high), very grave of feature, an old child who has seen much. She was carried in procession across sixteen countries, as far south as Australia and as far north as Trondheim, with events in 160 towns, on what was effectively a secular pilgrimage to raise awareness of refugees and especially refugee children.

With regard to people on the move, stories are key to their success as asylum seekers. These accounts resemble, in character and function, the pardon tales that in the past in France, for example, condemned criminals were permitted to write to the king to sue for grace. Only the author of the most dramatic and persuasive stories, the historian Natalie Zemon Davis shows, would succeed in capturing the ruler's attention and receiving amnesty. The way the story was told weighed more than the content; the more heartfelt, the stronger the chances of success. As the philosopher Bernard Williams argues in his book *Truth and Truthfulness*, convincing the listener of one's sincerity and consequently authenticity mattered more than giving an accurate report. In the seventeenth century, the subject seeking pardon told his or her story once, in the form of an epistle to the powers above; a refugee today must tell it again and again, and never deviate from the circumstances as given – from the first moment. The story can become a mark of identity that's a yoke, an insurmountable border in itself: you must not change your story.

The pardon tale has counterparts that have even greater currency in contemporary culture: the slave narrative, the psychological confession shaped by trauma, and the witness statement as presented to the Truth and Reconciliation Commission in South Africa. Acts of testimony, such as Mary Prince's blazing protest (1831) and Kate Drumgoold's *A Slave Girl's Story* (1891), brings to our ears across the years the singular and powerful voice of an individual, remembering what happened to her. Her experiences, like more famous earlier accounts such as Olaudah Equiano's (1789), are overwhelming documents of historical witness; they are narratives in which sincerity and authenticity are of paramount importance. They strike us as true; they speak truth, they tell things as they are, and it is crucial that they do so.

Contemporary examples of pardon tales or abolition memoirs are often restrained and controlled, and all the more devastating because their subjects have been through so much horror – and survived to tell the tale and warn us all not to let it go on, not to let it happen again. The reader feels awed by the life force that sustained them through their ordeals, by the dignity a human being can hold on to when undergoing unimaginable degradation. Many are outstanding acts of witness, witness as literature. A personal story, as told for example by the anthropologist Shahram Khosravi in his book *'Illegal' Traveller: An Auto-Ethnography of Borders* (2010), turns a harrowing chronicle of prolonged struggle and suffering into an argument for urgent rethinking of the human costs of displacement and the political response to the predicament of millions of people. An Iranian now settled in Sweden and teaching at the University of Stockholm, Khosravi turns his attention to the aftermath of migration, of deportation and of settlement. The Palestinian poet Yousif M. Qasmiyeh was born and grew up in Baddawi, one of the longest-established refugee camps for Palestinians in Lebanon; scenes from his childhood and adolescence offer rare, personal scenes, often piercingly tender, evoking the bonds of family and neighbourhood. Behrouz Boochani, the Kurdish-Iranian journalist who was held on Manus Island in Papua New Guinea for over six years at the orders of the Australian government, makes his case with blazing power in *No Friend But the Mountains*. The book was written on WhatsApp, message by message, text by text, fragment by fragment, clandestinely sent to a friend, Omid Tofighian, who then translated Boochani's words from Farsi (Persian) into English. The eventual book issues a lacerating indictment of Australia's policy towards asylum seekers: detaining them offshore, in effect concentrating them, indefinitely in utterly deplorable conditions. His lament is lit up by incisive analysis; it stands comparison with Primo Levi's memoir of Auschwitz, *If This Is a Man*, because Boochani relates how the structure of such a camp divides inmates against one another, encouraging them to dominate and coerce one another, just as Levi recalls how the arrangements of the *Lager* stoked tensions between the incarcerated. 'Oppression is not random but purposeful,' writes Boochani, 'designed to isolate and create friction amongst prisoners, leading to despair and broken spirits.' He compares its structure to a 'a Kyriarchial system', a term from feminist theological theory for a structure of oppression that is not hierarchical but intersectional.

All these accounts, and perhaps many more I have not come across, convey the deep severance from home that sanctuary seekers feel, even when their suit has been successful. The aftermath of migration may bring peace and security, but it does not ensure joy. The loss of home sounds keenly, an existential and indelible presence.

This form of first-person narrative, directly truth-telling, filled with a quality of raw witness, can help bring about shifts in public opinion. The sincere communication of lived sufferings has no equal in rhetorical power, partly because the experience of the narrator cancels the listener's or reader's instinctive mistrust of rhetoric. Precisely because of this, it offers the rest of us a literary mode of persuasion that is pre-eminent. But not everyone has such a story to tell. And not everyone can tell it well. Besides, who is permitted to tell it? Sharp questions about entitlement and appropriation are raised when the story is about someone's suffering. Boochani's experiences are of such an extremity that nobody else could have spoken of them in the first person.

The literature of witness, the relaying of lived experience, communicates the presence of an individual in words over time, while a visual portrait or self-portrait, taken from life, affirms your existence in the here and now. In both media, the subject is addressing the viewer and the artist in their own person from a moment when they were there. The Syrian Lebanese artist Mounira Al Solh has been portraying her fellow citizens and others from war-torn regions of the Middle East. She has called the series of drawings *I Strongly Believe in Our Right to Be Frivolous*, after a remark made by the poet Mahmoud Darwish. She approaches her sitters in graphic styles that vary in response to their personal circumstances, and she annotates the ruled, yellow legal-pad paper she uses with quotes from their conversation and life stories. Graphic, hand-drawn and written testimony of this special order makes the speaker/writer distinctive and visible. It resists the tendency, very pronounced in media reports on displaced people, of bundling everyone together in an undifferentiated mass. The photographs of 'huddled masses yearning to be free' in rubber dinghies or, after rescue, on the decks of Border Force launches or NGO vessels erases individuality and unwittingly, even when well intentioned, gives support to the dark visions of xenophobic politics, fears of 'swarms' and 'hordes'.

Many artists have likewise made visible the odysseys undertaken by border crossers young and old. Bouchra Khalili's maps were the first works of this kind I saw, in Paris: she asked arrivants to trace their routes from memory on a map while recounting the stages of their journey. In these videos we do not see their faces, only their hands, as we listen to their voices piecing together the tacking back and forth across the Sahel and the sea and many borders in Europe. Quiet and meditative, each piece is more eloquent than more dramatic renderings. The first-person voice here is almost neutral in its reassembling of the facts.

Testimony can be presented as memoir or autofiction and recast in poetry and novels as well as drama. Warsan Shire, who is Somali, was born in Kenya in 1988 and came to Britain as a toddler; she was appointed Young Poet Laureate in 2012. An especially poignant and now historic poem, 'Home' draws on her own uprooted infancy and then opens out into a magnificent anthem for the displaced everywhere:

you only leave home
when home won't let you stay.

And again, even more piercingly:

> you have to understand,
> that no one puts their children in a boat
> unless the water is safer than the land . . .

And yet again:

> i want to go home,
> but home is the mouth of a shark
> home is the barrel of the gun
> and no one would leave home
> unless home chased you to the shore . . .

The diva rock star Beyoncé was so passionately fired up by Shire's work that she adapted some of her fierce and feminist poems into lyrics on her album *Lemonade*. Shire now lives in Los Angeles, with her family, and has worked on a film, *Brave Girl Rising*, about young Somali women living in Dadaab, the vast camp in Kenya which is effectively a large Somali city.

The arrivants' testimonies play a crucial part in communicating their predicament, their individuality and their claims to justice and personhood, but they demarcate the self in ways that reflect how the human person is conceived in the host countries. Such modes of writing the self are commanding keen admiration in the form of autofiction. *I Love Dick* (1997) by Chris Kraus, *How Should a Person Be?* (2010) by Sheila Heti, the trilogy *Outline, Transit, Kudos*, by Rachel Cusk (2014–18), the novel *Crudo* (2018) by Olivia Laing and the six-volume autobiographical novel *My Struggle* (2009–13) by Karl Ove Knausgaard shelter under the generic term of fiction, but appeal to readers because they give a raw sense of lives as they have been lived; they are self-exposés, apparently disclosing hard truths about their subjects. Setting aside questions of solipsism or narcissism (though they are of interest, especially in owning up to abject states), these self-writers revel in the revelation of shame. Colin Burrow argues that Knausgaard's intensity of absorption in the everyday minutiae of his existence could be termed 'punitive realism' and that ultimately this obsessive tabulation of detail – to the point of tedium – is setting up a bulwark of truthfulness against cascades of fake news. 'In that respect,' writes Burrow with his customary acerbity, '*My Struggle* can be thought of as comfort food for the age of lies.'

Treating literature as a depositional space, where the subjects provide affidavits on their own stories, erects another kind of border, not a physical one in space, but a generic one that implicitly rules out imaginative projections into experiences that lie beyond lived circumstance. It treats stories as authentic only when they report what has happened from someone who was there. Yet Ben Lerner, reviewing Knausgaard, was unusual in concluding that *My Struggle* 'is a fictional farewell to literature'. The reader is led to accept that invention is tantamount to fraud and adopting an invented persona trespasses against others' rights to speak on their own behalf. (In the case of *I Love Dick*, Kraus set out to manufacture her lived material, which makes the avoidance of appropriation moot; the same goes for Knausgaard, since even his persona involves relations with others who must be aware they might become his material.)

Contemporary autofiction thus embodies a double anxiety: in an age that no longer relies on an underpinning of transcendental beliefs, the anxiety that I might disappear if the eventful (and less than eventful) reality of my feelings and memories is not captured and fixed on the page and, secondly, the anxiety that other people's minds – a nagging philosophical conundrum – lie behind the barbed wire of permitted exploration. The first anxiety recalls magical inscriptions which attempt to cover every eventuality in order to prevent something happening, in this case to keep the speaking/writing subject present – and alive. The second anxiety reminds us how important acts of imaginative storymaking are in exploring the interconnectedness of cultures and cross-correspondences across languages and epochs.

'The autobiographer writes', comments John Sturrock,

> in order to be received whole by those who read him; and the Common Reader at least reads autobiography in order to grasp the author as a whole – as if the reader's own integrity were being played back at him by the text. This wholeness may very well be fantasmal, and those theorists be right who argue that by its very nature a text denies rather than authenticates any notion of the writer as an integral being; but it

is a fantasm shared by autobiographers and readers alike and a crucial if unstated clause in the hypothetical 'contract' that binds them. To behave as if it were of no account is to ignore the real conditions under which autobiography has always so far been written and received.

In other words, Knausgaard, Kraus, Cusk and Heti, who even in some cases give their own names to the protagonists of their fictions, break with this tacit understanding that an autobiography presents a different mode of speech from a novel and choose to place their hybrid autofiction under the sign of personal truthful self-disclosure. The move evinces a psychological urgency to speak to the reader as to an intimate confidant, claim the territory of oneself as a story unfolding in time and forge personal existence in words, through the constitution of the I or self in language. As Sturrock goes on, 'The fortunes of autobiography are tied to the fortunes of the philosophies and ideologies of individualism that first helped it into existence and which have long sustained it in the West, and these show no signs of weakening.'

The mode of autofiction practised so successfully today takes off from this ground of traditional individualism and intensifies it. But the self in relation to the world in language could take a different route out of the bewilderment well put in the title of Heti's novel, *How Should a Person Be?*

Affirmation of individual uniqueness can also tend to isolation, and in the current global polity an acute form of alienation has brought about a new twist in the relation between self and world: as the digital databases distinguish each of us by our preferences and habits and increasingly pinpoint our desires to buy this or do that, our singularity becomes more and more precisely marked, as in DNA coding. But this individuality means only that we are atoms spinning in a mercantile vortex designed to subjugate us to its appetite. The relationship between identity and surveillance has governed the state's control of its citizens, and archival databanks, fingerprinting, iris recognition keep growing in order to triage desirables from undesirables (among whom migrants are increasingly relegated).

To my mind, certain political measures applied to the treatment of migrants conform to this view of truth-telling individualism, which assumes that nothing can be represented that has not happened to the speakers/writers, that the accounts must remain consistent and, by further implication, that only what lies within the ambit of their identity and circumstances should be considered legitimate material for them to utter.

Two alternative responses have been developing strongly to take possession of no man's land, to reactivate it and defy abandonment and negation. They both involve, paradoxically, resisting the dominion of the I. The first is to oppose the internet's effects of consumer identification by forming alternative collectives, assembling together, as in such projects as Refugee Tales: their communal acts of walking form a counter-assembly to the confinement of the detainees' fate. The second follows: to multiply and combine voices and develop a we-narrative, along the lines of the Greek chorus speaking together.

Poetry uses the first person with a freedom denied to prose: nobody challenges the authenticity of a lyric persona if the author's skill persuades us that they are being emotionally sincere. And in poetry, by contrast with prose, truthful utterance is not identical to factual accuracy. Biographers may later probe the facts and expose the poet as a dissembler and a hypocrite, but generally speaking readers accept the performance of sincerity from poets and do not demand a documentary warranty that they are telling the truth about what happened and how. Attitudes to the 'I' in a poem differ markedly from our expectations of a memoirist or a witness in court.

Theatre occupies a position between these two stances: a play such as *The Jungle* does not usually postulate a narrator or take a narrative position as such; the spectators are not usually asked to see the action from one particular protagonist's point of view: Macbeth, Hamlet are the focus of our attention and we enter Hamlet's horror and anguish when his father's ghost appears to him and his companions. We understand Macbeth's crisis when Banquo's ghost appears, but we also witness the scene through the eyes of others, on the battlements and at the banqueting table. (There are however plays which dramatize first-person works of fiction and retain that viewpoint in a running commentary, for example in *Jane Eyre* as adapted by Polly Teale.) When testimony is transposed on to the stage or dramatized for the screen, the audience accepts the necessity of technique, artifice, composition, excision and, to some extent, invention. In short, licence to embroider and shape the material.

Witnessing and confession are only varieties of utterance in the vast horizon of literary expression. Looking for further ways of making sanctuary, of taking up occupation of no man's land and making it home (if at all possible). Another way of thinking about stories would entail not replacing or abandoning witnesses, but supplementing it.

Several objections arise to placing the emphasis on testimony and valuing it only for its accuracy. For one thing, this approach overlooks the way memory works, its contingencies and fragmentation. Psychoanalysis and psychotherapies also dig into what happened in the past to understand an individual in the present and provide for a better future. However, the truthfulness of the analysand's self-disclosure is not taken to be objective nor a proof of their integrity. The process generally allows the analysand the benefit of the doubt: truth is what appears to be true to the one who remembers and revisits the event. In this respect, therapeutic approaches allow the subject to be unreliable.

This understanding does not extend to arrivants or refugees or migrants anywhere. And this constraint, which is understandable within the context of the law, limits the expressiveness of the asylum seeker. Legal entry requirements rely on forms of narrative, truth-telling in the first person; these expectations shape the stories they tell. Furthermore, the law demands that sanctuary seekers do not change their story – a discrepancy, a retraction, a new detail can cost someone their freedom of movement and their claim. The authorities are on the watch for fraud (the artist Lawrence Abu Hamdan was employed by the immigration authorities in the UK to listen to the recorded depositions of Syrian asylum seekers and ascertain from their Arabic, their accents and their particular *fusha* (vernacular) whether they were telling the truth about where they came from).

However, in relation to the wellbeing of the individuals caught up in the violence that has driven them out, these forms of narrative restrict the human spirit to a single genre of narrative; they narrow the potential for flourishing through imaginative engagement with the world. I remember asking a group of young men and women who had recently arrived in Sicily to tell a story, any story that they could remember that they had been told, a fable or legend, or that they might like to make up, and one of them looked at me in astonishment and exclaimed, 'You mean it doesn't have to be true?'

The imagination is forbidden territory, or so this young man had understood in the course of his travels so far. Yet the literature of imagination makes space for freedom of movement, to dwell in fantastic, speculative, hypothetical, irrealis territory.

Memories do not repeat accurately; there has been enough research into consciousness to establish that the human mind retains the memory of a memory, the story as it was last told by the one who remembers or someone else, rather than the original experience itself. We work eerily like computer memory, one instantiation of a document floating on top of another. Yet refugees are asked to repeat their story verbatim, and they struggle to meet the terms of admission as they do so. This procedure boxes them into a chronicle of abjection and closes down the possibility of an alternative ground to selfhood. Witness statement, confession, traumatic memory all depend on the subject's own lived experience, not on dreamed or imagined possibilities. Yet, both for the host communities where the displaced people arrive and for the arrivants themselves, a space for other ways of telling the story could inaugurate and mend and invigorate relations between them. But fantasy is relegated, intrinsically disadvantaged, and the continual interplay between memory and imagination denied. The single-subject narrative – what the Dutch call the ego-document – is in itself restrictive and a conventional form: most tellers of these tales necessarily present themselves as integers, obeying the tradition of the genre, which requires them to present themselves as such, rather than as kindred spirits in a group.

The welcome given in the UK and other countries to Ukrainian refugees from the war in their country, mostly women and children, shows how the law could be applied differently, and how the system can adapt and change and foster reciprocal exchanges between hosts and guests, arrivants and citizens.

Powerful and moving as first-hand testimony and individual tales are, they do not attempt to transfigure *Terra nullius* fundamentally, populate it with imagined and imaginable characters and their stories, to be shared by everyone who hears it. The contract between writer and reader in the cases of witness statements doesn't permit a speaking subject adopting an invented persona. Nor does it value received, traditional materials; and this can add to another loss – the loss of a shared culture, both from the past place of belonging and in the new places of arrival.

These effects of the dominance of testimony include restrictions which can be mapped on to a growing imposition of limits and borders, of policed frontiers. If we deny fluidity and freedom to a person's narrative voice, and ordain that it should match the biographical conditions and the real-life events of the writer, do we not, by extension, set up a wall around the displaced person who wants to make a new life in a new place, to refashion himself or herself? An arrivant, refugee, sanctuary seeker or migrant does not want to be limited by that label any more than I want to remain content with – and circumscribed by – the hand destiny dealt me as a woman of a certain class.

Yet the issue of appropriation remains live: can a writer use someone else's material – their life itself – even in a just cause? The poet and novelist Kei Miller wrote a notorious polemic against white writers voicing black characters. 'This man decides to take it on himself', he wrote, 'to tell the white woman that she is not one of us, that she don't speak for us or even to us.' The target may have been specific (she remained unnamed), but the general argument was plain: no trespassing. No entry. For literature is also a territory with borders, and who owns it, may occupy it, be included or excluded, are sharp questions. More recently, however, Miller conceded that the key is not whose material it is, but the respect shown it, and that a piece of writing – fact or fiction – needs to be embarked on not for commercial or exploitative reasons and must be carried out in language that blesses rather than curses. As Toni Morrison's first-person narrator wishes in her 1992 novel *Jazz*: 'I want to dream a nice dream for him, and another of him . . . I want to be the language that wishes him well, speaks his name, wakes him when his eyes need to be open.'

Looking at the question of appropriation in the larger context of the new walls and borders, it is possible to argue that writers trying to express what the detainees had been through were ourselves dissolving the boundaries on our own personhood and opening ourselves to another's consciousness, in a classic mode of storytelling. The nowhere man or woman was moving to centre stage and commanding us to listen and to identify, to unite with them. Witness literature can thus be viewed from yet another angle, as a move towards a shared humanitarian ethic, in Paul Gilroy's phrase, a collective resistance: 'Paranoid, parochial hostility to humanism and indeed to humanity, resonates most loudly behind fortified campus walls where the hip imperatives of identity politics: docile nihilism, resignation and complacent ethnic absolutism, reign unchallenged while the seductions of the Alt-right – to which they are kin – present a growing danger.' He expands on an ethics of mutuality, which can be reflected in what is written. 'The humanizing possibilities of conviviality and care', he writes, were shown in the aftermath of the fire in Grenfell Tower in London in 2017. 'In that instance, the survivors' emphasis on the human dimensions of their vulnerability to the flames was both telling and consistent. Stories of sympathy and solidarity were circulated against the effects of slow violence and official indifference. The language of humanity was central to the survivors' descriptions of their trauma and in the terms of the appeal that they made to the world – not to raise money, but in pursuit of attention or, as they put it, seeking clarity (based on commonality and heteropathic identification) rather than charity.'

In relation to such stories, we readers and spectators need to stay alert to the ambiguities of pity, which can make us feel good, suffering by proxy. Pity can imply superiority, too, and the recipient may feel a loss of self-respect at being pitied. I don't want to belittle the achievements of refugees and their supporters who campaign for reform by bringing into the public sphere the wasteland we have made of human rights and the right to asylum. While those who are caught in the no man's land of an asylum claim speak urgently and eloquently to those of us who have a fixed abode, citizenship and other forms of security, the emphasis on the individual belongs to a certain concept of the person, one that keeps personal freedom distinct from a vision of society as an ecosystem of mutually assured freedoms.

Amid a growing sense that we belong to an ecosystem, like mushrooms and trees, mutually interdependent and interconnected, there is a corresponding move away from the subjective 'I' towards a collective 'We'. Metaphors of melding and merging are beginning to act in some writings as a counterweight to the pressure of the self: from this perspective, no man's land may become a refuge where outcasts and fugitives can form a fellowship, a citizenry.

Svetlana Alexievich, the Belorussian journalist and chronicler (winner of the Nobel Prize in 2015), has undertaken immersive portraits of her countrymen and women by interviewing hundreds of her compatriots. The results, in books such as *Second-Hand Time* and *Chernobyl Prayer*, form a sequence of magnificent tragic chorales in which everyone is seen as part of an epic history (the French translation of the latter is *La Supplication*, which very eloquently links its elegy for the people of Chernobyl with the tradition of sanctuary seekers or suppliants).

In these books, her own first person is effaced; with the exception of minimal biographic introductions to each subject she has recorded, she absents herself from the flow of conversations, laments and memories she orchestrates. These are individual witness statements, across a sweep of characters and viewpoints and time; but, sounding together in a contemporary Greek tragic chorus, they fashion something larger, powerfully emotional – the prism flashing and flickering and leaving entry points like portals for the reader/audience to differ, agree, sympathize, recoil.

The American fiction writer George Saunders has long been concerned with the question of being human in the contemporary world of media and simulacra – from theme parks to virtual reality. His Booker Prize-winning novel *Lincoln in the Bardo* (2017) takes place in an eschatological interzone, a no man's land between life and death in the Buddhist scheme of last things in which the Bardo is limbo, teeming with the dead. President Lincoln's young son has just arrived in this cemetery in Washington, DC; the ghosts are all restless and chattering, awaiting the time when they will truly depart this world. The novel's tone is darkly, richly, naively comic, but his chorale of the undead communicates an acute sense of living in a state of transition, under the imminent threat of becoming utterly undone. Saunders's interest in digital hyperreality, evident in many short stories, is reprised here, where he explores metaphorically the half-life of media existence – the self as caught again and again on Facebook. The reader is given the proper names and the voices, diction, spelling are idiosyncratic for each character – often very wittily rendered. But the loss of vital signs in the post-mortem carnal body plunges all his characters into a dematerialized and undifferentiated state of personhood. The ghouls and spectres form a Greek chorus speaking in turn as they are each caught in a limbo waiting to be translated to heaven or hell.

'*Soumission totale à la realité*' (total submission to reality) is a phrase the writer Annie Ernaux has used about her method, and she has often written of her own experiences directly. However, in *The Years*, considered by many readers her most powerful book, which secured her the Nobel Prize in 2022, she drops the first-person singular for the first-person plural (*nous*, we) or adopts the gender neutral impersonal *on* (one) to present a chronicle cum elegy for her generation of women, their struggles and ideals – mostly failed or abandoned. *The Years* subordinates individual uniqueness to the possibility of collective memory. Luke Williams and Natasha Soobramanien, in their co-written novel *Diego Garcia*, about the forced displacement of the local Chagossian islanders in 1968–73, break conventional narrative focalization: they shift between first-person plural and third-person narrative to oscillate between different points of view and forge an innovatory 'we-narrative' that seductively enfolds the reader in the protagonists' consciousness.

The innovatory approaches of these writers to subjectivity sketch another mode of inhabiting place, by transvaluing the state of borderlessness and disappearance into a state of acknowledged, welcomed contiguity and even mergence into no man's land. *Outis*, the word for Nobody in Greek, becomes a significant player, a presence from another perspective, a connective link between isolated individuals. This dynamic inversion echoes many historic acts whereby negative labelling turns positively powerful.

Communality, conviviality – such conditions may seem mere decoration compared to the need for food and water, shelter, health, warmth, work and money. They are not luxuries but the necessary *ch'i* or breath of life for a person in a group or for society as a whole. D. W. Winnicott held that a baby needed – apart from those necessities as mentioned – to be *held in mind*, to have someone recognize their existence and keep them in mind. For the wellbeing of the hosts and the arrivants alike, conviviality is indispensable. Ways of growing that precious resource, immaterial though it may be, demand attention.

A connected stratagem arises from the resurgence of ritual, or secular acts of pilgrimage and assembly, and it returns us to no man's or no woman's land and the figure of Nobody. This mode of expression no longer grounds meaning in an individual voice and testimony to particular events and feelings particular to one person, but performs variations on the question: who is speaking?

This countervailing trend in contemporary writing thus passes beyond first-person subjectivity to return to much older way of occupying marginal territory – no man's or no woman's land – the we-speech of the Greek chorus in a tragedy such as Euripides' *The Trojan Women* or *Medea* or the you-speech of the exhortation, the lament, the blessing and the curse. In 2013, fifty Syrian women refugees in Jordan, who had never acted or been on stage before, transposed *The Trojan Women* into Arabic: *Queens of Syria* was performed on tour to widespread acclaim; a documentary film, directed by Yasmin Fedda in 2014, also drew enthusiastic audiences. The following year, the Italian playwright Roberto Cavosi adapted *The Persians*, Aeschylus' remarkable act of empathy with an enemy, and blended it with memories of Italy's horrific defeat in the First World War. In *I Persiani a Caporetto*, echoes of the Iraq war resonated laceratingly with the pleas of Darius' mother and the unfolding carnage.

The history of culture is filled with artefacts made by groups of people working together often from a theme, a tune, a symbol shared in common – from Homer's epics to Angkor Wat or Chartres cathedral, from a Kwakiutl masked dance ritual to a chamber ensemble or a jazz set. When the artist Kate Daudy was allowed to watch a heart transplant in progress on the operating table, she found in this ballet of nurses and doctors and their infinitely responsive actions to one another an eloquent metaphor for a society of collaboration and cooperation towards a common good.

Homeric visions of the afterlife, imitated closely by Virgil and then by Dante, evoke the numberless dead in another no man's land. The banks of the Styx form a liminal zone, where the departed crowd on the shore, holding out their arms to cross into the afterlife proper. They are not only numberless but featureless too, and insubstantial.

The poet and classicist Alice Oswald extends this sense of the fugitive contingency of each person by expressing herself as a writer through imagery of dissolution and erasure, merging into her subjects. Oswald's key verb for this form of metamorphosis is 'trans-shifting', a term she has taken from a small poem by Robert Herrick which she explores in 'The Art of Erosion', her first lecture as professor of poetry at Oxford in 2019. Dissolution is the theme, not a motif of anguish but a kind of salvation.

*Nobody*, a book-length poem, places the figure of the title at the centre of Oswald's rhapsodic evocation of the imagery of water in the *Odyssey*. When the Cyclops Polyphemus asks Odysseus who he is, he answers, 'Outis' (Nobody): it's riddling wordplay, born from his trickster nature, and cruel, for when the giant, blinded by Odysseus in his one eye, cries out to the gods that he has been cheated and violated, he can only shout, 'Nobody has done this to me!'. And so the gods turn away from him. In her poem Oswald mingles this sense of Nobody's paradoxical power with the epic's dominant imagery of water and the many marine beings – gods and goddesses, nymphs and monsters – who emerge from it and sink back into the waves. Her Nobody stands for all of us, and she hears the we-voice of this otherworldly throng, not in the Bardo, or on the banks of the Styx, but in the translucent wave and the spindrift – as she unfolds a lyrical narrative of dissolution into light and air and sea. The mood is ecstatic, and the ambition to disappear exhilarating. Her subject is Nobody and her chosen dynamic mode erasure.

In the original hardback, fragments of the poem floated across and down pages, between William Tillyer's watercolours, diffuse and splotchy as if painted in the rain, this surrender to abolition of contour accompanying the decentring and unnaming of the poet's self. Needless to say, Oswald's is a unique, marvellous voice and her negation of the autobiographical imperative highly original. But the whole burden of her song carries us into Nobody's land as a place of paradoxical reprieve, where nymphs and angels fuse with the elements. The movement is Ovidian – metamorphosis, the shedding of the mortal self and sublimation into a bird or a stream or a tree (she invokes Procne and Philomela). The performance piece she put on later, with music and images, lingers on the poem she explored in her lecture 'The Art of Erosion', where Herrick watches a fruit ripen from day to day, observing 'the colours steale into the Peare or Plum' and listening out for the soft sound of rain sliding into water. She writes, 'It is the merging melting sound of one transparency sliding into another, like two ghosts meeting in the underworld.' Then she asks the question, what would the sound of rain sliding softly into water sound like? – the very imperceptibility of such an event tuning her senses and ours as we listen. Without engaging directly with contemporary self-fashioning, Oswald radically undermines the premise that personhood must be achieved through acts of self-witnessing, self-naming and self-defining. Her vision of the self, trans-shifting through states of being, suspended like Nobody in the translucent wave, like light through a flask, may not appear connected to the pressing issue of border crossing and border crossers. Her poem invokes Homeric events but it is clearly not a narrative in the sense that autobiography or autofiction is – the stories it relates are mythic, elemental and nebulous, unanchored in the day to day. But this form of contemplation of being and belonging in the world eases the subject from the obligations of narcissistic realism and exact and stable identity definition. Such a concept of a person's interrelations with others, with us all, might lighten the burden of projecting a distinctive persona, and lessen the perceived threat of numberless strangers arriving on our shores.

When Colin Burrow identifies Knausgaard's assiduous attempts to pin down what happens to him as the ultimate refuge from the cascades of mendacious social media, he is diagnosing how the writer's defences have been wrongly set: he thinks he will be secured by his thousands of words, like a populist politician believing a wall will contain his people in their definitive and essential identity. Oswald implicitly counters this with a concept of inchoate reciprocity. Hers is a much less well-aired mode of taking ownership of no man's or no woman's land. As opposed to erecting barricades around identity, defining self with more and more data, Oswald's poetry sees each person in a process of fusion and merging and potential change, and this concept of the self corresponds to an understanding of habitat that refuses to put up borders between countries and fence in swathes of no man's land. Oswald embodies the act of living in words that matches rather than opposes the contingencies and rhythms of existence, the existential porousness of a person, and potential for transmutation. Her poet's voice is singular, exceptional and dazzling – individuality in creative acts mustn't be underestimated. Yet she is also committed to collective creativity and acts to revive the practice of communal making. Personal genius is not the only fountainhead of what we call culture; social interactivity can help, especially in times of dislocation and loss, to lay out common ground where incidentally another poet might rise and where in the meantime strangers may find a home.

Denise Riley, in a series of lectures on *The Voice of the Lyric* that she gave in Cambridge in 2024, develops a vision of quasi-anonymity and the impersonal personhood that opposes the current cult of the self and promotion of the Great I Am. Riley takes a different course from Oswald's self-abolition, one that is more fruitful regarding sanctuary as a possible social contract. She is feeling her way towards a more capacious, receptive and relational concept of the individual voice, not only where other persons are involved. We are all repositories of long legacies of sounds and images, bearer-beings of language (see Coda). She keeps her focus on poetry but what she says bears significantly on the broader tradition, on tales and songs, and chimes with the idea of sanctuary as a commonwealth of culture. She rejects definitions of lyric as subjective, confessional, soul-searching and self-exposing, and emphasizes instead the 'inhuman' aspects of the process, the autonomy of the voice that the poet produces; in her vision, poets act like receivers finely tuned to the culture around, which reach back in time far beyond their birth and are laid down in speech patterns, image clusters, sound and rhythm. Nursery rhymes, lullabies, patter and ditties move to these signifying waves and pass through our ears to our minds and onwards and outwards to the acoustic unconscious where narratives are stored and then spring up again.

# 8

# The Map Is Not the Territory

> Please help us, we are lost.
> We can't find the way anymore.
> Bertolt Brecht

The philosopher Alfred Korzybski coined a crisp and pungent phrase: 'The map is not the territory.' He was talking in terms of neurolinguistics and pointing out how our perceptions and beliefs as individuals and members of a society, gathered over time, form reality: they constitute the territory as it is experienced, whatever its actual reality. But this mode of reattaching oneself to a place that is not home but must become one, does not necessarily depend on transmitting an existing story – nor on inheriting one through historical or geographical bonds. It can evolve through mutual exchanges and invention: it can dream and speculate and comment and . . . even laugh.

A map includes names, and those names are depth charges of knowledge. Stories and memories are sunk into their matter: history has infused and shaped them, often going far back in time, but much has been forgotten or overlooked and processes of invention and imagination have also imprinted the map. Rather than seeing maps as palimpsests of historical events, a view which assumes vertical sequencing and even progress and evolution, adopting a different perspective – horizontal, lateral, spatial – better reflects the huge geographical dislocations that are taking place in our time. The place where you find yourself on the map matters – the place of your birth, perhaps, or the place you have arrived; these are the places where you belong or hope to belong. Remapping combines bearing witness (telling) with orienting yourself in the world (dwelling), as Bouchra Khalili shows, with memorable eloquence and sensitivity, in her 2016 video installation (see p. 227).

'More delicate than the historians' are the mapmakers' colours,' writes Elizabeth Bishop, but she was not perhaps altogether right. Mapmaking looks much less delicate now, and nowhere more so than in the regions which the majority of refugees are fleeing, Africa, the eastern Mediterranean and Central Asia; successive political and military arrangements have inscribed new borders and nations on the Middle East, from the Sykes–Picot Agreement of 1916 to the following year's Balfour Declaration and, more recently, the walls and settlements that the regime in Israel has built in Palestine. Aerial photographs taken by Fazal Sheikh in the Negev desert reveal, imprinted on the rocks and in the sand, the ghostly outlines of Bedouin encampments, cemeteries and other constructions, which have been taken over by official Israeli agricultural development and settlements, or otherwise obliterated. The Palestinian artist Jumana Emil Abboud has mapped the sites of springs and wells, many of them now choked and abandoned; her subjective, archaeological mappings give personal urgency to similar processes of erasure. Nothing is more crucial to survival than access to water; nothing gives greater power than controlling its distribution and its quality.

Maps are also ways of forging history when all around us in the twenty-first century the aftershocks of colonial mapping in Africa and the Middle East, are destabilizing the inhabitants. Brian Friel's play *Translations* dramatizes the renaming of Irish place names by the British military who were creating, in 1825–41, the maps of the Ordnance Survey; his drama has become a classic investigation – and indictment – of colonial processes more broadly, and has rightly been revived and revisited by different theatre companies. More recently, Kei Miller, who was born in Jamaica, returned to the topic in a sustained elegy-cum-essay, 'Sometimes I consider the names of places'. He then meditates in a spirit of injury and regret on the deceitfulness of established terms and lost words and, with their loss, lost peoples:

> Sometimes I consider the names of places: the West Indies. Or said another way: Western India

as if India was not enough.

And isn't it incredible that such a name should stick despite all geographic proof to the contrary. And maybe this is what place is – a distorted way of seeing, an insufficient imagining.

Cristobal, como se dice 'Taino' en español? Indio

Cristobal, como se dice 'Carib' en español? Indio

Cristobal, como se dice 'Guanahatabey' en español? Indio

What did it matter, our own names?

We are insufficiently imagined people from an insufficiently imagined place.

Miller then moves on to thinking on nowhere places:

So what will we call the thing between places?

No man's land becomes here an interzone where he – and others like him – might belong and become sufficiently imagined.

Bishop's and Miller's poems catch the potential of cartography for recovery and redress, for renewed, more sufficient, imaginative, sensitive draughtsmanship – for a revisioning of narrative memory, one that responds to the past but acts proleptically to dream of an alternative reality to come.

Historical projections and dreams – some deeply rooted in cultural memory, others more recent, also inform ancient maps: as invoked earlier, paramount examples would be the site of Troy, and the scenes of Jesus' sufferings and death and resurrection in Jerusalem, the Temple and the Via Crucis, or the Way of the Cross that he took to Calvary and that is followed by thousands of pilgrims every year. These most sacred sites are presented as if they are matters of historical record, though they are at best conjectures, the temporalities all jumbled, the evidence established by tradition and highly contested. Tradition – and hope – have turned them into history.

In the large family of imaginary maps, the most ancient of all – and in some ways the most naturalized and hence overlooked examples – represent the constellations as narratives. The connections drawn between the stars are filled with myths of gods and heroes, animals and monsters: the twelve signs of the Zodiac, Venus the Morning Star, the Hair of Berenice, Orion the Hunter, the Great Bear and the Little Bear are named by the Babylonians, Greeks, Romans and Arabs; the skies of Africa, Asia, and Australasia inspired different stories – the Milky Way is a dragon to the Chinese, a drift of sparks from a bonfire kicked by a dancing girl to the Khoisan people of Africa, a river flowing with fish to the First Nations of Australia, a stream of spilt corn to the Cherokee. The long cultural hegemony of Europe has eclipsed these narratives.

Star maps still conserve the most ancient dream scripts in human culture, and we don't question them at all – though the proximity of one star to another is an illusion of parallax from our vantage point on earth, and the constellations themselves are arbitrary impositions of pattern on random scatterings. (Newly discovered stars or phenomena

Finding patterns, perceiving stories: this star map of the night sky is filled with myths and was read for the foreknowledge it holds. Albrecht Dürer (1515).

are occasionally named after a luminary, but mostly identified by lustreless numbers.)

Imaginary maps are often drawn up by extrapolating from a landscape or townscape, which a writer or other artist — a composer, a painter — loves and inhabits, and recasts in their work, transfiguring it for better or worse, according to the precepts of fiction and the workings of their own mind and memory: Murasaki Shikibu's Kyoto in *The Tale of Genji*, Marcel Proust's Combray and Balbec, Thomas Hardy's Wessex. What has been less remarked on, however, is the way imaginary landscapes and townscapes map back on to real neighbourhoods: how Verona has become the place where Romeo and Juliet lived and loved and their families feuded, how Hardy's topography has returned and reconfigured Dorset and its environs. Some places have even been renamed after their fictional manifestations (Proust's country town has been renamed Illiers-Combray). These identifications add interest to a place for visitors, they sharpen their focus and make aspects appear: *Alice's Adventures in Wonderland* follows stations in the city of Oxford where the historical Alice (Liddell) lived, where the Revd Charles Dodgson took her for a boat ride on the river and, as Lewis Carroll, wrote down the stories of that golden afternoon for her. Further layers of narrative have been overlaid in Oxford on to Wonderland and coexist palimpsestically: Philip Pullman's *His Dark Materials* and J. K. Rowling's Harry Potter series (because the latter were partly filmed there) can both now be traced in the town's topography. Many deplore these confected effects of successful books, finding these mappings the product of a banal, theme-park mentality, fake news for the tourist trade. But I am not so leery of it: places are changed by the writings about them, and these infusions of story enrich their meaningfulness. Frequently, an imaginary site will take such hold of people's minds that they transpose it somewhere else and reproduce it often in multiple locations. Among imaginary mappings are acts of translation of one place to another. The child authors Katharine Hull and Pamela Whitlock, when they wrote *The Far Distant Oxus* (1937), palimpsestically superimposed their dream of Persia on to the familiar layout of Exmoor where they rode their ponies and forded streams, all of this transfigured into a faraway exotic land. There also exist many examples of straightforwardly imaginary maps: the delicately drawn charts of fantasy worlds, of Lilliput and Laputa et al. in *Gulliver's Travels*, the pirate's chart in *Treasure Island*, the Shire in Tolkien's *The Lord of the Rings*, and many others, and not only in books for children or in fantasy works for adults.

An imaginary homeland returns in contemporary literatures in English, not in the form of a lost birthplace or familiar house, but in a mental object, a site of reflection and metaphor. Writers in a variety of media are having recourse to an imaginary map which itself comes from a work of literature, not from direct experience. The Tuareg-Libyan writer Ibrahim al-Koni has called this a 'vagabond homeland' and for a nomad in exile like himself it can be found in fictive moorings.

Troy, the city that figures, as we have seen, in Greek epic and tragedy (Homer, Euripides) and in Latin poetry, especially the *Aeneid* and the *Metamorphoses* of Ovid, offers such a compass bearing. Am I simply peddling that old chestnut that classical humanism lives? I don't think so. Our contemporary war zones lie so geographically close to the scene of the Trojan war and its long aftermath that contemporary acts of memory and imagination are not superimposing a different set of coordinates on to the map but revisiting the same physical territory and remapping it. Narrating the fall of Troy has become a way of telling the story of today's wars. A reading list could include David Malouf's *Ransom*, a novel published in 2010, in which the Lebanese-Australian author movingly retells the scene from the end of the *Iliad* when Priam abases himself before Achilles to plead to be given the body of his son Hector, which the Greek hero has horribly violated after killing him. Highly wrought responses to the epics would also include the novel cum prose-poem *Achilles* by Elizabeth Cook (2003) and the prize-winning *The Lost Books of the Odyssey* by Zachary Mason, a dazzling, Calvinoesque sequence of revisioned episodes from the whole cycle of the Trojan war. These works are each of them unusual and remarkable in their own way, but they all slant their perceptions through the shared Matter of Troy and revisit the long-ago siege in Asia Minor in order to communicate thoughts about appalling violence and conflict we are engaged in now. That territory of Troy lies far off in time, yet that remote place of Bronze Age civilization has become a vivid site of recent and current hostilities: the island of Lesbos, where thousands of refugees from the Middle East are still being held, lies offshore within view of the heights of Pergamon.

The most potent example of this approach to thinking about home through a watermarked page, as it were, is Alice Oswald's *Memorial* (2012). It is a book-length poem to which she adds a subtitle – *An Excavation of the* Iliad – drawing attention to her work of exhuming pieces of the poem and reassembling them in a different shape and sequence. By shuffling the constituent elements of Homer's epic, she claims she has distinguished three different layers, as if analysing an archaeological tel. She has separated out from the narrative: first, a stratum which consists of a roll call of the dead, secondly, closely associated with the first, a threnody, in which the poem, in the manner of professional mourners of antiquity, remembers the ways the heroes died, and thirdly, a seam of pastoral poetry that gives the epic its famous, extended lyrical similes, inspired by scenes of domestic and daily existence both of people and of animals. She parts the strands and sets them out distinctively on the pages of her book: first the list of the fallen, by name. This litany unfolds over many more pages than one could imagine possible, and through the paper on which it is printed the reader can glimpse the phantom traces of those who have gone before and those who are to come. The mourning songs support this tally, filleting from the body of the poem the gory particulars that Homer gives for each death (the javelin through the cheek, the spear in the groin). The 'Homeric similes', scattered between these gruesome, ghastly reports of butchery, are transformed into flying illuminations. Each of them echoes lines from the *Iliad* that will return in Virgil's *Aeneid*, but they have been severed, for the most part, from their referents and allowed to stand independently, plangent passages of pastoral:

> Like a wind-murmur
> Begins a rumour of waves
> One long note getting louder
> The water breathes a deep sigh
> Like a land-ripple
> When the west wind runs through a field
> Wishing and searching
> Nothing to be found
> The corn-stalks shake their green heads

The similes' role as an oblique chorale gains strength from repetition: each of the stanzas beginning 'Like a . . .' is often repeated exactly. The pared-down simplicity gives the Homeric imagery an illuminist character, closer to the poetry of Eugenio Montale or Giuseppe Ungaretti than to classical epic's dramatic rhetoric. But the emotive use of *da capo*, avoided by those Italian precursors, produces an effect of uncertainty, as if summoning the healing vision only once cannot do enough, while saying it twice only draws attention to the insufficiency, ultimately, of lament.

Alice Oswald in person performs the long poem from memory and she underlines, in her preface, how she wants to place herself in the line of oral poets reaching back into antiquity, as the breath, in its living presence and warmth, carries more of a personal charge than the silent page. As mentioned before, the voice can reknit broken threads in the fabric and help coordinate one's place in the world, offering the possibility of finding others to whom one can reach out in like-mindedness.

Inventing history, supplying memories, identifying across boundaries of time, culture, geography, and staving off loneliness by planting signs to create mental companions – such an approach flouts every principle of authenticity. These stratagems appear to replace evidence with fictions. But if the material itself declares itself to be fiction, then the compact between the work and its receivers is clear. Troy becomes a secondary world, a place as imaginary as Fairyland, Erewhon, Utopia or Narnia. Literature – especially imaginative works of myth, legend, fairy tale and fable – reconfigures territory according to alternative measurements, names and pathways. It can map geographies of home on to surroundings that are not home: books and the stories they tell can house us, place us in the world when we are 'lost in place', when we are out of place.

Neighbourhoods share territory and those territories are saturated in stories – some of them historical and perhaps veridical and trustworthy, many of them legendary and fanciful. The work of a historian contributes fundamentally to this process, establishing the record on the one hand or fostering the myth on the other. Or, to look at the matter in a less binary and oppositional way, the historian weaves the story that brings out themes, people and events that signify for the audience, and this story changes according to the shifting values and dreams of a given period. *La Storia* – both story and history in Italian – develops in dynamic interactions between different epochs, the dead and the living: these can trigger fission, or assist fusion. The characteristic townscape of an Italian city, in Sicily as well as in Rome, speaks of the past to the present through monuments and memorials in a mode of storytelling that goes back to antiquity.

Today's theme parks offer imaginary remappings along these lines, for example. 'Instead of defining fiction in historical terms only,' writes Pavel, 'as the result of decayed myth, we should perhaps characterize it as well in terms of ontological landscaping and planning.' He calls the secondary or imaginary worlds projected in literature 'ontological landscapes' and comments perceptively on their interconnections with cultural memory and shared social norms: 'At the margins of ontological landscapes, one finds leisure worlds, or worlds for pleasure, which often derive from older discarded models. Each culture has its ontological ruins, its historical parks, where the members of a community relax and contemplate their ontological relics. Greek and Roman gods performed this function till late in the history of European culture.' Pavel is using ontological to refer to the shared religious world view of past civilizations, and I would include, within his leisure worlds, many varieties of sanctuary, including temples, churches and museums – though leisure is too restrictive a word to describe the function of such sites. They have become for many repositories of history, ideology and shared ideals but without commanding assent or declared allegiance to a religious system. Walking to Compostela, for example, has become part of a widespread quest for wellbeing for many pilgrims who do not profess faith in Christ or believe that the body of the apostle St James the Greater is buried in the shrine at the end of the long and austere journey. The nub of the issue is access: who is permitted to own the memories, to enter and enjoy the remains of a civilization as if they belong to them? For that to happen, in relation to the unhomed in the world today, the landscape needs to display marks that render it sacred for the stranger, recognizable, hospitable. Its hollowed state needs to be reversed.

For the poet Octavio Paz, memory work can be constitutive of experience as proleptic as well as retrospective:

> I am a history
> A memory inventing itself
> I am never alone
> I plant signs . . .

Planting signs metaphorically evokes the activity of the writer, storyteller or artist who does not chronicle events that have happened or transcribe an epiphany or report an experience, inner or outer, though the work may claim to be any one of those or all of them. But these writers/storytellers/artists make things up, knotting into the fabric of the story – the text, the woven thing – a series of events that may then take on the appearance of having happened. Some are enigmas, figures in the carpet, which await the interpreter to feel out later, and tease out the fullest implications. Elias Canetti in *Crowds and Power* discusses the brilliant efficacy of the Catholic church's methods of crowd control, and the influence of its time-tried rituals of bonding on the French Revolutionaries and, later and differently, on Fascists in Mussolini's regime and in the Third Reich. It is not necessary to endorse the uses of narrative and performance, of signs and relics, to enquire into their effects and their potential.

These may grow far beyond what their creators intended when they planted them. Indeed, the process of transmission should not be seen as a form of colonialist cartography. While it involves a figural layering of imaginary experiences on to the ground of the lived life, *planting signs*, such a way of being in the world does not obliterate but aims to enrich.

Imagination leads memory far more influentially than we allow or recognize: just to take one example, the places in Jerusalem associated with the life and death of Christ were discovered and mapped and visited by generations of pilgrims, and became the holiest sites on the planet for millions of Christians, on the basis of the stories told in the gospels, which are filled with contradictions, written according to literary conventions of allegory and prophecy, and give no hard evidence for a topography that was erased when the Romans laid waste to the city in 70 CE. Stories, transfigured and sealed into collective historical memories remapped the life of Jesus on to the streets and stones of Jerusalem: it was rebuilt in accordance with a shared narrative, although disputes of course continued about the exact position of this event or that.

The social historian Maurice Halbwachs is the great scholar of these themes. 'After Jerusalem had been conquered by the Crusaders,' he writes, in his magnificent and courageous work on the Holy Land and on collective memory,

> a new system of localization could retrieve these vestiges [of Christ's life], absorb them, but also modify them, thereby changing their appearance and meanings. Above all it allowed the emergence of a whole new flowering of consecrated sites, basilicas, churches, and chapels . . . The universal Christian community now took possession of the holy places and it wished to reproduce the image that it had constructed for itself throughout the centuries. This led to an abundant flowering of new localizations, much more numerous but also, most of the time, more recent.

As with the Flight into Egypt and the pilgrimage routes that trace the Holy Family's wanderings, the sites were animated by rituals and practices which developed after the holy places soon fell again into the hands of the 'infidels', and 'forms of devotion born in Europe . . . left their imprint on the consecrated sites and introduced new localizations that were entirely imaginary, such as, for example, the Via Dolorosa, based on the stations of the cross'. Halbwachs continues:

> Whatever epoch is examined, attention is not directed toward the first events, or perhaps the origin of these events, but rather toward the group of believers and toward their commemorative work. These [stones] are not traces of a human or supernatural individual but rather of groups animated by a collective faith that remains moving even if one does not really know its true nature. These groups evoked this individual, and those who were associated with him, in each epoch.

His arguments are central to the making of a sanctuary or holy place: the dynamics are governed by the community of believers, not by the god, prophet, saint, hero or heroine and their history.

The question now is, might these principles be adapted to create home for the unhomed?

In relation to the Holy Land, the routes to the holy places of Jerusalem developed long after the events they commemorate; centuries had passed before the corroborating stories were imprinted on the map of the city and its surroundings. This is the fruitful distinction between map and territory, which Korzybski's maxim expresses perfectly. A map presents us with geographical, geological and even civic facts, but territory encompasses meanings that come to us from beliefs and stories, which are often considered to be fused with history, but are projected: they are signs planted *in situ*. The place becomes a travelling text, and it then reproduces itself in artefacts that bear some written elements but are primarily material. For example, the Sakha stone in the Nile delta where the infant Jesus left his mark has been rubbed and kissed over centuries, until the impression has become much larger than a child's foot and indecipherable.

Footprints belong to a category of relics that aren't enfleshed; they're a type of secondary relic, neither an item of clothing nor an inanimate object that once made contact with the departed holy being but a vestigium of their passage, the impression that a holy body – of Buddha or Muhammad or Jesus or the Madonna or virgin martyr or other sainted being – once made on the earth. Like the fingerprints required by US border control, or the thumbprint that stands in for a signature, they give proof of presence. 'And did those feet in ancient time / Walk upon England's mountains green?' William Blake asks in his hymn 'Jerusalem'.

Such a relic preserves, in a literally vestigial form, a memory of a beloved being's bodily presence. It offers a symbolized link to a vanished person and charms the place because he or she once stood there; it offers a material warrant, impressed into the earth or rock, of the person *in absentia*. Footprints have become the focus of a cult in several shrines that serve as stations for pilgrims of varying faiths. They mirror the pilgrim's act of following in the footsteps of Jesus or other saint or subject of devotion. Before photography a footprint is an indexical sign par excellence: the mark of a solid body imprinting the surface it touches. It can also be copied and transmitted; the transit of relics from the Holy Land to western Europe in the form of replicas, miniatures, models, badges, charms and contact impressions and prints also applied to these precious signs of a now vanished holy presence. This crucial contact across the separation of death and the passing of time was then confirmed by further relics: pilgrims brought away prints of the footprints, made according to the same measurements or miniaturized. As Deborah Howard discusses in her splendid study of pilgrimage, taking the measurements of holy sites with a thread cut to the correct length offered a kind of surety that could be easily carried, close to the body, like an amulet. Even the wounds of the Saviour were measured in this way as an act of piety and imitation, and the results also kept in the form of a thread tied to the votary.

The prison cell adjacent to the church of the Holy Sepulchre in Jerusalem, which was on pilgrim routes from the earliest times, as Anthony Bale has explored in a fine and detailed paper, also included the relics of Jesus' footprints, and they inspired intense fervour: 'In this venerable cell we reflected, not without sorrow,' wrote one traveller, 'how the Lord Jesus wept therein, and awaited the torture of the Cross with equal dread and desire. We therefore entered it one by one, with sighs and groans, and each in turn bowed himself to the earth and kissed the footprints of our Saviour, and there we received indulgences.'

The chapel of the Ascension in Jerusalem enshrines the rock from which Jesus went up to heaven, and it is marked by the impression of his feet in two parallel depressions on a slab laid on the ground of the tiny circular shrine. In Cappadocia, one of the astonishing cave churches carved out of rock in the eleventh century is known as the 'Church of the Sandals', after a fresco which reproduces the miraculous imprints of Christ's feet after his Ascension; marvels and miracles grew up around them. Santa Cristina, patron saint of her hometown, Bolsena, in Italy, was horribly tortured by many means, including a fiery wheel and snakes that bit her, before being murdered by her father (see p. 107). When the torments failed to kill her, a millstone was hung around her neck, and she was thrown into the town's deep volcanic lake. But the stone refused to drown her. Instead, it bobbed to the surface as if made of balsa wood, and she rode on it like Venus on the half-shell and was gently wafted to shore. By a miracle, so that it should never be confused with any other rock, Cristina's footprints were imprinted on it.

The stone, with two tiny, parallel indentations, is enshrined in a crepuscular side chapel of the cathedral in her native town, in a Gothic tabernacle under a gold and mosaic sculpted canopy. I saw it there and found it had the true qualities of wonder, because its story is so wildly improbable and yet has the poetic logic of dreams.

In Ukraine in the fourteenth century, the Virgin Mary appeared in a vision to two monks and a shepherd and left a sign of her presence in the shape of a footprint from which rose a new spring. The shrine's power was consolidated by struggle, as often happens, and the icon recording the vision became the most sacred for Orthodox Slavs after an apocalyptic intervention of angels in the sky, fighting beside Mary, helped them lift the siege of Pochaev in 1675 and rout the Turkish army.

The Virgin's slipper, an analogous relic to the footprint, also became a much-loved wonder-working object of pilgrimage at Soissons in France and elsewhere. It in turn inspired a tertiary series of relics, votive souvenirs in the shape of her footprint, which would earn the pilgrim an indulgence of time in purgatory. The slippage here, from footprint to sandal and slipper and subsequently a print of its outline, acknowledges that the impressions are taken from the soles of the divine beings' footwear, so that in these instances direct contact with their flesh does not matter; this type of relic reveals the intuitive sense that a footfall embodies presence.

In Islam, this type of relic – one could call it a shadow relic, as in a photograph which is also a trace – figures all the more powerfully because it can convey presence without offering a likeness or a simulacrum; a footprint is not an image made by a human being who is claiming to be an *artifex* or creator, as only God can be. The footprints of the Prophet are among the holiest signs of his continuing presence, as are the footprints of the prophets and teachers who carry on his legacy, while the handprint of his daughter Fatima still appears on amulets and charms throughout the Mediterranean, North Africa and the Middle East (see Plate 8). The images also sometimes appear in the intricate interlace of Qur'anic quotation, blessings, magical formulae, amuletic eyes, Solomonic symbols (including the net by which the wisest of men captures and disempowers demons) on the talismanic scrolls rolled up tight and small in phylacteries worn next to the body for protection.

A footprint communicates the once corporeal substance of the dead, and it does so by embedding it in some cases in the actual earth, granting it an eternity of existence in solid rock and putting it on the map. The planting of a sign such as a footprint keeps in touch with the dead, their sillage, the trace of their being. By asserting presence, it makes claim to belonging. 'My land is where I set my feet' (*'La mia terra è dove poggio i piedi'*) is the defiant maxim hung up on a banner in the multi-ethnic café Moltivolti (Many Faces) in the Ballarò quarter of Palermo, where border crossers and asylum seekers, locals and tourists gather.

Such ways of dwelling, inventing histories, supplying memories and staving off homelessness by planting signs are stratagems born of longing and compensatory fantasy. But if the material itself declares itself to be a story, then the question of historical truth should no longer bear on the story's value as a story. Problems arise – and they certainly do – when the story demands belief of a fundamental and literal order.

In the introduction to the fiftieth-anniversary edition of *Mimesis*, Erich Auerbach's landmark study of representation in Western literature, Edward Said invokes a long and complex essay of Auerbach's called 'Figura'. *Figura* signifies a pattern within a text, a kind of figure in the carpet that is not immediately apprehensible but is structurally present in a form that enriches and directs the significance of the whole. Auerbach sets up a contrast between Odysseus and Abraham. 'The former is immediately present,' writes Said, 'and requires no interpretation, no recourse either to allegory or to complicated explanations. Diametrically opposed is the figure of Abraham, who incarnates "doctrine and promise" and is steeped in them. These are "inseparable from" him and "for that very reason they are 'fraught' with 'background' and [are] mysterious, containing a second, concealed meaning." And this second meaning can only be recovered by a very particular act of interpretation . . . figural interpretation.' The apparent meaning conceals another, as in that famous French warning on level crossings, *'Un train peut en cacher un autre'* ('One train can hide another'). The figure stands and moves in the present moment of the text under one's eyes, but the latent meanings both emerge in the past and look forward to the future: the narrowly averted sacrifice of Isaac prefigures the death of Jesus, for example, or the figure of Wisdom the Immaculate Conception of Mary. 'How much more fulfilling is the new idea that pre-Christian times can be read as a shadowy figure (*figura*) of what actually was to come.'

This figural method represents the German scholar's attempt, Said goes on, to negotiate 'between the Jewish and European (hence Christian) components of his identity'. The approach relates to Said's own way of reading contrapuntally. It was a traditional tool of medieval scholasticism, and is applied to the Song of Songs, for example, making it possible for this ecstatic and erotic sequence to enter the Bible, passing beyond the evident meaning of the words to descry a prophetic vision of mystical and spiritual union. Islamic exegesis also adopted the method, finding the highest Sufi metaphysics in the love lyrics and drinking songs of a poet such as Hafez, and his enraptured praise of wine and boys. This way of reading is explored in Henry James's great short story 'The Figure in the Carpet', but without a final epiphany.

The maps of cities present an account of the past concealed beneath their surface appearances analogously to a figure in the carpet, as Walter Benjamin and numerous writers have explored. Benjamin the flaneur has numerous progeny in his quest for unearthing the layers of meaning in the streets: Patrick Modiano searches out the past of Occupied Paris in the city today; W. G. Sebald's wanderings in East Anglia are matched by his meandering and melancholy reflections as he excavates the territory to create an archaeology of his own uprooted personal history. The activist writer Rebecca Solnit is a supreme chronicler of walking and writing and the hermeneutics of place, and has compiled atlases that are albums cum maps of personal experiences in San Francisco, New Orleans and New York: the literary imagination here reconfigures the territories by reassigning memories to this site or that. She begins on her own patch, San Francisco, and by interviewing and discussing with friends and locals how they inhabit their neighbourhoods, she draws up many different variations on the same ground plan, according to their personal paths and those of historical precursors in different fields of endeavour and art: gay SF, trade unions, ecological campaigners, lepidopterists, chefs. Each contributor has their own itinerary and landmarks, according to their sensibilities and interests, sexual orientation, passions and antipathies. Solnit is a fine practitioner of the new non-fiction, as meditation and polemic, satire and activism, memoir and self-questioning. She is present in the work with her particular concerns and intelligence in every twist and turn of the allusions and the interests but it is not autobiography or autofiction, because she does not claim to be giving a history of herself but offers through the experiences of fellow citizens a collective picture of the city. The speaking 'I' can be plural and collective, too. And it is more truthful to reveal the connectedness of the self with others from a prismatic and distributed point of view than to clothe oneself in the testifying authority of the first person.

The prismatic character of her approach allows the fictive modes of unreliability, inconsistency and ultimate unknowability to fork through and ignite her writings: her choice of Eadweard Muybridge as the subject of her book *River of Dreams* was no accident, as her variety of non-fiction admits that totality can't be achieved, that a galloping horse or a twirling dancer can only ever be grasped in fragments, in glimpses, high shutter-speed flashes.

The work of the artist Adam Dant takes this approach farther: he is a cartographer of buried histories, remembering marginal communities in London, but he has also created a series of mythological maps: locating Odysseus' wanderings across a London turned into the Mediterranean sea and the quest for the Golden Fleece in the financial district (see Plate 13).

Forgetting is also important: literature's memory work entails choices of figure and ground: what emerges, what recedes. Kazuo Ishiguro weaves a story around this theme in his novel *The Buried Giant*, which was received with some puzzlement at the time, but is a very fine fable about the quandary that history presents to the writer, packing and unpacking memories and history for the national consciousness. In this respect, the writer takes on the role of the *shabti* of ancient Egypt, whose name translates as whisperer and who perform their eternal tasks on behalf of the dead; these doppelgänger shades are the witnesses, the reporters, from the other side, figments proposing a chronicle to be shared.

The figural approach to narrative can yield the richest ways of engaging with a book and making it one's own, a habitation of the mind. A critic's task is to discern the meaning in the text, but that meaning will only become apparent afterwards, when the *Kulturbrille* (the cultural spectacles) and the frame of the reader are distanced from those of the writer. The literary scholar, working with figural analysis, looks into the text for what lay ahead at the time of writing, though it was not known to the writer or the book's readers then. In this sense, the interpreter is a scryer of signs.

This way of reading is creative; it generates meaning as well as perceives it. It is in many ways a storyteller's modus operandi, consciously adopted by the planter of signs in Octavio Paz's poem, and consciously or unconsciously practised by the builders of sacred cartographies, ontological ruins and subjective territories.

Mythic material demands this way of reading, which when applied allows an ethics of hope to flower, and opens a text to poetical truth-telling distinct from historical veracity or believability. This structure, oracular in meaning, architectural in form, endows the map with a chorale of voices, speaking in chords resonating across time: the past is prologue. Imaginative works of myth, legend, fairy tale and fable may map geographies of home on to surroundings that are not home: they can help to give us shelter, to take us home.

# 9

# In the Country of Words

> There are no sanctuaries
> Except in purposeful action
> Keorapetse Kgositsile

'Ours is a country of words,' wrote the late Palestinian poet Mahmoud Darwish, in a poem that speaks to all people who are on the move, displaced from their homes for reasons of war, persecution, necessity. In this famous poem, which has become something of an anthem for Palestinians everywhere, the exiled poet thinks of the words that form his memories; he alludes to the Psalms, from the Hebrew and other Bibles, to 'the tents of the prophets', invoking Moses, Abraham and Jesus, as well as Muhammad and the Qur'an, and refers to legends from the *Nights* about Solomon and his messenger the hoopoe. He also acknowledges Gipsy lore. Indeed, the whole poem not only celebrates nomadic tradition but itself reflects the larger culture itself, for he draws on the mingled languages and traditions of the eastern Mediterranean and its multi-layered memories.

The poem, an anthem for Palestinians in their country and in the diaspora, reaches out beyond this identity. Darwish rang changes on the strategic use of language and literature throughout his life, remembering writers with whom he had elective affinities – alive or dead. The words he uses may have been first written in Arabic, a language that, like ancient Greek and Latin in the past, ranges far and wide and connects disparate nations and even continents. His allusions in translation are intelligible because the words that make up 'a country of words' are not single locutions but image clusters and narrative allusions, as if we were contemplating a ruined mosaic wall where small, coloured stones still gleamed and the whole scene could be filled in – by mental projection – from the glint of a hoopoe's beak or the sound of a phrase. Many stories also dwell in a variety of languages and offer opaque images: the herb rampion ('Rapunzel') rarely makes an appearance in recipes, and spindles have long fallen into general disuse, yet these essential nodes of legends and fairy tales retain their meaning, and their power probably waxes through their unfamiliarity. Similarly, the landscape of the eastern Mediterranean and the characteristic tasks of nomadic and pastoral survival saturate biblical and Qur'anic narrative and imagery with profound effect, even where there is usually no shortage of rain and desert sands are far away. In the anglophone world, the language of the Psalms or the Song of Solomon or Jesus' imagery is charged with recognizable and wonderfully sensuous and evocative allusions because in the country of words they have taken root and have naturalized. The idea that displaced individuals and peoples might find themselves at home in such an immaterial zone acts as the guiding principle for remaking sanctuary now, when the classical and medieval sacred models of refuge are not replicable or practicable.

The country of words corresponds to the acoustic unconscious that Denise Riley explored in the lectures she gave on the lyric voice. She also explores the importance of listening, of picking up patterns and rhythms from one another and absorbing motifs and stories. Listeners assembled around a story that is being told in whatever medium (recitation, puppetry, shadowplay), may participate while there, and may in turn become transmitters. Sanctuary in our time needs this larger interpretation: a commons of imagination. 'The act of narration-translation itself,' Riley comments, 'in its generous openness and recognisable familiarity, can construct a temporary sheltering space, a kind of oral and aural sanctuary.'

'The country of words' receives a more political emphasis in the idea of 'the World Republic of Letters', the formulation of Pascale Casanova, which announces a conscious zone of liberty, equality and brotherhood, but slants the country of words towards print culture rather than performance or orature. Casanova argues that literature lays the ground of communities across barriers of language, ethnicity and geography, builds a polity of shared imaginings, a collectivity of stories, given and passed on. Her chosen term hints at an inheritance from the Hellenic, Latin, Arabic spheres of usage, except that in the current mingling and movements of peoples the trend is tilting towards an overlapping plurality of languages, creoles, macaronics; the novelist and EU interpreter Diego Marani proposed a new Esperanto he dubbed 'Europanto'. He offered a sample: '*Que would happen if, wenn du open your computero, finde eine message in esta lingua? No est englando, no est germano, no est espano, no est franzo, no est keine known lingua aber du under stande! Wat happen so? Habe your computero eine virus catched?*'

A world republic of letters can only come into existence by modifying ways of defining the nation state in relation to cultural capital; national literatures have always existed in international relationship with one another, Casanova argues, and have necessarily communicated beyond national borders in order to become visible to others and develop a sense of self. The Romantic nationalists, such as the Grimm Brothers, were vexed to discover that many of the fairy tales they thought authentically *echt* German had Italian and French antecedents. More recently, Casanova modified her original contrast between dominant and dominated literatures to propose instead a further political approach: 'the most important opposition is between combative literature and pacified or non-engaged ones'. Yet this need not be an opposition, but more a question of who is heard, of pricking up ears to register new frequencies.

Both these imagined models, the country of words and the world republic of letters, might appear to reprise the model of a collective unconscious, brimming with plots and characters and motifs that are shared by all peoples from the beginning of time, as in Jung's psychological theory and in twentieth-century structural folklore studies.

## The Ocean of Stories

'I'm producing so many stories at once,' the narrator tells us in Calvino's novel *If on a Winter's Night*, 'because what I want is for you to feel, around the story, a saturation of other stories that I could tell and maybe will tell or who knows may have already told on some other occasion, a space full of stories that is perhaps my lifetime, where you can move in all directions, as in space, always finding stories that cannot be told until

9. Bahram Gur, 'King of Kings', visits the Russian Princess in the Red Pavilion on the day of Mars, in a twelfth-century collection of Persian mystical allegories, in which the fierce Princess Turandot first appears. Nizami, *Haft Peykar*, Folio from a *Khamsa* (*Quintet*).

10. When the shipwrecked Aeneas, his son Ascanius (really Cupid in disguise), and his fellow Trojans, fleeing the destruction of their city, arrive in Carthage, Queen Dido shows them open-handed generosity. Francesco Solimena, *Dido Receiving Aeneas*.

11. After Aeneas leaves her and sails for Rome, Dido builds a pyre of his effects and love gifts and kills herself, in front of her sister's eyes. Guercino, *Death of Dido*.

12. The Brooklyn home of the Lubavitcher Messiah, the focus of an esoteric branch of modern Judaism, has been replicated in different countries. Andrea Robbins and Max Becher, *Ramat Shlomo, Jerusalem, Israel, Far View*, 2005.

13. *Opposite:* Artist-mapmaker Adam Dant projects the Trojans' quest for the Golden Fleece onto the streets of London's financial centre. Adam Dant, *Argonautica Londonensi* (*Jason and the Argonauts in London*).

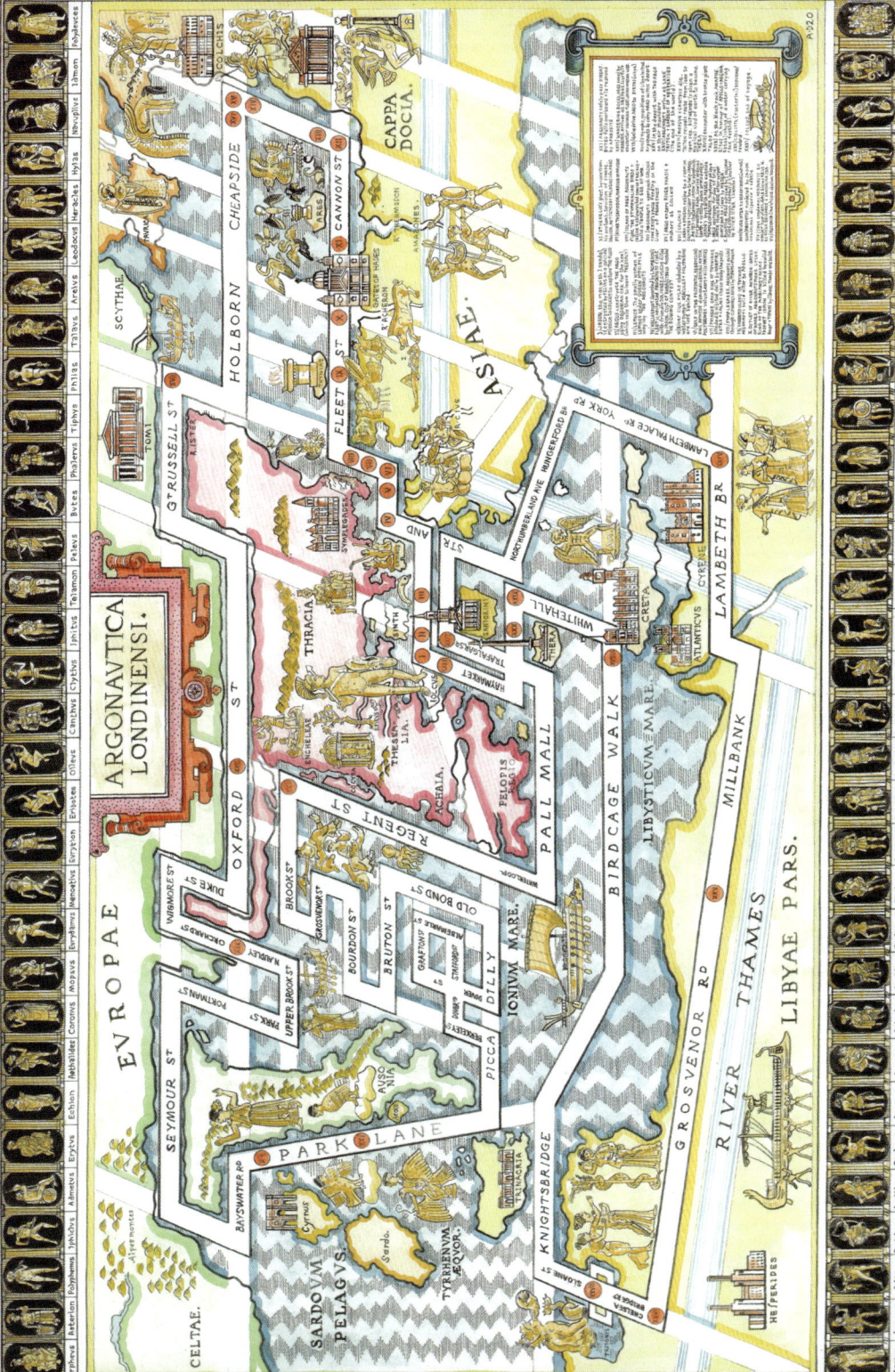

14a. (*Above*) Participants in the project Stories in Transit work towards the performance of 'The Tale of the Old Man and the Snake'. 14b and 14c. (*Below*) create portrait based on the statue of the Genius of Palermo and a traditional storyboard.

15. During the performance of 'One for You and One for Me', the storyteller, played by Numu Touray, asks the audience, 'Who was responsible?'

16a. (*Above*) In the Botanic Garden of Palermo, giant puppets of Gilgamesh and Enkidu are carried in procession by (*right-to-left*) Safoudiny ('Din') Diallo and Gassimou ('Maga') Magassouba, founding members of Stories in Transit. 16b (*Below*) On another occasion, in another venue, participants in the project enact the parable 'The Tale of the Old Man and the Snake'.

other stories are told first, and so, setting out from any moment or place, you encounter always the same density of material to be told.'

The phrase 'Ocean of Stories' echoes the title of an eleventh-century Sanskrit collection of animal wisdom tales, the *Kathāsaritsāgara* ('Ocean of the Streams of Stories'). Salman Rushdie plays wonderfully ingenious and prophetic variations on this metaphor in his children's story *Haroun and the Sea of Stories* (1990), one of his most lastingly high-spirited fictions, written for his son while Rushdie was in hiding after the fatwa. He imagines that the free-flowing Wellspring of All Stories has been taken over and polluted by the dictator Khattam Shud, 'the Prince of Silence and the Foe of Speech', whose name means 'all is finished'. He has shut down the tap and the stories are no longer flowing.

In Arabic, the root of the verb for watering – *rawaa* – happens to be the same as for storytelling: a storyteller is a *raawi*. 'There are lots of versions of the root,' the Arabist Philip Kennedy explains, 'including *riwaaya* which now means a story (or novel).' He adds, '*Rawiya* is to water, give a drink; while *rawaa* is to relate, narrate. A subtle distinction in modern Arabic is that *rawii* is thirst-quenching; while *rayyaan* is used for well-watered.' This image occurs in the title of a medieval collection of animal tales, *Solwan; or, Waters of Comfort* by the Sicilian Ibn Zafer (1104–1170/2). The translator comments: '"*Solwan*" is the plural of *Solwanah*, the name of a shell concerning which the Arabs believe that if a little water is poured upon it, and given to drink to one who is in love, he will immediately recover.'

I appreciate this deep insight of Arabic, as it looks on literature as a draught of pure water, a watershed, a delta, carrying its figments on its many currents, into its many aquifers and wells, because the chief gathering places where people talk, exchange memories and pass on their knowledge have always been waterholes, wells, fountains, working places for milling, laundry, cooking, washing, places where news has been given, information handed on, friendships and alliances made, and, I believe, imaginary stories further elaborated, remembered and transmitted. Narratives can heal, soothe, refresh and nurture growth, replenish and quench thirst, and they make their way like flowing water, unstoppably.

Rushdie's adoption of the deep-rooted metaphor is delightful and a brilliant, prophetic riposte to the death threat he'd received, which was indeed to lead to his near murder over three decades later in

2022. 'Narration is irrigation, irrigation is narration' doesn't encompass the all-important material circumstances – contact, encounter, historical movements of people, conditions of survival – that affect the transmission of stories and the flourishing of cultural expression. The country of words is the product of social and political currents; it can stand in for home when home is no longer there.

Fierce contests now blaze over history and memory, heritage and identity, and who tells the story and what story they tell has become an acute arena of struggle – and not only in dictatorships. Stories don't exist intrinsically as texts and are not confined to remain static between the covers of a book. A story acts like a cluster of iron filings that has been magnetized by a powerful but now distant source: it moves this way and that as new forces play upon it, it shifts its shape and size and sheds and picks up other bits and pieces, but unlike magnetized iron filings stories have voice – and receivers. They happen in dialogue with written texts, but are not constrained by writing or scribal culture; indeed, the internet and digital technologies are bringing out a revival of the bard or skald, griot, *raawi* and *hakawati* of the pre-Gutenberg era and have opened a vast seething arena for varieties of performance, recitation, speech, combining sound, image, voice. (Part of this revival is caught under the rubric 'spoken word'.) These bearers of words, interpreters and the scryers of signs, who speak the languages of literature and invite entry to others to understand their communications, through images and forms, patterns and devices, are inhabitants of the 'country of words', even when more and more barriers are going up to prevent movement across borders.

In his famous meditative poem 'An Ordinary Evening in New Haven', Wallace Stevens calls to mind:

> The spirit's speeches, the indefinite,
> Confused illuminations and sonorities,
> So much ourselves, we cannot tell apart
> The idea and the bearer-being of the idea.

Sound and sense are enmeshed, and babel and medley are not unintelligible, but the profound and necessary bearers of our sense of self and relation.

By allowing confusion to enter into play, Stevens's eavesdropping illuminates the role of stories today: they are not ways of reaching a solution; their acts of resolution are ambiguous and indeed, more often than not, failures. They communicate hurt and they do not lift the mystery of what happens, or clear the opacity of our understanding: Antigone, Medea, Orpheus, Snow White, Camar al-Zaman and any number of heroes and heroines of *The Thousand and One Nights*, as well as the figures discussed earlier in this book (Jesus and Mary, Dido, Turandot and riddle princesses), give us access to experience, and hold us precisely because there is no easy answer to their predicament. The effects of assuagement come from the telling, not the outcome. Stories are not theorems. At best they might be conjectures, but mostly they present baffling puzzles. Translation between languages and cultures can never be complete, nor should it attempt to be, as we have learned from colonialism. Stories tussle with these bequests from the past and these existential shortcomings.

In a fable called simply 'Metaphor', the Moroccan writer Abdelfattah Kilito pictures an orphaned she-camel wandering here and there taking up with one group, then another. This is the Arabic ode, he writes, and the camel is a porter, a bearer, a spreader, a copula:

> The ode, said the poets in former times, is a stray she-camel: you don't know where she'll end up.
>
> Lost in the immensity of the desert, she [the camel-ode] wanders looking for her nearest and dearest, animal and human. But it's not certain that she'll find them again. One day or other, the orphan will be taken in by persons unknown, who'll adopt her and she'll spend the rest of her days among them.
>
> Unless she wanders off again.
>
> Isn't it the fate of an ode to wander, to be a stranger everywhere?

But the fate of the stranger turns out not to be exclusion or stigmatization, but a different state, transnational:

> This was something known to the Arab poet of the desert. But he thought that his odes would never be read other than in Arabic. He was far from grasping that his she-camels, centuries later, would have

reached towns of which he had not the slightest idea: Berlin, Paris, London, New York.

Translated, interpreted, accompanied by commentaries, they now speak in foreign tongues.

With time, they'll doubtless forget the idiom of their original.

I would widen 'ode' to include stories, though poetry is easier to memorize especially when accompanied by music, and travels more securely.

Kilito has commented widely on travelling texts such as the Bible and *The Thousand and One Nights* and has compared his calling to the porters who feature so prominently in the *Nights*. He sees himself as a bearer-being, carrying the accumulated communications of the past. As mentioned before, narratives are mobile and diasporic; they are pods packed with *spories*, ready to break open and scatter, borne by different vehicles, media and bearers.

A story moves across time as well as space; its motion can be transcultural and multilingual and its burden historical or mythical and often both combined. (Some cultures, such as Italian, do not use a different word: *la storia* covers both, as already noted.) Translation loses the original language but gains others and thereby travels further and reaches more deeply; besides it may be that it is quite often a mistake to imagine there is a correct original.

Birds and animals communicate vital information with their howls, squeaks, cries, growls and purring, and these are utterances with elements of a story in them, about fear, pain, property and pleasure, but it is unlikely that an ant or a cricket, a cat or a mouse, relates what human beings call stories, that it invents plots and attributes thoughts and actions to imagined characters – as did La Fontaine, taking his cue from Aesop, among other collections of fables.

Digital media add to the swirling transmission and not always to disinform and mislead. In 2012, for example, the Franco artist Katia Kameli filmed a traditional storyteller from the famous square in Marrakesh, the Djemaa el-Fna, reciting a tale from his repertoire. Every inch the timeless figure of a *hakawati* or, in the Moroccan tradition, a *hlaïqya*, gaunt and rapt, the performer is wearing a well-worn djellabah and headcloth, standing against a backdrop of a ruinous building as he embarks in Arabic on a long, spiralling and marvellous romance of love and obstacles, wonders and triumphs.

On enquiry, it turned out that the source wasn't his grandmother or his nurse, but a 1964 vintage Bollywood film *Dosti*, directed by Satyen Bose. The storyteller, whose name is Abderrahim Al Azalia, specializes in reciting the plots of such films, while the derelict edifice in which he is performing is the grandiose, but unfinished Théâtre Royal, begun in the last century and abandoned. Against this forlorn backdrop, the storyteller stands, an emblem of the interconnection of past and present, traditional and modern. The Bollywood plot embroiders on a Persian original: this tale, like Turandot's, has wandered the world and come back again and is now going forth once more to new listeners' ears, who will transform it and bear it on.

As the Paris gallery which represents Kameli comments,

> the artist considers herself a translator. For Kameli, translation is not merely an exchange between two cultures or an act of transmission, it is an expansion of meaning and form. In Kameli's films translation is used as a tool that has the capacity to undermine binaries and destabilize hierarchical structures, especially concerning notions of authorship and the tenuous relationship between original and copy. Often, revisioning or rewriting narratives is purposefully accentuated in Kameli's work with the intention of calling attention to the ways in which global history is in fact much more impressionable and pliant than assumed. Her practice generates critical perspectives on world events, casting such events as mutable and reflexive.

The video presents the travelling tale as a foundation of a transnational community: during the séance the storyteller draws around him a circle of listeners, a node in the web of audiences which that story has previously gathered.

In a different part of the world, in Ireland at the end of the 1970s, when the Troubles were acute, some writers began publishing a magazine called *The Crane Bag*. The title comes from an eerie Irish myth that Aoife, the wife of the God of the Sea, stole from him the secret of writing; for this she was magically changed into a crane – a bird whose flight is a kind of sky writing, thought to be at the origin of the alphabet itself. The God of the Sea then took the skin of his wife and made it into a fishing net – the crane bag – and kept all his treasures in it, including writing: 'and when the sea was full, all the treasures were visible in it, but when the fierce sea ebbed, the crane bag was empty'. The magazine was dedicated to the imagination. Seamus Heaney wrote a foreword, a kind of manifesto for literature as a way of participating in society and history through acts of imagination: 'a mind [so] stretched between transcendence and politics produces exactly the kind of fibre from which this trawl-net of the mind is to be rewoven'.

Since that time, the kind of violence that convulsed Ireland is occurring in many places with a ferocity that inspires feelings of utter helplessness and despair. What can a writer do? What can culture achieve, if anything?

The long, long history of storytelling includes myriad alternative ways of shaping experience into narrative, and the most ancient cultures – Eastern and Western – have wrought some of the most eloquent expressions of courage, hope, resistance and, yes, resilience in these modes. Fabulism – making up stories – is not only a deep-rooted and peculiar mark of human beings, but its many genres (parables, romances, satires, fairy tales, animal fables, ballads, elegies, mythological tragedies and comedies) are tools of truth-telling, not as *cinéma-vérité* or reality TV but in the more elusive and more ancient forms of fabulation or poetic imagination. They also include tall tales, proverbs, jokes, riddles, old wives' nostrums. They have been fashioned over time, their authors mostly anonymous; they would have been recited and performed to a group rather than read in solitude, silently. The transmission of stories, Florence Dupont writes in her seminal study *The Invention of Literature*, was 'an event . . . [which] required the presence of speaking bodies'. She stresses the living, social character of these ways of reading and telling. In her conclusion, ominously called 'Writing and Death', she indicts the book: it is a tomb, even a cenotaph, 'In the absence of these bodies, when reduced to a book, writing was fated to draw attention to that absence.'

Above all, this ancient tradition is packed with supremely unlikely stories, almost defined by their improbability even as they set out to explain the origin of things or the workings of destiny or the extremes of passion – Odysseus' encounters with the one-eyed Polyphemus or with the goddess Athena in the form of a sea eagle, or the metamorphoses of young men into flowers, women into mountains, springs and trees. The Greek philosopher Sallustius, a committed believer in the Olympians, captures the eternal present of mythic events and beings with his aphoristic remark, 'All this did not happen at any one time but always is so . . .'

The stories' internal narrators may be nameless or famous – Ulysses, Helen of Troy, Sinbad. Their external authors are sometimes mythical themselves, like Homer or Shahrazad, or they may be historical, recognized messengers of knowledge about human existence – Aeschylus, Virgil, El Nizami. They are likely to have drawn on what they had lived at first hand, but they do not present themselves as eyewitnesses. They may have invented it all or their forerunners may have. To these ancient literary mythological works, many newer genres have been added: speculative histories, above all, filling in the gaps in the record. The tradition's many registers and moods range through the whole gamut of communicating subtleties and nuances, with irony taking pride of place. The oldest stories in the world – often about lions and jackals and other beasts – like the Arabic Aesop, called *Kalilah wa Dimnah*, are directed at princes and laced with caustic comment about tyranny and its prerogatives. Proverbs crystallize the lessons of such tales, from Aesop to Ibn al-Muqaffa to La Fontaine (dog in the manger, sour grapes, crying wolf): these are fossils of cautionary, often comic, tales saturated in world-weariness about the ways of the strong against the weak, the ruthlessness of the powerful, the stupid trustfulness of ordinary people; casting animals as the protagonists, the form seems to go back to the beginnings of the species. The compendia travelled the globe: their age-old wisdom, hard-headed and rueful, makes the reader/listener smile and then leaves a bittersweet aftertaste. These fables and fantasies exemplify the narrative device of masquerade: beasts, monsters, divinities and prodigies like volcanoes, meteors and Fata Morgana provide fertile, versatile and intrinsically entertaining ways of asking important questions and thinking about values. They offer a mask for utterances that might otherwise be difficult for the powerless to consider, let alone utter.

The tradition counts on stories to tell the truth, but its receivers are also aware that the truth that stories have been telling for so long has not dented the swollen brutality of tyrants one jot. During the period when I was immersed in *The Thousand and One Nights*, reading the stories told by a woman under threat for her life, about injustice and cruelty and violence, in an attempt to persuade her husband, the ruler with murder in mind, to think and behave and govern with mercy instead, my thoughts kept turning to . . . Assad in Syria, Putin and so many others across the world. In spite of this pessimistic history of failing and failing again, stories still matter crucially: the tyrants would not be recognized as being what they are without them; they would not be restrained at all and would act with total impunity. The rolls of barbed wire will not be taken away when someone recasts the received idea of the enemy. But something may shift a little.

In the current global upheavals, thousands have crossed the Mediterranean into Europe, the majority making landfall in southern Italy, on the island of Lampedusa off the coast of Sicily. These arrivants come from Asia – from Pakistan, Bangladesh – and from Africa, especially from the countries of the Maghreb and the Sahel, as well as from the Middle East and the eastern Mediterranean, the original source of so much European lore. They know and are carrying with them an array of myths and fables, family stories and memories, and they mostly think that we, in the host countries where they have landed, are not interested in such things. Lacking an expectation of esteem, something invaluable is being left to waste.

The Mandé people of West Africa, from Mali, the Gambia and neighbouring regions, from which many border crossers have started out, developed a cosmology that is wonderfully rich and strange and very little known. Comparable in many ways to Sumerian origin myths, it relates the conflict between twin deities, one good, one evil, descended from the seeds of none other than an hibiscus flower. The story twists and turns, imagining the origin of the great River Niger that flows through the region, and strikes many contemporary resonances around drought and flooding. It is a cycle of oral stories, recorded partially by French ethnographers (Mali having been part of France's colonial empire) and they have not yet, at least to my knowledge, travelled or been translated and reimagined. Ben Okri treated Yoruba beliefs with freewheeling imagination in his 1991 novel *The Famished Road,* and the novelist Marlon James, who was born in Jamaica, has been excavating and repurposing his heritage by drawing on African mythology in his ongoing *Dark Star* trilogy. In this spirit of reinvigorating heritage, the most audacious venture – to my mind, an exceptionally exciting one – took place in 2007 in Bamako, the capital of Mali, on the River Niger. *Bintou Wéré: The Opera of the Sahel* is about migration, and it centres on an asylum seeker, a woman who is hoping and waiting to make the crossing to Italy so that her unborn child, the consequence of a rape, will enjoy a safer future. The creation of the opera gathered together a production team, musicians, singers and dancers from several different nations and languages in the region; this work, unprecedented in its vision and powerful in execution (I have only seen the filmed version from 2017), was performed in the dramatic open-air setting of a specially built platform on the banks of the River Niger. A *passeur* or trafficker figures as a highly ambiguous magician, able on the one hand to fulfil the migrants' hopes and on the other showing himself to be utterly ruthless and undependable. The first libretto was by Wasis Diop who, after scourging critical advice from Achille Mbembe, refashioned his early draft in full consciousness of the North–South dialectics involved. With another poet, Koulsy Lamko, he set out to forge 'a new poetics' from the encounter – from the productive fission – between African ritual and masquerade and the grand operatic traditions of Europe. Mbembe wrote, 'To think of the opera as a genre may sound peculiar to African ears, given the singularity of its emergence in Europe and its seemingly rigid rules . . . the task will be . . . to domesticate this form . . . so as to rejuvenate it . . .'

Ten years later the writer and scholar Manthia Diawara made a film of the opera. Although it preserves valuable records of the live production, Diawara recombines the many elements to produce a new opus on film, an exhilarating and tragic '*chaos-opéra*' – a term Diawara has adopted from the work of Édouard Glissant. Including footage of the original production, Diawara introduced new elements and new members of the cast, removed some scenes and intercut the performance with documentary records of Syrians fleeing their homes and, from an earlier era, of Jews in flight from Nazi Germany. Diawara was born in Bamako and raised partly in Guinea, and after he fled the civil wars in the region was able to make his new home in the USA, where he is a professor at NYU. He wanted to focus on the opera's topicality: his '*chaos-opéra*' enacts 'an encounter between words, music and dance, which attempts to make sense of human movements and the new cultures that are born out of them'. He wanted 'to show that, throughout human history, such movements, migrations and immigrations have often resulted in the creation of new and dynamic humanities, rather than negative and fearful human products'.

## Forewarning and Forestalling

The ways stories reveal truth rather than document reality require imaginative stratagems. They do not photograph what took place, but paint possibilities with eyes closed out of the dreaming, thinking, creative faculties. Anxiety now clusters around narratives' power to imprint expectations and shape actions and future ends. And books, the purveyors of stories and histories, are not a good in themselves, as Margaret Atwood has warned; their contents can be and have often been dangerous. The directions literature takes are not intrinsically ethical, needless to say. Some books are trouble, by design; sometimes, trouble follows by happenstance, occasionally when writers are brave and outspoken. The reception of a work of literature, a poem, play, novel, biography, essay or any other form of literature, can be life-threatening for the author, in many countries where the state keeps a close watch. The many genres of fabulism, such as the animal tales, have grown up to evade censorship: the unlikelihood of their conventions – talking beasts, magical reprieves – masking barbed shafts against identifiable targets.

The poet W. H. Auden, discussing the imaginary zones of speculative or hypothetical fiction, adopted the term 'secondary world', which had been used by J. R. R. Tolkien and C. S. Lewis, and declared, 'Every normal human being is interested in two kinds of worlds: the Primary, everyday, world which he knows through his senses, and a Secondary world or worlds which he not only can create in his imagination, but also cannot stop himself creating . . . Stories about the Primary world may be called *Feigned Histories*; stories about a Secondary world myths or fairy tales.'

The folk and fantasy tradition has however long been scorned as escapist and foolish – old wives' tales. For example, Thomas Love Peacock roundly denounced the Romantics for 'wallowing in the rubbish of departed ignorance, and raking up the ashes of dead savages to find gewgaws and rattles for the grown babies of the age'. He named names: 'Mr. Scott digs up the poachers and cattle-stealers of the ancient border. Lord Byron cruizes for thieves and pirates on the shores of the Morea and among the Greek islands. Southey wades through ponderous volumes of travels and old chronicles, from which he carefully selects all that is false, useless, and absurd . . . Mr. Wordsworth picks up village legends from old women and sextons . . .' He went on: 'Mr. Coleridge superadds . . . the dreams of crazy theologians and the mysticism of German metaphysics, and favours the world with visions in verse, in which . . . sexton, old woman, Jeremy Taylor, and Emanuel Kant are harmonized into a delicious poetical compound . . .'

This is spirited, funny, verbal peacockery indeed and with hindsight we can laugh. But the shafts are deadly in their accuracy – from a certain vantage point. Percy Bysshe Shelley wrote back instantly to tell Peacock, who was a friend, that he was going to reply, but in his *Defence of Poetry* Shelley sounds less hurt that exhilarated as he unequivocally rebuts Peacock's general conclusion that imaginative literature has no role in modern society, which needs science and politics only.

In spite of Shelley's blazing oratory, those direct taunts that Peacock issued against ballads, old wives' tales and superstition did somehow stick and the stigmatized material shifted sideways into children's literature. Not only into poetry, but into prose forms such as the tale, the novella, the full-length fantasy novel, and today, increasingly, the series, both in print and in audio and film. The broad genre that includes myths, fairy tales, horror, romance, science fiction and many other forms with children or young adults as the target audience and readership provided an open horizon which was also a safe place to express strong views – some of them moralizing and filled with Christian piety (Hans Christian Andersen, Charles Kingsley, C. S. Lewis), but many dissident and polemical and even visionary: Lewis Carroll, George MacDonald, Christina Rossetti, Angela Carter, Philip Pullman.

Most suggestively of all, at the end of the *Defence*, Shelley also declares, 'Poets . . . are the mirrors of the gigantic shadows which futurity casts upon the present . . .' This is the nub: the task of capturing those shadows from the future has been seized by writers for young audiences – often with young heroes and heroines. They act to elude those limits which André Gide, in *Les Nourritures terrestres*, glumly recognizes: 'The present would be full of every future if the past had not already projected History upon it.' These new Romantics imagine and reimagine the world as if it might be other than the consequence of past troubles: Carroll speaks with Alice, her questions are his questions; he voices through her sturdy common sense his own feelings about his society's absurd conventions, cruelties and arbitrary justice; Ruskin writes an ecological fable for Effie, 'The King of the Golden River', announcing a triumph of kindness over greed and selfishness; Pullman's demons, his moribund Old Testament God and his alternative parallel worlds deliberately revoke the story of the Fall and open up a vision of a possible, different society. Such legislative visions are not free from controversy: Pullman rails against C. S. Lewis for his didacticism; passionate condemnation erupts over Tolkien's demonized orcs and Harry Potter's use of magic.

When Shelley termed poets unacknowledged legislators, he was opposing Keats, who famously wrote to a friend, 'We hate poetry that has a palpable design upon us . . .' However, many fine poetical writers now, especially writing with a child in mind, often have palpable designs. In the long nineteenth century, fairy tales, so often filled with the 'motiveless malignancy' that Coleridge noted in Iago, develop a powerful undertow of moral principle, wishful hope and idealistic dreaming.

Projecting secondary worlds to reflect on present experience helps address the latter directly. 'Symbolic distance is meant to heal wounds,' writes Pavel. '. . . But the cure cannot work unless it is somehow shown to pertain to actuality. Symbolic distance must be complemented by a principle of relevance.' He continues, 'since we need an alien space in which to deploy the energy of the imagination, there have always been and always will be distinct fictional worlds – but we may also use close fictional worlds for mimetic purposes, in order to gather relevant information or just for the pleasure of recognition'.

The art of words is not intrinsically ethical. Rather it is amoral, ambivalent; a story is not a reliable remedy – we all know how narratives act to entrench prejudice, and we are witnessing forces of reaction busily commandeering them to their own ends. In his recent polemical study *Seduced by Story: The Use and Abuse of Narrative*, the eminent literary critic

Peter Brooks recants his 1984 book *Reading for the Plot*, which hugely influenced the 'narrative turn' in literary studies. Forty years on, he now deplores the widespread acceptance of story as a paramount value in fiction and in lived lives, and the concurrent emphasis on affect, so strongly in evidence in the way news items are now reported. He calls for a return to analytic reading, to the ideals of objective evaluation and to quest for a historical account rather than an emotive response. Turning to the question of stories' status, he draws a distinction: are they ontological or epistemological? That is, do they precede experience or shape the understanding of it? Does someone who explores the role of narrative in life see 'narrative as constitutive of human existence, and human beings defined as *Homo narrans*, or rather conceive narrative as the mental instrument that humans use to make sense of an otherwise unorganized existence'? This does not seem to me to present alternatives. Each of us will be dealt a set of circumstances that frame our identity, provide us with a story, and this context is indeed constitutive of our existence. But everyone is also able, when prompted and inspired to do so, to reflect upon the hand that destiny has dealt and reconfigure and reimagine it. This does not mean that repurposing the story will effect a change to the conditions in which our life is unfolding, but it does mean that an individual's experience of those conditions might not be merely passive and receptive. It can be transformed – the monster reimagined, the degraded subject transvalued, the personal tragedy made endurable by being recognized as the fate of others, too.

Several contemporary responses to the Matter of Troy, as we have seen in this book, communicate mercy, pity, despair and a hunger for justice through scenes of carnage and cruelty inspired directly by the *Iliad* and its afterlives: poetry, song, story, the imaginative representations of art are not necessarily vehicles of sweetness and light. The story of Medea, in the tragedies written by Euripides and Seneca, have inspired numerous revisionings in recent years, from Ted Hughes's versions to a play by the Kuwaiti writer Sulayman Al Bassam. The latter transposed the story to the Middle East today and recast Medea as a social-media influencer who is driven to support terrorism, is imprisoned and silenced. Evils can and must be remembered, and need to be so, as warnings – even while they are being averted by the power of fair words, 'the bread of faithful speech', in the marvellous phrase of

Wallace Stevens. The step from accepting a reality and telling it with a difference does make all the difference, and it is a step that can be taken if not in fact then in imagination. To think that stories are simply consolatory misses the quality of their truth-telling, which often exceeds the horrors of experience (think of the outlandish crimes in Greek tragedy, the cannibal mothers in fairy-tale favourites, such as Perrault's version of 'Sleeping Beauty' or the Grimms' 'The Juniper Tree'.)

I believe, with Paul Ricoeur, that artefacts created by the power of the imagination can reach more deeply and broadly than the finest scholarly criticism, and that the main arena of struggle is fantasy, fantasy taken broadly speaking to embrace supernatural narratives, from hagiography to fairy tales. These are forms of storytelling that flourish in popular milieux, among less valued elements of society, often subject to condescension and mockery from their own clergy and prelates. Consequently, they enjoy the supreme distinction of being intrinsically informal and unofficial, tending to heterodoxy, and extending opportunities beyond the control of hegemonic arbiters. Anna Della Subin's recent study *Accidental Gods* discusses wittily but never mockingly other people's beliefs even when they seem ridiculous – like worshipping Prince Philip as a god. Throughout her book, she probes what needs the worship meets among the people who perform it; even more significantly, she also trusts, ultimately, the beneficent potential of active imagination and its products. She defiantly declares, 'Myth *is* enlightenment. And it summons us to the work of transformation. It seeks to find the origin, the cause, the reasons why things are the way they are, and thus to shape the future. Different ideas of divinity determine what form political rule should take.'

Many forms of fiction that are caught under the broad shelter of the term 'fantasy' have a two-fold function in the making of sanctuary: as prophecy, stories are told to bring about a desired future, and, more crucially, to prevent some calamity. A prophetic story thus does not necessarily include manifest fortune-telling or prediction or oracles; fulfilment may take place without the story's knowledge of its own significance. Several writers and tellers of stories, novelists and fabulists, are writing from a perspective of 'as if'. They are posing the root question of the prophet Jeremiah, 'When shall it once be?' (Jeremiah 13: 27), rather than taking up the vantage point that claims, 'and so it was'. Gérard Genette points out the paradox that, while 'it seems evident that the narrating can only be subsequent to what it tells, this obviousness has been belied for many centuries by the existence of "predictive" narrative in its various forms (prophetic, apocalyptic, oracular, astrological, chiromantic, cartomantic, oneiromantic, etc.), whose origin is lost in the darkness of time'.

*Providential* structures do not always claim that they command cause and effect, rather the opposite, presenting events as fated. In forms of *inadvertently coded* prolepsis, the prophecy is not enunciated as such but has to await its decipherers, who will be later readers/redactors/translators. It is we, the audience or readers, who must discover the oracle in the narrative, which acts as a seer: the invitation to read figurally effectively hands over to writers or storytellers a field of possibility, for they can rely on a circle of readers and listeners who, expecting them to be writing hermeneutically, will decipher the hidden figures in the carpet of their narratives. A strong difference thus distinguishes conscious and unconscious prolepsis; the latter device is undergoing reinvigoration, too, by readers of modern and contemporary fiction. Prolepsis in imaginative works of literature becomes a powerful form of 'as if'.

The unintended prescience of literary imagination has come to play a vital part in current cultural values. In relation to certain books, truth-telling takes place independently of the intention of the work's creators or its former readers: the text comes to seem prophetic – as if it has an unconscious that speaks. The promise of figurative suggestion underlies William Burroughs's advocacy of a similar palimpsestic process, his cut-up technique. As Burroughs writes, 'When you cut into the present the future leaks out.' Many compelling stories exercise their hold on us because they appear to have seen further and deeper than their forebears or contemporaries: the very short animal fable 'Jackals and Arabs', written by Kafka in 1917, tells of an endless desert war, an unbreakable cycle of carnage driven by gleeful antagonism, mutual stubborn incomprehension and an immutable commitment to continued hostility. Kafka condenses this apocalyptic epic into a fragment and brings into play a symbol that, like the key in 'Bluebeard' or the mirror of the Snow Queen in Andersen's fairy tale, condenses into a banal and domestic instrument a world of danger: a pair of small rusty scissors that has been travelling through the desert for ever, waiting to be used to kill. 'Marvelous creatures, aren't they? And how they hate us!' are the closing lines of this lacerating fable.

It would be an overstatement to claim writers *are* prophets, or to demand that they should set out to be, according to Shelleyan ideas of the poet's calling or according to readings that cast Kafka as a visionary who foresaw the bureaucratic tyranny of the twentieth century. But I am arguing that stories in themselves move to a hermeneutic dynamic that yields meaning for the receivers, at different times, in different places. Heidegger's axiom applies: 'I do not speak language, language speaks me.' Or rather, 'I do not make stories, they make me.'

The British anthropologist Alfred Gell formulated the useful phrase 'art as agency' for activities in any medium that set out to intervene in the world and make things happen or prevent the worst. In this way, storytelling seeks to assure the survival of the audience, as a group or as individuals.

The revival of fabulism, often under the star of Kafka, Borges and Samuel Beckett, acts in accordance with magical thinking chiefly when, on behalf of readers and audience, it issues a challenge to the future, in an attempt at self-protection through far-sightedness, a form of prophylaxis to ward off the threats the story envisages. This further function of storytelling corresponds to the anthropological view of ritual performances and their processes: mimetic, when the celebrants represent the life force in order to secure its continuity and their own survival; sacrificial, when participants set out to placate the forces of danger by offering up something valuable in exchange for mercy or even a reward; and, the most deep-rooted and simple motive of all, the apotropaic mode, when performers seek to anticipate calamity and forestall it. As A. E. Stallings puts it in a very tender poem set in the intimate and domestic scene of putting a child to bed:

> The tales that start with *once* and end with *ever after*,
> All, all of the stories are about going to bed,
>
> About coming to terms with the night, alleviating the dread
> Of laying the body down, of lying under a cover.

Coming to terms with the night, she writes, alleviating the dread, are what the makers of stories are trying to do.

Made-up stories may seem to possess uncanny foreknowledge, unbeknown to themselves, as in Kafka's fables, or be deliberately conceived as mimetic, as J. G. Ballard's off-centre fictions show. Foreshadowings are not always conscious. Le Guin imagined alternative worlds with awe-inspiring ingenuity and sympathy, melded with strongly ironic judiciousness, too – in *The Left Hand of Darkness* (1969) and *The Dispossessed* (1974) for example. She is bold and far-sighted, and though she has millions of readers her clarity and her warnings have not prevented dangerous authoritarian developments in the US and beyond. The most sobering recent examples of prophetic fiction would be *The Handmaid's Tale* by Margaret Atwood, which was published in 1988, and *Parable of the Sower* by Octavia Butler, which came out in 1993, during an era when civil liberties which had been won and enshrined in law in the US, including rights of women over their reproductive role, seemed unshakeable. Both Atwood and Butler write politically charged fables, and they have inspired others to think of imagination as an instrument of warning: a beacon lit on a hill to tell others of dangers approaching.

*The Handmaid's Tale* was triumphantly adapted for television, decades after its first publication, thereby reaching audiences in their millions through a contemporary mass medium of storytelling. Sometimes what begins as record turns into fantasy: figments of imagination can take up occupation of memory more deeply than factual accounts and factual accounts have a way of turning fantastical as time passes: Herodotus presented himself as a historian and was enjoyed as such, but is now chiefly read as a teller of marvellous tales – wonderfully rich, entertaining, erudite, but not documentary reports, or what we consider history, at least not consistently.

Anachronism is home ground for mythical time, as Ted Hughes shows again and again when he detonates seismic shocks of modernity in his 'translations' of Ovid's metamorphoses; similarly, Alice Oswald also catches us up into simultaneous time when she 'excavates' the *Iliad* in her poem *Memorial* and beams up in front of our eyes the hero Hector who:

> used to nip home deafened by weapons
> To stand in full armour in the doorway
> Like a man rushing in leaving his motorbike running
> All women loved him

As discussed before, Troy was then, but it is also now.

It is however in the very nature of such stories that within the demarcated space of the story – be it told on the page or on some kind of stage – the events that are re-enacted and revisioned announce ways of connecting to immediate experience and bring news of what might be. The stories they pass on act as foretokens.

Fiction of all kinds also fills in gaps in the historical record, attend to the undocumented dead and reawaken the voices of the unheard. The Angolan writer José Eduardo Agualusa, who writes in Portuguese, told an interviewer, 'We know almost nothing about our pasts . . .' He meant the past that is not written down in the annals of the Portuguese empire. The journalist then asked, 'Do you think a made-up past can come to define someone's future, too?' Agualusa replied, 'Yes, no doubt about it: by making up a past you're able to alter your future.'

This is at first sight shocking, especially when fake news is such a deadly weapon in political ambitions, but on reflection some of the acknowledged masterpieces of contemporary fiction set out to act as Agualusa describes: to name a very few authors who draw deeply on history and reimagine it and, in retrospect, can be seen to have altered attitudes in the present and therefore affected the future: John Steinbeck, Aleksandr Solzhenitsyn, Toni Morrison. The sense of a literary mission to meet loss with new, invented testimony is rising among novelists and their audiences. The list could go on and on.

Stories represent a handful of earth scattered on to the common ground of culture, to add to its solidity and salience. With this last, we enter the rough crosscurrents where liberal humanism meets charges of appropriation. The current critique of the humanist tradition demands consideration, but without being too glib I argue that attention to local particularities and formerly overlooked and even disparaged forms of literature from marginalized cultures can flourish on the common ground, as constituent and vital elements of it. Revisioning existing materials, reinventing them, through creative translation as well as reformulations, has been growing as the main dynamic of this process, as for example in Maria Dahvana Headley's recasting *Beowulf* as a novel of contemporary warfare, in *The Mere Wife* (2018); it is significant that she has also published a superb translation of the poem, updated to a streetwise vernacular: it opens, 'Bro!'

None of these uses of stories – prescience and prophylaxis, simultaneity and visibility in time, cross-fertilization and community – lie in the control of the author, the storyteller or the reader – or the editor, publisher, press representative or critic. Or not entirely. All of these actors play a part, of course, but the fortunes of a story or body of a writer's work remain ultimately unpredictable, ungameable. They depend on a conjunction of circumstances at the time of the book's appearance and then, over the longue durée, a whole confluence of other imponderables. Simply put a story has a life of its own – as is clearly shown by the spread of rumour and slander before social media, but it can also happen with stories that are not poisoning the wellspring.

Recent developments in literary criticism have begun to explore the human mind according to the methods of cognitive studies, and the findings reinforce that call of Seamus Heaney's for engagement through imagination. 'Human cognition is alert, attentive, responsive,' writes Terence Cave, author of *Thinking with Literature*.

> Above all, it is *imaginative*: it can think beyond the constraints of immediate experience, do strange things with words, conjure up futures and histories of all kinds, bring to life people who never existed and invent for them plausible stories and environments. Despite the tangible evidence that this is so, the word 'cognition' has traditionally been used to refer to the rational knowledge-seeking processes of the mind as opposed to other modes of engagement with the world.

Memory and imagination were long considered faculties apart, enclosed in different physical parts of the head: Leonardo intuited, in a drawing of the cross-section of the brain, how intertwined they are, and neuroscientists have now shown that when we conjure up a hypothetical scene (as in writing fiction) we use the same mental regions as when we remember something that happened to us. 'Literature is neither a sideshow nor a side-issue in human cultures,' writes Cave. Peter Brooks similarly stresses the cognitive vitality of literature and calls ardently for more attention to the complexity of fiction, through close reading and sharpened tools of analysis so that readers/listeners can discern the lies, sentimentality and other manipulative stratagems in a narrative. But such acts of imagination also sharpen antennae in response to truth-telling.

The thinking imagination, developed by literature, stimulates a stance of alertness and questioning: what Cave calls 'epistemic vigilance'. When it comes to education in life and the detection of falsehood, critical reading is the best school; given the power of social media to sow rumours, such alertness is a vital defence, a serum against malice.

## Transluminations

Translations and versions of old stories (not only classical myths and traditional tales such as those found in *The Thousand and One Nights*) have flowed thick and fast recently. In John Dryden's still valuable scheme, translation took three forms: 'Metaphrase' and 'Paraphrase' come close to what is generally accepted now as the task of a translator who is not to betray the original. But Dryden's third category, 'Imitation', allows creative freedoms and emulation as an ideal pursuit of a writer. *Imitatio* was a rhetorical discipline and was taught to Shakespeare among others as part of the school curriculum, with fruitful effect. Imitation in this Renaissance sense carries no stigma of plagiarism nor of appropriation.

Various alternative terms have been proposed to convey the new trend toward free retellings. Anne Washburn calls her rendering of Euripides' *Iphigenia in Aulis*, a 'transadaptation'; Jeanette Winterson has borrowed 'cover' from the music industry to describe her prose novella inspired by *The Winter's Tale*. Oswald's term, 'trans-shifting', has already been mentioned, as well as her 'excavation' of the *Iliad*. *Transluminación*, an inspired play on words by the Chilean poet Andrés Ajens, captures 'how translation is a form of reading and writing that creates new work, new conversations'. Ajens uses both Spanish and Andean in his work. *Translucinar*, another of his suggestions, points to the illuminating power of translation and its potential to enhance, but it also hints at instability, for it combines ideas of *translucency* and *lucidity* with the more ambiguous and subjective state of *hallucination*. The wordplay can be taken further: while *transluminación* tips the idea towards the Apollonian pole, *transluciferation* suggests the Dionysiac. The editors of a special issue of the journal *Chain*, which was dedicated to the topic of *translucinación*, commented: 'what interested us was the relentless utopian drive within any act of translation. For no matter what translation does, it still represents the need for one culture to speak and learn about another through the other culture's words.' It is commonly regretted that something is 'lost in translation', but the history of past cultural exchanges shows rather the opposite, that much is gained. The translator Nick Caistor, after noticing that a Victorian edition of Leonardo's notebooks carried the credit line 'Arranged and rendered by . . .', suggested an analogy with flower arranging, but a better analogy would be music: stories are made up of motifs and themes that have travelled culturally across local languages and media; they can be shuffled and rearranged and played with almost infinite variations.

Perhaps because English is hardly an endangered language, nor exactly homeless, possessiveness about texts as homelands of the imagination does not reach in the UK the intense pitch of national identification found in France. After Nicolas Sarkozy, then minister of the interior, publicly disparaged the seventeenth-century novel *La Princesse de Clèves* by Mme de La Fayette, saying that there was no point reading such books from the past, or knowing about such things in the present day, French men and women all over the country rose up and organized a mass read-in of the novel aloud in public as a protest. The novel became a bestseller, an effect which lasted for three years. It took its place besides other symbols of the national culture as a treasured *lieu de mémoire*.

In the culture of Arabic and Farsi speakers, this sense of dwelling in language and its vehicles has far greater presence because poems circulate orally and through other channels. For example, Shiraz, the birthplace of the Sufi poet Hafiz, a fortune-teller working in the market would ask his trained pigeon to pick out, from a heap on a tray in front of him, a folded paper which the petitioner would then open and read; the prophecies written therein were all taken from the poetry of Hafiz, still widely known in Iran and often quoted. The Egyptian scholar and novelist Radwa Ashour also reports, from a very different social milieu, how she and her family exulted in their common knowledge of poetry. How they dwelt in words. In her interwoven memoir and fiction *Spectres*, written in 2010, she recalls her childhood visits to aunts and other members of the family. Umm Duqduq, an older, grandmotherly figure, coaxed by her young visitors, would tell fables – wisdom stories featuring clever monkeys and talking date palms, playful and witty but carrying an undertow of sorrow. One of her tales about a whole menagerie coming to grief ends with the Nile crying out, 'And I, Water, will flow no more!'

The folk tradition commingles in Radwa Ashour's experience with the classical poetry of Al-Mutanabbi, whose complete works were edited by her grandfather Abdel Wahhab Azzam. She captures the exuberant poetic polyphonic games that she and her husband, Mourid Barghouti, played with their son Tamim, as they struck up a loving rivalry, quoting strophes of Al-Mutanabbi learned by heart in a counterpoint that resolves into a hymn of delight. They trade quotations back and forth from other poets – some from the classics, others their own – challenging one another in high spirits to spin new lines and antiphonal responses in rhythm and rhyme. In these scenes of loving alliance, dwelling in language happens when they are united and dwelling together once again at home in Cairo after all the displacements they, and most especially Mourid, suffered during their lives.

The religious and ethnic tensions that are causing, alongside the fight to control resources (water, oil), so much of the current flight of people from the Middle East and Africa, are creating cultural diasporas. Refugees, whether in camps and other places of exclusion or settling within societies where they are to live, are establishing and will continue to establish communities – translated communities – of people who will need to negotiate their place in relation to the local culture and vice versa.

In 2016, the United Nations declared that cultural heritage is a human right and thereby opened a new horizon for the survival of beleaguered communities, recognizing at the same time the vital role that cultural heritage plays in establishing social bonds. UNESCO has since identified intangible artefacts, such as songs and stories, as part of that cultural heritage. The compass points of heritage are set not by material goods alone, but by immaterial artefacts: by acts of making, with sounds and images spoken, recited, performed, passed on. These creations may eventually be set down in books or recorded in a durable medium, but they also travel by other ethereal conduits, especially in the age of the internet when they are at one and the same time vigorous and fragile. They may inhere in things, containers of memories and history and imagination. In 2003, when UNESCO first declared protection for intangibles, the implication was that this applied principally to the culture of unlettered peoples – to orature. This viewpoint needs adjusting: highly literate civilizations also flourish through oral and digital – performed, played – media.

Cultural and literary transmission of myth and story involves a process of constant, deep and fruitful metamorphosis. These metamorphoses take place in dialogue with written texts, but are not constrained by writing; indeed, mobile narratives are a dynamic feature of contemporary culture because the internet and digital technologies have opened up a vast arena for varieties of performance, recitation, speech, combining sound, image, voice and translation. The traffic in myths is rising with the strong and omnipresent return of acoustics to communication – we have entered a hybrid era, in which the oral is no longer placed in opposition to the literate. Audio books are described as 'performed' rather than read, and certainly the actors involved dramatize them, able to voice a myriad characters in a way unattainable through silent reading. Although Jorge Luis Borges commented that he had always imagined 'Paradise will be a kind of library,' it is worth remembering that the great writer was himself blind for a great part of his life, and he was read to – books for him were *sounded*.

Attitudes to newly arrived strangers, ranging from welcome to rejection, are always rooted in certain social and historical values, and these are not fixed: ideas of who to accept and who to exclude depend above all on a shared sense of place and history. This is an immense topic, but within it the ancient law of sanctuary plays a special part; it was a safe place instituted by words, by consensus around a story. Such 'holy' sites and their histories, sacred and secular, reveal the decisive interplay between ideas about self and world, purity and impurity; works of literature and art are vitally involved in these processes of consecration and desecration and, through the vicissitudes in the lives of mythic and dramatic protagonists, the reader/audience can trace the contours of a larger picture about changing common values and the bonds between individuals and society.

In stories, people have come together, using their imaginations to embroider a common tapestry, to explore tensions and conflicts and dreams of hope, to lay out rules of conduct and to test the limits of convention, to work out ethics. Listening to the voices of the makers of stories that do not speak the language of injustice and intolerance, tuning in to the imagination and memories of our forerunners and our neighbours, weaving counter-myths – these are, it seems to me, acts of stewardship at the heart of culture.

The country of words is a storehouse of old stories, Babylonian, Indian, Greek, Arabic, Latin, Hebrew, Fula, Swahili and in many other languages. My contention – my hope – is that thinking with stories can bring into being a country of words beyond the borders of nation and language, that the shared invention and retelling of stories, performed and recited and animated, can contribute to fashioning 'a community of fate', in the eloquent phrase of the comparatist, Bruce Robbins, help individual and social survival, connect a remembered past with present circumstances and build relations in the future. Refugees, migrants and arrivals, while stripped of their possessions, still own their minds, and these hold rich material – knowledge made of poems, stories and memories, songs and proverbial lore. But building the country of words involves reinventing stories and memories, and very fierce conflicts erupt over numerous issues, not least immigration (think only of the current struggle over gender identity, statues and legacies). As Bruce Robbins writes,

> The present is always different [from the past], because one can act in and on the present as one cannot act on even an identical situation (if such a thing exists) in the past. A secular version of fate is a political community that, like the nation-state, at least has a possibility of controlling what its members do and suffer and adding to those who can count as members . . .

He goes on to warn,

> it does not follow that we fulfil our moral responsibilities merely by reading strenuous fiction. Literature, whether strenuous or not, is valuable not because it can substitute for collective agents like the nation-state – it cannot – but because it can motivate us to build and inhabit collective agents, whether national or (increasingly, hopefully) transnational. Some years later, we may in this way be able to remember

that, faced with the demands of our moment, we at least did what we could.

Imagining future outcomes is one way for stories to intervene in history and experience: sometimes to warn, at other times to hope, sometimes to prevent developments – or attempt to. Making stories together may also add a bit of lightness and laughter in difficult times and moves the storymakers towards finding the key to a place where someone might feel a little more at home.

The bearers of stories, writers and storytellers, the *hakawati*, the *raawi*, the rhapsodes, the bearers of words, can build bridges, shelters and sanctuaries.

Since I became ever more deeply immersed in thinking about mysterious mythological works – *The Epic of Gilgamesh*, the stories of the Trojan war, *The Thousand and One Nights*, Celtic legends and Norse sagas – the supernatural forces in these stories, personified as gods, fairies or jinn, seemed more and more to embody the power that the stories themselves possess to determine destiny. They represent not only the destiny of the characters subject to magic inside the story, but our fate, too, the fate of the story's receivers.

The travelling tale Edward Said explored in relation to exile radiates out from the voice of the storyteller or the printed page and materializes in territory and things, which it infuses with significance, significance which arises from the features of the story. A story may be mobilized to entrench nationalistic and religious separatism and partisan histories; but the same process of imprinting stories on a landscape and into objects can also work towards opening minds to difference and thereby to tolerance, ecumenically. These deep-rooted political and religious principles can be applied in secular contexts too. That we are the story we tell has become a cliché, but I think it has profound significance especially in times of violent uprootings and horrendous losses at every level, literal and figurative. It is all too frequently that culture – including education in the arts and humanities – is set aside, regarded as a luxury. Refugees – arrivants – are often severed from families and friends as well as from their geography of home, and one of their needs that must command attention is the need for culture. It will develop spontaneously, of course: making music, confabulation, art, masking, storytelling cannot be altogether stifled. Yet creating conditions in which expression can flourish and exchanges can take place remains vital, even when other resources are stretched.

## Postscript

Storytelling can change someone's fate: the German literary critic Marcel Reich-Ranicki, in his memoir *Mein Leben* (1999; English translation, *The Author of Himself*), relates his remarkable odyssey as a Jewish refugee from the Nazis and his survival against the odds. Marcel was born in Warsaw, his wife Teofila (Tosia) in Łódź; they were both in their early twenties when they managed to escape the pogrom in the Warsaw Ghetto. They found shelter with a Polish couple, a Protestant typesetter called Bolek and his wife Genia, who lived in an isolated suburb of the city, and hid them – sometimes in their basement, at other times in the attic. The Polish hosts were not however acting out of altruism or rebellion; they themselves were short of everything. The arrangement was that the young Jewish fugitives would roll hundreds of cigarettes, working at night in the cellar by the light of carbide or oil lamps in order to conceal this contraband activity; the money earned went on vodka for Bolek. They were fed, but barely, and were always hungry, and above all, constantly frightened of being denounced and turned over to the authorities. But the couple did not betray them, and in a chapter called 'Stories for Bolek', Reich-Ranicki describes how their relationship underwent a subtle and remarkable change: 'Incredible though it may seem,' he writes, 'here, quite unexpectedly, I had a reunion with literature . . .'

> One day [Genia] suggested that I should tell them a story, preferably a thrilling one. From that day onwards, as soon as it was dark, I would tell all kinds of stories . . . for hours, for weeks, for months. These had but one aim – to entertain my hosts. The better they liked a story, the better we were rewarded – with a slice of bread, with a few carrots. I did not invent any stories, not a single one. Instead, I told them whatever I could remember . . . dramatically heightened shortened versions of novels and novellas I had read, or of plays and operas, even films, I had seen . . .

His repertory passed from Goethe to *Aida*, from Flaubert to *Rigoletto*.

Unlike Shahrazad, Marcel Reich-Ranicki does not overlook his own circumstances when he takes up Heinrich von Kleist's peculiar and hallucinatory tale *The Prince of Homburg* and retells it for us in the same way he told it for his hosts in his precarious refuge. After Marcel has unfolded to them the plot of Kleist's play, Bolek explodes, 'The devil take the Germans, all of them! But this Herr Hamburg, I like him! He is shit-scared of death – as we all are. He wants to live. He doesn't give a monkey's for honour and glory. He is afraid, but he's not ashamed, he speaks up about his fear. *Those who want to live let others live too.*'

The space of story has cleared a new shelter – a kind of sanctuary – for the four of them together. The plots did not have to capture their circumstances mimetically to bring about potent recognition, for its listeners to feel that this man, however remote his social setting, belonged to them. The Prince of Homburg, living by an elaborate and remote aristocratic code, is transformed – without friction – into Bolek's *semblable*, his brother in suffering.

Shahrazad, in *The Thousand and One Nights*, does not invent any stories either, or so we are told at the beginning – she remembers them because she's an avid reader. Just as Sultan Shahryar is changed by the experience of listening, so in occupied Poland storytelling could help save a young Jewish couple.

In this way the stories Marcel told day after day from his hiding place acted as a point of triangulation between potentially hostile or dangerous elements. Like an ingredient which, when added to a chemical mixture may neutralize its poison, his remembered and retold stories kept him, his wife – and his hosts – alive and safe from June 1943 to September 1944: 'we continued to produce thousands of cigarettes every night, and during the long evenings I continued to tell stories of girls in love, young princes and old kings, winter's tales and midsummer night's dreams'.

Then the Russian army arrived and a soldier appeared at the door and freed them. Later, Reich-Ranicki naturally never forgot 'the Warsaw typesetter who risked his life to save mine'.

# Coda

## Stories in Transit

> Those old composers were such fools:
> they wrote melodies only for the happy times
> festivals, grand banquets, celebrations.
> None of them thought to make a music for real life,
> music that would salve our wounds
> and soothe our bitter griefs . . .
> We need a tune when there's no food to eat.
> 
> Euripides

In a closely shuttered side room of the Puppet Museum, Palermo, in the heart of the old city, scores of puppets are hanging, sitting, standing; from the four quarters of the world, mingling with many paladins and Moors of the *Orlando* cycle and the odd Sirena and Dragon. It was one of the early workshops in the project Stories in Transit, which had begun in 2016 in Sicily and is still continuing to engage young arrivants in storytelling and other forms of imaginative play. I was sitting on a rug with two or three others, while another group across from us was trying out different musical instruments and choruses; on our part we were struggling a bit with the racket. I said something about a story from *The Thousand and One Nights* and Din Diallo, a young Guinean, who was across from me, looked thoughtful and said, 'That reminds me of something my grandfather used to tell me.'

Like many who make the crossing of the Mediterranean, Safoudiny

Diallo (to give his full name) had not brought anything with him from Guinea, where civil strife had destroyed his family and their home, and besides, the journey to Europe had taken him through many countries and across many borders – and through many ordeals where he would have lost anything he had started out with. He began telling us, in French, which was then his principal language after Fula, a complicated, nested tale, 'L'Histoire du chasseur, le fils du roi, et le cerf enchanté' ('The Story of the Huntsman, the King's Son, and the Enchanted Deer'; see pages 298–301).

Din was the first of the sanctuary seekers who, during those early days of Stories in Transit, passed on a traditional story. Before then we had drawn on world myths and well-travelled fairy tales. Din had been a vivid presence at the workshops from the start: in November 2016, during the first full-scale workshop, he played Gilgamesh in the promenade cum pageant cum parade that meandered through the Botanical Gardens of Palermo. Enkidu the wild man was played by Gassimou Magassouba, known as Maga, with whom he had made fast friends on the boat coming over; Maga would also prove a mainstay of the project overall. The day had opened with a terrific thunderstorm, so we were worried that the puppets and the splendid boat that the group has made would be wrecked. But the sky cleared suddenly and the wind dropped, and when we reached the Orto Botanico birds were singing joyously at being so deliciously bathed, the leaves on the trees and plants shone in their newly-washed freshness and the light was entirely beautiful, the colours of the greens and yellows bright and vigorous. The performance wound its way through the gardens under the flowering orange, lemon, pomegranate, mango and kapok trees, fallen petals and ripe grapefruit scattered on the ground. The whole marvellous place felt like Eden.

At one point towards the end of the performance, after the serpent has stolen the plant of immortality from the sleeping hero, a little girl, aged around seven or eight, turned to me indignantly, Alice-like, and protested, 'Non è la pianta dell'immortalità. È un carciofo!' (That isn't a plant of immortal life. It's an artichoke!). Her mother responded, 'Tesoro, artichokes are a bud, you see, and they open up into something else, so they can give a sense of hope.'

These forays into *Gilgamesh* were hardly theatre in the sense that Peter Brook achieved with his international cast interpreting *The*

*Mahabharata*. The project's aim was conviviality, involvement, exchanges, fellowship – and it succeeded in this far more than all those involved had hoped. The process matters, not the product. The atmosphere is the product. Participants assemble peacefully, and the project is not looking for stars. On each occasion, the involvement, inventiveness and sheer high spirits of all participants reached a state of what can only be thought of as self-forgetfulness – which after all is one form of happiness.

Din and Maga had arrived in Sicily having spent more than two years on the road, crossing the Sahara on foot and working in the labour camps of Libya to take a boat across the Mediterranean. They were among eighty pupils enrolled in CPIA Palermo 1, a school now chiefly attended by refugees who are unaccompanied minors. Originally an institution for drop-outs, it still includes Italian students (and some second-generation migrants), including some girls. The Scuola Superiore F. Ferrara also took part. Clelia Bartoli, a human rights academic at the University of Palermo, had volunteered to opt out of her job at the university to teach the newly arrived young people instead; she became an inspiration and moving force in the work of Stories in Transit.

I had expected many refugees from the war in Syria, but they have mostly fled to neighbouring countries, including Turkey, Jordan and Greece, where they are still housed in the vast UNHCR camps (around 80,000 in Zaatari; 40,000 in Azraq – though at the time of writing, with the fall of the Assad regime, many are perhaps able to return home). Stories in Transit, as it has developed, collaborates predominantly with 'minorenni', aged under eighteen who, according to international law, cannot be imprisoned or detained and have a right to education. This context allows a volunteer group, like Stories in Transit, to work with them in different venues in comparative freedom. Besides Guinea, many more West African nations, peoples and languages were represented by this first cohort of participants – the Gambia, Mali, Côte d'Ivoire, Burkina Faso, Niger – as well as Egypt, Libya, Tunisia, Bangladesh. During recent, subsequent Stories in Transit visits, young men and women from Chad, Nigeria, Sudan, Guinea-Bissau and Morocco have taken part. All had travelled through Libya, where the conditions are ruthless. The journalist Sally Hayden, in *My Fourth Time, We Drowned: Seeking Refuge on the World's Deadliest Migration Route* (2022), gives a detailed, harrowing account of the lawlessness and horror of the situation as it was in 2018–21, when she was reporting on the region.

～

Flight, the loss of home and the loss of bearings have been recurrent themes in my writing, and the recent intensity of the refugee situation made me feel quite helpless to do anything, as it does us all. I was looking at images of camps with their endless rows of tents or huts, and no focal points or gathering places, and wondering how these new cities – many of the inhabitants spend decades living there – could be given some qualities of home. Could literature in its broadest sense offer an alternative shelter? Then I noticed, from an image published by Save the Children, that a refugee child named Farah had drawn a crowd around the water supply.

Like the water sources, laundries and washing places where news and stories used to be exchanged, like the magic well in so many fairy tales where encounters take place and carry the characters over into another dimension of reality, the water delivery arriving in a camp created a place of exchange and fellowship; it exemplified the Arabic association of narration, thirst-quenching and irrigation.

Since the 1970s I had often visited Sicily – I first did research there for my study of the cult of the Virgin Mary published in 1976. Valentina Castagna, who is a lecturer in English literature at the University of Palermo and a translator, is a colleague and has become a friend and the lynchpin of Stories in Transit. She told me how, around the year 2015, she had volunteered as an interpreter in the city courts where asylum cases are heard. The petitioners whose words she voiced in Italian, were English speakers from former British colonies, now members of the Commonwealth, such as Nigeria. One case affected her deeply: an old man, dignified, upstanding and sincere (she said with feeling) was told by the judge: 'I have no alternative but to order you to be deported back to your country.' He himself sounded regretful, Valentina said. She duly translated his words and at that point, she remembered, the sanctuary seeker fell to his knees and begged the judge not to pass this sentence. He was weeping as he described the future that certainly lay ahead for him. Valentina was still translating as best she could, but she found speaking the judge's words and the suppliant's pleas excruciating. (I once heard Archbishop Tutu during a public interview in London being asked about the worst ordeals the Truth and Reconciliation Commission had undergone. He reflected and then commented, musingly, that he often thought of the plight of the interpreters who, day after day, week in week out, had had to relive, in the voice of one victim after another, the sufferings the court was recording.)

There are rarely funds for repatriations. Failed asylum seekers try to survive under the radar, to disappear. Their stateless, paperless, homeless, unprotected condition makes them rich pickings for the Mafia and other clandestine operators, who offer their protection in return for their labour.

Valentina and I, who spend most of our time reading and writing, felt and still feel useless as we saw the expulsion of populations, the flight of so many, the prolonged establishment of camps and detention centres, the profusion of borders everywhere and the utter waste of huge sums on supposed deterrents such as the plan to transport asylum seekers to a third country – Rwanda, in the case of the failed Conservative policy. At the beginning of this wave of hostility, Valentina and I asked ourselves if there was something we, as academics and writers, could do. Exploring the forms sanctuary has taken during the writing of this book led me to see the important part stories play in developing a sense of being at home. Clelia, Valentina and I decided we would try to create a space of sanctuary by making up stories, retelling old ones, playing various games with the arrivants. Strangers in a strange land are often severed from family and friends as well as from the familiar geography of home, and they often arrive singly, having lost companions on the way. They're in need of the conviviality that making art, music, poetry, song together, as well as eating, laughing together, can provide. *Convivencia* is our aim – between us and the arrivants, and among the arrivants themselves; after all, they come from many different places, with different languages, faiths, customs. We would exchange images, ideas, fragments, stories, which could be woven into the fabric of belonging; such group activities might help overcome barriers of language and difference and develop a place of refuge for displaced individuals. It was important for us to eat together, and to let the arrivants speak and take charge of the stories and their direction. Our band of *nessi* (links, as in *connessione*, connection – 'facilitator' sounds too heavy) come from various spheres:

theatre, music, art, animation, writing. We would try to build a sanctuary that is not a physical site, but a sanctuary of the mind.

I have another powerful, selfish motive: I don't want to breathe the oppressive miasma of hostility, mistrust, contempt that greets refugees seeking sanctuary. I am the daughter of a southern Italian mother who came to England with very little English (a smattering of popular song lyrics, like 'Tea for Two') and no formal education or training, from a war-battered, famously backward region, and flourished. I am married to an Australian whose Jewish forebears fled the tsar's conscriptions and pogroms. We both have grandparents who were illiterate. I want to inhale another, brighter air in relation to the strangers who come from elsewhere. The ones we work with have landed, they are now in Europe, and meeting them on different terms from those of the immigration authorities, the courts and the camps can re-establish values that I for one hope are still central to the way of life that we want to flourish, and that drew them in the first place to come to countries – democracies – like the UK. I am not at all alone in this desire: at the time of writing, there have been mass expressions of solidarity with the victims of recent horrific riots of far-right, nativist protesters, who have attacked mosques, hostels where asylum seekers are housed, shops and even libraries.

For millennia Sicily has been the crossroads where Europe, Africa and Asia meet. It is the largest island in the Mediterranean and has been a site of exceptionally rich cultural exchange since at least the Phoenicians – the epoch when the historical Carthage became a Phoenician colony. Arabic used to be spoken and written in Sicily, before civil conflict between rival emirs there weakened Muslim power and gave the Norman Franks, who had coexisted with their Arab predecessors for a century, the chance to take over the whole of the island. A part of Palermo displays street signs in Arabic to remember this history, and of course the local cuisine draws on its spices and flavours too. For a time, the cultural conversations continued, with Moorish artisans working on the Normans' magnificent monuments, such as the palace of the Norman kings and the Cappella Palatina in Palermo and, in nearby Monreale, the duomo, where they laid the mosaic marble floor, each square a different pattern, each one more ingenious and kinetic than the next.

The island has seen perpetual cross-fertilization in every kind of human activity, from growing apricots to religious cults to narrative transmission. Strategically placed at the sea's centre, it has long acted as a powerful transmitter – a huge server – of endlessly shifting archives of stories. In the nineteenth century, for example, the daughter of the Swiss consul in Messina, Laura Gonzenbach (1842–78), collected fantastic local fairy tales she had heard and translated them into German, circulating them to colleagues and friends. Her work, which was eventually published in 1870, influenced the course of European fairy literature. She herself was inspired by the activities of Giuseppe Pitrè, a doctor from Palermo and a pioneer of literary ethnography. Greek, Arabic, Norman, Arthurian and romance traditions intermingled and continue: Morgan le Fay, in legend King Arthur's half-sister, still conjures illusions of castles in the air over the straits of Messina.

In Arabic, the equivalent of 'Once upon a time' – 'It was and it was not' – conveys conscious relish in the playful ambiguity of the material. In Italian the word *fiaba* applies to both legends and epics, forms of story which have historical roots in lived events but are nevertheless punctuated by fantastic episodes of enchantments and wonders. Sicilian puppet plays still stage characters from the Arthurian cycle of heroic chivalry as dramatized in the epics of Tasso and Ariosto, filled with memories of Crusader history and of the ambivalent relations between Moors and Christians. To this group of cross-culturally inflected *aja'ib* belong the animal fables told by the Sicilian Arab Ibn Zafer in the twelfth century, and the comic antics, now relayed mostly for children, of Giufà, the scapegrace and fool, who is always in trouble.

Soon after our first visit, and encouraged by Clelia Bartoli, several of the young arrivants who had joined in the workshops of Stories in Transit formed themselves into a cooperative called Giocherenda, from a Fula word meaning cooperation, negotiation, unity. It echoes the Italian verb *giocare*, to play, as in *giocando*, playing, and seemed to fit the group's aims.

They have devised storytelling toys, games and devices such as story dice, *acchiapparicordi* (memory prompt cards), and a collaborative role-playing game called the *La Ronda dei desideri*, the wheel of wishes. By design, none of the games they offer is competitive and luck does not feature strongly; all involve group discussion of strategy. Giocherenda have also been importing African wax-printed cottons, and they make

The baobab tree offers shelter, a place for stories, and is the emblem for the group Giocherenda in Palermo, founded by sanctuary seekers in 2016.

bags, computer sleeves, notebooks and all kinds of garments, sometimes on request from customers (Din and another, Daouda, had been taught tailoring back home). With some local and EU funding, they opened a shop cum workshop, and until the pandemic interrupted everything they had also established a busy diary of engagements in schools and at fairs and festivals all over the island encouraging play and performance – collaboratively, not competitively. This splendid initiative continues the process that lies at the heart of Stories in Transit: to open communication and create ties among the arrivants themselves, with the city of Palermo and its inhabitants, and to enjoy making up stories – incidentally a form of activity that does not take anyone else's job.

The tale that Din related early on, 'The Huntsman, the King's Son and the Enchanted Deer', proved a rich source of many retellings. It's a spirited imbroglio of politics and enchantment, comedy and sorrow, one tale looped inside another in the manner of *The Thousand and One Nights*, and it echoes animal fables from the medieval Arab collection *Kalilah wa Dimnah*. Each repeated warning points to the danger of haste, the necessity of calm deliberation and the fallibility of rulers. The story is a morality tale, bloody and outlandish, wholly directed at pointing out the follies of tyrants. Over several workshops, another promenade cum play developed, with puppetry, song and animated film.

## 'The Tale of the Huntsman, the King's Son and the Enchanted Deer'

Din began, in French:

> A young man living with his mother is having difficulty finding a wife, when his mother suggests, 'Stay here and work for me and maybe when I die, you'll be able to marry.'
> And so it turns out. His mother dies and he marries a good woman.
> One day, his wife tells him that she's had a dream, and he must tell her when he is going out hunting again, as the dream has foretold that he must take a lot of food and drink with him, as he will meet someone who will bring them great fortune.
> Soon after, he sets out to go hunting and his wife prepares a lot of food and drink. In the forest, he comes upon an animal and begins giving chase, and then, as he lifts his gun and shoots, at that very same moment, someone else also lifts his gun and shoots the animal.
> The two men begin discussing who can claim the kill:
> 'The animal is mine.'
> 'No, it is mine.'
> The huntsman suggests that, before they dispute the spoils, they should introduce themselves:
> 'Who are you?' he asks.
> 'I am the son of a king,' replies the other, 'and I was lost in the forest.'
> The huntsman shares his food and drink, and then shows him the way through the forest. The king's son invites him to come home with him.
> On the way, a branch of a tree is about to fall on the prince's head but the huntsman saves him, and then, when they arrive at the prince's house, they go in to rest, but the huntsman hears a great wind and it rises and fans a fire and the house burns down. The huntsman then hears a voice crying out, in a wild wail, 'You chased that animal, and it was my son. He wanted to escape you and you did not let him go. I will never forgive you.'

With the prince's wife, the prince and the huntsman set out again to find another place to shelter and there they retire to rest. But a huge snake enters their room. The huntsman wakes and kills the snake with his knife, cutting the animal in two. Blood spreads everywhere and the princess wakes up and, seeing the carnage, faints clean away. When the prince wakes up, he sees his wife covered in blood and denounces his friend, the huntsman, as the murderer.

He orders him to be arrested and he is taken away by the guards to prison – from which nobody ever reappears.

When they reach the gates of the fort, the gatekeepers tell them that the old king has died and everyone inside is mourning him for forty days, and they cannot enter by those gates but should go round to another entrance.

Meanwhile, the huntsman tells the guards, 'Listen, I have a story to tell you:

Once upon a time there was a king who had a bird, and the bird was very very old. But one day, the bird came back from the forest and was entirely transformed, young and beautiful again.

'How come?' asks the king, and the bird tells him he's eaten the fruit of a tree in the forest. The king demands to have some of this fruit; he wants to plant it in his garden, and eat it himself.

When the tree has borne fruit, he asks one of his entourage to taste it beforehand, and the man falls down dead.

The king turns on the bird and accuses it of planning his death. The bird protests her innocence, but the king wrings her neck.

Around the same time, there were two very old courtiers who were working for the king, but they could no longer do so and were plunged into poverty, so the king decided they must die. He orders them to eat the same fruit, but when they ate it, they were refreshed and reinvigorated, and became young again.

So the king has the tree investigated and it turns out that a snake was living in the tree and contaminating the fruit.

The king understood that he had acted wrongly, and that the bird who had brought him the fruit had been right all along.

They're making their way to the second set of gates, when the huntsman says to his guards, 'Excuse me, I have another story to tell you:'

Once upon a time there was a mother of a baby and they had a pet cat who looked after the baby like a nursemaid, sleeping beside her to protect her.

One day when the mother had left to go to the market, a huge snake entered the room and wanted to kill the baby. But what happened? The cat seized the snake's head between its teeth and bit it off. There was blood everywhere and all over the baby. The cat dragged the head of the snake outside. When the mother came back and saw her baby covered in blood, she jumped to the conclusion that the cat had fallen asleep at her post and let a disaster happen, or that the cat had attacked her baby, but that in any case, her child was dead.

She took her broom and beat the cat to death.

But almost immediately, after the cat nursemaid had been killed, the baby woke up and then the mother saw, outside the house, the head and the body of the huge snake.

She reproached herself bitterly for her rage, but it was too late. The cat nursemaid was dead.

At the moment that the huntsman finishes his second tale, the wife of the king's son regains consciousness, and she asks her husband, 'Where is your friend?'

He explains what has taken place, how he thought his friend had killed her and had ordered the guards to take him away.

His wife told him, 'No! He saved our lives!'

The young prince says, 'If it is not too late, tell him to come back to us.'

When they received this order, the guards let the huntsman go and he returned to the prince and princess.

Meanwhile, the king's son has inherited the throne from the old king who'd died, and he decides to share his power with his friend the huntsman, and they begin working together as if they were brothers.

This is how the story happened, this is how things turned out and how the dream of the huntsman's wife proved to have foreseen the future.

But what does it tell us?

If we understand the story, that it is not right to rush to judgement.

If you rush, you will spoil things.

It is so very important to be patient, to look into the matter before you act.

This is what I wanted to say.

Thank you.

And so Din closed his tales within a tale.

~~~

By the following year and our next visit, Din could tell the story in Italian to a new cohort of arrivants (the arrivants are young and pick up languages quickly as they cross from country to country on their way to Europe). One of the tales embedded in the overall structure – 'The

The happy ending of 'The Huntsman, the King's Son and the Enchanted Deer'.
Gassimou Magassouba and Safoudiny Diallo perform the tale (2016).

Cat and the Baby' – has recognizable counterparts in Aesop and other fables and it inspired one group to compose a lullaby for the cat nursemaid to mew to her charge: it is a high point of the film that the young people were making under the guidance of Joan Ashworth and Lee Shearman, both of them professional animators.

The stories the young people passed on often emphasized the ethic of listening, absorbing and helping, and the moral Din put to his audience is characteristic of the wisdom tradition. Numu Touray, one of Din's friends from the hostel, presented a show on Radio Asante, the arrivants' local station, and had originally invited him on to the programme to tell the story of 'The Huntsman'; Numu was its star presenter and disc jockey, and he then staged a comic parable about a village spooked by a rumour (a presage of social media disinformation).

## 'One for You and One for Me'

Numu began, in English:

> My name is Numu Touray, from the Gambia, and I live now in Italy at the Centro Asante, Palermo.
> Once upon a time there was a village that had a magnificent grove of mango trees growing inside the cemetery. One summer, the villagers came together to discuss the crop, and agreed that for another month no one should pluck the mangoes from the trees. Once they had agreed on this, they also said that this agreement would not be enough: 'We will have to get a watchman for this cemetery, to keep an eye on the mangoes.'
> It was all set up and going well; the watchman was doing a very good job. One evening, however, he came to the graveyard and realized he had forgotten something. He decided to rush home and fetch what he needed and then come back to his post. [In the performance, the actor made as if he had forgotten his mobile phone.] He went, and two boys, who were waiting outside the cemetery, saw him leave and jumped into the cemetery to pick the mangoes. They gathered as many as they could and went and sat down to share the mangoes between the two of them.

Their arms were so full of mangoes that on their way to another part of the cemetery, they passed by the gate of the cemetery, where they dropped two mangoes.

*Listeners, concentrate on the two mangoes dropped at the gate.*

The two boys went on to distribute the mangoes between themselves:

'One for you – one for me – one for you – one for me – one for you – one for me – one for you – one for me.'

And so on.

They continued sharing out their load, when the watchman returned. He heard a noise coming from the graveyard:

'One for you – one for me – one for you – one for me.'

He said to himself, 'How is this possible? I left nobody in here and now I hear people saying "One for you – one for me". What could this be?'

So he thought and pondered and he finally settled on an idea: 'It's a graveyard and there are dead people buried there, and maybe angels are distributing the dead souls.' And the more he thought the more he believed that there were angels in the graveyard distributing the dead among them. 'I have to go home!' he concluded. 'And inform the head of the village and the religious leader. They are the most two important people in the village and will know what to do.'

He ran home very fast, very afraid because he thought that, once the angels had finished distributing the dead, they would be coming for the living. He went to the head of the village first, who was sleeping, and said, 'Please you need to get up! There's a big problem in the village.'

The man answered, 'How can you come into my house at this time of the night and wake me?'

'There is a problem!'

'Then tell me the problem.'

The watchman said, 'There are angels in the cemetery and they are distributing the dead people – and when they finish with the dead people they will surely be coming for us.'

The head of the village said, 'That is not possible. How can the angels – angels don't act this way!'

'This is the truth – I've seen it, I've heard them. There is no dispute, so let's try and find a solution rather than keep on talking.'

'OK, well, I can't do anything, so let us go and see the religious leader and see what he will say.'

They went and knocked on the religious leader's door and asked him to come outside, repeating the watchman's call: 'Please come out! There is a problem in the village.' Out he came, and they said, 'There are angels are in the cemetery and they are distributing the dead people and we believe if they finish with the dead they are coming for us. Tell us what can we do.'

The religious leader said, 'You people don't know what you are saying. Angels don't act this way – angels cannot come and distribute dead people.'

The watchman said, 'I respect you so much and don't want to say anything foul, but believe me – there are angels in the cemetery and they are distributing the dead people.'

The religious leader admitted, 'This is strange . . . let's go and see.'

So they went to see what was going on in the graveyard where the mangoes grow. They all went along until, as they were approaching the cemetery, the watchman said, 'You see, they know what I'm saying so I cannot go any nearer. The two of you have to go – me, I cannot go.'

They said, 'OK – we will see whether what you are saying is true or not.'

The two of them stood at the gate to listen to what was going on inside, and the head of the village and the religious leader heard the same noise in the cemetery, saying:

'One for you – one for me – one for you – one for me.'

They looked at each other, saying, 'It seems to be true!'

As they were listening, the two boys finished distributing the mangoes.

*You remember there were two mangoes at the gate? Great.*

The boys said, 'OK, we have finished this. But the two at the gate?'

The head of the village and the religious leader thought that they were talking about the two of them at the gate and they said, 'This is true – now they have finished with the dead people, they are coming for us!'

So, they decided to run away and go to the village. When they reached the village they called everybody and said, 'Please come out! There is a big problem in the village. The watchman is right. The angels have distributed the dead people – they have finished and they are coming for us. We were at the gate and they said they were coming for the two of us and we ran away. They could not get us. So, everybody, pack your clothes; pack whatever you can. Let's leave this village. The village is not safe.'

Everybody left the village. The village was abandoned, just like that.

Now, this is the end of this story. But there is a question, which is this:

*Among the three parties – the head of the village and religious leader, the watchman and the thieves – who is the cause of the abandonment of the village?*

*If it is the watchman, why do you say it is the watchman?*

*If it is the two boys, why do you say so?*

Ghosts in the cemetery flap, gibber and squeak,
in 'One for You, and One for Me' (2018).

*If it is the head of the village and the religious leader, why is it so?*
This is the end of the story.
I would like you now to listen to everybody's comments.

Numu starred in the performance, and directed others in the parts, while musicians accompanied the action with sound effects (See Plate 15). We were gathered under the magnificent branches and aerial roots of one of the banyan trees that grow in the Giardino Girabaldi, Piazza Marina in the old city of Palermo, and the performance had drawn quite an audience, who rose to the occasion with gusto, deliberating who was to blame. The acting was inventive, especially the part of the sleepy head of the village who absolutely did not want to wake up when the alarm was raised.

Afterwards, Numu explained, with a lot of humour but also intensity of feeling: 'The reason for this story is to tell the leaders – I know many people will say that "It is the watchman's fault, he wasn't doing his job right," or "It is the boys' fault because they didn't respect the rules" – but this story is meant for leaders. It lays the blame on the leaders, that is, the head of the village and the religious leader. Because if you are in power, remember that there will be thieves, that you will have armed robbers, you will have liars, you will have every kind of human being, so it depends on you to know how to treat all these kinds of people. The religious leader and the headman of the village should not just jump to conclusions and make an announcement that everybody should leave when they haven't undertaken any thorough investigation.'

The verdict of the audience, arrived at after a lively and entertaining debate, enthusiastically endorsed his view.

## Genius Loci

Taking our cue from the idea that 'The map is not the territory' Stories in Transit invited participants to wander through the city where they now live and draft their own maps of Palermo. Most of them are housed in institutions far from the city centre and aren't yet familiar with it. The plan was to gather sights and sounds towards making story maps and thereby strengthen their sense of place.

We met at Moltivolti, the popular multi-ethnic restaurant-café in the old town, provided paper and pencils, split up into small groups, then set out in different directions for the Vucciria market, through the warren-like streets of the ancient Arab quarter of the Kalsa.

Going for a walk, equipped with notebooks, offered the arrivants a way of making their new home less strange. Infusing their surroundings with history and stories, compiling a street map and so creating personal but also common territory would lead them, it was hoped, to know a bit better the place where they find themselves and to know it in a different way from taking pictures on their phones. After some initial inhibition and protests ('I don't know how to draw!'), they plunged in with much laughter, making sketches of the washing hanging from the windows, the geraniums, the chairs out on the street where neighbours reminisce and gossip in the evening, the stringy cats, the gorgeous sun-drenched stands of fruit and vegetables, the head of a gleaming swordfish, the wording of street signs (*Zona Pedonale; Vietato lo Skateboard*), inscriptions, slogans and graffiti which speak and bristle all over the crumbling walls of Palermo. But the locals also reacted in most encouraging ways. I had worried about walking through the narrow streets with a large gaggle of asylum seekers, and we had broken up into smaller clusters of six to ten each, but still. There was no hostility, only curiosity: '*Che cosa state facendo?*' (What are you doing?), locals passing the time of day in the street as is their custom asked in surprise rather than with suspicion. The same impulse that draws onlookers in a gallery to the artist making a copy at an easel prompted bystanders to peek at these young people's notebooks. 'We are making a map of the things we see and are interested in . . .' This answer seemed to intrigue rather than threaten. No disapproval was shown. The walk and the process had diminished the strangeness of the incomers in the eyes of their hosts.

The maps were drafted on large sheets of paper and their drawings collaged and assembled in the hall of the convent of Santa Chiara, where welcome and solidarity have been extended since the time of Danilo Dolci in the 1950s and 1960s. Don Enzo, the tall, powerfully built, genial *parocco* (parish priest) in charge, continues in Dolci's courageous spirit – no dog collar or canonicals for him – and offered us the use of his courtyard and spaces free of charge. Only one nun was left in the convent, and she would play with children of the neighbourhood every afternoon.

'Thinking *is* mobility,' the neuroscientist Chris Frith has remarked. Motion is memory, too, as pianists exemplify as they practise for days to internalize a piece until they no longer need a score. When something hovers at the edges of consciousness, Frith continues, we often try to reposition ourselves mentally and try and think back to where we were at the time, often pivoting physically to recapture the memory: this is a deep form of somatic consciousness. These ideas about knowing a place where one finds oneself, turning a street map into a personal but also common territory inspired one of the most fruitful methods that the project has adopted. The resulting collective maps inspired jubilation – we *nessi* were taken aback by the enthusiasm that making them inspired.

Our various itineraries took us past images of the city's tutelary deity, its *genius loci*, the *Genio di Palermo* (The Genius of Palermo), of which there are many. This mysterious figure became the centre of the maps and later inspired a new story.

An old, bearded king, he's enthroned, with a very large scaly snake wound around his right leg and torso and rearing up to nurse – showing its fangs – at his breast. The most fascinating early image, a statue erected in 1483, is known locally as '*Palermu lu Grandi*', and survives – just – in a small, ruinous Renaissance square, the Piazza del Garraffo, in the Spanish quarter of the old city. The dilapidated figure is set into an outdoors altarpiece, from which all the original elaborate ornament and sculpture has vanished. It's a secular variation on the tabernacles and sacred way stations that dot the walls and mark the crossroads and street corners, where offerings of photos and flowers, handwritten entreaties and thank-yous lie shrivelling.

Local Spanish merchants commissioned the sculpture of the Genio in gratitude for their prospering on the island, and in its day, the monument presented a humanist alternative to the local saint, Santa Rosalia. The statue still plays the part of a classical neighbourhood guardian, a Roman *lar*, the district or household god to whom altars were raised at the intersection of *vici* in ancient Rome. The community would gather at these crossroads to worship and plead for protection. In many ways the old king looks like a river god – he wears a pointed diadem like Poseidon/Neptune's – and he may express gratitude for the city's water supply: the name Garraffo comes from an Arabic word meaning abundance of water, and the Oreto river used to flow into the fountain which stood in the middle of the piazza.

'*Palermi li Piccolo*', a smaller version, stands atop a beautiful carved fountain of the same period, inside the Palazzo Pretorio, a grand enclave where the local government meets. Set on an ornate column, like a Paschal candle or a saint's pillar, he carries on the rim of the fountain an inscription: '*Panormus conca aurea suos devorat alienos nutrit*' (Palermo of the golden shell devours its own and nourishes strangers). These ominous words identify the old king as Panormus (Palermo) itself; he would appear to embody the proverbial phrase 'nurturing a serpent in one's bosom', which harks back to a traditional, classical animal fable (to which Voltaire gives a fine bitter twist in *Candide*: 'To caress the serpent that devours us and hug him close to our bosoms till he has gnawed into our hearts?'). Yet the inscription has been generally taken to be a memorial to Sicilian generosity, business sense and even altruism, praising the city and its citizens: commemoration rather than commiseration. Palermitani are proud of the Genio; he recalls their deep-rooted cosmopolitanism, their long-term hospitality to *xenoi*.

The inscription would then be a rare statement of the facts, from their point of view: Palermo devours its own and nourishes strangers. In this case, the evolution of the figure into a talisman of the city's openness to arrivants would ring with contemporary significance. Nevertheless, it seems contrary for a community of foreign merchants, trading from the Vucciria market district, to put up a monument to the danger of fostering foreigners like themselves. The message the figure proclaims must surely concern the fundamental nature of the city, its generosity and plenitude, and its deep-rooted, symbiotic relations with incomers. Yet it is a troubling motto for a city that has been receiving waves of strangers for millennia.

The Genio, emptied of history and material associations, still remains the symbol of Palermo, a brand image, comparable to Michelangelo's *David* in Florence, the *Manneken Pis* in Brussels, the Eiffel tower in Paris, though he is rather less celebrated. He numbers among those monuments that the Prince of Salina, Don Fabrizio, in Lampedusa's classic novel *Il Gattopardo*, invokes in his bitter remarks about his country to the Piedmontese envoy Chevalley in November 1860, six months after Garibaldi and the Mille landed at Marsala in the historic war of unification. The Genio belongs among:

these monuments of the past, too, magnificent but incomprehensible because we did not set them up and yet they stand around us like beautiful mute ghosts; all these regimes that disembarked here armed from who knows where, and were quickly attended to, soon detested, and always unintelligible, expressed themselves only through works of art that are enigmas to us and the most concrete extractions of taxes, which were then spent elsewhere; all these things have formed our character which remains so conditioned by outside disasters as well as by a terrifying insularity of spirit.

The Genio may be one of those beautiful mute ghosts, but could he be heard? Could he be reanimated?

During our Stories in Transit workshops, we let the imagery speak in whatever way the observer chose to hear. Part of our approach is to work with the matter to hand and shake it up, break it down and reassemble it in a new form. If the Genio is issuing a xenophobic warning, then that is to be seized and confronted – and reconfigured. But the obscurity of the statue's meaning, the odd and compelling strangeness of the relations between old man and snake, the figure's importance as the emblem of the city, coupled with the very ambivalence of the old Latin tag, deepens its emptiness as a sign and makes it rich potential storymaking material.

The centre of Palermo still carries the scars of heavy bombing in the Second World War, by the Allies from 1940 onwards; the worst attacks in 1943 were followed by retaliatory bombing from the Luftwaffe. These modern ruins, now streaked and scrawled all over with huge angry graffiti, still stand after decades of failure to rebuild; they have become a tourist landmark. The spectacle of the wreckage beside the busy markets and crowded streets might establish a connection, I thought, between the Sicilian past and these young people, who have often fled violence of every kind.

Amadou Diallo, another founding member of Giocherenda who, like Din Diallo (no relation), fled the civil strife in Guinea, began reimagining the meaning of the mysterious king with his snake: the creature isn't venomous, he declared, but most people mistake its nature. He then developed a full backstory, a fine example of translating personal experiences into a fabulous narrative: a burning village, ostracism and expulsion

Palermo's Genius Loci, an old man entwined with a serpent which bites his breast, appears all around the city. Pietro de Bonitate, 1483.

from home, a long arduous journey, the search for food and water, and the arrival in a strange place where one is perceived as a danger and an alien.

## 'The Tale of the Old Man and the Snake'

Once upon a time there was a village where the inhabitants were accustomed to cutting down and setting fire to the trees of the forest in order to grow their crops. In doing so, they had killed all the snakes that lived there, except for one small snake that escaped.

One day an old man came upon him and decided to take him home and raise him. However, his neighbours, seeing the old man feeding a snake, were afraid and they ran him out of the village – in fact, they thought that the snake was their enemy.

The old man ran away, ran with the snake and, after walking a lot, fell asleep under a tree. At that moment the snake moved away and, after some time, wanting to go back, approached the wrong tree. A man was sleeping there too! Gilgamesh! It was evening and the snake was famished so fell upon the first thing he saw: it was the plant of eternal youth!

When he found the old man he bit him and the plant of eternal youth, which had made the snake change his skin, gave the old man immortality!

The next day the old man set off again and ultimately found refuge in Palermo. Everyone who met him there, seeing that the snake did not hurt him, thought it magic. But the old man explained to them that the snake loved him because he had always been kind to him.

~~~

This is a wistful fable about the need for kindness and the rewards of generosity. It is an incomer's supplication expressed as a picaresque tale of misadventures and eventual safety. Amadou may have a trace memory of the ancient classical fable, but he spontaneously and decisively interpreted the snake and the Genio's strange embrace as infusing the old man with new vigour.

During workshops to perform Amadou's tale of the Genio, we adopted the mode of local Sicilian *cantastorie*, or story singers, who, like their counterparts in India, Japan and the Middle East, hang up a scroll or banner behind them, a kind of storyboard, and then enact the scenes accompaniment by percussion and other instruments (See Plates 14a and 14b). We made masks and props (the snake, the flames of the burning village, the angry villagers who drove out the old man and his nursling). New elements surfaced as we worked on the story: one of the *pupari* (puppeteers) told us that in the Sicilian countryside the farmers use snakes as diviners of water sources – a certain species will lead them to an underground stream or aquifer. Others in the group came up with the idea that the old man, the Genio, could ride on the snake he has adopted to cross the sea to reach Palermo.

These elements were also included in the storyboard painting and the performance. The scenes of the burning down of the village, the villagers later blaming the old man and chasing him away inspired especially vigorous action. It was, in its own way, a miniature *chaos-opéra*, which closed on a note of hope that was also a plea, a supplication: 'From the old man's wisdom, the Palermitani learned to be kind to others. And from that time onwards, the Genio of Palermo watches over the city and reminds its inhabitants to be welcoming.' (See Plate 14c).

Stories like these, which we heard from Din, Amadou, Numu and others, offered us the chance to cross-pollinate elements with traditional material such as tales from *The Thousand and One Nights* and the *Epic of Gilgamesh*. They were made to be performed and printing them as if they were written works does not capture their liveliness. We treated them like soft clay, to be moulded, pulled and patted into different shapes.

~

We were planning to return regularly, but in February 2020 our group was met at the airport in Palermo by a cordon of red-uniformed nurses, thermometers at the ready. We passed through them and worked for three days at Giocherenda, but the lockdown spread from Italy to the UK and time went by (I had problems with my health as well) and we were only able to return in November 2023. Around forty young people joined us on the Friday, brought by their teachers from the same school as before, the CPIA – renamed CPIA 'Nelson Mandela'. These recent arrivals included many young women from Bangladesh and Morocco as well as young men from the Maghreb, West Africa and Syria.

At the weekend they came back of their own free will (no school) to continue exploring scenes from 'The Second Dervish's Tale', part of the cycle of 'The Porter and the Three Ladies of Baghdad' from the *Nights*, which tells of a prince transformed into a monkey by a wicked jinni, and ends with a dizzying sequence of animal metamorphoses.

I picked this particular story because on this visit, after a long gap, we didn't have a story collected from the group, and the dramatic finale of this tale had great potential, for re-enactment, masks and sound effects. The struggle between a princess jinniya, who is a great magician, with the evil jinni who has turned the prince hero into a monkey, takes the form not of a fight with weapons but of a sequence of transformations, one animal into another, on and on, twisting and soaring, now fish, now bird, now fruit; finally the evil jinni turns himself into a pomegranate, bursts and scatters seeds everywhere. The princess magician becomes a cockerel and gobbles up the seeds – all except one. She manages to turn the monkey back into a prince, but that final uneaten seed proves her undoing – it bursts into flame. In the story both princess and jinni are consumed, but in the version we explored at that most recent workshop we concentrated on the magical restoration of the prince to human shape.

This kind of fugue of metamorphoses is known as a 'witches' duel' and is found in folklore far and wide, including in the legend of Taliesin and the Sorcerer's Apprentice. (I didn't refer to it during this workshop under this Folklore studies rubric, a witches' duel, because a witch may have a malignant, frightening charge for some of the arrivants.) The story was performed by the Lebanese storyteller Wafa' Tarnowska. The young people started work on masks, puppets, costumes and accompanying noises (music is not quite the *mot juste*) to bring it on to the stage. Giocherenda's founding members, Din, Amadou and others, took charge of the interpretation; the atmosphere was excited, joyous, and the teachers were enthusiastic – the young women had hardly spoken at all in class, and now they were playing, mingling, performing (and several who were veiled took off their veils, unprompted, see Plates 16a and 16b). There was much laughter and delight (and at the end spontaneous dancing) at what they had achieved. As Mahmoud Darwish once said, 'I strongly believe in our right to be frivolous.'

This return after a long interruption was not as successful as some of our earlier visits. We hadn't prepared enough (not enough ideas about the dialogue, not enough crêpe paper). But Stories in Transit is also a process of learning for everyone involved.

Sanctuary has taken the form of a sacred precinct or holy mountain, a secret enclave or a safe and private refuge, but it is above all a disposition and an idea that underpins actions. One thing that has also however become unequivocally clear on every visit: young men and women who have crossed into Europe from the Global South do not find it irrelevant to think together about a story and make it leap into life – it came as it were naturally. Play is perhaps a human way for strangers to come together and to find one another less strange.

Building the country of words will always involve contradictory stories and memories. The problems are enormous, and consensus can only be partial, nor is it desirable for it to be otherwise (it is dictatorships that impose uniformity).

Confronted with the virulence of the antagonism at a political level to arrivants from the Global South, these workshops represent a tiny effort and can achieve very little; the stories are not making a claim to be literature, but a playscript for improvisation. Faced with the numbers of displaced people, such an enterprise as Stories in Transit is not even a pebble tossed into a sea of troubles. As I worked on this book, the difficulties came to seem intractable – on the one hand, hostility to strangers and incomers, most particularly towards young black men, has been mounting all over Europe, the Middle East and the United States. And the situation has been worsening. In 2016 the enlightened, much loved, anti-Mafia campaigner and mayor of Palermo Leoluca Orlando was stressing the historical role of Sicily as the hub of the Mediterranean, a bridgehead from Africa to Europe; he spoke a language of openness and welcome and put in place many positive schemes of study and training. He defied the then minister of the interior, Matteo Salvini (now, at the time of writing, back in government), who had closed the ports to rescue vessels and ordered civil servants to refuse to issue *permessi di soggiorno* (leave to remain), the necessary document for an asylum seeker to attend school and be recognized in civil society. When officials were scared to defy the new law, Orlando undertook to sign the forms himself. Meanwhile on the mainland, in Riace in Calabria, another mayor, Domenico 'Mimmo' Lucano, initiated a programme of reclaiming abandoned orchards and fields and reinvigorating other social services by employing immigrants rather than incarcerating them.

Both these officials are no longer in post. As I write, President Trump's government is overseeing the deportation of thousands of Latin American immigrants, and doing so by executive order. In Italy, the far-right-wing government led by Giorgia Meloni of the party Fratelli d'Italia now have their representatives in power in many cities, including Palermo, and their anti-migrant pronouncements are unrelenting.

Stories in Transit is an attempt to put into practice principles which have been active in making sanctuary. My position is also founded in a certain degree of pessimism: that humanity being a storytelling, story-bearing species – *homo narrans/homo ludens* – there is no way out of the quandary that we invent and pass on stories that suit us and serve our needs, that falsehood stalks the imagination. And needs can match interests. However, I agree with Cornel West when he remarked, 'I cannot be an optimist, but I am a prisoner of hope.'

I am also a prisoner of hope. In this book I have been trying to understand the principles on which the ancient and medieval practice of sanctuary was founded, and the work has led me to believe (I am hardly alone in this) that the history of storymaking and storytelling shows that stories encode values, so the task before us is to find stories that can be 'strong enough to help' – to adapt the question George Seferis put and Seamus Heaney reprised. They were speaking of poetry, but their words can be extended more broadly to culture in general. I cannot offer a policy solution to the flows of people seeking a better life in countries where rights to move, to work, to speak and their consequent liberties have been shaped over time – to find sanctuary in the deep sense of a place of freedom and safely from harm. But my hope consists in trying to shift opinion, to lessen fear, to dissolve the miasma of suspicion, prejudice and hostility that is damaging host as well as guest, citizen and arrivant. In her sermon the day after President Trump's inauguration, the Bishop of Washington, D.C., asked him to show mercy to undocumented migrants: 'In fact, we are more like one another than we realize', she said, 'we need each other.'

To achieve the recognition of this common ground, this mutual need, a new *xenia* needs to come into being, a renewed ethic of hospitality and a revived sense of sanctuary, a fresh ethos, which is composed of ideas and beliefs, formed and carried by stories. Stories in Transit replicates a social gathering – as it were round the well, the hearth, the campfire – and explores travelling texts, in the form of stories, histories, songs, poems, believing they make a difference and will prove strong enough to help.

# Acknowledgements

I have many debts of gratitude to friends and colleagues who generously read drafts in progress: Denise Riley's constant inspiration and incisive comments have been invaluable; Peter Boxall gave me courage to continue wrestling with the topic; Ali Smith also read a draft and spurred me on; Dan Gunn most kindly applied his toothcomb; Clare Finburgh gave me meticulous comments and inspiring suggestions. The book would be the lesser without all their insights; remaining mistakes and muddle are down to me.

Several conversations, lectures and events, which took place over the course of researching sanctuary, sharpened questions and showed the way. My colleagues at Birkbeck have been a support and a continual source of inspiration: special thanks to Julia Bell, Luisa Calè, Jacqueline Rose, Olivia Sheringham, and Sue Wiseman, and to former colleagues Isobel Armstrong, Anthony Bale, Lynne Segal and Leslie Topp, founder of the excellent Compass Project. I would also like to express profound thanks to the Warden and Fellows of All Souls College, Oxford: for inviting me to a Two-Year Fellowship in 2013–15, when I took the first steps towards this book, and for support in further related endeavours. The Warburg Institute has always been a reservoir of knowledge, and I owe a great deal to Paul Taylor's wide-ranging scholarship. I am also grateful to Sally Shuttleworth and Matthew Reynolds for the invitation to give the Weidenfeld Lectures at St Anne's, Oxford, in 2015–16; to Ahdaf Souief and Mariam Said for the opportunity to focus my thoughts, first for the Edward Said Memorial Lecture, in Cairo in 2009, and later, in New York in 2023. Thank you to David Herd and the organisers of the T. S. Eliot Memorial Lecture at the University of Kent (2017); to the Oxford Refugee Studies Centre for the Barbara Harrell-Bond Memorial Lecture (2019); to Fiona Macintosh and Alicia Stallings, inspiring collaborators on the Sanctuary Study

Day (2024); to Michael Hrebeniak and his students at The New School of the Anthropocene; to Mark Dorrian, of Edinburgh University, for the invitation to give the Carnegie Lecture (2024), and to his colleagues and students who took part in the subsequent Study Day. Mary Kay Wilmers, Alice Spawls and Jean McNicol, past and present editors of the *London Review of Books*, and Sam Kinchin-Smith, of the podcast series *Close Readings*, have provided a vital forum in which to explore and test ideas; at the *New York Review of Books*, Eve Bowen has been a most considerate editor, generous yet exacting. To the writers, translators, poets and their representatives, who have given permission for me to quote their works, my very warm thanks – to Tamim al-Barghouti, Philippe Beck, the family of Seamus Heaney, Abdelfattah Kilito, Alice Oswald, Wang Ping, Robin Robertson, Mariam Said, Michael Schmidt, Alicia Stallings. Regarding some quotations, every effort has been made to reach the relevant rightsholder. Please do get in contact so I can update future editions.

Several artists are a continuing inspiration: Chiara Ambrosio, Adam Dant, Kate Daudy, Aura Satz. The family and estate of Donald Rodney kindly allowed me to reproduce a black and white image of his 'In the House of my Father'. Tanya Peixoto and her exceptional Bookartbookshop supported the research and the project Stories in Transit with her inimitable hospitality and depth of reading. Alongside them, many others guided me to the right reference or allusion: Lisa Appignanesi, Omar Berrada, An Van Camp, Dinah Casson, Terence Cave, Richard Davenport-Hines, Peter Davidson, David Herd, Peregrine Horden, Neil Kenny, Adrian May, Alan Moses, Ruth Padel, Omar-Hussein Radjy, Catriona Seth, Oliver Taplin, Mariam and Shawkat Toorawa, Chris Wickham, Peter Wiseman, and more besides, whom I am sorry not to mention by name.

The Holberg Foundation cleared the way for me to develop the project Stories in Transit. Lauren Bon and the Metabolic Studio, and Camilla Toulmin and the International Institute for Environment and Development made possible the workshops in Palermo. I can't find words to say how much I owe everyone who took part, especially in Palermo: Valentina Castagna and Clelia Bartoli above all, and Daria Settineri, Maria Vaccaro, and the teachers from the CPIA school: Lucia Barbera, Nicoletta Campisi, Leda Parisi, Nilla Palmieri and others. My infinite gratitude goes to the many former refugees and asylum seekers, most especially Safoudiny 'Din' Diallo, Amadou Diallo, and Numu Touray, who told the stories we worked with (they refused the fee offered them by the project, so it has been donated to their association, Giocherenda). Many others contributed to the activities: Bandiougou Diawara, Dawda Barry, Mustapha Conteh, Gassimou (Maga) Magassouba, Omar Sillah, Ibrahim Ture. Over the years, the participating musicians, puppeteers, writers, and artists have become too many to name, but heartfelt thanks to Joan Ashworth, Sally Bayley, Stephen Brichieri-Colombi, Selma Dabbagh, Marcia Farquhar, Jem Finer, Spike Gascoigne, Ben Haggarty, Mark Haworth-Booth, Antonia Karaisl, Mercedes Kemp, Yousif Latif Jaralla, Rich Nielson, Badia Obaid, Rosie Oddy, Sarah Riggs, Lee Shearman, David Swift, Philip Terry, Wafa Tarnowska, and Liz Wickett.

David Godwin, my agent, introduced me to the publisher, Arabella Pike, who trusted me to write this book when it was a sketch: my thanks to them both. Peter James copy-edited scrupulously and patiently (errors remaining are mine); Sam Harding and Eve Hutchings worked most spiritedly to bring it to press. I wish I could find more eloquent and original words to show my feelings for the support that friends and allies – Rachel Kneebone, Roger Malbert, Maggie Simmons and Anna Della Subin – have given me along the difficult way. Hannah Machover's many inspirations, interests and resourcefulness have sustained the making of this book. Conrad Shawcross, my son, continues to give me my compass bearings; and I could not have written the book without Graeme Segal, my beloved, patient and understanding companion.

Kentish Town,
1 May, 2025

# Permissions

The page numbers below reflect where the following extracts appear in *Sanctuary*.

*Culture and Imperialism*, Edward Said © 1993. Used by kind permission of The Wylie Agency (UK) Limited. (p.15).

*Sophocles: Four Tragedies: Oedipus the King, Aias, Philoctetes, Oedipus at Colonus* trans. Oliver Taplin © 2015. Reproduced with kind permission of The Licensor through PLSclear. (p. 22).

*Station Island*, Seamus Heaney © 1984. Reproduced with permission of Faber and Faber Ltd. (p. 102).

'Things We Carry on the Sea', reprinted with permission from *My Name is Immigrant* by Wang Ping, 2020. Hanging Loose Press. (p. 116).

*The Spirit Level*, Seamus Heaney © 1996. Reproduced with permission of Faber and Faber Ltd. (p. 125).

*Out of Place: A Memoir*, Edward Said © 1999. Used by kind permission of The Wylie Agency (UK) Limited. (pp. 139–140).

*Redress of Poetry*, Seamus Heaney © 1995. Reproduced with permission of Faber and Faber Ltd. (p.146).

'The Noble Rider and the Sound of Words', *The Necessary Angel: Essays on Poetry and the Imagination*, Wallace Stevens © 1942. Reproduced with permission of Faber and Faber Ltd. (p. 146).

'The Shelter of Stories', *Winter Pollen: Occasional Prose*, Ted Hughes © 1994. Reproduced with permission of Faber and Faber Ltd. (p.213).

*The Language of Autobiography: Studies in First Person Singular*, John Sturrock © 1993. Reproduced with permission of The Licensor through PLSclear. (pp. 229–230).

'Sometimes I consider the names of places', Kei Miller © 2019. Reproduced with kind permission of *PN Review 249*, vol. 46, no. 1 (September–October 2019). (pp. 243–244).

'Vrindaban', from *Collected Poems 1957–1987*, Octavio Paz © 1971. Reproduced with kind permission of Carcanet Press. (pp. 250–1).

*Memorial*, Alice Oswald © 2011. Reproduced with permission of Faber and Faber Ltd. (p. 248, p. 279).

Introduction to *Mimesis* by Erich Auerbach, Edward Said © 2003. Used by kind permission of The Wylie Agency (UK) Limited. (p. 256).

'An Ordinary Evening in New Haven', *Collected Poems*, Wallace Stevens © 1950. Reproduced with kind permission of Faber and Faber Ltd. (p. 264).

'Metaphor', *Archaeology*, Abdelfattah Kilito © 2012. Used with kind permission of the author. (pp. 265–60).

'Another Bedtime Story', *This Afterlife: Selected Poems*, A. E. Stallings © 2012. Reproduced with kind permission of Carcanet Press. (p. 278).

*The Author of Himself: The Life of Marcel Reich-Ranicki*, Marcel Reich-Ranicki © 2001. Used with permission of Princeton University Press. Permission conveyed through Copyright Clearance Center, Inc. (p. 288).

# Illustrations

## Integrated Images

p. 19: The Frid Stol, Sprotborough Church, South Yorkshire, *c.* 1100 (*Public domain*).

p. 25: Cassandra seeks sanctuary at the statue of Athena, fourth century BCE, National Museum of Archaeology, Naples (*Album / Alamy Stock Photo*).

p. 29: Santa Rosalia's grotto, Monte Pellegrino, Palermo (*Chris Hellier / Alamy Stock Photo*).

p. 49: Pilgrimage tattoos (*Tattoo handmade by JONA: tattoos lauretani of Loreto, https://www.tatuaggilauretani.it*).

p. 52: Giovanni Domenico Tiepolo, *The Flight into Egypt*, 1750–1753 (*The Picture Art Collection / Alamy Stock Photo*).

p. 61: Winifred Gill, *The Childhood of Jesus*, 1920s (© *Bodleian Libraries, University of Oxford*).

p. 64: Matareya near Cairo, from map by Matteo Pagano, Venice, 1549. From *The True Description of Cairo*, ed. Nicholas Warner (*Public domain*).

p. 67: Rembrandt van Rijn, *The Flight into Egypt*, Etching, *c.* 1628, Rijksmuseum, Amsterdam (*Public domain*).

p. 76: Neuschwanstein Castle, near Munich, built by King Ludwig of Bavaria, 1845–86 (*Sorin Colac / Alamy Stock Photo*).

p. 76: Disneyland's Sleeping Beauty Castle, Anaheim, California (*Chad McDermott / Alamy Stock Photo*).

p. 79: Relics of Christ's life on Earth, kept in S. Croce in Gerusalemme, Rome (*Fabrizio Troiani / Alamy Stock Photo*).

p. 80: The Ruthwell Cross (*South West Images Scotland / Alamy Stock Photo*).

p. 86: Piero della Francesca, *The Dream of Constantine*, 1464, San Francesco, Arezzo (*Public domain*).

p. 88: St Helena identifies the True Cross, print of the copy published by Thomas Fisher, 1804–7, after original frescoes, Guild Chapel of the Holy Cross, Stratford-upon-Avon (*Florilegius / Alamy Stock Photo*).

p. 112: Ludovico Mazzanti, *Joseph di Cupertino in Ecstasy*, 1767, Santuario di S. Giuseppe di Cupertino, Osimo (*Public domain*).

p. 114: Exterior of la Santa Casa, engraving (*colaimages / Alamy Stock Photo*).

p. 115: Pilgrim souvenir bowl, made with Santa Polvere, date unknown (*The Fitzwilliam Museum, Cambridge*).

p. 126: Andrea Sansovino and others, La Santa Casa, exterior (*Paolo Reda – REDA & CO / Alamy Stock Photo*).

p. 129: The interior of the Holy House of Loreto (*Odyssey-Images / Alamy Stock Photo*).

p. 130: Lorenzo Lotto, *The Recanati Annunciation*, c. 1534–35, Civic Museum of Villa Colloredo Mels, Recanati. (*Public domain*).

p. 133: Commemorative medal of the battle of Párkány, 1683, issued by Pope Innocent XI, 1678– 89, (© *Numismatics.hu*).

p. 136: The Temple Church in London, engraving (*Public domain*).

p. 143: Donald Rodney, *In the House of My Father*, 1996–7 (*By kind permission of the estate of Donald Rodney*).

p. 157: Sebastian Brant, *The Death of Dido,* from his edition of Virgil's *Aeneid*, Hans Grüninger's workshop, Strasburg, c. 1500 (*Public domain*).

p. 165: Jean-Auguste-Dominique Ingres, *Virgil Reading the Aeneid to Augustus, Livia, and Octavia*, Musée des Augustins, Toulouse, 1812 (*Public domain*).

p. 167: Carl Ludwig Becker, *Othello Relating his Adventures to Desdemona*, 1880, Musée national de Wroclaw, Breslau (*Public domain*).

p. 187: Pedro de Cordoba as Prince Calaf in Karl Voll Moeller's 'Chinoiserie in Three Acts', a reprise of *Turandot, Princess of China,* Max Reinhardt's Berlin production the year before. New York, 1912 (*Public domain*).

p. 189: The cover of the score by Giacomo Puccini, *Turandot*, Milan, Casa Ricordi, 1926 (*Public domain*).

p. 191: Gertrud Eysoldt as Turandot in *Turandot, Princess of China*, directed by Max Reinhardt, with incidental music by Ferruccio Busoni, 1911 (*Public domain*).

p. 201: Portrait engraving of Carlo Gozzi (*Public domain*).

p. 208: 'Tom Tit Tot', illustrated by Maginel Wright Barney, *The Young and Field Literary Readers, Book 2* (*Project Gutenberg*).

p. 213: Maps of Lilliput and Laputa from Jonathan Swift's *Gulliver's Travels*, 1726 (*Public domain*).

p. 218: Rohingya refugees gather in no man's land, the border zone between Myanmar and Bangladesh, 2018 (*YE AUNG THU / Getty Images*).

p. 245: Albrecht Dürer, *Imagines coeli Septentrionales cum duodecim imaginibus zodiac*, Nuremberg, 1515 (*Andrew Fare / Alamy Stock Photo*).

p. 297: The logo of Giocherenda (*www.giocherenda and www.storiesintransit.org*).

p. 301: Gassimou Magassouba and Safoudiny Diallo, 'The Huntsman, the King's Son and the Enchanted Deer', International Puppet Museum Antonio Pasqualino, Palermo, September 2016 (*Photo: Lee Shearman, Stories in Transit*).

p. 305: Rehearsal for 'One for You and One for Me' (*Photo: Richard Nielsen, Stories in Transit*).

# First plate section

1a. The Dome of the Rock (*Nick Brundle Photography*).
1b. Durham Cathedral (*mattbuck*).
2. Anthony Van Dyck, *Madonna del Rosario*, Palermo, 1623–4.
3. Paolo Cagliari (Veronese), *Rest on the Flight into Egypt*, c. 1572, National Gallery, London.
4. Paolo Cagliari (Veronese), *The Dream of Saint Helena*, c. 1570, National Gallery, London.
5a. Stavelot Triptych of the True Cross, c. 1156–58, Morgan Library and Museum, New York.
5b. Piero della Francesca, *The Legend of the True Cross*, detail, San Francesco, Arezzo, 1452–66 (*DEA / S. VANNINI / Getty Images*).

6. Giambattista Tiepolo, *The Flight of the Holy House of Loreto*, 1743 (*Getty Center*).
7. Caravaggio, *The Madonna of the Pilgrims / di Loreto*, 1604–6, Sant' Agostino, Rome.
8. The footprints of Iman Reza, from a dispersed *Falnama*, Iran, Qazvin, Safavid period, mid-1550s to early 1650s (*Album / Alamy Stock Photo*).

## Second plate section

9. From El-Nizami, *Haft Peykar*, Folio from a *Khamsa* (*Quintet*), (d. 1209).
10. Francesco Solimena, *Dido Receiving Aeneas*, 1710, National Gallery, London (*Heritage Images / Getty Images*).
11. Giovanni Francesco Barbieri (Guercino), *The Death of Dido, 1631* (*DEA / S. VANNINI / Getty Images*).
12. Andrea Robbins and Max Becher, *Ramat Shlomo, Jerusalem, Israel, Far View*, 2005 (*Courtesy of Max Becher and Andrea Pobbins*).
13. Adam Dant, *Argonautica Londonensi* (*Courtesy of Adam Dant*).
14a. Participants of Stories in Transit Workshop VI, making 'The Tale of the Old Man and the Snake' story banner, September 2018 (*Photo: Nicola Chemotti, Stories in Transit*).
14b. Stories in Transit Workshop V, Map-making, April 2018 (*Photo: Marina Warner, Stories in Transit*).
14c. Stories in Transit Workshop VI, Rehearsal of 'The Tale of the Old Man and the Snake', September 2018 (*Photo: Hannah Machover, Stories in Transit*).
15. Stories in Transit Workshop VI, Numu Touray storytelling, 'One for You, and One for Me', Giardino Garibaldi, Palermo (*Photo: Richard Nielsen, Stories in Transit*).
16a. Stories in Transit Workshop IV, Gassimou Magassouba and Safoudiny Diallo, Botanic Gardens, Palermo (*Photo: Lee Shearman, Stories in Transit*).
16b. Stories in Transit Workshop VI, Performance, 'The Tale of the Old Man and the Snake', Giardino Garibaldi, Palermo (*Photo: Richard Nielsen, Stories in Transit*).

# Notes

**Epigraphs**

p. vii  'lights in the distance': Italo Calvino, *Invisible Cities*, trans. William Weaver (London: Penguin, 1997), p. 48.

p. vii  'purely secular grace?': Denise Riley, 'All, as a rule, fall towards their wound', in her *Lurex* (London: Picador, 2022), p. 43.

**Introduction**

p. 1  'carried as a guest': Horace, *Epistles*, 'To Maecenas', line 15, my translation. An alternative goes: 'where the storm drives me I turn in for shelter', https://la.wikisource.org/wiki/Epistulae_(Horatius)/Liber_I The Royal Society's motto, *'Nullius in verba'*, is taken from line 14.

p. 1  hospitality: a sanctuary: Antony Bale suggests that I am remembering the opening scene of *The Hunchback of Notre Dame* (1939), but the image in my mind brings up a Robin Hood-like figure rather than Charles Laughton's powerful portrayal of Quasimodo.

p. 2  *hollowed* ground and *hallowed* ground: Marcus Doel, 'Proverbs for Paranoids: Writing Geography on Hollowed Ground', *Transactions of the Institute of British Geographers* (1993), pp. 377–94, quoted in Jordan Savage, '"What the Hell Is a Flowery Boundary Tree?"': *Gunslinger*, *All the Pretty Horses* and the Postmodern Western', *Journal of American Studies*, vol. 46, issue 04 (November 2012), pp. 997–1008.

p. 2  'Is a sanctuary a cell?': Antony Gormley, film accompanying exhibition *Body Politic* at White Cube Gallery, Bermondsey, 22 November 2023–28 January 2024.

p. 2  'entangled with history': James Crawford, *The Edge of the Plain: How Borders Make and Break our World* (London: Canongate, 2022), p. 22.

p. 2  'only ever be *told*': Ibid., p. 22. See my review, 'No Freedom to Move', *New York Review of Books*, 23 November 2023.

p. 2 different parts of the world: Oxford University became a University of Sanctuary in 2023, with two colleges, Somerville and Mansfield, leading the way. Other UK universities that have also been recognized by the Sanctuary movement include Edinburgh and Kent. A full list can be found here: https://data.cityofsanctuary.org/universities/list

p. 3 'out of place': Edward Said's memoir, *Out of Place* (New York: Knopf, 1999), passim.

p. 3 'lost in place': Susan Stewart, *The Ruins Lesson: Meaning and Material in Western Culture* (Chicago: University of Chicago Press, 2020), p. 249.

p. 3 phrase of Benedict Anderson: Benedict Anderson's book *Imagined Communities: Reflections on the Origin and Spread of Nationalism* (London: Verso, 1983) established the concept.

p. 4 the term 'homelooseness': James Wood, 'On Not Going Home', *London Review of Books*, 20 February 2014.

p. 6 'invasion' and swarms: Hein de Haas, *How Migration Really Works: 22 Things You Need to Know About the Most Divisive Issue in Politics* (London: Viking, 2023), pp. 15–30 and passim.

p. 6 opportunity and skills: Wendy Brown, *Walled States, Waning Sovereignty* (New York: Zone Books, 2010), passim.

p. 6 They are leaving behind: Haas, *How Migration Really Works*, ibid., pp. 93–108.

p. 7 'your mountainish inhumanity': Thomas More, addressing a crowd of Londoners who are baying for the blood of strangers, asks them to think of themselves in the strangers' situation. The speech comes from *Sir Thomas More*, a play on which several writers collaborated, including Shakespeare. It is the only extant holograph in Shakespeare's hand. For the full speech, see: https://myshakespeare.com/hamlet/the-strangers-case-speech-sir-thomas-more and for the context Emma Smith on: https://www.english.ox.ac.uk/ten-minute-book-club/shakespeare-sir-thomas-more

p. 7 of immigrant workers: https://www.unhcr.org/refugee-statistics/ see also: https://www.bbc.co.uk/news/articles/cgrnn8zxdego

p. 7 impossible to grasp: https://blogs.worldbank.org/dev4peace/2019-update-how-long-do-refugees-stay-exile-find-out-beware-averages

p. 7 been born there: Yousif M. Qasmiyeh, *Writing the Camp* (Llandysul: Broken Sleep Books, 2021).

p. 7 the undifferentiated mass: There were 75,340 asylum applications (main applicants only) in the UK in the year ending September

2023, similar to the number in the year ending September 2022 but 10 per cent lower than the previous peak (84,132 in 2002). In the year ending September 2023, there were 41,858 initial decisions made on asylum applications, over two and a half times more than in the previous year. This is higher than the pre-pandemic levels of decisions (20,766 decisions were made in 2019) and the most initial decisions since 2004 (46,021 decisions). Three-quarters of the initial decisions in the year ending September 2023 were grants of refugee status, humanitarian protection or alternative forms of leave. Since 2021, the grant rate has been over 70 per cent – substantially higher than in pre-pandemic years when only around one-third of applications were successful at initial decision. Prior to this latest period, the highest grant rate was over thirty years ago: 82 per cent in 1990. https://www.gov.uk/government/statistics/immigration-system-statistics-year-ending-september-2023/summary-of-latest-statistics As this book goes to press, the statistics have been updated till September 2024 and classified differently: 73,000 individuals arrived by 'Legal and Humanitarian routes', 30,000 by 'small boats'. There were 100,000 claims for asylum, 7,000 'Enforced returns', 24,000 'Voluntary returns', 23,000 'Port returns' and 1,700 people placed in detention. https://www.gov.uk/government/statistics/immigration-system-statistics-year-ending-september-2024

p. 8 they are with us: Jacques Derrida and Anne Dufourmantelle, *Of Hospitality: Anne Dufourmantelle Invites Jacques Derrida to Respond*, trans. Rachel Bowlby (Stanford: Stanford University Press, 2000).

p. 8 Second World War: Edward Kamau Brathwaite, *The Arrivants: A New World Trilogy* (Oxford: Oxford University Press, 1967), passim. This edition combines in one volume his books of poems *Rights of Passage, Islands* and *Masks*.

p. 8 a neighbouring one: https://www.unhcr.org/refugee-statistics/

p. 8 (... asylum seekers are housed): See Brian Bilston's remarkable palindromic poem 'Refugees': https://www.up.edu/garaventa/files/fildg%20files/refugees.pdf

p. 8 exoduses in the past: Haas, *How Migration Really Works*, pp. xx–xx.

p. 11 (Edward Said's term): Edward Said, 'Traveling Theory', in his *The World, the Text, and the Critic* (London: Vintage, 1991), pp. 226–47.

p. 11 border-crossing capacities: See Alex Ross, 'Post-Apocalyse Now', *New Yorker*, 5 February 2024, for a very informed review of the vital contemporary music scene in Ukraine.

p. 12   subjunctive and conditional tenses: From 'irrealis' in linguistics, the speculative or hypothetical mood, conveyed by the subjunctive ('I may go to the ball'), conditional ('I would go to the ball if I had glass slippers)', jussive ('You shall go to the ball!') or optative tense ('I wish to go to the ball!'). It is cognate with 'reality', from the 'realis' mood referring to events that are known to have taken place or not to have taken place, for which the indicative tenses, present and past, are used. André Aciman has explained, 'Grammarians call this unthinkable, imponderable, impalpable, fluid, transitory, incoherent zone the irrealis mood, a verbal mood to express what might never, couldn't, shouldn't, wouldn't possibly occur but that might just happen all the same.' André Aciman, 'Underground', *Harvard Review*, no. 50 (2017), pp. 58–67, https://www.jstor.org/stable/45210611; and Edmund de Waal, 'Farewell to an Idea: Garry Fabian Miller and the irrealis mood', Introduction to Garry Fabian Miller, *In the Dark Room* (Oxford: Bodleian Publishing, 2023), p. 224; see also https://en.wikipedia.org/wiki/Irrealis_mood

p. 12   representations of experience: Jonathan Swift, Lewis Carroll, Franz Kafka, Jorge Luis Borges and Angela Carter are among the masters of irrealis literature. At the time of writing, I am making a podcast series, 'Fiction and the Fantastic', for the *London Review of Books Close Readings*, which explores these writers and more: https://www.lrb.co.uk/podcasts-and-videos/podcasts/close-readings/fiction-and-the-fantastic-the-thousand-and-one-nights

p. 12   fate of arrivants: There is one three-screen version and another five-screen installation. See Isaac Julien, *Riot*, 2013, MoMA, New York; https://www.royalacademy.org.uk/art-artists/work-of-art/the-leopard-western-union-small-boats

p. 13   by the pandemic: See www.storiesintransit.org for the project's history and continuing activity.

p. 14   'we become historical': Hannah Arendt, *The Human Condition* (Chicago: University of Chicago Press, 1958), p. 97.

p. 14   I am indebted: See the Acknowledgements and the Bibliography.

p. 14   the stranger-guest: Derrida and Dufourmantelle, *Of Hospitality*; see also Jonathan Rée, 'No Foreigners', reviewing Jacques Derrida, *Hospitality*, vol. 1, eds. Pascale-Anne Brault and Peggy Kamuf, trans. E. S. Burt, and *Hospitality*, vol. 2, eds. Brault and Kamuf, trans. Kamuf (Chicago: University of Chicago Press, 2023, 2024), in *London Review of Books*, 10 October 2024, pp. 5–8.

p. 14 entrench dominant ideologies: Roland Barthes' series of essays, collected in 1957 and published by Les Lettres Nouvelles as *Mythologies*, mounted the most devastating critique of myths as ideology.

p. 15 'dismantle the master's house': Audre Lorde, 'The Master's Tools Will Never Dismantle the Master's House', in her *Your Silence Will Not Protect You* (London: Silver Press, 2017), pp. 89–93.

p. 15 new 'integrative realities': 'Merely to urge students to insist on one's own identity, history, tradition, uniqueness may initially get them to name their basic requirements for a democracy and for the right to an assured, decently humane existence, but we need to go on and to situate these in a geography of other identities, peoples, cultures, and then to study how, despite their differences, they have always overlapped one another, through unhierarchical influence, crossing, incorporation, recollection, deliberate forgetfulness, and of course, conflict . . . The fact is, we are mixed up with one another in ways that most national systems of education have not dreamed of. To match knowledge in the arts and sciences with these *integrative realities* is, I believe, the intellectual and cultural challenge of the moment' (italics added). Edward Said, *Culture and Imperialism* (London: Vintage, 1994), p. 331.

p. 15 viable, humane society: Given the current drift towards strident ethnic nationalism with neo-fascist proclivities in Italy, Sweden, Hungary and France, as well as in Britain and the United States, and the growing influence of conspiracy theories, it could not be more crucial to contest claims to ownership of tradition. Edward Said warned over twenty years ago: 'Between the extremes of discontented, challenging urban mobs and the floods of semi-forgotten, uncared for people, the world's secular and religious authorities have sought new, or renewed modes of governance. None has seemed so easily available, so conveniently attractive as appeals to tradition, national or religious identity, patriotism. And because these appeals are amplified and disseminated by a perfected media system addressing mass cultures, they have been strikingly, not to say frighteningly effective.' Ibid., p. 327.

p. 17 'a hypothetical mode': Paul Ricoeur, *Oneself as Another*, trans. Kathleen Blamey (Chicago: University of Chicago Press, 1992), p. 170.

p. 18 'purely secular grace?': Denise Riley, 'All, as a rule, fall towards their wound', in her *Lurex* (London: Picador, 2022), p. 43.

## Part One: A Kind of Freedom

p. 19  *Measure for Measure* II. ii. 44–6.

## Chapter 1: Laws: A Brief History of Sanctuary

p. 21  'an unbreakable shield': Aeschylus, *The Suppliants*, line 190, in the literal version communicated to me by Daniel Byam Shaw, who has translated the play as *The Asylum Seekers*: private communication, 22 November 2024. Philip Vellacott in his 1961 translation gives 'An altar is stronger than a fortress' (Harmondsworth: Penguin, 1983), p. 59.

p. 21  ledge of 'unchiselled rock': Sophocles, 'Oedipus at Colonus', in *Sophocles, Four Tragedies: Oedipus the King, Aias, Philoctetes, Oedipus at Colonus: A New Verse Translation*, trans. Oliver Taplin (Oxford: Oxford University Press, 2015), line 19, p. 221; published in paperback as *Oedipus the King and Other Tragedies* (Oxford: Oxford University Press, 2022).

p. 21  'pure to tread': Ibid., line 38, p. 222.

p. 21  'Earth and Dark': Ibid., lines 39–40, p. 222.

p. 21  will come about: Ibid., lines 89–91, p. 225.

p. 22  'if you refuse it': Ibid., lines 175–7, p. 228.

p. 22  their sacred ground: Ibid., lines 466–92, pp. 240–2.

p. 22  grants him sanctuary: Robert Garland, *Wandering Greeks: The Ancient Greek Diaspora from the Age of Homer to the Death of Alexander the Great* (Princeton: Princeton University Press, 2014), p. 115.

p. 22  the Homeric dictionary: Georg Autenrieth, *A Homeric Dictionary*, ed. Robert Porter Keep (London: Macmillan, 1908), p. 299.

p. 22  as divine property: See Gunnel Ekroth, 'A Room of One's Own? Exploring the *temenos* concept as divine property', in Matthew Haysom, Maria Mili and Jenny Wallenstein (eds.), *The Stuff of the Gods: The Material Aspects of Religion in Ancient Greece*, ActaAth-4°, 59 (Acta Instituti Atheniensis Regni Sueciae (Stockholm: Swedish Institute at Athens, 2024), pp. 69–82, https://doi.org/10.30549/actaath-4-59 Ekroth does point out that walls were later built to enclose such holy places. However, at the major temple to Zeus in Olympia, 'Apparently there was no need for a proper wall for more than 500 years.' Ibid., p. 71.

p. 22  Chorus calls Oedipus: Sophocles, *Oedipus at Colonus*, trans. Taplin, line 1563, p. 283.

p. 23   declared a failed state: The list of failed states is very controversial. Currently they are: https://worldpopulationreview.com/country-rankings/failed-states

p. 23   'the same as you . . .': Sophocles, *Oedipus at Colonus*, trans. Taplin, line 1335, p. 275.

p. 23   'lowest of the low': Ibid., lines 1380–5, p. 276.

p. 24   withdrawn her protection: Thucycides, *The Peloponnesian War*, trans. Richard Crawley (London: Dent, 1910), 1.126, https://www.perseus.tufts.edu/hopper/text?doc=Perseus%3Atext%3A1999.01.0200%3Abook%3D1%3Achapter%3D126 and Plutarch, *Life of Solon*, ed. and trans. Bernadotte Perrin (Cambridge, Mass.: Loeb Classical Library, 1914), ch. 12, https://penelope.uchicago.edu/Thayer/E/Roman/Texts/Plutarch/Lives/Solon*.html. I am very grateful to Ruth Padel for telling me about this historical incident.

p. 25   palladium (protector) of Troy: Lykophron, *Alexandra*, trans. Simon Hornblower (Oxford: Oxford University Press, 2022), lines 246–372, p. 13.

p. 25   or abortive homecomings: Ibid., lines 348–72, and Explanatory Notes, pp. 72–3.

p. 26   were commonly flouted: Garland, *Wandering Greeks*, pp. 123–5.

p. 26   'uterus on the loose': Ted Hughes, *Shakespeare and the Goddess of Complete Being* (London: Faber & Faber, 1992), p. 11.

p. 27   'bronze-stepped threshold': Sophocles, *Oedipus at Colonus*, trans. Taplin, line 56, p. 223.

p. 30   and to pray: Rosalia Sinibaldo (c.1130–60?) was the daughter of a local nobleman. Her remains, discovered on 15 July 1624, were identified by an inscription in Latin, and were then translated to the cathedral amid huge rejoicing and interred in a gigantic silver *urna* or sarcophagus created by the leading baroque silversmiths Francesco Rivelo and Matteo Lo Castro. Alessandro Giuliana-Alajmo, *S. Rosalia ed it suo eremitaggio nella grotto del Monte Quisquina* (Palermo: Trinacria, 1953), pp. 4–10.

p. 30   echo her name: *Van Dyck in Sicily*, Dulwich Picture Gallery (2012), displayed five surviving paintings of Santa Rosalia.

p. 31   'a heavy door': Rev. J. Charles Cox, *The Sanctuaries and Sanctuary Seekers of Medieval England* (London: George Allen & Sons, 1911), pp. 121–2.

p. 32   'baying at their tail': Benjamin Myers, *Cuddy* (London: Bloomsbury, 2023), p. 196.

p. 32  blessing are related: See Giorgio Agamben, *Homo Sacer: Sovereign Power and Bare Life* (Stanford: Stanford University Press, 1998), and Walter Burkert, *Homo Necans: The Anthropology of Ancient Greek Sacrificial Ritual and Myth* (Berkeley: University of California Press, 1986).

p. 32  tempers to settle: In some places the right to sanctuary lasted longer: in Edinburgh, for example, the debtors' sanctuary around Holyrood Abbey was dissolved as late as 1880. https://www.atlasobscura.com/places/sanctuary-stones

p. 32  rest of their lives: At various times, some crimes were excluded: the Duchess of Gloucester was refused sanctuary at Westminster in 1441 after she had been accused of witchcraft. Gradually more and more offences were added to the list; by the reign of Henry VIII, treason, rape, sacrilege, arson, robbery and murder all debarred claims to sanctuary. Douglas Smith, *The Sanctuary at Durham* (Newcastle-on-Tyne: Frank Graham, 1971), pp. 6, 28–9.

p. 33  'the loneliness shall': Myers, *Cuddy*, p. 197.

p. 33  play, and the sacred: Roger Caillois, *Les Jeux et les hommes: Le masque et le vertige* (1958; revised and enlarged, Paris: Gallimard, 1967).

p. 33  'Pax!' or 'Cruces!': Iona and Peter Opie, *The Lore and Language of Schoolchildren* (1951; New York: New York Review Books, 2001), pp. 143–4, 150, 152.

p. 33  and . . . become inviolable: https://francisalys.com/childrens-game-24-pandemic-games/

p. 34  hoping to reach: Caillois defines four different types of games, corresponding to competition (*agon*), chance (*alea*), simulacrum (mimicry) and vertige (*Ilinx*): *Les Jeux et les hommes*, p. 47.

p. 35  flight was debt: Cox, *The Sanctuaries and Sanctuary Seekers*, p. 136; Benjamin Michael Woodring, '"Oft Have I Heard of Sanctuary Men": Fictions of Refuge in Early Shakespeare' (doctoral dissertation, Harvard University, 2014), https://dash.harvard.edu/handle/1/12274302 p. 138, quoting Chris Fitter, *Radical Shakespeare: Politics and Stagecraft in the Early Career* (New York: Routledge, 2012), pp. 175, 177.

p. 36  purer, way of life: Ronald B. Sakolsky and James Koehnline (eds.), *Gone to Croatan: Origins of North American Dropout Culture* (New York: Autonomedia, 1993), interprets the message left by the vanished colonists of Virginia as meaning they had abandoned the enterprise of settlement; the retreats of hippies, dropouts, off-grid survivors would then figure as a form of modern sanctuary.

p. 36   riot or trouble (usually): Woodring, '"Oft Have I Heard"', p. 175, quoting Fitter, *Radical Shakespeare*, p. 219; Northrop Frye, *Anatomy of Criticism* (Princeton: Princeton University Press, 1957), pp. 182–4.

p. 37   terms and justice: The example of Ukrainian refugees to the UK in 2022 when they were welcomed into family homes and subsequently rehoused presents a far more desirable functioning of sanctuary than sequestration in a hotel or detention in a People Removal Centre.

p. 37   of boot camp: Woodring, '"Oft Have I Heard"', p. 173.

p. 37   completed the process: In 1531 the option of abjuration and exile was ended by Henry VIII; in 1624, James I declared 'no Sanctuary or privilege of Sanctuary shall hereafter be allowed in any case'. Smith, *The Sanctuary at Durham*, pp. 28–9.

p. 38   and twenty yeomen: Harley Ms 4292, quoted by Cox, *The Sanctuaries and Sanctuary Seekers*, pp. 136–7.

p. 38   actual places of refuge: Woodring, '"Oft Have I Heard"', pp. 145–8.

p. 38   all as a holy refuge: In Spain in the great pilgrimage city of Santiago de Compostela stood the Royal Hospital, an institution independent of both church and state, where sanctuary could be sought. A platform encircled by elaborate posts linked by heavy chains now marks the sanctuary area. The label qualifies the eligible: murderers, highwaymen and other criminals were barred from entering. My thanks to Dinah Casson and Alan Moses for sending me this information after their visit to Compostela.

p. 39   temple at Corinth: Ekroth, 'A Room of One's Own?', p. 71.

p. 40   forfeited his life: Cox, *The Sanctuaries and Sanctuary Seekers*, p. 127; https://www.realyorkshireblog.com/post/beverley-s-frith-stool-and-the-right-of-sanctuary

p. 42   dangerous no-go areas: Walter Scott, in *The Fortunes of Nigel* (Edinburgh: Archibald Constable, 1822), relishes the notoriety of such areas and fuelled their dangerous reputation, probably unjustly.

p. 42   Jungle in Calais: John Levin, 'The Debtor Sanctuaries of London' is an ongoing blog, and richly informative: https://alsatia.org.uk/site/

p. 42   (... than I ever could): Alongside Cox, *The Sanctuaries and Sanctuary Seekers*, see David Cadman and John Carey (eds.), *Sanctuary* (London: Temenos Academy, 2006) and Shannon McSheffrey, *Seeking Sanctuary: Crime, Mercy, and Politics in English Courts, 1400–1550* (Oxford: Oxford University Press, 2017).

p. 42   put into practice: Among many efforts, see https://data.cityof sanctuary.org/universities/list In 2016, Birkbeck College, London opened the Compass Project programme for asylum seekers: https://www.bbk.ac.uk/professional-services/access/compass-project

p. 43   Roman law in particular: Karl Shoemaker, *Sanctuary and Crime in the Middle Ages* (New York: Fordham University Press, 2011), pp. 29–43.

p. 44   within universities, Colleges: See note 46 above.

p. 45   support and information: https://sanctuaryeastbourne.org/

p. 45   rights and mutual obligations: See Lyndsey Stonebridge, *Placeless People: Writing, Rights, and Refugees* (Oxford: Oxford University Press, 2018), and Hein de Haas, *How Migration Really Works: 22 Things You Need to Know About the Most Divisive Issue in Politics* (London: Viking, 2023).

p. 45   prize for their creation: The architects were Kimmo Lintula, Niko Sirola and Mikko Summanen of K2S Architects Ltd.

p. 47   many visitors/pilgrims: *Sam's Eden*, CCA Derry/Londonderry, 7 July–9 September 2023, https://www.ccadld.org/exhibitions/sams-eden

## Part Two: Sites of Memory

p. 49   'history of facts': Jocelyn Wogan Browne, Ford Lecture, 23 January 2025. Quoted with kind permission.

### Chapter 2: Traces: The Flight into Egypt

p. 51   'alchemy of the word': '*Depuis longtemps . . . J'aimais la littérature démodée, latin d'église, livres érotiques sans orthographe, romans de nos aïeules, contes de fées, petits livres de l'enfance, opéras vieux, refrains niais, rythmes naïfs . . . La vieillerie poétique avait une bonne part dans mon alchimie du verbe.*' Arthur Rimbaud, '*Alchimie du verbe*', in his *Une Saison en enfer* (Brussels: M.-J. Poot, 1873). My translation.

p. 52   hope of transformation: Susan Stewart, *The Ruins Lesson: Meaning and Material in Western Culture* (Chicago: The University of Chicago Press, 2020), pp. 1–20.

p. 53   the imagined realm: Thomas G. Pavel, *Fictional Worlds* (Cambridge, Mass.: Harvard University Press, 1989), p. 138.

p. 53   'tracery of a pattern': Italo Calvino, 'La Mappa delle metafore', in his *Sulla Fiaba*, ed. Mario Lavagetto (Turin: Einaudi, 1988), pp. 129–46.

p. 54 'the termites' gnawing': Italo Calvino, *Invisible Cities*, trans. William Weaver (London: Secker & Warburg, 1974), p. 10.

p. 54 listeners and readers: See Jorge Luis Borges, 'The Apocryphal Gospels', in his *The Total Library: Non-Fiction, 1922–1986* (London: Penguin, 2000), pp. 515–16.

p. 55 'common cultural heritage': Stephen J. Davis, *Christ Child: Cultural Memories of a Young Jesus* (New Haven: Yale University Press, 2014), p. 161.

p. 55 'Islamic Near East': Ibid.

p. 55 Muslim imaginary and faith: See Muna Tatari and Klaus von Stosch, *Mary in the Qur'an*, trans. Peter Lewis (London: Gingko, 2021).

p. 55 also honour her: 'And We made the Son of Mary and his mother a wonder': Sura 23:48, The Believers. *The Qur'an*, trans. Tarif Khalidi (New Delhi: Penguin, 2009), p. 276.

p. 55 act of 'special reverence': Tarif Khalidi (ed. and trans.), *The Muslim Jesus: Sayings and Stories in Islamic Literature* (Cambridge, Mass.: Harvard University Press, 2003), p. 44.

p. 55 symbol of Mary: See Tatari and Stosch, *Mary in the Qur'an*, pp. 283–311; Karl-Josef Kuschel, *Christmas and the Qur'an*, trans. Simon Pare (London: Gingko, 2017), pp. 183–206; Khalidi (ed. and trans.), *The Muslim Jesus*, pp. 43–5.

p. 56 Youakim Moubarac (1924–95): Moubarac was the student of the orientalist Louis Massignon; in his photograph on his Wikipedia page he looks a dead ringer for the pin-up priest on the pious calendars sold to pilgrims in Rome (!): https://en.wikipedia.org/wiki/Youakim_Moubarac

p. 56 Christianity and vice versa: See Mouchir Basile Aoun, *The Arab Christ: Towards an Arab Christian Theology of Conviviality*, trans. Sarah Patey (London: Gingko, 2022), pp. 343–78.

p. 56 'common cultural heritage': Maria Couroucli, Introduction to Dionigi Albera and Maria Couroucli (eds.), *Sharing Sacred Spaces in the Mediterranean: Christians, Muslims, and Jews at Shrines and Sanctuaries* (Binghampton and Indianapolis: Indiana University Press, 2012), p. 5.

p. 56 social and secular sense: M. A. Vauchez (ed.), *La Religion civique a l'époque médiévale et moderne (chrétienté et islam)*, Actes du colloque de Nanterre, 21–23 Juin 1993, Collection de l'École Française de Rome no. 123 (Rome: École Française de Rome, 1996).

p. 56   have a child (Sura 19: 15): Sura 19, Mary. *Qur'an*, trans. Khalidi, pp. 241–7; Kuschel, *Christmas and the Qur'an*, p. 101.

p. 57   'any human being': *Qur'an*, Sura 19, trans. Khalidi, p. 243.

p. 57   'and a fountain' (Sura 23: 50): *Qur'an*, trans. Khalidi, p. 276.

p. 57   church in Old Cairo: Sara Allam, 'Holy Family in Egypt – Christ leaves "footprint" on Xois rock', *Egypt Today*, 31 October 2017, https://www.egypttoday.com/Article/6/30175/Ep-5-Holy-Family-in-Egypt-Christ-leaves-%E2%80%98footprint%E2%80%99.

p. 58   piety in Spain: William A. Christian Jr, *Local Religion in Sixteenth-Century Spain* (Princeton: Princeton University Press, 1989).

p. 58   performed by the child Jesus: M. R. James (ed. and trans.), *The Apocryphal New Testament* (1924; rev. edn Oxford: Clarendon Press, 1996), pp. 38–80.

p. 58   youth of the child Jesus: *The Arabic Gospel of the Infancy* is 'a late compilation'. It was first edited as late as 1697. Ibid., pp. 80–4.

p. 59   'shade of a palm tree': Chapter XX of the Pseudo-Matthew has directly inspired many works of art about the Flight into Egypt. Ibid., p. 75.

p. 60   at its deliciousness: The source for this delightful aetiology is eluding me, but I can't have made it up.

p. 60   bring them to life: Davis, *Christ Child*, p. 162.

p. 62   molest the family: James, *Apocryphal New Testament*, p. 81, gives more sources for story of the thieves, including a retelling by Aelred of Rievaulx who dramatizes the moment when the good thief as he is dying on the cross next to Jesus remembers meeting him as a child thirty years before.

p. 62   maid for his (second) wife: It should be noted here that a pioneering editor of these manuscripts was E. A. Wallis Budge, keeper of the British Museum's Egyptian and Middle Eastern collections, including Ethiopic literature. He influenced the children's writer E. Nesbit (with whom he had an *amitié amoureuse*); she consulted him about the details of her story *The Amulet*, for example. His palaeographical, historical and scholarly work thus flowed into the fiction of enchantment.

p. 63   (... the Syriac version): James, *Apocryphal New Testament*, p. 81.

p. 63   creates balm (or balsam) trees: Ibid., James adds that these passages are 'an Egyptian interpolation, not earlier than the twelfth century'.

p. 63 (... true balsam is gathered): Nicholas Warner (ed.), *The True Description of Cairo: A Sixteenth-Century Venetian View*, 3 vols (Oxford and London: Arcadian Library, 2006), vol. 2, pp. 56–9; François Savary, comte de Brèves, *Relation des voyages de Monsieur de Breves, tant en Grece, Terre-Saincte et Aegypte, qu'aux royaumes de Tunis & Arger* (Paris: Nicolas Gasse, 1628), and Richard Pococke, *A Description of the East and Some Other Countries*, vol. 1: *Observations on Egypt* (London: W. Bowyer, 1743), give vivid travellers' accounts of the shrine over a century apart. I tell this story in a different mode in Marina Warner, *Inventory of a Life Mislaid: An Unreliable Memoir* (London: William Collins, 2021), pp. 237–49.

p. 64 'Pharaoh's fig' still stands: I gave the Edward Said Memorial Lecture at the American University in Cairo in 2009, and Ahdaf Soueif, the writer and founder of Palfest, was my host, and most generously took me to see the shrine.

p. 64 fold up into the present: According to Michel Foucault's third principle defining the heterotopia: '[it] has the power to juxtapose in a single real place several spaces, several locations which are in themselves incompatible. Thus, the theatre has a whole series of places on the rectangle of the stage which are foreign to each other; thus, the cinema is a very curious rectangular room, at the back of which, on a two-dimensional screen, a three-dimensional space is projected; but perhaps the oldest example of these heterotopias, in the form of contradictory locations, is the garden.' Michel Foucault, 'Des Espace Autres' (March 1967), *Architecture Mouvement Continuité*, October 1984, trans. Jay Miskowiec, https://web.mit.edu/allanmc/www/foucault1.pdf

p. 65 Coptic church in the garden: Benoît de Maillet and Jean-Baptiste Le Mascrier, *Description de l'Égypte: contenant plusieurs remarques curieuses sur la geographie ancienne et moderne de ce païs, sur ses monumens anciens, sur les mœurs, les coutumes, & la religion des habitans, sur le gouvernement & le commerce, sur les animaux, les arbres, les plantes, &c.* (Paris: Louis Genneau and Jacques Rollin, 1735).

p. 66 feature of Islamic piety: See for example, this magic bowl from the Saffavid period, Iran: https://www.britishmuseum.org/collection/object/W_1984-0128-1 Water that was used to rinse the bowls was given to the sick to drink and considered a remedy – an example of ritual ingestion.

p. 67   effects of exile: *Young Rembrandt*, an exhibition of his work at the Ashmolean in Oxford, 10 August–1 November 2020. I am most grateful to its curator, An Van Camp, for her helpful insights. Personal communication, 25 July 2022.

p. 68   and enjoy themselves: See Albera and Couroucli (eds.), *Sharing Sacred Spaces*.

p. 68   they made flourish: J. W. McPherson, *The Moulids of Egypt (Egyptian Saints-Days)* (Cairo: N. M. Press, 1941): I'm grateful to Amir-Hussein Radjy for this reference.

p. 69   Matarea is one: Ibid., pp. 129–30.

p. 69   'in his old age?': Ibid., p. 131.

p. 69   serious and violent hostility: Mayeur-Jaouen, 'What Do Egypt's Copts and Muslims Share?', pp. 148–73.

p. 69   overcoming another fiend: Elizabeth Wickett, *Seers, Saints and Sinners: The Oral Traditions of Upper Egypt* (London: I. B. Tauris, 2012), pp. 75–98, 129–30; also Maria Couroucli, 'Saint George the Anatolian: Master of Frontiers', in Albera and Couroucli (eds.), *Sharing Sacred Spaces*, pp. 118–40.

p. 70   Egyptian Book of the Dead: Elizabeth Wickett, *For the Living and the Dead: The Funerary Laments of Upper Egypt, Ancient and Modern* (London: I. B. Tauris, 2009).

p. 71   'nicer than any man?': Virginia Woolf, *Jacob's Room* (London: Vintage, 1992), p. 5.

p. 71   one of her colleagues: Gary Younge, 'Scapegoating the Immigrant', *New York Review of Books*, 17 October 2024, pp. 20–3.

p. 71   'and it's acceptance': Matthew Phillip, 'A Home and a Sanctuary', *Tate Etc.*, issue 62 (Summer 2024), pp. 60–3, https://www.tate.org.uk/tate-etc/issue-62-summer-2024/matthew-phillip-notting-hill-carnival

p. 72   series of moulids: https://www.nationalgallery.org.uk/about-us/press-and-media/press-releases/the-triumph-of-art-jeremy-deller-commission-for-bicentenary-announces-partners-in-each-nation-of-the-uk

p. 73   Salman Rushdie's phrase: Salman Rushdie, 'The Empire Writes Back with a Vengeance', *The Times*, 3 July 1982.

p. 74   a made-up story: J. M. Coetzee, *The Childhood of Jesus* (London: Vintage, 2014), p. 137.

p. 74   groups or larger gatherings: Ed Vulliamy, 'Sam Lee: "There is a difference in the songs Gypsies sing"', *Observer*, 28 October 2012, https://www.theguardian.com/music/2012/oct/28/sam-lee-gypsy-folk-music I have this CD Sam Lee, *Old Wow* (London: Cooking Vinyl, 2021); see also samleesong.co.uk

p. 74    gave him lashes three: https://mainlynorfolk.info/lloyd/songs/thebitterwithy.html and samleesong.co.uk.

p. 75    sow and plant them?: Vulliamy, 'Sam Lee'.

p. 75    the silver screen: Pavel, *Fictional Worlds*, p. 141.

p. 75    'history of European culture': Ibid.

## Chapter 3: Relics: Helena Dreams of the Cross

p. 78    'We live in things': Virginia Woolf, *Between the Acts* (London: Hogarth Press, 1941), p. 55.

p. 78    'remedy for our sins . . .': Ambrose's sermon on the death of Theodosius acclaimed Helena – see A. R. Birley, 'St. Helena, Discoverer of the True Cross (250–330)'; Julia Hillner, *Helena: Mother of the Empire* (Oxford and New York: Oxford University Press, 2022), pp. 309–16; https://www.brown.edu/Research/Breaking_Ground/bios/St.%20Helena_Flavia%20Julia%20Helena%20Augusta.pdf

p. 81    'mocked us both together': *The Dream of the Rood*, ed. and trans. Roy M. Liuzza, *Old English Anthology* (Peterborough, Ont.: Broadview Press, 2014), pp. 187–91 at p. 188; see also https://www.poetryfoundation.org/poems/159129/dream-of-the-rood-translation The cross speaks to the dreamer in words that are partly inscribed in runes on the Anglo-Saxon Ruthwell Cross, now in Scotland.

p. 81    The long poem *Elene*: Cynewulf, *Elene*, trans. Charles W. Kennedy (Cambridge, Ont.: In Parentheses Publications, Old English Series, 2000). The precious manuscript is kept in the Italian town of Vercelli, hence its name 'the Vercelli book'.

p. 83    practice dear to God: Eusebius, *Life of Constantine*, ed. and trans. Averil Cameron and Stuart G. Hall (Oxford: Clarendon Press, 1999), p. 138.

p. 84    'sacralization of space': Jacques le Goff, *In Search of Sacred Time: Jacobus de Voragine and* The Golden Legend (Princeton: Princeton University Press, 2014), p. 177.

p. 84    'profoundly imagistic time': Ibid., p. 179.

p. 84    'came and bit me!': Jacobus de Voragine, *The Golden Legend: Readings on the Saints*, trans. William Granger Ryan, 2 vols (Princeton: Princeton University Press, 1993), vol. 2, p. 173.

p. 85   'able to carry it': John Calvin, *A Treatise on Relics*, trans. Count Valerian Krasinski (Edinburgh: Johnstone, Hunter, 1870), https://dbooks.bodleian.ox.ac.uk/books/PDFs/600107864.pdf

p. 85   (178 million cubic centimetres): *The Legendary History of the Cross: A Series of Sixty-Four Woodcuts*, from a Dutch book published by [John] Veldener A.D. 1483, ed. and intro. John Ashton (London: T. Fisher and Unwin, 1887) https://www.hellenicaworld.com/Religion/JohnAshton/en/TheLegendaryHistoryOfTheCross.html

p. 85   in Greek, Latin and Syriac: For the three streams of legendary material that flowed into the traditional story of St Helena, see: https://roman-emperors.sites.luc.edu/helena

p. 85   cross will be made: Jacobus, *Golden Legend*, trans. Ryan. The book unfolds the story in two principal entries: 'The Feast of the Finding of the Holy Cross', vol. 1, pp. 277–84; 'The Exaltation of the Holy Cross', vol. 2, pp. 168–73.

p. 86   'raised to the heights': Ibid., vol. 2, p. 168.

p. 90   'matronage' in Byzantium: Leslie Brubaker, 'Memories of Helena: Patterns in Imperial Female Matronage in the Fourth and Fifth Centuries', in Liz James (ed.), *Women, Men and Eunuchs: Gender in Byzantium* (London: Routledge, 1997), pp. 52–75.

p. 90   said to be a *stabularia*: Ambrose (*De obit. Theod.*, 42), quoted in A. R. Birley, 'St. Helena, Discoverer of the True Cross', https://www.brown.edu/Research/Breaking_Ground/bios/St.%20Helena_Flavia%20Julia%20Helena%20Augusta.pdf

p. 90   'different from strumpets': Philostorgius (*Hist. Eccl.*, 2.16), quoted in Jan Willem Drijvers, 'Helena Augusta', https://roman-emperors.sites.luc.edu/helena.htm

p. 90   when he was baptized: Averil Cameron and Stuart G. Hall, Introduction to Eusebius, *Life of Constantine*, ed. and trans. Cameron and Hall, pp. 41–2.

p. 91   restored and reopened: I am grateful to the British School at Rome for organizing a visit to the Mausoleum, and to Loredana Ottomano for acting as my guide.

p. 91   two are intertwined: However, it may also be possible that her journey to the East was a political act of conciliation. People living in the east of the empire may have been dissatisfied with Constantine's radical (religious) reforms, which included e.g. the replacement of many officials by Christian dignitaries and the rigorous suppression of pagan cults. Furthermore, Constantine's popularity may have suffered severe damage from murdering his wife Fausta and his son Crispus in 326. A reason why Helena travelled to the East may therefore have been to appease malcontents among the local inhabitants. Hillner, *Helena*, pp. 208–14.

p. 91 'Aug. 18. Rome, *b. Colchester*': Annotations made by Helen Roeder, Photographic Collection, Warburg Institute. My thanks to Paul Taylor for this information.

p. 92 landed in Totnes: Her identity as an ancient Briton also intersects with the figure of Cunobelinus, another client king of the Romans, whose capital was Colchester and who is remembered in the figure of Cymbeline in Shakespeare's late, British play.

p. 92 attempting to fly: Geoffrey of Monmouth, *Historia Regum Britanniae*, ed. Acton Griscom (London: Longmans, Green, 1929), pp. 338–40. This edition prints the Latin text with a translation of the Welsh Ms. LXI of Jesus College, Oxford.

p. 93 weekly ceremonies here: *L'Histoire mouvementée de notre église*, leaflet-guide in the church, n.d.

p. 95 rumbled and wailed: Evelyn Waugh, *Helena* (1950; London: Penguin, 1963), pp. 24–5.

p. 96 (... 'The Subaltern's Love Song', 1941): John Betjeman, 'A Subaltern's Love Song', in his *Collected Poems* (London: John Murray, 1978), https://poetryarchive.org/poem/subalterns-love-song/

p. 96 there alone lies Hope: Waugh, *Helena*, p. 159.

p. 97 to do and did it: George Weigel, *The Truth of Catholicism* (London: HarperCollins, 2002), https://www.georgeweigel.com/evelyn-waugh-1903-2003/

p. 97 palace of her son: Robert Cassanelli and Emilia Stolfi (eds.), *Gerusalemme a Roma: La Basilica di Santa Croce e le reliquie della Passione* (Milan: Jaca Books, 2012).

p. 98 from the sacred origin: Mother-of-pearl models of the Holy Sepulchre are in the British Museum and the Ashmolean Museum, Oxford.

p. 99 teeth and real hair: Samuel Butler, *Ex Voto: An Account of the Sacro Monte or New Jerusalem at Varallo-Sesia* (London: A. C. Fifield, 1909), pp. 40–2. The principal artist was known as Tabachetti, but several others were involved.

p. 101 'memory of the same': Edmund Matyjaszek, 'Walsingham in Ballad, Poetry, and Prose', *Walsingham: Richeldis 950: Pilgrimage* and History, Proceedings of the Richeldis 950 Historical Conference, March 2011 (Walsingham: RC National Shrine, 2012), pp. 47–79 at p. 47.

p. 101 doors in welcome: The poignant documentary *Relics and Roses*, dir. Michael Whyte (2011), follows the UK tour of the relic, https://www2.bfi.org.uk/films-tv-people/5bb098e3931b30 see also Adam Gabbatt, 'Relics of St Thérèse of Lisieux arrive in London', *Guardian*, 12 October 2009, https://www.theguardian.com/world/2009/oct/12/st-therese-lisieux-relics-london

p. 102 several of them recent: I am most grateful to the writer and artist Chiara Ambrosio for telling me about this shrine.

p. 102 critique and celebration: Christian Boltanski and Cornelia Parker are pre-eminent artists in this mode. See exhibition catalogue *Cornelia Parker*, ed. Andrea Schlieker (London: Tate, 2022); see also Mark Dion's *Tate Thames Dig* (1999).

p. 102 and waken from: Seamus Heaney, *Station Island* (London: Faber & Faber, 1984), p. 87.

p. 103 by daily prayers: See Marina Warner, 'Holy Shape Shifters', review of Harriet I. Flower, *The Dancing Lares and the Serpent in the Garden: Religion at the Roman Street Corner*, New York Review of Books, 7 June 2018.

p. 104 ( . . . have toured Europe): The Museum of Innocence: https://www.masumiyetmuzesi.org/en/zi-yaret-g%C3%BCn-ve-saatleri. I saw the touring version of the show.

p. 104 reaching the sacred today: Eugenio Trías, 'Thinking Religion: The Symbol and the Sacred', in Jacques Derrida and Gianni Vattimo (eds.), *Religion*, trans. David Webb (Cambridge: Polity Press, 1998), pp. 95–110: see p. 110, note 6 in particular.

p. 105 *Seas of Red*: Paul Cummins and Tom Piper's installation *Blood Swept Lands and Seas of Red*, Tower of London, July–November 2014, was extended in response to huge public demand, http://www.hrp.org.uk/TowerOfLondon/poppies

p. 106 in that period: See Mairi MacDonald, 'The Guild of the Holy Cross and its Buildings', in J. R. Mulryne (ed.), *The Guild and Guild Buildings of Shakespeare's Stratford* (Farnham: Ashgate, 2013), pp. 13–30.

p. 106 out of purgatory: Susan Dunn-Hensley, 'The Return of the Sacred Virgin: Memory, Loss, and Restoration in Shakespeare's Later Plays', in Dominic T. S. Janes and Gary F. Waller (eds), *Walsingham in Literature and Culture from the Middle Ages to Modernity* (Farnham: Ashgate, 2010), pp. 185–98.

p. 107 (... now partially restored): See Emily Howe, Henrietta McBurney, David Park, Stephen Rickerby and Lisa Shekede, *Wall Paintings of Eton* (London: Scala Publishing, 2013), passim, and a short story, Marina Warner, 'Filigrana Italiana', in Michel Jeanneret and Nicolas Ducimetière (eds), *The Italian Renaissance: A Zest for Life* (Oxford: Legenda, 2018), pp. 127–39. On the lower register on the same south side of the chapel, the story of the travails of the empress falsely accused of adultery unfolds in eight exquisitely painted and very busy scenes; they follow the wronged heroine from persecution to triumph. The story is much more familiar from romance and fairy tale than from hagiography, and it's a surprise to find it dramatized in this liturgical setting. In plays and poetry it takes many forms (Patient Griselda, that nastiest of instruction manuals on wifely virtue, recounted by Boccaccio in the *Decameron*, Day 10, Tale 10, being the most famous): Boccaccio, *Decameron*, trans. G. H. McWilliam (Harmondsworth: Penguin, 1980), pp. 813–27; https://web.archive.org/web/20210130215324/http://sites.fas.harvard.edu/~chaucer/special/authors/boccaccio/boc10-10.html

p. 107 they use to assault her: Jacobus, *The Golden Legend*, trans. Ryan, 2: 334–41.

p. 107 through the eye: Ibid., 1: 385–7. (Her name is here spelt Christina.)

p. 107 limited facsimile edition: I was kindly shown this rare book by Sarah Hosking: *16 Plates of the Paintings in the Chancel, including the legend of the Holy Cross and the murder of Thomas Becket* (London: Nichols & Sons, 1836). Only 120 copies were printed. Computer-generated reconstructions of the chapel as it was can be seen at http://www.heritagetechnology.co.uk/portfolio

p. 107 group of local needlewomen: The project was led by Norma Whittard at the request of the verger at the time, Robin Smart. I am very grateful to Andrew Holtom for sending me Tim Raistrick's photographs of these embroideries as well as descriptions of each one by Mairi MacDonald, and to Sarah Hosking for her information and help throughout.

p. 109 'block of toilets': Quoted by Eamonn Gearon, 'In Makkah', *TLS*, 29 May 2015, p. 30, from Ziauddin Sardar, *Mecca: The Sacred City* (London: Bloomsbury, 2015).

p. 110 to a collective story: The Church in Wales declared on 19 April 2023 that the cross will be made available for veneration to both the Anglican and Catholic churches in Wales: https://www.churchinwales.org.uk/en/news-and-events/the-cross-of-wales-will-lead-coronation-procession/

## Chapter 4: Dust: The Flying House of Loreto

p. 111 'where to put it': A child in a refugee camp gave this answer to a journalist/NGO worker, but their name and when and where they uttered these words are lost, which sadly corresponds to the circumstances. I heard this from Oliver Marlow, one of the students in the audience, to whom many thanks, after a talk I gave for the New School of the Anthropocene on 13 December 2024.

p. 111 'oh blessed place!': Paolo Agelli, *Vita del Beato Giuseppe da Copertino*, trans. Christopher David Costanzo (North Charleston, SC: CreateSpace Independent Publishing Platform, 2014), p. 143, quoted in Carlos Eire, *They Flew: A History of the Impossible* (New Haven: Yale University Press, 2023), pp. 128–9.

p. 111 'off the ground': Eire, *They Flew*, p. 128.

p. 115 church still proclaims: I transcribed the inscriptions in the church of Loreto; for their author, see Peter Davidson, 'Perceptions of the British Isles and Ireland among the Catholic Exiles: The Case of Robert Corbington SJ', in David Worthington (ed.), *British and Irish Emigrants and Exiles in Europe, 1603–1688* (Leiden: Brill, 2010), pp. 315–22, https://doi.org/10.1163/ej.9789004180086.i-346.69

p. 116 their new surroundings: https://www.unhcr.org/uk/news-and-stories/special-features/seeds-hope

p. 116 in mushroom clouds: 'Things We Carry on the Sea', from *My Name is Immigrant* by Wang Ping, 2020. Hanging Loose Press. See https://poets.org/poem/things-we-carry-sea

p. 118 verify the events: Marijan Bradanović and Emanuel Hoško, *Mary's Trsat*, trans. Živan Filippi (Zagreb: Turistika naklada, 2011).

p. 118 remember its brief sojourn: Ibid.

p. 118 Carlo II to the Pope: Cartularia Culizanense fol. 181, which I saw in the Museum of the Shrine at Loreto.

p. 118 the fourteenth century: H. Thurston, 'Santa Casa di Loreto', in *The Catholic Encyclopaedia* (New York: Robert Appleton Company, 1912), retrieved from New Advent: http://www.newadvent.org/cathen/13454b.htm See also *Guida al santuario di Loreto*,

Delegazione Pontificia per il Santuario della Santa Casa-Loreto (2013), pp. 3–19.

p. 119 (... attracts votaries again): https://www.chch.ox.ac.uk/cathedral/visiting/pilgrimage

p. 120 it should stand: *Walsingham: Richeldis 950: Pilgrimage and History*.

p. 120 remember the devastation: 'The Pynson Ballad', which tells the whole story of the shrine's foundation, is dated to the mid-fifteenth century: https://www.walsinghamanglicanmedieval.org.uk/pynson.htm

p. 120 Walsingham, oh, farewell!: https://www.walsinghamanglicanmedieval.org.uk/arundel.htm It is known as 'The Arundel Ballad', though it is no longer attributed to the Earl of Arundel. The first edition is in the Bodleian Library, Oxford. I am most grateful to Edmund Matyjaszek for his help with the literary references to Walsingham in his article 'Walsingham in Ballad, Poetry and Prose', in *Walsingham: Richeldis 950: Pilgrimage and History*, Proceedings of the Richeldis 950 Historical Conference, March 2011 (Walsingham: RC National Shrine, 2012), pp. 47–79, and his pamphlet *Walsingham: England's Nazareth – Story of the Shrine in Poetry and Prose* (Ryde: Isle of Wight Catholic History Society, c.2012). See also Susan Stewart, *The Ruins Lesson: Meaning and Material in Western Culture* (Chicago: University of Chicago Press, 2020), pp. 110–11.

p. 122 a huge sum: '*J'y lessai pres de 50 bons escus pour ma part*': Michel de Montaigne, *Journal de Voyage*, ed. Louis Lautrey (Paris: Hachette, 1906), p. 285. My translation.

p. 122 'old and tumbledown': '*Le lieu de la devotion, c'est une petite maisonete fort vieille et chetifve*': Ibid. My translation.

p. 123 courtesan of the time: Lena, or Maddalena Antognetti: in Ricardo Bassani and Fiora Bellini, *Caravaggio assassino: la carriera di un 'valenthuomo' fazioso nella Roma della Controriforma* (Rome: Donzelli, 1994), pp. 201–14; https://it.wikipedia.org/wiki/Madonna_dei_Pellegrini#cite_ref-13

p. 123 feet to the Madonna: Gian Pietro Bellori, *Le vite de' pittori, scultori et architetti moderni* (Rome: Mascardi, 1672), pp. 202–15; see Evelina Borea's edition (Rome: Einaudi, 1976), pp. 211–33, quoted in https://it.wikipedia.org/wiki/Madonna_dei_Pellegrini#cite_ref-3

p. 123 around the same time: Pietro Teramano, *Trāslatio miraculosa ecclesie beate Marie virginis de Loreto* (Rome: Eucharius Silber, c.1500).

p. 123 them and the roof: see numerous prints, of the sixteenth and seventeenth centuries, in *La historia della chiesa di Santa Maria di Loreto* (Loreto: Carilo, 1993), pp. 47, 107, 111, 151, 214–15, 317.

p. 123 'lord Jesus Christ': *'Ecclesia beate Mariae de Loreto fuit Camera domus beate M V B Matris domini nostri J C.'* Teramano, *Trāslatio miraculosa*. My translation.

p. 123 'age of twelve': Ibid.

p. 124 'so it was done': *'qui videntes multa misteria divina fuisse facta in dicta camera: decreverunt de communi consensu omnium de dicta camera facere unam ecclesiam in honorem et memoriam B. Mariae Virginis; et ita factum fuit.'* Ibid.

p. 124 'faith of Mohammed': *'dimisit fidem Christi: et recepit fidem Mahemet'*. Ibid.

p. 124 this chosen church: *'prelibatam Ecclesiam'*. Ibid.

p. 124 'fights broke out': *'maximas discordias et lites venerunt'*. Ibid.

p. 124 the public way: *'in viam communem'*. Ibid.

p. 124 'traces of the foundations': *'vestigia fundamentorum'*. Ibid.

p. 125 'Blest Lady of Loreto': Transcribed by me *in situ*. The English version is reproduced in *La Historia della Chiesa di Santa Maria di Loreto* (Loreto: Carilo, 1993), p. 497. See also Davidson, 'Perceptions of the British Isles and Ireland Among the Catholic Exiles: The Case of Robert Corbington, SJ'.

p. 125 'survives translation true': Seamus Heaney, *The Spirit Level* (London: Faber & Faber, 1996), p. 50.

p. 125 'rose and flew': Heaney sent me the earlier version in a letter dated 19 April 1995. 'This floated up a couple of months ago,' he wrote, 'and I kept meaning to send it to you. You don't know of any pictures or illustrations of the "translation" – or is it? a translation, maybe not – of the house? It would make a lovely cover for a book – all Marian blue and gold leaf . . .' In this draft of this poem, the last two lines ran:

> I lift my eyes to them, in an unmeta-
> physical need for the beautiful and true.

In the published version, these last two lines, admittedly rather weak, are transformed into a much richer statement – a profession of faith, which picks up the earlier metaphorical twining of print and vision.

p. 127 over twenty years: Yves-Marie Bercé, *Lorette aux XVIe et XVIIe siècles: Histoire du plus grand pèlerinage des Temps modernes* (Paris: Presses de l'Université Paris-Sorbonne, 2011), pp. 123–4.

p. 127 classical Renaissance art: The artists who worked on the monument include Andrea Sansovino, D. d'Amia, the Lombardi and Della Porta brothers and Niccolò Tribolo. See Floriano da Morrovalle, OFM, *Loreto nell'arte* (Loreto: Congregazione Universale della Santa Casa di Loreto, 1965); Floriana Grimaldi, *La chiesa di Santa Maria di Loreto nei documenti dei secoli XII–XV* (Ancona: Archivio di Stato, 1984).

p. 129 someone to focus on: Jacques Le Goff, *In Search of Sacred Time: Jacobus de Voragine and* The Golden Legend (Princeton and Oxford: Princeton University Press, 2014).

p. 133 run by nuns: Abbé Pierre Coural, *Solitude de Nazareth: Maison religeuse et industrielle, fondée à Montpellier en 1841, dans le but de recevoir sans rétribution, et sous la direction des Soeurs de Marie-Joseph, les jeunes filles libérées sortant des prisons et des maisons centrales* (Montpellier: Grollier, 1843).

p. 133 Laundries in Ireland: The events inspired an artists' project at Rua Red in Dublin, https://visualartists.ie/events/a-mary-magdalene-experience-grace-dyas-at-rua-red/ as well as Claire Keegan's acclaimed novel *Small Things Like These* (London: Faber & Faber, 2021).

p. 133 the word 'Solitude': Patrick Modiano, *Dora Bruder* (Paris: Gallimard, 1997), p. 41.

p. 133 in the foundations: Two coins of Gui II de la Roche, the last Duke of Athens, minted in 1291–8: Bercé, *Lorette*, p. 310.

p. 133 the eastern Mediterranean: The herringbone grooves on the stones are characteristic of masons' methods in the Middle East and are unknown in Italy; to my surprise, in 2014 I saw similar herringbone traces of the masons' tools on stones in the excavated areas near the Pyramids in Egypt.

p. 134 brought the relic: Anon. [Congrezione Universale della S. Casa], *Storia Illustrata della Santa Casa / Illustrated History of the Holy House* (Loreto: Donati Editore, 2010).

p. 135 border of his cope: https://en.numista.com/catalogue/exonumia 318554.html

p. 135 coast near Loreto: The painting hangs in the local Pinacoteca Civica, Iesi.

p. 136 ex votos and model ships: It is called the chapel of the Votive Gifts and the chapel of Candles.

p. 137 and their efficacy: Walter Benjamin, 'The Work of Art in the Age of Mechanical Reproduction', in his *Illuminations: Essays and Reflections*, ed. Hannah Arendt, trans. Harry Zohn (New York: Schocken Books, 2007), pp. 217–52.

p. 137 San Pancrazio, Florence: Damiano Neri, *Il S. Sepolcro Riprodotto in Oriente* (Jerusalem: Franciscan Printing Press, 1971), pp. 81–7. Diarmaid MacCulloch has noted how through acts of spatial imagination Jerusalem can be recreated here when Jerusalem there is no longer accessible. Diarmaid MacCulloch, 'The Chief Inhabitant', review of Simon Sebag Montefiore, *Jerusalem: The Biography*, *London Review of Books*, 14 July 2011, https://www.lrb.co.uk/the-paper/v33/n14/diarmaid-macculloch/the-chief-inhabitant

p. 137 at a much smaller scale: Bani Hashim Mosque, Rabdan Al Maqta, Abu Dhabi.

p. 138 doppelgängers far and wide: George Prochnik, '770 is here! Bricks, aura and the multiplication of the Lubavitcher Messiah', *Cabinet*, 3 November 2022, https://www.cabinetmagazine.org/kiosk/prochnik_george_3_november_2022.php The essay draws on the photographic work of Andrea Robbins and Max Becher, 770 (2005), https://robbinsbecher.com/projects/770/

p. 138 'skills at replication': Hillel Schwartz, *The Culture of the Copy: Striking Likenesses, Unreasonable Facsimiles* (New York: Zone Books, 1996), p. 378.

p. 138 'heart of our history': Mourid Barghouti, *I Was Born There, I Was Born Here*, trans. Humphrey Davies (London: Bloomsbury, 2012), p. 64.

p. 139 'reduction of all history': Ibid., p. 195.

p. 139 Palestinians before 1948: Said's maternal great-grandfather Yousif Badr was perhaps the first native Evangelical minister in Lebanon, while his maternal grandfather Shoukri Musa converted to Christianity in Chicago, became a missionary and in 1911 founded the first Baptist church in Nazareth. Hilda Musa, Edward's mother, was born in Nazareth four years later, went to school in Beirut and on her marriage to Wadie Said at the age of eighteen in 1932 lived first in Jerusalem and then in Cairo. The family continued to visit Nazareth regularly, where Hilda's mother, known as Teta, had remained throughout the turbulent decades of Israel's foundation and after, until her death in 1990. See Jean Makdisi Said (Edward

Said's sister), *Teta, My Mother and Me: An Arab Woman's Memoir* (London: Saqi Books, 2005), pp. 247–65; see also Edward W. Said, *Out of Place: A Memoir* (London: Granta, 1999), p. 12, and Naim Atallah, *The Old Ladies of Nazareth* (London: Quartet Books, 2004).

p. 140 'a place to return to . . .': Said, *Out of Place*, p. 119.

p. 140 about the Holy Family: Ibid., pp. 119, 123.

p. 140 'wouldn't last three days': 's'il etoit permis d'en amporter, il n'y en aurait pas pour trois jours'. Montaigne, *Journal de Voyage*, p. 287.

p. 140 (. . . until the 1940s): I saw examples in the Museo Antico-Tesoro nel Palazzo Apostolico, Loreto; John Miller, *The Philosophy of Tattoos* (London: British Library, 2021), illustrates the engraving of the Jerusalem pilgrim on p. 30 but does not discuss the custom.

p. 140 punishment in hell: Bercé, *Lorette aux XVIe et XVIIe siècles*, pp. 29–33, figs 2–3; I also saw examples in the museum at Loreto.

p. 141 'of language and of life': John Ruskin, *Seven Lamps of Architecture* (London: Smith, Elder, 1849), 8.234, quoted in Lawrence Gasquet, '"That Golden Stain of Time": The Ethics of the Dust from Ruskin to Jorge Otero-Pailos', https://courtauld.ac.uk/research/research-resources/publications/courtauld-books-online/ruskins-ecologies-figures-of-relation-from-modern-painters-to-the-storm-cloud/13-that-golden-stain-of-time-the-ethics-of-the-dust-from-john-ruskin-to-jorge-otero-pailos-lawrence-gasquet/#top Otero-Pailos is an architect whose installation in Westminster Hall, under the auspices of Artangel, explored Ruskin's ideas: https://www.artangel.org.uk/project/the-ethics-of-dust/

p. 141 'city of God': John Ruskin, *The Ethics of the Dust: Ten Lectures to Little Housewives on the Elements of Crystallisation* (London: Smith, Elder, 1866), p. 231.

p. 142 'real of our reality': Duane Michals, *The House I Once Called Home* (London: Enitharmon Press, 2003), no page numbers.

p. 143 some Palestinian earth: Raja Shehadeh, *Language of War, Language of Peace: Palestine, Israel and the Search for Justice* (London: Profile Books, 2015), (p. 62), quoted in James Crawford, *The Edge of the Plain: How Borders Make and Break Our World* (Edinburgh: Canongate, 2023), pp. 160–1. *Land of Aeolia*, Ilias Venezis's piercingly nostalgic autobiographical novel (1943) about the flight of Greeks from Anatolia at the beginning of the twentieth century, closes with the exodus of the family. The child narrator's grandmother leaning on her husband's breast finds a lump there: he has wrapped earth from their farm in a kerchief under his shirt. Trans. Therese Sellers (Limni, Evia: Denise Harvey, 2020).

p. 143 self, house and home: The Tate website states, 'The sculpture also exists as a separate work, *My Mother. My Father. My Sister. My Brother* 1996–7': https://www.tate.org.uk/art/artworks/rodney-in-the-house-of-my-father-p78529 A retrospective of his oeuvre was shown in 2024 in Nottingham: https://www.nottinghamcontemporary.org/whats-on/donald-rodney-visceral-canker/?mc_cid=6c50116be6&mc_eid=91383ddoed It will tour to the Whitechapel Gallery, London, in 2025.

p. 144 'all his homes': https://www.ellislandfarm.co.uk/

## Chapter 5: Bonds: The Migrant Queen

p. 146 pressure of reality: Wallace Stevens, 'The Noble Rider and the Sound of Words', in his *The Necessary Angel: Essays on Poetry and the Imagination* (New York: Vintage, 1951), p. 36, as quoted in Seamus Heaney, *The Redress of Poetry* (London: Faber & Faber, 1996), p. 1.

p. 146 (. . . those who suffer too): Virgil, *Aeneid*, I:628–30, trans. Robert Fagles (London: Penguin, 2006), p. 68; Shadi Bartsch in her recent version – *Vergil: The Aeneid: A New Translation* (London: Profile Books, 2020), p. 22 – gives the lines a more direct expression: 'Knowing / pain, I can learn to help the pain of others.'

p. 148 (. . . my own free will): Virgil, *Aeneid* IV:361, trans. Bartsch, p. 84.

p. 149 Arab worlds: Elissa: Sources for the story include a lost history by Timaeus of Tauronemium, Sicily, *c.* 256–360 BCE; a fragment of an epic poem by Gnaeus Naevius, who died at Utica in 201 BCE, where appears a passage which might or might not be part of a conversation between Aeneas and Dido; and Servius' commentary on Varro (first century BCE) in which Dido's sister Anna killed herself for love of Aeneas (4: 682; 5: 4).

p. 150 'boots in crimson': Virgil, *Aeneid* I:409–10, trans. Fagles, pp. 58–9.

p. 151 long, twisting, dark . . .: Virgil, *Aeneid* I:411–15, trans. Fagles, p. 59.

p. 152 and her possessions: *Aeneid* I:605, trans. Fagles, p. 64.

p. 153 certain narrative elements: Many more dates have been suggested for the cities' foundation, but Virgil was wishfully exercising narrative licence in synchronizing the fall of Troy and the reign of Pygmalion in Tyre with the origins of Carthage and Rome. Josephus, the author of the first-century CE *History of the Jews*, provides a chronology that dates the reign of Pygmalion in Tyre to 831–785 BCE plausibly enough to convince Peter Wiseman.

p. 153 first century BCE: Gnaeus Pompeius Trogus in his *Philippic Histories*, as rendered in a digest or epitome made by Junianus Justinus in the third century CE, describes the early history of Carthage, 18: 4–6: https://www.livius.org/sources/content/the-founding-of-carthage/

p. 154 she sees them: In this historical version Dido inspires a cult, and metamorphoses into the monstrous and bloodthirsty goddess Tanit, who was worshipped at the Tophet, a site which, when excavated in the 1970s, appeared to confirm the practice of human sacrifice, especially of infants. See Paolo Xella, Josephine Quinn, Valentina Melchiorri and Peter van Dommelen, 'Cemetery or sacrifice? Infant burials at the Carthage Tophet: Phoenician bones of contention', published online by Cambridge University Press, 22 November 2013, https://www.cambridge.org/core/search?filters%5BauthorTerms%5D=Paolo%20Xella&eventCode=SE-AU

p. 155 such barbaric ways: *Aeneid* I:648–9, trans. Fagles, p. 65.

p. 156 'underfoot – you'll see . . .': *Aeneid* IV:610–14, trans. Fagles, p. 144.

p. 156 'against my will': *Aeneid* IV:610–14, 617, trans. Fagles, p. 144.

p. 156 could gnaw it off: *Aeneid* IV:644–5, trans. Fagles, p. 145.

p. 158 'endless war!': I haven't given quotations in the original in most cases but this is a speech that deserves reproducing in full.

> *tum vos, o Tyrii, stirpem et genus omne futurum*
> *exercete odiis, cinerique haec mittite nostro*
> *munera. nullus amor populis nec foedera sunto.*
> *exoriare aliquis nostris ex ossibus ultor*
> *qui face Dardanios ferroque sequare colonos,*
> *nunc, olim, quocumque dabunt se tempore vires.*
> *litora litoribus contraria, fluctibus undas*
> *imprecor, arma armis: pugnent ipsique nepotesque.*
> (That is my prayer, my final cry – I pour it out
> with my own lifeblood. And you, my Tyrians,
> harry with hatred all his line, his race to come;
> make that offering to my ashes, send it down below.
> No love between our peoples, ever, no pacts of peace!
> Come rising up from my bones, you avenger still unknown,
> to stalk those Trojan settlers, hunt with fire and iron,
> now or in time to come, whenever the power is yours.

> Shore clash with shore, sea against sea and sword
> against sword – this is my curse – war between all
> our peoples, all their children, endless war!)
> 
> Aeneid IV:774–84, trans. Fagles, p. 149

p. 158 'slaughter of a queen': Marlowe, *Dido, Queen of Carthage*, V. i.294, in Christopher Marlowe, *The Complete Plays*, ed. Frank Romany and Robert Lindsey (London: Penguin, 2003), p. 66.

p. 158 that be never league . . .: Ibid., V. i. 304–9.

p. 159 *This Orient Isle*: Jerry Brotton, *This Orient Isle: Elizabethan England and the Islamic World* (London: Allen Lane, 2016); many plays and operas reflect the intermingling of cultures across the Mediterranean in the period, e.g. Francesco Cavalli's 1644 opera *L'Ormindo*, at the Wanamaker Playhouse, 25 March–12 April 2014.

p. 159 that Ovid stages: Ovid, *Heroides*, 'Dido to Aeneas', in *Ovid's Heroines: A Verse Translation of the* Heroides, trans. Daryl Hine (New Haven: Yale University Press, 1991), pp. 69–78; 'Dido to Aeneas', in Clare Pollard, *Ovid's Heroines* (Hexham: Bloodaxe Books, 2013), pp. 49–55.

p. 160 be your last loss . . .: Pollard, *Ovid's Heroines*, p. 54.

p. 160 Dido destroyed herself: Ovid: '*Praebuit Aeneas et causam mortem et ensem. / Ipsa sua Dido concidit usa manu*', trans. Pollard, ibid., p. 55.

p. 161 'like a dear sister': Ovid, *Fasti*, trans. Anne and Peter Wiseman (Oxford: Oxford University Press, 2011), III:524ff., pp. 54ff.

p. 161 'a symbolic homicide': Attilio Mastrocinque, 'Late Antique Lamps with Defixiones', *Greek Roman and Byzantine Studies*, vol. 47 (2007), pp. 87–99 at p. 96.

p. 161 'complete, at rest': *Aeneid* III:830, trans. Fagles, p. 126.

p. 163 buried in her heart: '*At regina gravi iamdudum saucia cura / vulnus alit venis et caeco carpitur igni.*' *Aeneid* IV:1–3, trans. Fagles, p. 127.

p. 163 through her bones: *Aeneid*, I:785–6, trans. Fagles, p. 69.

p. 163 'does not matter which': Aelius Donatus, *Life of Virgil*, 31–2, http://virgil.org/vitae/

p. 164 perform a futile rite: *Aeneid*, VI:1017–21, trans. Fagles, p. 211.

p. 164 'each of the verses': Donatus, *Life of Virgil*, 31–2, http://virgil.org/vitae/Donatus

p. 166 'should weep for her?': See Marina Warner, '"Come to Hecuba": Theatrical Empathy and Memories of Troy', in *The Shakespearean International Yearbook*, vol. 11: *Special Issue: Placing Michael*

Neill – *Issues of Place in Shakespeare and Early Modern Culture*, ed. Jonathan Gil Harris (Farnham: Ashgate, 2012), pp. 61–87.

p. 166 falsehood and imputation: The First Folio also has 'my travellours' history' (I. iii), but the preferred reading comes from the First Quarto 'my travailous history', i.e. beset by troubles, which fits better with the general drift of Othello's narrative. The phrase 'but not instinctively I did consent' from the First Folio has generally been changed to 'not intentively' from the First Quarto to convey Othello's lack of designs upon Desdemona. See the full and splendid edition by Michael Neill: William Shakespeare, *Othello: The Moor of Venice* (Oxford: Oxford University Press, 2006).

p. 166 'feeling taking shape': Jason Allen-Paisant, 'Self-Portrait as Othello I', in his *Self-Portrait as Othello* (Manchester: Carcanet, 2023), pp. 43–5 at p. 45.

p. 168 beneath their shoulders: John Mandeville, the chief source for the existence of the so-called 'Monstrous Races', probably never left his fireside. See Shakespeare, *Othello*, ed. Neill.

p. 169 'against / badmind': Allen-Paisant, 'Othello Walks', in his *Self-Portrait as Othello*, p. 46.

p. 170 'to an outside world': Ibid., p. 53.

p. 171 role of knight errant: I was lucky enough to see a production at the Edinburgh Festival in 2007. I have a DVD: Cavalli, *La Didone*, with Les Arts Florissants, conductor William Christie, with Anna Bonitatibus and Kresimir Spicer (Opus Arte, 2011).

p. 173 'greatly enriches both': Lucy Hughes-Hallett, 'A dual spin on Virgil', *New York Sun*, 21 August 2007.

p. 173 Purcell's lyric masterpiece: Henry Purcell, *Dido and Aeneas*, libretto by Nahum Tate, with Susan Graham, Ian Bostridge et al., Le Concert d'Astrée, conducted by Emmanuelle Hahn (CD: Veritas 72435 45605 2 1, 2003); also a DVD with the Orchestra of the Age of Enlightenment, conductor Christopher Hogwood, with Sarah Connolly and Luca Meachem, at the Royal Opera House (Opus Arte, 2009).

p. 173 *Les Troyens*: The CD I have is a recording of a concert performance: Berlioz, *Les Troyens*, performed by the London Symphony Orchestra, conductor Colin Davis with Michelle DeYoung, Ben Heppner et al., LSO Live, Barbican, London, 2000; also a DVD: Berlioz, *Les Troyens*, Metropolitan Opera Orchestra, Chorus and Ballet, conductor James Levine, with Jessye Norman, Plácido Domingo et al., directed by Fabrizio Melano, New York, 1983. See also https://lsolive.lso.co.uk/products/lsooo10-berlioz-les-troyens?srsltid=AfmBOoroRLN7viL11-Dms309I1S5kLOi345xORf2jiGigJZ_oTGCbq4W.

p. 174 'we become historical': Hannah Arendt, *The Human Condition* (Chicago: University of Chicago Press, 1958), p. 97.

p. 174 'on the involuntary': W. H. Auden, 'The World of Opera', in his *Secondary Worlds* (London: Faber & Faber, 1968), p. 88.

p. 175 'the local clans': Depicted with fascination in French orientalist paintings by Horace Vernet and others, including Delacroix, whose *Le Sultan de Maroc entouré de sa garde et de ses officiers* Baudelaire admired extravagantly: 'Salon de 1845', in Baudelaire, *Oeuvres complètes*, ed. Marcel A. Ruff (Paris: Seuil, 1968), pp. 204–24 at p. 206.

p. 175 Let them quake: Hector Berlioz, *Les Troyens*, Act III, finale, CD of the concert performance, Barbican, London, 2000. My translation.

p. 176 with their destruction: Ibid.

p. 178 points of their boots: Erri De Luca, 'Coro', in *Solo Andata: Righe che vanno troppo spesso a capo* (Milan: Feltrinelli, 2014), p. 35. My translation.

p. 178 spread like manure: Ibid., p. 25. My translation.

p. 178 you have suppressed: Ibid., p. 35. My translation.

p. 179 'the art of words': Ursula K. Le Guin, 'Speech in Acceptance of the National Book Foundation Medal for Distinguished Contribution to American Letters', https://www.ursulakleguin.com/nbf-medal By kind permission. Copyright © 2014 Ursula K. Le Guin.

p. 180 moving, subtle story: Ursula K. Le Guin, *Lavinia* (London: Phoenix Books, 2009).

p. 180 'he is quiet': Ibid., p. 26.

p. 181 satirize Roman pomp: Errolyn Wallen, *Dido's Ghost*, premiered at the Barbican on 6 June 2021; Frederic Wake-Walker directed: https://www.barbican.org.uk/whats-on/2021/event/didos-ghost-live-from-the-barbican

**Chapter 6: Tales: The Riddle Princess**

p. 183 'true love of mine': the tune is known as 'Scarborough Fair'; see Hugh Haughton (ed.), *The Chatto Book of Nonsense Poetry* (London: Chatto & Windus, 1988), pp. 164–5.

p. 184 out into the night: See William Ashbrook and Harold Powers, *Puccini's Turandot: The End of the Great Tradition* (Princeton: Princeton University Press, 1991).

p. 185 country in consequence: Yevgenia Belorusets, *Lucky Breaks*, trans. Eugene Ostashevsky (London: Pushkin Press, 2022). Reviewed by Marcel Theroux, *Guardian*, 2 June 2022, https://www.theguardian.com/books/2022/jun/03/lucky-breaks-by-yevgenia-belorusets-review-war-stories-from-ukraine

p. 186 I shall overcome!: Libretto by Giuseppe Adami and Renato Simoni, trans. Anon: https://www.murashev.com/opera/Turandot_libretto_English_Italian The DVD I have is Giacomo Puccini, *Turandot*, with the Metropolitan Chorus and Orchestra, conductor James Levine, with Eva Marton, Plácido Domingo et al., directed by Franco Zeffirelli, New York, 1988.

p. 188 the Aarne-Thompson-Uther Index: Stith Thompson, *Motif-Index of Folk-Literature: A Classification of Narrative Elements in Folk-Tales, Ballads, Myths, Fables, Mediæval Romances, Exempla, Fabliaux, Jest-Books, and Local Legends* (Helsinki: Suomalainen Tiedeakatemia, Academia Scientiarum Fennica, 1932), 6 vols, vol. x, pp. xx–xx.

p. 188 streets of Milan: Anon., Programme, *Rigoletto* (Cardiff: Welsh National Opera, Autumn 2024), pp. 17–22; see also Francesco Izzo, 'Music and drama in Verdi's *Rigoletto*', in the same programme, p. 16.

p. 190 'Mozart and others': https://www.bellperc.com/blogs/repertoire/carl-maria-von-weber

p. 190 'you want by force!': Han Seung Hee and Jin Seok Jeon, *One Thousand and One Nights*, trans. Hye Young Im and J. Torres, adapted J. Torres (Seoul: Seoul Cultural Publishers, 2004; New York: Yen Press, 2005). I am very grateful to Mariam and Shawkat Toorawa for giving me a copy of the book, which I would never have discovered on my own.

p. 190 Edward Said defined: Edward M. Said, 'Travelling Theory', in his *The World, the Text, and the Critic* (London: Vintage, 1991), pp. 226–47.

p. 191 a characteristic topic: For a clear stemma of the manuscripts and subsequent retelling see Youssef Mogtader and Gregor Schoeler, *Turandot: Die persische Märchenerzählung* (Wiesbaden: Reichert Verlag, 2017), p. 130.

p. 192 courtly and sophisticated circles: Peter Chelkowski, Introduction to El Nizami, *Mirror of the Invisible World: Tales from the* Khamseh *of*

Nizami, adapted and trans. Peter J. Chelkowski, with an essay by
Priscilla P. Soucek, Foreword by Richard Ettinghausen (New York:
Metropolitan Museum of Art, 1975), pp. 1–10; Nezâmî, *Le Pavillon
des sept princesses*, ed. and trans. Michel Barry (Paris: Gallimard,
2000), 'Récit de la princesse des slaves sous le pavillon rouge de
Mars', pp. 301–27.

p. 192 'the prophetic veil': Chelkowski, Introduction to El Nizami, *Mirror
of the Invisible World*, p. 9.

p. 193 'shadow of light': Nezâmî, *Le Pavillon des sept princesses*, p. 307
('*Y entortillait des noeuds dans l'eau à en paraître perles et du noir de son
calame, telle boucle noire de houri, jétait sur son tableau comme une ombre
de lumière*'). My translation.

p. 193 day of Mars: Nezâmî, 'Récit de la princesse des slaves sous le
pavillon rouge de Mars', pp. 301–27; Chelkowski, 'The Seven
Princesses', in El Nizami, *Mirror of the Invisible World*, ed.
Chelkowski, 'The Red Pavilion', pp. 88–4.

p. 193 the dead queen: see *The Arabian Nights: Tales of 1001 Nights*, ed.
Robert Irwin, trans. Malcolm C. Lyons, 3 vols (London: Penguin,
2008), vol. 2, pp. 518–45; and Marina Warner, *Stranger Magic:
Charmed States & the Arabian Nights* (London: Chatto & Windus,
2011), pp. 54–63.

p. 194 (*The Thousand and One Nights*): François Pétis de La Croix, *Les Mille
et Un Jours: Contes persans*, (eds.) Pierre Brunel, Christelle Bahier-
Porte and Frédéric Mancier (Paris: Honoré Champion, 2006),
pp. 303–4, 307–9, 457–76, 508–60.

p. 194 'universally, is Fable': *Spectator*, no. 183, 29 September 1711 and
no. 512, 17 October 1712. https://muse.jhu.edu/pub/50/edited_
volume/chapter/3487110

p. 195 'four more volumes': See Robert Irwin, *The Arabian Nights: A
Companion* (London: I. B. Tauris, 2004), pp. 14–21; and Warner,
*Stranger Magic*, pp. 12–15.

p. 195 'his hands in 1675': Christelle Bahier-Porte, Introduction to Pétis
de La Croix, *Mille et Un Jours*, pp. 229–75.

p. 195 'a learned Cabbalist': '*{le} célèbre Dervis Moclès, que la Perse met au
nombre de ses grands personnages. Il étoit Chef des Sofis d'Ispahan . . . {et}
il passoit pour un scavant Cabaliste.*' Ibid., pp. 331–3. My translation.

p. 195 working with others: Pierre Brunel, Préface to Pétis de La Croix,
*Mille et Un Jours*, pp. 213–27; one of the stories, 'Histoire du Prince
Seyf El-Mulouk', ibid., pp. 605–29, also appears in a slightly

different version in the full cycle of *The Thousand and One Nights*, but not in Galland's translation. See 'The Story of Saif al-Muluk and Badi' al-Jamal', in *Arabian Nights*, trans. Lyons, vol. 3, pp. 95–145.

p. 195 'knew a thousand Tales': *'une vieille Esclave Arabe qui sçavoit mille fables'*. She links her source to Lokman, an oriental counterpart of Aesop. Marie-Catherine d'Aulnoy, *Les Contes des fées* (Paris: Claude Barbin, 1710), pp. 108–9.

p. 195 set of *Arabian Nights*: Hanna Diyab, *The Book of Travels*, ed. Johannes Stephan, trans. Elias Muhanna, 2 vols (New York: New York University Press, 2021), and Paulo Lemos Horta, *Marvellous Thieves* (Cambridge, Mass.: Harvard University Press, 2017), pp. 18–21, 42, 54.

p. 196 'Fairy Way of Writing', Joseph Addison, *Spectator*, 1 July 1712.

p. 196 many oriental variations: *Le Cabinet des fées, ou Collection choisie des contes des fées et autres contes merveilleux*, ed. Charles-Joseph Mayer, 41 vols (Geneva: Chez Barde, Manget, 1785–6).

p. 197 the 'neck riddle': Eleanor Cook, *Enigmas and Riddles in Literature* (Cambridge: Cambridge University Press, 2006), pp. 233–4.

p. 199 'through your painting': *'je le trouve plus vain qu'amoureux, un peu étourdi, en un mot ce qu'on appelle un jeune homme . . . Ma chère Sutlumemé, vous avez beau peindre les hommes avec les plus belles couleurs, leurs défauts percent toujours au travers de vos peintures.'* Pétis de La Croix, *Mille et Un Jours*, p. 561.

p. 199 origins of the stories: Pétis de La Croix, The *Persian and Turkish Tales*, trans. William King, 2 vols (London: Richard Ware, 1739), https://archive.org/details/bim_eighteenth-century_the-persian-and-the-turk_1714_1

p. 199 plotlines in these stories: Justin Huntly McCarthy, *Persian Tales* (London: Chatto & Windus, 1892), https://catalog.hathitrust.org/Record/009774778

p. 199 a boring book?: Abdelfattah Kilito, *Arabs and the Art of Storytelling: A Strange Familiarity*, trans. Mbarek Sryfi and Eric Sellin (Syracuse, NY: Syracuse University Press, 2014), pp. 116–25.

p. 199 (. . . Chinese fairy play): Carlo Gozzi, *Turandot. Fiaba chinese teatrale tragicomica in cinque atti Opere edite ed inedite del Co: Carlo Gozzi*, 2 vols (Venice: Giacomo Zanardi, 1801), vol. 2.

p. 200 departure from Venice: Gozzi's highly entertaining, blithe autobiography, *Memorie inutili* (Useless Memoirs), 3 vols (Venice: Palese, 1797), gives his side of the story.

p. 202 *The Turandot Suite*: Ferruccio Busoni, Orchestra Filarmonica della Scala, conductor Riccardo Muti (CD: Warner Classics 50999 4 56324 2 6, 2010).

p. 202 'heart of an hysteric': Ashbrook and Powers, *Puccini's Turandot*, pp. 56–7.

p. 202 'power of one's imagination': Marina Volok, 'Metropolitan Acting Studio: Vakhtangov's Princess Turandot', http://sites.google.com/site/arttheatrestudio/vakhtangov-s-princess-turandot

p. 203 of such material: The wiki page gives a fuller summary: https://en.wikipedia.org/wiki/Turandot_(Gozzi)

p. 203 'worthy of pity!': http://www.murashev.com/opera/Turandot_libretto_English_Italian

p. 204 in their country: Ukrainian Chorus and Ballet Theatre, Kyiv, Sembla presents Opera International, Ellen Kent Productions, the New Theatre, Oxford, 3 March 2023.

p. 206 death is one!: https://www.murashev.com/opera/Turandot_libretto_English_Italian

p. 207 in turn utterly smitten: 'The Tale of Qamar al-Zaman and Princess Budur', in *The Arabian Nights*, trans. Lyons, vol. 2, pp. 693–807.

p. 208 'The Sea Hare': https://www.surlalunefairytales.com/oldsite/authors/grimms/191seahare.html and https://www.grimmstories.com/en/grimm_fairy-tales/the_sea-hare David Hockney illustrated several of the Grimms' tales early in his career, for a delectable tiny edition (London: St Petersburg Press, 1970); for the last riddle of 'The Sea Hare', in a very enigmatic move, he envisages the boy hidden inside the princess's body – her womb? My thanks to Laura Harty for drawing my attention to his interpretation.

p. 209 find out his name: Colin Radford, 'Wittgenstein and "fairy tales"', *Merveilles & Contes*, vol. 2, no. 2 (December 1988), pp. 106–10.

p. 209 saw it any more: 'Tom Tit Tot'. In this very lively demotic version, the good-for-nothing girl protagonist makes a bargain with the 'impet' to marry him in return for his magical spinning; when she learns his name, she's released: 'that gave an awful shriek and away that flew into the dark, and she never saw it any more'. We are not told what her husband thinks when she can no long spin such quantities of yarn. https://sacred-texts.com/neu/eng/eft/eft02.htm

p. 210 phrase of André Jolles: André Jolles, *Simple Forms: Legend, Saga, Myth, Riddle, Saying, Case, Memorabile, Fairytale, Joke*, trans.

Peter J. Schwartz (London: Verso, 2017). As his subtitle shows, he examines fundamental, popular forms of stories that circulate.

p. 211 Kazakhstan in Central Asia: See B. E. Juniper, *The Story of the Apple* (Portland, Ore.: Timber Press, 2006).

## Part Three: The Shelter of Stories

p. 213 worlds we live in: Ted Hughes, 'Myth and Education', in his *Winter Pollen: Occasional Prose*, ed. William Scammell (London: Faber & Faber, 1994), p. 143.

## Chapter 7: In No Man's Land

p. 215 does not exist: Philippe Beck, 'Liminal Poem', in his *Didactic Poetries*, trans. Nicola Marae Allain (Cambridge: New Equipage Publishing, 2016). I have lightly adapted the translation.

> *le moi et le toi ordinaires*
> *font des efforts*
> *pour devenir un Toi*
> *avant l'arrivée supposée*
> *au grand Moi*
> *qui n'existe pas*

See Philippe Beck, *Poésies didactiques* (Paris: Gallimard, 2001).

p. 215 to each other: Wendy Brown gives an incisive account of walling in and walling out, with a diagram of the multilayered Saudi–Iraqi border; since she wrote, Trump has won a second term, and barriers and borders all over the world have grown yet more complex. Wendy Brown, *Walled States, Waning Sovereignty* (New York: Zone Books, 2010), pp. 7–42.

p. 215 'a zone of abandonment': Noam Leshem and Alasdair Pinkerton, 'Re-inhabiting no-man's land: genealogies, political life and critical agendas', *Transactions of the Institute of British Geographers*, vol. 41, no. 1 (2016), pp. 41–53.

p. 215 no man's land: Louis Imbert, 'Israël configure Gaza à sa main', *Le Monde Hebdomadaire*, 11 May 2024, pp. 8–9.

p. 215 'sterile security zones': Brown, *Walled States*, p. 50.

p. 216 with this expedition: Leshem and Pinkerton, 'Re-inhabiting no-man's land', pp. 41–53; also listen to https://www.bbc.co.uk/sounds/play/p032mlf1

p. 216 *The Land in Between*: Ursula Schulz-Dornburg, *The Land in Between: Photographs from 1980 to 2012* (London: Mack Books, 2018); see also https://www.schulz-dornburg.com/en/vanished-landscapes-iraq-mesopotamia

p. 216 their occupation seriously: An example of this jest-in-earnest would be the Kingdom of Redonda, an uninhabited rock in the Caribbean, which is ruled by a chosen writer. The most recent elected sovereign was the Spanish novelist Javier Marías (d. 2022), who relates the tradition's origins in his 1989 novel *All Souls*, trans. Margaret Jull Costa (London: Harvill Press, 1992). See also Michael Hingston, *Try Not to Be Strange: The Curious History of the Kingdom of Redonda* (Windsor, Ont.: Biblioasis, 2022). I had the honour of being enrolled by Javier Marías in 2022, just before his death, as the Duchess of Phantasmagoria (!).

p. 217 as bodily scarification: Sophie Ristelhueber, *Fait* (1992) and *Irak* (2001), http://www.sophie-ristelhueber.fr/

p. 217 burned into their hide: Denise Riley explains that the word 'maverick' arose after the lawyer Samuel Maverick kept unbranded cattle roaming in Texas.

p. 221 started Refugee Tales: David Herd, *Walk Song* (Swindon: Shearsman Books, 2022) and *Writing Against Expulsion in the Post-War World: Making Space for the Human* (Oxford: Oxford University Press, 2023).

p. 222 claim to sanctuary: I didn't use their real names in the published story, and here I have used initials so as to respect their privacy. Marina Warner, 'The Mother's Tale', in David Herd and Anna Pincus (eds.), *Refugee Tales II* (Manchester: Comma Press, 2017).

p. 222 from Latin America: John Washington, *The Dispossessed: A Story of Asylum and the US–Mexican Border and Beyond* (London: Verso, 2020).

p. 224 and raised money: *The Jungle* was written by Joe Murphy and Joe Robertson, and directed by Stephen Daldry and Justin Martin. I saw it at the Playhouse Theatre, London in 2019. https://www.goodchance.org.uk/thejungle

p. 224 especially refugee children: https://www.walkwithamal.org/ The making of the play and the life in the Jungle also became the subject of a powerful documentary, filmed by Sue Clayton, who has been working with refugees since 2012. She recorded the clearing of the camp by the authorities (it moved to another site, and has been destroyed again, only to move on and assemble again nearby). Roberta Lentini, 'On the ethics of inclusion and the politics of cultural mediation: Sue Clayton in conversation with Roberta Lentini', *InVerbis Lingue Letterature Culture*, Issue 1 (January–June 2018), pp. 35–50.

p. 224 and receiving amnesty: Natalie Zemon Davis, *Fiction in the Archives: Pardon Tales and Their Tellers in Sixteenth-Century France* (Cambridge: Polity, 1988).

p. 225 an accurate report: Bernard Williams, *Truth and Truthfulness* (Princeton: Princeton University Press, 2002), pp. 1–7, 172–205.

p. 225 happened to her: Mary Prince, *The History of Mary Prince: A West Indian Slave*, ed. Sara Salih (London: Penguin, 2004).

p. 225 of historical witness: Olaudah Equiano, *The Interesting Narrative of the Life of Olaudah Equiano, or Gustavus Vassa, the African, Written by Himself* (Philadelphia: Press at Toad Hall, 2007).

p. 226 family and neighbourhood: Yousif M. Qasmiyeh, *Writing the Camp* (Llandysul: Broken Sleep Books, 2021).

p. 226 (Persian) into English: Behrouz Boochani, *No Friend But the Mountains*, trans. Omid Tofighian (London: Picador, 2019), https://en.wikipedia.org/wiki/Behrouz_Boochani

p. 226 'and broken spirits': Robert Manne, '*No Friend But the Mountains* review: Behrouz Boochani's poetic and vital memoir', *Sydney Morning Herald*, 10 August 2018, https://www.smh.com.au/entertainment/books/no-friend-but-the-mountains-review-behrouz-boochanis-poetic-and-vital-memoir-20180801-h13fuu.html

p. 226 hierarchical but intersectional: Elisabeth Schüssler Fiorenza, 'Introduction: Exploring the Intersections of Race, Gender, Status and Ethnicity in Early Christian Studies', in Laura Nasrallah and Elisabeth Schüssler Fiorenza (eds), *Prejudice and Christian Beginnings: Investigating Race, Gender, and Ethnicity in Early Christian Studies* (Minneapolis: Fortress Press, 2009), pp. 1–25.

p. 227 and life stories: Clare Gilman and Roger Malbert, *Drawing in the Present Tense* (London: Thames & Hudson, 2023), pp. 246–9.

p. 227 distinctive and visible: Sophie Herxheimer, poet and artist, has long been taking down personal stories while at the same time making graphic drawings of what they are telling her, in one-to-one sessions organized by various refugee support groups.

p. 227 I saw, in Paris: http://www.bouchrakhalili.com/the-mapping-journey-project/

p. 229 'the age of lies': Colin Burrow, 'Fiction and the Age of Lies', *London Review of Books*, 20 February 2020.

p. 229 'farewell to literature': Ben Lerner, 'Each cornflake', *London Review of Books*, 22 May 2014.

p. 230 written and received: John Sturrock, *The Language of Autobiography* (Cambridge: Cambridge University Press, 2010), pp. 288–9.

p. 230 'signs of weakening': Ibid., p. 289. He goes on to castigate those who 'approach autobiography in a spirit of deconstructive bile, out of dislike for the political, social and religious belief systems which can be invoked to explain it'. I hope I have not fallen into this category; I see the demand for self-justification from migrants as a form of political authority that limits their potential for narrative.

p. 232 (... they came from): Lawrence Abu Hamdan has since founded Earshot, 'the first agency for sound and acoustic analysis dedicated to open-source investigators and the field of human rights': https://en.wikipedia.org/wiki/Lawrence_Abu_Hamdan

p. 234 or even to us: Joshua Surtees and Alison Flood, 'Kei Miller essay about white women sparks tensions among Caribbean writers', *Guardian*, 2 May 2018, https://www.theguardian.com/books/2018/may/02/kei-miller-essay-about-white-women-sparks-tensions-among-caribbean-writers?CMP=share_btn_fb Kei Miller, 'The White Women and the Language of Bees', *PREE*, 13 April 2018, https://preelit.com/2018/04/13/the-white-women-and-the-language-of-bees/

p. 234 'need to be open': Toni Morrison, *Jazz* (London: Chatto & Windus, 1992), p. 161.

p. 235 'a growing danger': Paul Gilroy, 'Refusing Race and Salvaging the Human', Holberg Lecture, University of Bergen in Norway, 4 June 2019, https://www.youtube.com/watch?v=Ta6UkmlXtVo

p. 235 'rather than charity': Quinn Slobodian, 'Safe havens', *New York Review of Books*, 23 May 2024, https://www.nybooks.com/articles/2024/05/23/safe-havens-butler-to-the-world-bullough/

p. 236 'submission to reality': I heard this remark during a conversation with Annie Ernaux which I attended at the French Institute,

Edinburgh, during the Edinburgh International Festival, 21 August 2019.

p. 237 failed or abandoned: Annie Ernaux, *The Years*, trans. Alison L. Strayer (London: Fitzcarraldo, 2018), originally published as *Les Années* (2008).

p. 238 drew enthusiastic audiences: https://das-kabarett.blogspot.com/2015/11/i-persiani-caporetto-di-roberto-cavosi.html; https://www.trojanwomenproject.org/queens-of-syria-film; https://www.wildyak.co.uk/queens-of-syria

p. 238 the unfolding carnage: https://www.teatrobiondo.it/produzioni/i-persiani-a-caporetto/

p. 238 kind of salvation: Alice Oswald, 'The Art of Erosion' (2019), http://podcasts.ox.ac.uk/art-erosion

p. 239 dynamic mode erasure: Alice Oswald, *Nobody*, with watercolours by William Tillyer (London: 21 Publishing, 2018; paperback, Jonathan Cape, 2019).

p. 239 'meeting in the underworld': Oswald, 'The Art of Erosion'.

p. 240 through a flask: The artist-photographer Garry Fabian Miller, whose life's work involves camera-less capture of light, has collaborated with Alice Oswald on the pamphlet *As Colours Steale* (Totnes: The Letter Press, 2019), inspired by Robert Herrick, https://www.theletterpress.org/product/as-colours-steale/

p. 241 impersonal personhood: Denise Riley, 'The Voice of the Lyric?', Clark Lectures, given in spring 2024, Trinity College, Cambridge: 'The "Inhuman" Aspect of Lyric Poetry', https://www.youtube.com/watch?v=r_RjkJAkzqA; 'The Impersonal Personal', https://www.youtube.com/watch?v=gvE5rsxoLqI; 'Something There Is That Talks Within', https://www.youtube.com/watch?v=Om6-dotWLg4; 'On the "Voice of the Poem"', https://www.youtube.com/watch?v=EMZnANrbGk8

## Chapter 8: The Map Is Not the Territory

p. 242 the way anymore: Bertolt Brecht, *The Collected Poems*, ed. and trans. Tom Kuhn and David Constantine (New York: Liveright Publishing, 2015), p. 830.

p. 243 'the mapmakers' colours': Elizabeth Bishop, 'The Map', in her *Collected Poems* (London: Chatto & Windus, 2004), p. 3, originally published in *North and South* (1946).

p. 243 or otherwise obliterated: Eyal Weizman and Fazal Sheikh, *The Conflict Shoreline: Colonization as Climate Change in the Negev Desert* (Göttingen and Brooklyn: Steidl with Cabinet Books, 2015); see also Eyal Weizman, 'The Politics of Verticality', Rice University's Baker Institute for Public Policy, http://www.bakerinstitute.org/events/1360

p. 243 processes of erasure: Jumana Emil Abboud, *In Aching Agony and Longing I Wait for You by the Spring of Thieves* (London: Black Dog Publishing, 2019); see also Marina Warner, *Forms of Enchantment: Writings on Art and Artists* (London: Thames & Hudson, 2018), pp. 173–82.

p. 243 'names of places': Kei Miller, 'Sometimes I consider the names of places', *PN Review* 249, vol. 46, no. 1 (September–October 2019), pp. 21–3, https://www.pnreview.co.uk/cgi-bin/scribe?item_id=10575 pp.21-23.

p. 244 thing between places?: Ibid., p. 22.

p. 248 their green heads: Alice Oswald, *Memorial: An Excavation of the* Iliad (London: Faber & Faber, 2012), p. 14.

p. 249 'lost in place': Susan Stewart, *The Ruins Lesson: Meaning and Material in Western Culture* (Chicago: University of Chicago Press, 2020), p. 249.

p. 250 'landscaping and planning': Thomas G. Pavel, *Fictional Worlds* (Cambridge, Mass.: Harvard University Press, 1986), p. 143.

p. 250 'of European culture': Ibid., p. 141.

p. 250 and austere journey: Henry Chadwick, *Priscillian of Avila: The Occult and the Charismatic in the Early Church* (Oxford: Clarendon Press, 1976), proposes convincingly that the body in the shrine was in fact the remains of Priscillian, who was condemned as a heretic and a sorcerer *c.*385 and then venerated clandestinely by his fervent followers.

p. 251 I plant signs . . .: Octavio Paz, 'Vrindaban', in *Configurations*, trans. Lysander Kemp (New York: New Directions, 1971), pp. 140–9.

p. 252 'stations of the cross': Maurice Halbwachs, *On Collective Memory*, trans Lewis A. Coser (Chicago: University of Chicago Press, 1992), p. 234.

p. 252 in each epoch: Ibid., pp. 234–5.

p. 254 tied to the votary: Deborah Howard, 'Venice as Gateway to the Holy Land: Pilgrims as Agents of Transmission', in Paul Davies,

Deborah Howard and Wendy Pullan (eds), *Architecture and Pilgrimage, 1000–1500: Southern Europe and Beyond* (Farnham: Ashgate, 2013), pp. 87–110.

p. 254 'we received indulgences': Felix Fabri, *The Book of the Wanderings*, quoted in Anthony Bale, 'God's Cell: Christ as Prisoner and Pilgrimage to the Prison of Christ', *Speculum: A Journal of Medieval Studies*, vol. 91, no. 1 (January 2016), pp. 1–35 at p. 22.

p. 254 grew up around them: Çarıklı Kilise (the Sandals church) – the Ascension fresco (dated to the eleventh century) at the entrance to the church is said to be an exact copy of the one in the church of the Ascension in Jerusalem. https://www.cappadociahistory.com/post/sandal-church-%C3%A7ar%C4%B1kl%C4%B1-kilise

p. 255 shape of her footprint: Anthony E. Dundon, 'The Lady's Slipper', *Marist Messenger*, 28 February 2021, https://www.maristmessenger.co.nz/2021/02/28/the-ladys-slipper/#:~:text=Relics%20are%20regarded%20as%20a,for%20the%20sick%20and%20infirm

p. 256 Auerbach's called 'Figura': Edward Said, Introduction to his *Mimesis*, pp. ix–xxxii, quoting Auerbach, 'Figura', in his *Scenes from the Drama of European Literature: Six Essays* (Gloucester, Mass.: Peter Smith, 1973).

p. 256 'interpretation . . . figural interpretation': Ibid., p. xx.

p. 256 'actually was to come': Ibid., p. xxi.

p. 257 'components of his identity': Ibid.

p. 257 uprooted personal history: For example, W. G. Sebald, *The Rings of Saturn*, trans. Anthea Bell (New York: New Directions, 1998).

p. 257 this site or that: J.-B. Pujoulx, writing in Year 8 of the French Revolution, suggested that new arrivals from e.g. the south of France might feel more comfortable in Paris if the *quartiers* had street names and rivers that were familiar from their own home territory. This idea materializes in such US districts as Little Serbia and Little Koreatown, and in the Chinatowns of cities such as Los Angeles and London. Pujoulx doesn't mention colonists' widespread practice of naming provinces and cities after home countries or cities they had left behind: New Caledonia, New York and sometimes without the 'new' label, for example Boston. J. B. (Jean Baptiste) Pujoulx, *Paris à la fin du XVIIIe siècle, ou, Esquisse historique et morale des monumens et des ruines de cette capitale: de l'état des sciences, des arts et de l'industrie à cette époque, ainsi que des moeurs et des ridicules de ses habitan* (Paris: B. Mathé, 1801), pp. 77–84.

p. 258 of the first person: Solnit has recently published an anguished lament for her city, now hollowed out by the mega-rich who have made mind-boggling fortunes in tech companies, and whose high-end way of living has seen the end of neighbourhood and community, low rents, cooperatives, walking and chance encounters. See 'In the Shadow of Silicon Valley', *London Review of Books*, 8 February 2024.

p. 258 those of the writer: *Kulturbrille* is the term suggested by Franz Boas, the anthropologist. Thanks to Denise Riley for identifying the source.

## Chapter 9: In the Country of Words

p. 260 in purposeful action: Keorapetse Kgositsile, 'Notes from No Sanctuary', in his *Collected Poems, 1969–2018* (Lincoln, Nebr.: University of Nebraska Press, 2023), pp. 78–80.

p. 260 war, persecution, necessity: Mahmoud Darwish, 'We Travel Like All People', in his *Unfortunately, It Was Paradise*, trans. Munir Akash and Carolyn Forché, with Sinan Antoon and Amira El-Zein (Berkeley, Los Angeles and London: University of California Press, 2003), p. 11.

p. 260 alive or dead: Marwan A. Hamdan, 'Mahmoud Darwishe's [sic] Voicing Poetics of Resistance: A Receptionist Review', *International Journal of Humanities and Social Science*, vol. 6, no. 10 (October 2016), https://www.ijhssnet.com/journals/Vol_6_No_10_October_2016/25.pdf. See also Robyn Creswell, *The Ruins: Arabic Poetry in an Age of Extremes* (New York: Farrar, Straus & Giroux, forthcoming). My thanks to the author for sharing his work with me.

p. 261 appearance in recipes: In a short story called 'The Difference in the Dose', I explore the associations with parsley in other similar stories, for example 'Petrosinella' by Giambattista Basile, and 'Persinette' by Charlotte Rose Caumont de La Force. See Marina Warner, *Fly Away Home* (Cromer: Salt Publishing, 2014), pp. 197–215.

p. 261 the lyric voice: Denise Riley, 'The Voice of the Lyric?', Clark Lectures, given in spring 2024, Trinity College, Cambridge, https://www.trin.cam.ac.uk/news/the-clark-lectures-2024-a-voice-of-the-lyric-denise-riley/

p. 261 'and aural sanctuary': Personal communication, November 2024.

p. 262 given and passed on: Pascale Casanova, *The World Republic of Letters*, trans. M. B. DeBevoise (Cambridge, Mass.: Harvard University Press, 2007), and 'Literature as a World', *New Left Review*, no. 31 (January/February 2005), pp. 71–90.

p. 262 'eine virus catched?': Diego Marani, *Ein Europanto Sample Documento* (1997), https://en.wikipedia.org/wiki/Europanto

p. 262 'or non-engaged ones': Pascale Casanova, 'Combative Literatures', *New Left Review*, no. 72 (November/December 2011), pp. 123–34 at p. 133, trans. Nicholas Gray: 'As long as ago as 1986 Fredric Jameson wrote, "I would propose that all third world texts are allegorical, and allegorical in a very specific mode: they should be read as national allegories, even when, or perhaps I should say, above all when their forms have come from representational mechanisms that are eminently western, such as the novel."'

p. 263 'material to be told': Italo Calvino, *If on a Winter's Night a Traveller* (New York: Harcourt Brace Jovanovich, 1981), p. 109.

p. 263 'story (or novel)': Philip Kennedy, personal communication, 4 August 2016.

p. 263 'for well watered': Philip Kennedy, personal communication, 2 February 2025.

p. 263 'will immediately recover': Ibn Zafer, *Solwan; or, Waters of Comfort*, ed. Michele Amari, English trans. Anon. (1852; BiblioLife LCC, n.d.), p. 124.

p. 264 'bearer-being of the idea': Wallace Stevens, 'An Ordinary Evening in New Haven', in his *Collected Poems* (New York: Vintage, 1990), pp. 465–89 at p. 466.

p. 264 self and relation: I called an exploratory study day, held in Oxford in 2016, 'Bearer Beings: Portable Stories in Dislocated Times', https://www.youtube.com/watch?v=vr7bRvg39n4

p. 266 idiom of their original: Abdelfattah Kilito, 'Métaphore', in *Archéologie: Douze Miniatures* (Brussels: BookLeg DABA Maroc, 2012), p. 18, trans. Clare Finburgh Delijani and Marina Warner as 'Metaphor', in *Archaeology: Twelve Miniatures*, https://www.thewhitereview.org/poetry/archaeology-twelve-miniatures/

p. 266 a correct original: Creswell, *The Ruins*.

p. 267 wonders and triumphs: Katia Kameli, *The Storyteller*, https://kadist.org/work/the-storyteller/ I saw the film in her solo show 'What Language Do You Speak Stranger?' in the Mosaic Rooms, London, in September 2016.

p. 267 mutable and reflexive: Katia Kameli, Kadist, Paris, https://kadist.org/people/katia-kameli/

p. 268 'bag was empty': This is only one variation; there are other versions which cast Aoife as a captive of the god of the sea, bound to him for 200 years. Robert Graves, 'The Crane Bag', quoting from the book he is reviewing, Anne Ross, *Pagan Celtic Britain: Studies in Iconography and Tradition* (New York: Columbia University Press, 1967), *New York Review of Books*, 29 June 1967.

p. 268 'is to be rewoven': Seamus Heaney, Preface, in M. P. Hederman and R. Kearney (eds.), *The Crane Bag Book of Irish Studies (1977–1981)* (Dublin: Blackwater Press, 1982), no page numbers.

p. 268 'of speaking bodies': Florence Dupont, *The Invention of Literature: From Greek Intoxication to the Latin Book*, trans. Janet Lloyd (Baltimore and London: Johns Hopkins University Press, 1999), pp. 248–9.

p. 268 'attention to that absence': Ibid., pp. 248–9.

p. 269 'but always is so . . .': Sallustius, *Concerning the Gods and the Universe*, ed. and trans. Arthur Darby Nock (Cambridge: Cambridge University Press, 1926), paragraph IV, p. 9.

p. 270 an hibiscus flower: Barbara C. Sproul, *Primal Myths: Creating the World* (San Francisco: Harper, 1979), pp. 66–75; Jan Jansen and James R. Fairhead, 'The Mandé Creation Myth, by Germaine Dieterlen, as a Historical Source for the Mali Empire', *Journal of West African History*, vol. 6, no. 2 (Fall 2020), pp. 93–114.

p. 271 *Dark Star* trilogy: Marlon James won the Booker Prize in 2014 with *A Brief History of Seven Killings*, his book about the death of Bob Marley. At the time of writing, the first two volumes of his mythological trilogy have appeared: *Black Leopard, Red Wolf* (2019) and *Moon Witch, Spider King* (2022).

p. 271 traditions of Europe: Koulsy Lamko, *Bintou Wéré: African Opera*, ed. Els Van Der Plas, trans. El Hadji Moustapha Diop (Amsterdam: Prince Claus Fund/Sahel Opera Foundation, 2017), pp. 153–91.

p. 271 'as to rejuvenate it . . .': Ibid., pp. 124–9. It was sung multilingually under the direction of Massambou Wélé Diallo to a soundtrack of traditional African songs and Italian arias. For the 2017 film version see Manthia Diawara, *Bintou Wéré: An Opera of the World*, https://maumaus.org/resources/Maumaus_An-Opera-of-the-World_Manthia_Diawara_text.pdf

p. 272 'fearful human products': Manthia Diawara, 'Postface', in Lamko, *Bintou Wéré*, pp. 148–52; Diawara, *Bintou Wéré: An Opera of the World*: https://maumaus.org/resources/Maumaus_An-Opera-of-the-World_Manthia_Diawara_text.pdf

p. 272 'myths or fairy tales': W. H. Auden, *The Complete Works: Prose: Volume V: 1963–68* ed. Edward Mendelson (Princeton, N.J.: Princeton University Press, 2015), p. 237. I am indebted to Richard Davenport-Hines for this reference.

p. 273 'babies of the age': Thomas Love Peacock, *The Four Ages of Poetry*, in *Peacock's Four Ages of Poetry, Shelley's Defence of Poetry, Browning's Essay on Shelley*, ed. H. F. B. Brett-Smith (Oxford: Basil Blackwell, 1923), pp. 3–29 at p. 15.

p. 273 'delicious poetical compound . . .': Ibid., pp. 15–16.

p. 274 'principle of relevance': Thomas G. Pavel, *Fictional Worlds* (Cambridge, Mass.: Harvard University Press, 1986), p. 145.

p. 274 'pleasure of recognition': Ibid., p. 148.

p. 275 'otherwise unorganized existence': Peter Brooks, *Seduced by Story: The Use and Abuse of Narrative* (New York: New York Review Books, 2023), p. 13.

p. 275 imprisoned and silenced: Sulayman Al Bassam, I MEDEA (2021), performed at the London Shubbak Festival, Stone Nest, London, 2023, https://www.shubbak.co.uk/imedea/

p. 276 of hegemonic arbiters: Mark I. Wallace, Introduction to Paul Ricoeur, *Figuring the Sacred: Religion, Narrative, and Imagination*, ed. Mark I. Wallace, trans. David Pellauer (Minneapolis: Fortress Press, 1995), pp. 5ff.

p. 276 'political rule should take': She adopts the term 'mythopolitics' from the philosopher Carl Schmitt. Anna Della Subin, *Accidental Gods: On Men Unwittingly Turned Divine* (London: Granta Books, 2021), p. 275.

p. 276 'When shall it once be?' (Jeremiah 13: 27): 'I have seen thine abominations, even thine adulteries, and thy neighings, the lewdness of thy whoredom, on the hills in the fields. Woe unto thee, O Jerusalem! thou wilt not be made clean; how long shall it yet be? when shall it once be?'

p. 277 'darkness of time': Gérard Genette, trans. Jane E. Lewin, with a Foreword by Jonathan Culler, *Narrative Discourse* (Oxford: Basil Blackwell, 1980), p. 216.

p. 277 'future leaks out': William S. Burroughs, *Break Through in Grey Room* (recordings, 1960–76), http://www.allmusic.com/album/

break-through-in-grey-room-mw0000326529/credits The poet Caroline Bergvall, who acknowledges the inspiration, quotes this as: 'The future leaks through the cuts of the present.' See http://www.asymptotejournal.com/visual/eva-heisler-caroline-bergvall-propelled-to-the-edges-of-a-languages-freedom/

p. 278 this lacerating fable: Franz Kafka, 'Jackals and Arabs' (1917), in his *The Complete Short Stories*, trans. Willa and Edwin Muir (London: Vintage Classics, 1992), pp. 407–11.

p. 278 prevent the worst: Alfred Gell, 'The Technology of Enchantment and the Enchantment of Technology', in Fiona Candlin and Raiford Guins (eds), *The Object Reader* (London: Routledge, 2009), pp. 209–28; see also Alfred Gell, *Art and Agency: An Anthropological Theory* (Oxford: Clarendon Press, 1998).

p. 278 under a cover: A. E. Stallings, 'Another Bedtime Story', in her *This Afterlife: Selected Poems* (London: Carcanet, 2022), p. 109.

p. 279 'women loved him': Alice Oswald, *Memorial: An Excavation of the Iliad* (London: Faber & Faber, 2012), p. 72.

p. 280 act as foretokens: See Marina Warner, 'The Politics of Translation', *London Review of Books*, 11 October 2018.

p. 280 'alter your future': Paulo Polzonoff Jr, 'An Interview with José Eduardo Agualusa', *Words Without Borders* (September 2007), http://www.wordswithoutborders.org/article/an-interview-with-jos-eduardo-agualusa

p. 281 engagement with the world: Quoted with kind permission of Terence Cave from an unpublished paper, 2015. See also: Terence Cave, *Thinking with Literature* (Oxford: Oxford University Press, 2015), and his *Live Artefacts* (Oxford: Oxford University Press, 2022), in which this argument is fully developed.

p. 281 'in human cultures': Ibid., p. 12.

p. 282 *Iphigenia in Aulis*, a 'transadaptation': Performed in September 2015 by the Classic Stage Company in New York; see Alexis Soloski, 'Iphigenia in Aulis review – an epic reinvented in flowery festivalwear', *Guardian*, 18 September, 2015, https://www.theguardian.com/stage/2015/sep/17/iphigenia-in-aulis-review-an-epic-reinvented-in-flowery-festivalwear

p. 283 'other culture's words': Jena Osman and Juliana Spahr (eds.), *Chain 10: translucinación* (Philadelphia: Temple University Press, 2003). The translator Mireille Gansel invokes as an analogy for the work of translation the transhumance, or pastoral peoples' annual migration, when they move their flocks to higher ground in summer. For her, *humus* or earth stands for culture, and lays the emphasis on the necessary amphibian character of translators, in her opinion; they must be at home in different habitats. There lingers also a tribute to humanism – translation being central to humanities studies and the pleasures of a shared tradition. Mireille Gansel, *Translation as Transhumance*, trans. Ros Schwartz (London: Les Fugitives, 2017).

p. 284 'flow no more!': Radwa Ashour, *Spectres*, trans. Barbara Romaine (London: Arabia Books, 2010), p. 117.

p. 284 establishing social bonds: UN General Assembly, Resolution adopted by the Human Rights Council on 30 September 2016, https://documents.un.org/doc/undoc/gen/g16/227/55/pdf/g1622755.pdf

p. 284 that cultural heritage: UNESCO, Text of the Convention for the Safeguarding of the Intangible Cultural Heritage, https://ich.unesco.org/en/convention. See Warner, 'The Politics of Translation'.

p. 287 'did what we could': Bruce Robbins, 'Prolepsis and Catastrophe', unpublished paper kindly lent by the author, published in a different form as 'Many Years Later: Prolepsis in Deep Time', *Henry James Review*, vol. 33, no. 3 (September 2012), pp. 191–204.

p. 288 films, I had seen . . .: Marcel Reich-Ranicki, *The Author of Himself: The Life of Marcel Reich-Ranicki*, trans. Ewald Osers with an Introduction by Jack Zipes (Princeton: Princeton University Press, 2001), pp. 193–205 at pp. 200–1.

p. 289 *'others live too'*: Ibid., p. 201.

p. 289 'to save mine': Ibid.

## Coda: Stories in Transit

p. 290 no food to eat: Euripides, *Medea*, trans. Robin Robertson (London: Vintage, 2008), pp. 14–15.

p. 290 Puppet Museum, Palermo: Stories in Transit, Palermo, http://www.museodellemarionette.it/index.php?option=com_content&view=article&id=598:storie-in-transit&catid=90&Itemid=665&lang=it

p. 291 started out with: See Din Diallo's account of his journey in Natalya Din-Kariuki, Subha Mukherji and Rowan Williams (eds.), *Crossings: Migrant Knowledges, Migrant Forms* (Santa Barbara: Punctum Books, forthcoming), https://punctumbooks.com/titles/crossings-migrant-knowledges-migrant-forms

p. 291 Botanical Gardens of Palermo: Stories in Transit IV, http://www.storiesintransit.org/workshops/storiesintransitiv/ The epic was retold

p. 291  in the workshop, in Arabic by Badia Obaid, in French by the storyteller Wafa' Tarnowska and in Italian by Yusuf Jaralla, who fled Iraq in the 1990s and settled in Sicily.

p. 291 felt like Eden: A short video of the workshop, filmed and edited by Letizia Gullo, is available at https://youtu.be/x65nZOS4axo?si=gtqBfXqnp_PkmYGu

p. 292 (... able to return home): The UN website reported in 2024 that only around 18 per cent of Syrians in Jordan who have fled the war are living in camps: https://www.unhcr.org/jo/ This figure will have changed if the fall of Assad does allow many to return.

p. 292 in comparative freedom: A record of each workshop can be found at http://storiesintransit.org A report by Marina Warner on the two first workshops in 2016, one in Oxford and one in Palermo, has been published in the *Marvels & Tales* journal under the title 'Report: Bearer-Beings and Stories in Transit/Storie in Transito', https://digitalcommons.wayne.edu/marvels/vol31/iss1/9/

p. 293 an alternative shelter?: Marina Warner, 'Losing Home, Finding Words: Transformations of Story', Holberg Lecture, 2015, https://www.youtube.com/watch?v=AaLrl9qFHRA

p. 293 thirst-quenching and irrigation: Philip Kennedy, personal communication, 4 August 2016.

p. 294 failed Conservative policy: In 2024, the Brothers of Italy government of Giorgia Meloni made an agreement with Albania to transport asylum seekers to a new facility they have subsidized, in a part of the country that is desolate because locals have been leaving for decades; this camp consists of containers, which sleep 3,000 inmates, and the plan is to process thousands of claims swiftly in the belief that many will be found invalid and the asylum seeker deported. Jean-Baptiste Chastand, 'En Albanie, l'aubaine du centre Italien de migrants', *Le Monde Hebdomadaire*, 16 November 2024, p. 4.

p. 295 art, animation, writing: Through the patient negotiations of Professor Valentina Castagna with the Liceo Ferrara, one of the schools where asylum seekers are enrolled, and with the support of CPIA teachers such as Clelia Bartoli, the pupils were given permission to come and join Stories in Transit instead of their ordinary classes.

p. 296 European fairy literature: Laura Gonzenbach, *Beautiful Angiola: The Lost Sicilian Folk and Fairy Tales of Laura Gonzenbach*, and *The*

*Robber with a Witch's Head: More Stories from the Great Treasury of Sicilian Folk and Fairy Tales Collected by Laura Gonzenbach*, ed. and trans. Jack Zipes (London: Routledge, 2003 and 2004).

p. 296 pioneer of literary ethnography: Giuseppe Pitrè, *The Collected Sicilian Folk and Fairy Tales of Giuseppe Pitrè*, ed. and trans. Jack Zipes and Joseph Russo, 2 vols (London: Routledge, 2008).

p. 296 always in trouble: see F. M. Corrao ed., *Le storie di Giufà* (Palermo: Sellerio, 2009).

p. 296 cooperation, negotiation, unity: See https://giocherenda.it/en/about-us/

p. 297 collaboratively, not competitively: The shop is at 25, Avenida Aragona, Palermo 90133, a street leading to the Piazza della Rivoluzione, where another statue of the Genio, by an anonymous sixteenth-century artist, stands on the mossy fountain in the centre of the square. He is looking up at the sky – in hope, for he serves here to commemorate the end of Spanish rule in Sicily. The statue had been removed by the Bourbon viceroy after the 1848 uprising and was then set up in its present position in 1860, in honour of the insurgency that had begun in this part of Palermo. The tablet recording this struggle for the island's freedom attracted the attention of several in our group and they copied out the rousing inscription: 'QUESTO MARMO / SIMBOLO TEMUTO DI LIBERTA / SOTTRATTO DAGLI OCCHI DEL POPOLO / DALLA INQUIETA TIRANNIDE / IL POPOLO VINCITORE RIPOSE / IN 1860' (This marble, awesome symbol of Liberty, stolen from the eyes of the people by restless tyranny, the victorious people set up again in 1860): https://upload.wikimedia.org/wikipedia/commons/b/ba/Iscrizione_fontana_del_genio.jpg

p. 297 follies of tyrants: 'The Huntsman, the King's Son, and the Magic Deer', in Din-Kariuki, Mukherji and Williams (eds.), *Crossings*. The tale also features in the Stories in Transit VI workshop: https://storiesintransit.org/workshops/storiesintransitvi/

p. 300 'nursemaid was dead': Denise Riley points out that it is 'the same as the Welsh fable about the faithful hound Gelert, who saves his master's baby from an attacking wolf, only to be killed himself by his returning master who misinterpreted the bloody scene'. Personal communication, November 2024. It is classified in the Aarne-Thomson Index as Folktale 178A. See D. E. Jenkins, *Bedd Gelert: Its Facts, Fairies, & Folk-lore*, poetry trans. the Rev. H. Elvet

Lewis, Introduction by John Rhys (Portmadoc: Llewelyn Jenkins, 1899).

p. 302 them professional animators: The making of the film was halted by the lockdowns, but we hope somehow to pick up the thread. In the meantime, Joan Ashworth has edited the pieces together and the result was shown at the BookartBookshop in London's Pitfield Street in February–March 2024. Find out more about these displays here: https://storiesintransit.org/info/babs/

p. 302 'One for Me': Numu Touray's story, from his grandmother, told during Stories in Transit performance, September 2018. Reproduced with his kind permission. Transcribed and edited by Hannah Machover.

p. 308 Chris Frith has remarked: See *Gingerella (Rockafela)*, with Chris Frith, written and directed by Alex Reuben, 2028, http://www.alexreuben.com/home/gingers

p. 308 there are many: Images of the Genio appear in numerous sites, in piazzas, on fountains and in the Palazzo Pretorio or City Hall, in various media – in marble, mosaic, paint. The earliest Genio, standing in the Piazza del Garaffo, has been restored; it was sculpted by Pietro de Bonitate in 1483 and enshrined in an elaborate architectural setting, designed by the eminent architect of Sicilian baroque Don Paolo Amato. This grand assemblage has gradually fallen into ruin thanks to adverse developments ranging from the bombing of the Second World War to decades of casual neglect and deliberate theft and vandalism (the allegorical statues in the niches on either side of the Genio disappeared as recently as 1992).

p. 308 at his breast: Pietro Gulotta, 'La Fontana del Garraffo. Un progetto estetico e iconologico di Paolo Amato da restituire alla città', 2017, https://www.academia.edu/39262382/La_Fontana_del_Garraffo_Un_progetto_estetico_e_iconologico_di_Paolo_Amato_da_restituire_alla_citt%C3%A0

p. 309 middle of the piazza: The local church of the Spanish community – Sant'Eulalia dei Catalani – also stood in the Piazza del Garaffo, dating from the time when the Spanish Bourbons were the ruling power in Sicily; local Spanish merchants commissioned the sculpture of the Genio and formulated the inscription in gratitude for their great good fortune on the island.

p. 309 '( . . . gnawed into our hearts?'): An echo of the Palermitan motto, that the city devours its own, has often been struck recently in relation to the turmoil in the UK during the schism wrought by Brexit. The proverbial warning is attributed to the French royalist Jacques Mallet du Pan, who in his pamphlet *Considérations sur la nature de la Révolution de France, et sur les causes qui en prolongent la durée* (1793) addressed his fellow Frenchmen in a lacerating, impassioned jeremiad. Translated into English at the time, the pamphlet is known to have been read by and to have influenced William Pitt. https://archive.org/details/malletdupanfrencoomalluoft

p. 310 insularity of spirit: Giovanni Tomasi di Lampedusa, *Il Gattopardo* (Milan: Feltrinelli, 1958), pp. 212–13. My translation. See Giovanni Tomasi di Lampedusa, *The Leopard*, trans. Archibald Colquhoun (London: Collins and Harvill Press, 1960), p. 146.

p. 310 potential storymaking material: Other statues of the Genio adorn fountains which used to draw water from the rivers that flowed through the city: the Oreto and the Papireto, so called from the papyrus that used to grow there. Beneath the city of Palermo the Arab rulers, from the ninth to the eleventh century, constructed a network of *qanat* channels, deep underground tunnels which lift water from ground aquifers to the surface – they are open to visitors and still working. See, for example, this tour: https://wearepalermo.com/news/qanats-palermo/

p. 312 kind to him: Created by Amadou Diallo in April 2018, performed in September that year. See here: http://www.storiesintransit.org/workshops/storiesintransitvi/

p. 313 sequence of animal metamorphoses: 'The Story of the Second Dervish', in *The Arabian Nights: Tales of 1001 Nights*, ed. Robert Irwin, trans. Malcolm C. Lyons, 3 vols (London: Penguin, 2008), vol. 1, pp. 76–90.

p. 314 'right to be frivolous': Mahmoud Darwish, interview in *Bomb* (Fall 2002), https://bombmagazine.org/articles/2002/10/01/mahmoud-darwish/, quoted by Mounira Al Solh: https://artmejo.com/mounira-al-solh-i-strongly-believe-in-our-right-to-be-frivolous/

p. 315 no longer in post: In 2021 Lucano was given thirteen years in jail for abetting illegal migration – the sentence was later reduced to eighteen months.

p. 316 'prisoner of hope': A tweet from Cornel West on 12 January 2013: http://twitpic.com/buebex Since then the phrase has become proverbial.

p. 316 'strong enough to help': Seamus Heaney, quoting George Seferis, in his *The Redress of Poetry* (London: Faber & Faber, 1996), p. 9.

p. 316 'we need each other': The Right Rev. Mariann Edgar Budde, 'Contempt is a dangerous way to lead a country', *Guardian*, 24 January 2024, https://www.theguardian.com/commentisfree/2025/jan/24/bishop-mariann-edgar-budde-sermon-that-enraged-donald-trump

# Selected Bibliography

Adolph, Anthony, *Brutus of Troy and the Quest for the Ancestry of the British* (Barnsley: Pen and Sword, 2015).
Agamben, Giorgio, *Homo Sacer: Sovereign Power and Bare Life*, trans. Daniel (Stanford: Stanford University Press, 1998).
Agamben, Giorgio, *State of Exception* (Chicago: University of Chicago Press, 2005).
Agamben, Giorgio, *Pulcinella: Or Entertainment for Children*, trans. Kevin Attell (London and Calcutta: Seagull Books, 2019).
Agbabi, Patience, Polly Atkin, Jean 'Binta' Breeze, Fred D'Aguiar, Helen Dunmore and Bernardine Evaristo, *I Have Found a Song: Poems and Images about Enslavement to Mark the Centenary of the Abolition of the Slave Trade Act* (London: Enitharmon Editions, 2010).
Agulhon, Maurice, and Pierre Nora, *Les Lieux de mémoire* (Paris: Gallimard, 1992).
Ahmad, Omar Khaled, Nibal Al Alow, Safa Khaled Algharbawi, Omar Abdellatif Alndaf, Rayan Mohamad Sukkar, Safiya Badran, Fatima Omar Ghazawi, Samih Mahmoud and Hiba Mareb, *Shatila Stories* (London: Peirene, 2018).
Aikins, Matthieu, *The Naked Don't Fear the Water: An Underground Journey with Afghan Refugees* (London: Fitzcarraldo, 2022).
Albera, Dionigi, and Maria Couroucli (eds), *Sharing Sacred Spaces in the Mediterranean: Christians, Muslims, and Jews at Shrines and Sanctuaries* (Binghampton and Indianapolis: Indiana University Press, 2012).
Anderson, Benedict, *Imagined Communities: Reflections on the Origin and Spread of Nationalism* (London: Verso, 1983).
Appiah, Anthony Kwame, *Cosmopolitanism: Ethics in a World of Strangers* (New York: W. W. Norton, 2006).
*The Arabian Nights: Tales of 1001 Nights*, ed. Robert Irwin, trans. Malcolm C. Lyons (London: Penguin, 2008).
Arendt, Hannah, *The Human Condition* (Chicago: University of Chicago Press, 1958).

Armitage, Simon, *Sir Gawain and the Green Knight* (London: Faber & Faber, 2018).

Ashour, Radwa, *Spectres*, trans. Barbara Romaine (London: Arabia Books, 2010).

Auden, W. H., *Secondary Worlds* (London: Faber & Faber, 1968).

Bagnoli, Martina, Holger A. Klein, C. Griffith Mann and James Robinson (eds), *Treasures of Heaven: Saints, Relics and Devotion in Medieval Europe* (London: British Museum Press, 2011).

Bale, Anthony, *A Travel Guide to the Middle Ages: The World Through Medieval Eyes* (London: Viking, 2023).

Barenboim, Daniel, and Edward W. Said, *Parallels and Paradoxes: Explorations in Music and Society*, ed. Ara Guzelimian (London: Bloomsbury, 2002).

Barghouti, Mourid, *I Was Born There, I Was Born Here*, trans. Humphrey Davies (London: Bloomsbury, 2012).

Barthes, Roland, *Mythologies*, trans. Annette Lavers (New York: Hill & Wang, 1973).

Bartoli, Clelia, *Chile Revolts: From the Uprisings to the Constitutional Process* (Turin: Accademia University Press, 2022).

Barush, Kathryn R., *Art and the Sacred Journey in Britain, 1790–1850* (London: Routledge, 2016).

Bate, Jonathan, *Shakespeare and Ovid* (Oxford: Oxford University Press, 1994).

Bayley, Sally, *The Private Life of the Diary: From Pepys to Tweets – A History of the Diary as an Art Form* (London: William Collins, 2021).

Beloff, Zoe, *Between Worlds: An Asylum Seeker in America* (Maastricht: Charles Nypels Lab, 2018).

Benjamin, Walter, *Illuminations: Essays and Reflections*, ed. Hannah Arendt, trans. Harry Zohn (New York: Schocken Books, 2007).

Bercé, Yves-Marie, *Lorette aux XVIe et XVIIe siècles: Histoire du plus grand pèlerinage des temps modernes* (Paris: Presses de l'Université Paris-Sorbonne, 2011).

Bergvall, Caroline, *Drift* (Brooklyn: Nightboat Books, 2014).

Betts, Alexander, and Paul Collier, *Refuge: Transforming a Broken Refugee System* (London: Penguin, 2018).

Bianchi, Herman, *Justice as Sanctuary: Toward a New System of Crime Control* (1994; Eugene, Ore.: Wipf & Stock, 2010).

Boccaccio, *Decameron*, trans. G. H. McWilliam (Harmondsworth: Penguin, 1980), pp. 813–27.

Boochani, Behrouz, *No Friend But the Mountains*, trans. Omid Tofighian (London: Picador, 2019).

Borges, Jorge Luis, *The Total Library: Non-Fiction, 1922–1986*, ed. Eliot Weinberger, trans. Esther Allen, Suzanne Jill Levine and Eliot Weinberger (London: Penguin, 2001).

Boxall, Peter, *The Possibility of Literature: The Novel and the Politics of Form* (Cambridge: Cambridge University Press, 2024).

Brathwaite, Edward Kamau, *The Arrivants: A New World Trilogy: Rights of Passage, Islands, Masks* (Oxford: Oxford University Press, 1973).

Brooks, Peter, *Seduced by Story: The Use and Abuse of Narrative* (New York: New York Review Books, 2022).

Brown, Wendy, *Walled States, Waning Sovereignty* (New York: Zone Books, 2010).

Brubaker, Leslie, 'Memories of Helena: Patterns in Imperial Female Matronage in the Fourth and Fifth Centuries', in Liz James (ed.), *Women, Men and Eunuchs: Gender in Byzantium* (London: Routledge, 1997), pp. 52–75.

Brundin, Abigail, Deborah Howard and Mary Laven, *The Sacred Home in Renaissance Italy* (Oxford: Oxford University Press, 2018).

Burden, Michael, *A Woman Scorn'd: Responses to the Dido Myth* (London: Faber & Faber, 1998).

Burkert, Walter, *Homo Necans: The Anthropology of Ancient Greek Sacrificial Ritual and Myth* (Berkeley: University of California Press, 1986).

Burrow, Colin, *Imitation* (Oxford: Oxford University Press, 2019).

Byam Shaw, Daniel, 'Asylum Seekers', translation of Aeschylus, *The Suppliants*, 2024 (unpublished, kindly lent by the translator).

Cadman, David, and John Carey (eds), *Sanctuary* (London: Temenos Academy, 2006).

Caillois, Roger, *Les Jeux et les hommes: Le masque et le vertige* (1958; revised and enlarged edn, Paris: Gallimard, 1967).

Calvino, Italo, *Le città invisibili* (Turin: Einaudi, 1972); trans. as *Invisible Cities* by William Weaver (London: Penguin, 1997).

Calvino, Italo, *Sulla Fiaba*, ed. Mario Lavagetto (Turin: Einaudi, 1988).

Calvino, Italo, *The Literature Machine: Essays*, trans. Patrick Creagh (London: Vintage, 1997).

Calvino, Italo, *If on a Winter's Night a Traveller*, trans. William Weaver (London: Vintage, 1998).

Calvino, Italo, *Six Memos for the Next Millennium*, trans. Geoffrey Brock (London: Penguin, 2016).

Casanova, Pascale, *The World Republic of Letters*, trans. Malcolm DeBevoise (Cambridge, Mass.: Harvard University Press, 2007).

Cassirer, Ernst, *The Philosophy of Symbolic Forms*, vol. 2: *Mythical Thought*, trans. Ralph Manheim (New Haven: Yale University Press, 1965).

Cave, Terence, *Thinking with Literature: Towards a Cognitive Criticism* (Oxford: Oxford University Press, 2016).

Chambers, Iain, and Marta Cariello, 'At History's Edge: The Mediterranean Question', *New Formations*, no. 106 (2022), pp. 6–24.

Chartres, Richard, 'Sanctuary in the Christian Tradition: St Ethelburga, Bishopsgate', in David Cadman and John Carey (eds), *Sanctuary* (London: Temenos Academy, 2006), pp. 15–24.

Clayton, Sue, *Activist Volunteers in the European Refugee Crisis* (London: Goldsmiths Press, 2020).

Clifford, Sue, and Angela King, (eds.), *Local Distinctiveness: Place, Particularity and Identity* (London: Common Ground, 1993).

Coetzee, J. M., *The Childhood of Jesus* (London: Vintage, 2014).

Coetzee, J. M., *The Schooldays of Jesus* (London: Vintage, 2017).

Coetzee, J. M., *The Death of Jesus* (London: Vintage, 2019).

Colasanti, Arduino, *Loreto* (Bergamo: Istituto Italiano d'Arti Grafiche, 1910).

Coleman, Simon, and John Elsner, *Pilgrimage Part and Present: Sacred Travel and Sacred Space in the World Religions* (London: British Museum, 1995).

Collingwood, R. G., *The Philosophy of Enchantment: Studies in Folktale, Cultural Criticism, and Anthropology*, ed. David Boucher, Wendy James and Philip Smallwood (Oxford: Clarendon Press, 2007).

Compass Group (Birkbeck) and Konik, Anna, *Silence Heard Loud* (Poznań: Municipal Gallery Arsenal, 2021).

Conte, Salvatore, *Dido sine veste: Il Codice di Virgilio* (Cologno Monzese: Lampi di Stampa, 20 2012).

Cook, Eleanor, *Enigmas and Riddles in Literature* (Cambridge: Cambridge University Press, 2006).

Cook, Elizabeth, *Achilles* (London: Methuen, 2002).

Cox, Revd J. Charles, *The Sanctuaries and Sanctuary Seekers of Medieval England* (London: George Allen & Sons, 1911).

Crabman (Phil Smith), *Mythogeography: A Guide to Walking Sideways* (Axminster, Devon: Triarchy Press, 2010).

Crawford, James, *The Edge of the Plain: How Borders Make and Break Our World* (Edinburgh: Canongate, 2023).

Davies, Paul, Deborah Howard and Wendy Pullan (eds), *Architecture and Pilgrimage, 1000–1500: Southern Europe and Beyond* (Farnham: Ashgate, 2013).

Davis, Natalie Zemon, *Leo Africanus Discovers Comedy: Theatre and Poetry Across the Mediterranean* (Toronto: Centre for Renaissance and Reformation Studies, 2021).

Davis, Stephen J., *Christ Child: Cultural Memories of a Young Jesus* (New Haven: Yale University Press, 2014).

Dean, Tacita, and Jeremy Millar, *Place (Art Works)* (London: Thames & Hudson, 2005).

De Luca, Erri, *Solo Andata: Righe che vanno troppo spesso a capo* (Milan: Feltrinelli, 2014).

Derrida, Jacques, *Archive Fever: A Freudian Impression*, trans. Eric Prenowitz (Chicago and London: University of Chicago Press, 1998).

Derrida, Jacques, and Anne Dufourmantelle, *Of Hospitality: Anne Dufourmantelle Invites Jacques Derrida to Respond*, trans. Rachel Bowlby (Stanford: Stanford University Press, 2000).

Derrida, Jacques, and Gianni Vattimo (eds), *Religion*, trans. David Webb (Cambridge: Polity Press, 1998).

Din-Kariuki, Natalya, Subha Mukherji and Rowan Williams (eds), *Crossings: Migrant Knowledges, Migrant Forms* (Santa Barbara: Punctum Books, forthcoming).

Diyab, Hanna, *The Book of Travels*, ed. Johannes Stephan, trans. Elias Muhanna, 2 vols (New York: New York University Press, 2021).

Doig, Allan, *Liturgy and Architecture: From the Early Church to the Middle Ages* (Farnham: Ashgate, 2008).

Duffy, Eamon, 'On "Sacred" and "Secular" Time?', in Duffy, *The Stripping of the Altars: Traditional Religion in England, 1400–1580* (New Haven: Yale University Press, 1992), pp. 46–52.

Duffy, Eamon, *Royal Books & Holy Bones: Essays in Medieval Christianity* (London: Bloomsbury, 2018).

Dupont, Florence, *The Invention of Literature: From Greek Intoxication to the Latin Book*, trans. Janet Lloyd (Baltimore and London: Johns Hopkins University Press, 1999).

Euripides, *Helen*, trans. Frank McGuinness (London: Faber & Faber, 2009).

Foster, R. F., *On Seamus Heaney* (Princeton: Princeton University Press, 2020).

Francis, Gavin, *The Bridge Between Worlds: A Brief History of Connection* (Edinburgh: Canongate, 2024).

Francis, Pope, *Let Us Dream: The Path to a Better Future* (New York: Simon & Schuster, 2020).

Garland, Robert, *Wandering Greeks: The Ancient Greek Diaspora from the Age of Homer to the Death of Alexander the Great* (Princeton: Princeton University Press, 2014).

Gell, Alfred, *Art and Agency: An Anthropological Theory* (Oxford: Clarendon Press, 1998).

Gell, Alfred, 'The Technology of Enchantment and the Enchantment of Technology', in Fiona Candlin and Raiford Guins (eds), *The Object Reader* (London: Routledge, 2009), pp. 209–28.

Georgy, Fathy S., *The Flight of the Holy Family to Egypt* (Cairo: Dar Nubar, 1998).

Gillett, H. M., *Walsingham: The History of a Famous Shrine* (London: Burns Oates & Washbourne, 1946).

Gilmour, Andrew, *The Burning Question: Climate and Conflict – Why Does It Matter?* (Berlin: Berghof Foundation, 2024).

Gozzi, Carlo, *Turandot. Fiaba chinese teatrale tragicomica in cinque atti. Opere edite ed inedite del Co: Carlo Gozzi*, 2 vols (Venice: Giacomo Zanardi, 1801).

Grese, Robert E., and John R. Knott (eds), 'Reimagining Place', *Michigan Quarterly Review*, special issue, vol. XL, no. 1 (Winter 2001).

Grimaldi, Floriano, *La historia della chiesa di Santa Maria di Loreto* (Loreto: Cassa di risparmio di Loreto, 1993).

Grimaldi, Floriano, and Katy Sordi, *Pittori a Loreto: Committenze Tra '500 e '600: Documenti*, (Ancona: Soprintendenza per i beni ambientali e architettonici delle Marche, 1988).

Grimm, Jakob and Wilhelm, *The Complete Fairy Tales of the Brothers Grimm*, ed. and trans. Jack Zipes (New York and London: Bantam, 1992).

Haas, Hein de, *How Migration Really Works: 22 Things You Need to Know About the Most Divisive Issue in Politics* (London: Viking, 2023).

Halbwachs, Maurice, *On Collective Memory* (selections from *Topographie légendaire des évangiles en terre sainte / The Legendary Topography of the Gospels in the Holy Land* [1941] and *Les Cadres sociaux de la mémoire / The Social Framework of Memory* [1952]), trans. Lewis A. Coser (Chicago: University of Chicago Press, 1992).

Hall, Stuart, *Familiar Stranger: A Life Between Two Islands*, ed. Bill Schwarz (London: Allen Lane, 2017).

Han, Byung-Chul, *The Disappearance of Rituals: A Topology of the Present*, trans. Daniel Steuer (Cambridge: Polity Press, 2020).

Harmon, Katherine, *You Are Here: Personal Geographies and Other Maps of the Imagination* (New York: Princeton Architectural Press, 2004).

Harney, Stefano, and Fred Moten, *The Undercommons: Fugitive Planning & Black Study* (New York: Minor Compositions, 2013).

Harter, Christopher, Anthony Tedeschi and Jodine Perkins (eds), *Places of the Imagination: A Celebration of Worlds, Islands, and Realms & Imaginary and Constructed Languages*, The Lilly Library, 2006 [exhibition catalogue] (Indiana: Indiana University Libraries, 2006).

Hayden, Sally, *My Fourth Time, We Drowned: Seeking Refuge on the World's Deadliest Migration Route* (New York: Melville House, 2022).

Heaney, Seamus, *The Redress of Poetry: Oxford Lectures* (London: Faber & Faber, 1995).

Heaney, Seamus, *Finders Keepers: Selected Prose, 1971–2001* (London: Faber & Faber, 2002).

Heller-Roazen, Daniel, *Absentees: On Variously Missing Persons* (New York: Zone Books, 2021).

Herd, David, *Walk Song* (Swindon: Shearsman, 2022).

Herd, David, *Writing Against Expulsion in the Post-War World: Making Space for the Human* (Oxford: Oxford University Press, 2023).

Herd, David, and Anna Pincus (eds), *Refugee Tales I, II, III* and *IV* (Manchester: Comma Press, 2016, 2017, 2019, 2021).

Hillner, Julia, *Helena: Mother of the Empire* (Oxford and New York: Oxford University Press, 2022).

Homer, *The Iliad*, trans. Robert Fagles (London: Penguin 1992).

Homer, *The Iliad of Homer*, trans. Richmond Lattimore (Chicago and London: University of Chicago Press, 1951).

Horta, Paulo Lemos, *Marvellous Thieves: Secret Authors of the Arabian Nights* (Cambridge, Mass.: Harvard University Press, 2019).

Howard, Deborah, 'Introduction' (with Paul Davies) and 'Venice as Gateway to the Holy Land: Pilgrims as Agents of Transmission', in Paul Davies, Deborah Howard and Wendy Pullan (eds), *Architecture and Pilgrimage, 1000–1500: Southern Europe and Beyond* (Farnham: Ashgate, 2013), pp. 1–20, 87–111.

Howe, Emily, Henrietta McBurney, David Park, Stephen Rickerby and Lisa Shekede, *Wall Paintings of Eton* (London: Scala Publishing, 2012).

Howes, Graham, *The Art of the Sacred: An Introduction to the Aesthetics of Art and Belief* (London: I. B. Tauris, 2007).

Hughes, Ted, *Shakespeare and the Goddess of Complete Being* (London: Faber & Faber, 1993).

Hughes, Ted, *Winter Pollen: Occasional Prose*, ed. William Scammell (London: Faber & Faber, 1994).

Huizinga, Johan, *Homo Ludens: A Study of the Play-Element in Culture* (London: Routledge & Kegan Paul, 1949).

Irwin, Robert, *The Arabian Nights: A Companion* (London: I. B. Tauris, 2004).

Jacobus, Mary, *On Belonging and Not Belonging* (Princeton: Princeton University Press, 2022).

James, M. R. (ed. and trans.), *The Apocryphal New Testament* (1924; rev edn Oxford: Clarendon Press, 1996).

Janes, Dominic T. S., and Gary F. Waller (eds), *Walsingham in Literature and Culture from the Middle Ages to Modernity* (Farnham: Ashgate, 2010).

Jeffrey, Alex, Colin McFarlane and Alex Vasudevan, 'Rethinking Enclosure: Space, Subjectivity and the Commons', *Antipode*, vol. 44, no. 4 (2012), pp. 1247–67.

Jolles, André, *Simple Forms*, trans. Peter J. Schwartz (London: Verso, 2017).

Kennedy, Philip F., *Recognition in the Arabic Narrative Tradition: Discovery, Deliverance and Delusion* (Edinburgh: Edinburgh University Press, 2016).

Khalidi, Tarif (ed. and trans.), *The Muslim Jesus: Sayings and Stories in Islamic Literature* (Cambridge, Mass.: Harvard University Press, 2003).

Khosravi, Shahram, *Illegal Traveller: An Auto-Ethnography of Borders* (London: Palgrave Macmillan, 2010).

Kilito, Abdelfattah, *Archéologie: Douze Miniatures* (Brussels: BookLeg DABA Maroc, 2012), trans. Clare Finburgh Delijani and Marina Warner as 'Metaphor', in *Archaeology: Twelve Miniatures*, https://www.thewhitereview.org/poetry/archaeology-twelve-miniatures/

Kilito, Abdelfattah, *Arabs and the Art of Storytelling: A Strange Familiarity*, trans. Mbarek Sryfi and Eric Sellin (Syracuse, NY: Syracuse University Press, 2014).

Kristeva, Julia, *Strangers to Ourselves*, trans. Leon S. Roudiez (New York: University of Columbia Press, 1991).

Kuschel, Karl-Josef, *Christmas and the Qur'an*, trans. Simon Pare (London: Gingko, 2017).

Lamko, Koulsy, *Bintou Wéré: African Opera*, ed. Els Van Der Plas, trans. El Hadji Moustapha Diop (Amsterdam: Prince Claus Fund/Sahel Opera Foundation, 2017).

Le Goff, Jacques, *In Search of Sacred Time: Jacobus de Voragine and* The Golden Legend (Princeton and Oxford: Princeton University Press, 2014).

Le Guin, Ursula K., *Lavinia* (New York: Harcourt, 2008).

Le Guin, Ursula K., *The Carrier Bag Theory of Fiction* (1988; London: Ignota, 2019).
Le Guin, Ursula K., *Space Crone* (London: Silver Press, 2023).
Levin, Boaz, Hanno Loewy and Anika Reichwald, *Say Shibboleth! On Visible and Invisible Borders* (Hohenems: Jüdisches Museum Hohenems, 2018).
Logue, Christopher, *War Music* (London: Faber & Faber, 2000).
MacGregor, Neil, 'Making the History We Need: Civic Engagement in Rethinking the Past', Palliser Lecture, 2021, 21st Century Trust and Salzburg Global Seminar, 4 December 2021.
Macintosh, Fiona, and Justine McConnell, *Performing Epic or Telling Tales* (Oxford: Oxford University Press, 2020).
McPherson, J. W. (Joseph Williams), *The Moulids of Egypt (Egyptian Saints-Days)* (Cairo: N. M. Press, 1941).
McSheffrey, Shannon, *Seeking Sanctuary: Crime, Mercy, and Politics in English Courts, 1400–1550* (Oxford: Oxford University Press, 2017). Also see her website, 'Sanctuary Seekers in England, 1394–1557', https://sanctuaryseekers.ca/
Malouf, David, *Ransom* (London: Chatto & Windus, 2010).
Marlowe, Christopher, *Dido, Queen of Carthage* (1594), in Christopher Marlowe, *The Complete Plays*, ed. Frank Romany and Robert Lindsey (London: Penguin, 2003), pp. 1–67.
Mason, Zachary, *The Lost Books of the Odyssey* (London: Jonathan Cape, 2010).
Matyjaszek, Edmund, 'Walsingham in Ballad, Poetry, and Prose', in *Walsingham: Richeldis 950: Pilgrimage and History*, Proceedings of the Richeldis 950 Historical Conference, March 2011 (Walsingham: RC National Shrine, 2012), pp. 47–80.
Mazzara, Federica, *Reframing Migration: Lampedusa, Border Spectacle and Aesthetics of Subversion* (Oxford: Peter Lang, 2019).
Mazzara, Federica, and Maya Ramsay (eds), *Sink Without Trace: Exhibition on Migrant Deaths at Sea* (London: P21 Gallery, 2019).
Meinardus, Otto F. A., *The Holy Family in Egypt* (Cairo: The American University in Cairo Press, 1986).
Mogtader, Youssef, and Gregor Schoeler, *Turandot: Die persische Märchenerzählung* (Wiesbaden: Reichert Verlag, 2017).
Molesworth, Helen, with Ruth Erickson, *Leap Before You Look: Black Mountain College, 1933–1957* (Boston: Institute of Contemporary Arts, and New Haven: Yale University Press, 2016).

Mondzain, Marie José, *Accueillir: Venu(e)s d'un ventre ou d'un pays* (Paris: Les Liens qui Libèrent, 2023).

Morales, Helen, *Pilgrimage to Dollywood: A Country Music Road Trip Through Tennessee* (Chicago: University of Chicago Press, 2014).

Morrill, John, 'In Wracks of Walsingham: Dissolution and its Consequences', in *Walsingham: Richeldis 950: Pilgrimage and History*, Proceedings of the Richeldis 950 Historical Conference, March 2011 (Walsingham: RC National Shrine, 2012), pp. 97–112.

Morrison, Toni, *The Origin of Others* (Cambridge, Mass.: Harvard University Press, 2017).

Ibn al-Muqaffa, *Kalilah and Dimnah: Fables of Virtue and Vice*, ed. Michael Fishbein, trans. Michael Fishbein and James Montgomery (New York: New York University Press, 2021).

Nezâmî, *Le Pavillon des sept princesses*, ed. and trans. Michel Barry (Paris: Gallimard, 2000).

Niero, Antonio, *The Basilica of Santa Maria della Salute* (Venice: KINA Italia / L.E.G.O. S.p.A. Editions, 2015).

Nizami, El, *Mirror of the Invisible World: Tales from the Khamseh of Nizami*, adapted and trans. Peter J. Chelkowski, with an essay by Priscilla P. Soucek, Foreword by Richard Ettinghausen (New York: Metropolitan Museum of Art, 1975).

O'Brien, Steven, *Britannic Myths* (London: Holland House Books, 2017).

Ó Carragáin, Éamonn, *Ritual and the Rood: Liturgical Images and the Old English Poems of the Dream of the Rood Tradition* (London and Toronto: The British Library and University of Toronto Press, 2005).

Onne, Eyal (ed.), *Jerusalem: Profile of a Changing City* (Jerusalem: Mishkenot Sha'ananim and The Jerusalem Institute for Israel Studies, 1985).

Opie, Iona and Peter, *The Lore and Language of Schoolchildren* (1959; New York: New York Review Books, 2001).

Oswald, Alice, *Memorial: An Excavation of the* Iliad (London: Faber & Faber, 2011).

Oswald, Alice, *Nobody*, with watercolours by William Tillyer (London: 21 Publishing, 2018; (paperback, Jonathan Cape, 2019).

Ovid, *Ovid's Heroines: A Verse Translation of the* Heroides, trans. Daryl Hine (New Haven: Yale University Press, 1991).

Pavel, Thomas G., *Fictional Worlds* (Cambridge, Mass.: Harvard University Press, 1986).

Payne, Alina, 'The Portability of Art: Prolegomena to Art and Architecture on the Move', in Diana Sorensen (ed.), *Territories and Trajectories: Cultures in Circulation* (Durham, NC, and London: Duke University Press, 2018), pp. 91–109.

Paz, Octavio, *Configurations*, trans. Lysander Kemp (New York: New Directions, 1971).

Perec, Georges, *Espèces d'espaces: Journal d'un usager de l'espace* (Paris: Seuil, 1974).

Pétis de La Croix, François, *Les Mille et Un Jours: Contes persans*, ed. Pierre Brunel, Christelle Bahier-Porte, and Frédéric Mancier [with *Histoire de la sultane de Perse et des vizirs*, ed. Raymonde Robert and Abbé Jean-Paul Bignon and *Les Aventures d'Abdalla*, ed. Raymonde Robert] (Paris: Honoré Champion, 2006).

Phillips, Adam, and Barbara Taylor, *On Kindness* (London: Penguin, 2010).

Pollard, Clare, *Ovid's Heroines* (Hexham: Bloodaxe Books, 2013).

Popescu, Lucy (ed.), *A Country of Refuge* (London: Unbound, 2016).

Pullan, Wendy, Maximilian Sternberg, Lefkos Kyriacou, Craig Larkin and Michael Dumper, *The Struggle for Jerusalem's Holy Places* (New York: Routledge, 2013).

Qasmiyeh, Yousif M., *Writing the Camp* (Llandysul: Broken Sleep Books, 2021).

*The Qur'an*, trans. Tarif Khalidi (New Delhi: Penguin, 2009).

*Refugee Tales* (all volumes) (London: Comma Press, 2016).

Reich-Ranicki, Marcel, *The Author of Himself: The Life of Marcel Reich-Ranicki*, trans. Ewald Osers with an Introduction by Jack Zipes (Princeton: Princeton University Press, 2001).

Ricoeur, Paul, *Oneself as Another*, trans. Kathleen Blamey (London and Chicago: University of Chicago Press, 1992).

Ricoeur, Paul, *Figuring the Sacred: Religion, Narrative and Imagination*, ed. Mark I. Wallace, trans. David Pellauer (Minneapolis: Fortress Press, 1995).

Riley, Denise, *The Words of Selves* (Stanford: Stanford University Press, 2000).

Riley, Denise, *Lurex* (London: Picador, 2022).

Rizzo, Alessandra and Karen Seago, 'Introduction: The aesthetics of migration: Reversals of marginality and the socio-political translation turn', in Rizzo and Seago (eds), 'Translating the margin: Lost voices in aesthetic discourse', *InVerbis: Lingue Letterature Culture* (Palermo: Università degli Studi, Anno VIII, n. 1 (2018), pp. 7–32.

Robbins, Bruce, and Paulo Lemos Horta (eds), *Cosmopolitanisms* (New York: New York University Press, 2017).

Robertson, Joe, and Joe Murphy, *The Jungle* (London: Faber & Faber, 2018).

Roodenburg, Herman, 'Summary in English', in Roodenburg, *Onder censuur. De kerkelijke tucht in de gereformeerde gemeente van Amsterdam, 1578–1700* (Hilversum: Verloren, 1990).

Rubin, Miri, *Mother of God: A History of the Virgin Mary* (London: Penguin, 2010).

Ibn al-Sai, *Consorts of the Caliphs: Women and the Court of Baghdad*, ed. Shawkat M. Toorawa, trans. Editors of the Library of Arabic Literature (New York: New York University Press, 2015).

Said, Edward W., *The World, the Text, and the Critic* (London: Vintage, 1991).

Said, Edward W., *Culture and Imperialism* (London: Chatto & Windus, 1993).

Said, Edward W., *Out of Place: A Memoir* (London: Granta Books, 1999).

Said, Edward W., *Reflections on Exile and Other Literary and Cultural Essays* (London: Granta Books, 2001).

Said, Edward W., 'Introduction to the Fiftieth-Anniversary Edition', in Erich Auerbach, *Mimesis: The Representation of Reality in Western Literature* (Princeton and Oxford: Princeton University Press, 2003), pp. ix–xxxi.

Saussy, Haun, *The Ethnography of Rhythm: Orality and Its Technologies* (New York: Fordham University Press, 2016).

Scaraffia, Lucetta, *Loreto* (Bologna: il Mulino, 1998).

Schwartz, Hillel, *The Culture of the Copy: Striking Likenesses, Unreasonable Facsimiles* (New York: Zone Books, 1996).

Scott, Joan W., 'Echo: History and the Construction of Identity', *Critical Inquiry*, vol. 27, no. 2 (Winter 2001), pp. 284–304.

Scott, Joan W., 'Storytelling' (Forum: Holberg Prize Symposium: Doing Decentred History), *History and Theory*, no. 50 (May 2011), pp. 203–9.

Segatto, Diego, Isshaq Al-Barbary and Elena Isayev (eds), *Xenia: Campus in Camps Collective Dictionary* (Exeter: University of Exeter, 2017).

Sennett, Richard, *The Craftsman* (London: Penguin, 2009).

Shakespeare, William, *The Riverside Shakespeare*, ed. Frank Kermode et al. (Boston: Houghton Mifflin, 1972).

Shakespeare, William, *Othello: The Moor of Venice*, ed. Michael Neill (Oxford: Oxford University Press, 2006).

Al-Shaykh, Hanan, *One Thousand and One Nights* (London: Bloomsbury, 2013).

Shoemaker, Karl, *Sanctuary and Crime in the Middle Ages, 400–1500* (New York: Fordham University Press, 2011).

Silk, Dennis, *Retrievements: A Jerusalem Anthology* (2nd edn; Jerusalem: Keter Publishing House, 1977).

Simpson, David, *Engaging Violence: Civility and the Reach of Literature* (Stanford: Stanford University Press, 2022).

Singer, Stella A., 'Walsingham's Local Genius: Norfolk's "Newe Nazareth"', in Dominic T. S. Janes and Gary F. Waller (eds), *Walsingham in Literature and Culture from the Middle Ages to Modernity* (Farnham: Ashgate, 2010), pp. 23–34.

Sjón, *The Whispering Muse*, trans. Victoria Cribb (London: Telegram, 2012).

Smith, Ali, *Artful* (London: Hamish Hamilton, 2012).

Smith Ali, *Seasonal Quartet*, 4 vols. *Autumn, Winter, Spring, Summer* (London: Hamish Hamilton, 2016–20).

Smith, Ali, *Gliff* (London: Hamish Hamilton, 2024).

Smith, Douglas, *The Sanctuary at Durham* (Newcastle-on-Tyne: Frank Graham, 1971).

Solnit, Rebecca, *Infinite City: A San Francisco Atlas* (Berkeley and Los Angeles: University of California Press, 2010).

Solnit, Rebecca, and Joshua Jelly-Schapiro, *Nonstop Metropolis: A New York City Atlas* (Berkeley and Los Angeles: University of California Press, 2016).

Solnit, Rebecca, and Rebecca Snedeker, *Unfathomable City: A New Orleans Atlas* (Berkeley and Los Angeles: University of California Press, 2013).

Sophocles, *Four Tragedies: A New Verse Translation*, trans. Oliver Taplin (Oxford: Oxford University Press, 2015).

Sproul, Barbara C., *Primal Myths: Creating the World* (San Francisco: Harper, 1979).

Stallings, A. E., *Olives* (Evanston, Ill.: TriQuarterly Books/Northwestern University Press, 2012).

Steedman, Carolyn, *Dust* (Manchester: Manchester University Press, 2001).

Stewart, Susan, *On Longing: Narratives of the Miniature, the Gigantic, the Souvenir* (Durham, NC: Duke University Press, 1993).

Stewart, Susan, *The Ruins Lesson: Meaning and Material in Western Culture* (Chicago: University of Chicago Press, 2020).

Stonebridge, Lyndsey, *Placeless People: Writing, Rights, and Refugees* (Oxford: Oxford University Press, 2018).

Stonor Saunders, Frances, with photographs by Kaupo Kikkas, *What Would You Take?* (2018) and *What Would You Take? Ukraine: Stories of Escape* (2023), 12 Star Gallery, Europe House.

Subin, Anna Della, *Accidental Gods: On Men Unwittingly Turned Divine* (London: Granta Books, 2022).

Tarnowska, Wafa', *The Seven Wise Princesses: A Medieval Persian Epic* (Concord, Mass.: Barefoot Books, 2000).

Tatari, Muna, and Klaus von Stosch, *Mary in the Qur'an*, trans. Peter Lewis (London: Gingko, 2021).

Tearne, Roma, *The House of Small Things* (Nottingham: Angel Row, 2002).

Te Brake, Wayne P., *Religious Peace, Then and Now* (Eugene, OR: Cascade Books, 2022).

Teramano, Pietro, *Trāslatio miraculosa ecclesie beate Marie virginis de Loreto* (Rome: Eucharius Silber, *c.* 1500).

Trías, Eugenio, 'Thinking Religion: The Symbol and the Sacred', in Jacques Derrida and Gianni Vattimo (eds), *Religion*, trans. David Webb (Cambridge: Polity Press, 1998).

Trilling, Daniel, *Lights in the Distance: Exile and Refuge at the Borders of Europe* (London: Picador, 2018).

Vergil, *The Aeneid: A New Translation*, trans. Shadi Bartsch (London: Profile Books, 2020).

Vince, Gaia, *Transcendence: How Humans Evolved Through Fire, Language, Beauty, and Time* (London: Penguin, 2020).

Virgil, *The Aeneid*, trans. Robert Fagles (London: Penguin, 2006).

Voragine, Jacobus de, *The Golden Legend: Readings on the Saints*, trans. William Granger Ryan, 2 vols (Princeton: Princeton University Press, 1993).

Warner, Marina, *Stranger Magic: Charmed States & the Arabian Nights* (London: Chatto & Windus, 2011).

Warner, Marina, 'The Politics of Translation', *London Review of Books*, 11 October 2018, https://www.lrb.co.uk/the-paper/v40/n19/marina-warner/the-politics-of-translation.

Warner, Marina, 'Living in a Country of Words: The Shelter of Stories', in Charles Fernyhough (ed.), *Others: Writers on the Power of Words to Help Us See Beyond Ourselves* (London: Unbound, 2019), pp. 233–51.

Warner, Marina, 'Out Loud: The Experience of Literature in the Digital Space', in Susheila Nasta with Rukhsana Yasmin (eds), *Brave New Words* (Oxford: Myriad Editions, 2019).

Warner, Marina, 'The Shelter of Stories', Carnegie Lecture, Edinburgh, 2024.

Warner, Marina, and Valentina Castagna, 'Stories in Transit/*Storie in transito*: Storytelling and arrivants' voices in Sicily', in Claudia Gualtieri (ed.), *Migration and the Contemporary Mediterranean: Shifting Cultures in Twenty-First-Century Italy and Beyond* (Oxford: Peter Lang, 2018), pp. 223–43.

Warner, Marina, 'Communities of Fate: Magical Writing and Contemporary Fabulism', in A. Hölter (ed.), *The Languages of World Literature: The Many Languages of Comparative Literature* (Berlin: De Gruyter, 2024), pp. 31–50, https://doi.org/10.1515/9783110645033-002

Washington, John, *The Dispossessed: A Story of Asylum and the US–Mexican Border and Beyond* (London: Verso, 2020).

Washington, John, *The Case for Open Borders* (Chicago: Haymarket Books, 2024).

Waugh, Evelyn, *Helena* (1950; London: Penguin, 1963).

Weil, Simone, 'Iliad, or the Poem of Force', in Simone and Rachel Bespaloff, *War and the Iliad*, trans. Mary McCarthy (New York: New York Review Books, 2005), included with Rachel Bespaloff, *On the Iliad*.

Weinberger, Eliot, *Angels & Saints* (New York: New Directions Books and Christine Burgin Books, 2020).

Wickett, Elizabeth, *For the Living and the Dead: The Funerary Laments of Upper Egypt, Ancient and Modern* (London: I. B. Tauris, 2009).

Wickett, Elizabeth, *Seers, Saints and Sinners: The Oral Traditions of Upper Egypt* (London: I. B. Tauris, 2012).

Williams, Bernard, *Truth and Truthfulness: An Essay in Genealogy* (Princeton: Princeton University Press, 2002).

Winnicott, D. W., *Playing and Reality* (London: Tavistock Publications, 1971).

Woodring, Benjamin Michael, '"Oft Have I Heard of Sanctuary Men"': Fictions of Refuge in Early Shakespeare' (doctoral dissertation, Harvard University, 2014).

Worpole, Ken, *New Jerusalem: The Good City and the Good Society* (London: The Swedenborg Society, 2017).

Ibn Zafer, *Solwan; or, Waters of Comfort*, ed. Michele Amari, English trans. Anon. (1852; BiblioLife LCC, n.d.).

# Index

Aachen Cathedral 79
Abboud, Jumana Emil 243
Abu Hamdan, Lawrence 232
Acre, fall of (1291) 113, 117
Adami, Giuseppe 204–5
Aeneas 146–66, 172, 173, 175–6, 180–1, *Plate 10*
Aeschylus 24, 26
Agamben, Giorgio 220
agricultural calendar 70
Agualusa, José Eduardo 280
Ajax the Lokrian 25
Ajens, Andrés, *Transiluminación* 282
*Aladdin* 190
Alexievich, Svetlana 235–6
Algeria 100, 175, 177
*Ali Baba* 190
Allen-Paisant, Jason, *Self-Portrait as Othello* 166–7
Alsatia 42
Alÿs, Francis 32
Ambrose, St 78
Andalusia, Spain 56
Andersen, Hans Christian 273, 277
Anderson, Benedict 3
Anglican church 121
animal reserves 4
Anna (Dido's sister) 153, 155–6, 158, 159–61, 181
Anna Perenna 160
Anne of Austria 119
Aoun, Mouchir Basile 56
Al-Aqsa mosque, Jerusalem 63, 137
apocrypha 58–68, 61, 72–4
*Arabian Nights* see *Thousand and One Nights, The*
*Arabic gospel of the Infancy* 58, 60, 61–3, 72
Arendt, Hannah 14, 174

arrivants 3, 8, 22–3, 147, 227, 294, 296, 301, 313–14
art galleries 47
Arthurian legends 92
'Arundel Ballad' (anon) 120
Ash Wednesday 117, 141
Ashour, Radwa, *Spectres* 283–4
Ashworth, Joan 302, 373
Assad, Bashar al- 270
assembly 65–6, 72, 83, 104, 237, 292
asylum seekers 4, 7, 8, 44, 221–4, 232, 270, 293–4
asylums 132–3
Athelstan 39–40
Atwood, Margaret, *The Handmaid's Tale* 272, 279
Auden, W. H. 174, 272
Auerbach, Erich, *Figura* 256
Augustus, Emperor 90, 127, 148, 154, 160, 163–4, 165, 166
d'Aulnoy, Marie Catherine, *Contes des fées* 195
autofiction 220, 228–30

Bale, Anthony 254
Ballard, J. G. 279
balsam trees 63–5
barbed wire fences 217–18, 270
*Barca Nostra*, (2016) art work 13
Barefoot Carmelites 125
Barghouti, Mourid 138–9
Barocci, Federico 66
barricades 8, 215, 217
Barthes, Roland 108
Bartoli, Clelia 292, 294, 296
Basil, Bishop 94
Basile, Giambattista, *Pentamerone* 199, 202
Basílica de San Francisco, Arezzo 86

Al Bassam, Sulayman 275
Becket, Thomas 40, 105, 120
Beckett, Samuel 278
Belorusets, Yevgenia 185
Benjamin, Walter 137, 257
*Beowulf* (anon) 207, 280
Berlin Wall 142, 215
Berlioz, Hector, *Les Troyens* 173–6
Betjeman, John 95–6
Beverley Minster 37–40
Beyoncé 228
Bible, the
  apocrypha 58
  Book of Numbers 22
  Book of Psalms 260
  Deuteronomy 22
  Gospel of St Luke 56, 114
  Gospel of St Matthew 51–3
  Jeremiah 276–7
  Joshua 22
  New Testament 54, 72
  Old Testament 5, 53, 54, 185, 218, 274
  Song of Songs 131, 257
*Bintou Wéré: The Opera of the Sahel* (contemporary opera) 271
Bishop, Elizabeth 243, 244
Black, Freda 74–5
Black Madonnas 29, 128
Blake, William, 'Jerusalem' 98
*Blood Swept Lands and Seas of Red* (Tower of London poppies) 104–5
Boccaccio, Giovanni 343
Boochani, Behrouz, *No Friend But the Mountains* 226
Books of Hours 60
Borges, Jorge Luis 278, 285
Bosch, Hieronymus, *Garden of Earthly Delights* 59
boundaries 2, 22, 35, 39–40, 76, 100, 201, 249
Bourgeois, Louise 107
Bramante, Donato 127
Brathwaite, Edward Kamau, *The Arrivants* 8
breaches, of sanctuary 40–1
Brooks, Peter, *Seduced by Story: The Use and Abuse of Narrative* 274–5, 281, 292
Brothers Grimm 208–9, 262, 276

Brotton, Jerry, *This Orient Isle* 159
Brown, Peter 99
Brown, Wendy 6
Browne, Thomas 31
Brubaker, Leslie 90
Buchel, Christoph, *Barca Nostra* 13
Budde, Mariann Edgar, Bishop of Washington, D.C. 316
Burchard of Mount Zion 63
burial goods 132
Burns, Robert 144
Burroughs, William 277
Burrow, Colin 228–9, 240
Busoni, Ferruccio, *The Turandot Suite* 202
Butler, Octavia, *Parable of the Sower* 279
Butterfield, William 93
Byron, Lord 273

*Cabinet des fées, Le* 196, 199
Caillois, Roger, *Les Jeux et les hommes* 33, 34, 332
Caistor, Nick 283
Calle, Sophie 34
Calvin, John 85
Calvino, Italo 53–4, 262–3
camps, 'temporary' 7
Camus, Albert, *Le Premier Homme* 177
Canetti, Elias, *Crowds and Power* 251
Canterbury Cathedral 40, 120
Caravaggio, *La Madonna dei Pellegrini* 122–3, Plate 7
carnivals 30, 71–2
Carroll, Lewis, *Alice's Adventures in Wonderland* 246, 274
Carthage 146–7, 149, 151–3, 159–60, 173, 176–7, 295
Casanova, Pascale 261–2
Cassandra (Alexandra) 25, 25
Castagna, Valentina 293–4, 371
'The Cat and the Baby', fable, 301–2
Catherine of Aragon 121
Catholicism
  Anglo-Catholic revival 121
  art and 66, 98
  crowd control 251
  forced conversion to 56
  high altar 42
  Mary and 55
  persecution and 85, 221

popes 102, 109, 127, 135
Reformers and 106
rosaries 17, 116
St Dismas 62
saints and 69, 96, 119
Cavalli, Francesco 171–2
Cave, Terence, *Thinking with Literature* 281–2
caves 35, 51, 57, 60, 82–3, 147, 254
Cavosi, Roberto, *I Persiani a Caporetto* 238
Caxton, William 89, 106
Cervantes, Miguel de C, *Don Quixote* 195
*Chain* (journal) 282–3
Chapel of Sant'Agostino, Rome 122
Chapel of St Helena, Paris 93, 137
Chapel of the Ascension, Jerusalem 254
charity auctions 105
Charles III 109–10
Chartres Cathedral 79
Chaucer, Geoffrey 38, 101, 106, 221
Chelkowski, Peter, *Mirror of the Invisible World* 192
Chetwode, Penelope 95
Chevalier, Ulysse, *Notre Dame de Lorette* 134
Chiesa del Gesù Nuovo, Naples 102
Christina (Cristina, St) 107, 254
Christ Church Cathedral, Oxford 116
Christian, William Jr 58
Christianity
    Arab 138, 139
    cult practices 98
    early 10, 53, 54, 58, 88, 90, 100, 131
    Islam and 55–6, 68
    maps and 251
    medieval 87
    Oriental 56
    relics and 82
    sanctuary and 43
Church of S. Maria of Nazareth, Venice 125
Church of Saint-Leu-Saint-Gilles, Paris 93
Church of Santa Croce, Rome 97, 99
Church of the Holy Sepulchre, Jerusalem 130

Church of the Holy Virgin, Cairo 51
churches, history of sanctuary in 29–32
*Cinderella* (castle) 76, 76, 190
Coel, King 91–2
Coetzee, J. M. 72–4
Colchester 92–3; St Helen's chapel 93–4
Coleridge, Samuel Taylor 273
collective memory 144, 237, 252
Cologne Cathedral 85
*commedia dell'arte* 135, 199–202, 204, 209
common ground 16, 63, 186, 191, 206, 240, 280, 286, 307–8, 316
commons 4, 14, 17, 55, 66, 68, 70–2, 181, 190–1, 238, 261
Constantine 81, 82, 87–8, 90–1, 96
Constantius 90, 91, 92, 94–6
Cook, Capt. James 144
Cook, Elizabeth, *Achilles* 247
copies 120, 128–9, 137–8
Coptic Church 51, 65, 69, 70, 137
Corbington, S.J., Robert 124–5
Correggio, *Madonna della Scodella* 66
cosmopolitanism 7
Counter-Reformation 98–9, 124–5, 127, 128
Coural, Abbé Pierre 133
Cox, Revd J. Charles, *The Sanctuaries and Sanctuary Seekers of Medieval England* 31, 38
CPIA 'Nelson Mandela' school 292, 313
Cranach, Lucas, *Saint Helena with the Cross* 91
*Crane Bag, The* (magazine) 267–8
Crawford, James 2
Cristina, St 107, 254
crosses, stone 39
cultural heritage 55, 56, 284–5
curses 161
Cusk, Rachel, *Outline, Transit, Kudos* 228, 230
Cuthbert, St 31
Cylon of Athens 24

Dant, Adam 258, *Plate 13*
Darwish, Mahmoud 139, 227, 260, 314

Daudy, Kate 116, 238
Davis, Natalie Zemon 224
Davis, Stephen J. 55
De Luca, Erri, *Solo Andata (One-Way Ticket)* 178–9
debtors' sanctuaries, London 42
Deller, Jeremy, 'The Triumph of Art' 72
Demilitarized Zones (DMZs) 215, 217
deportation 7, 44, 220–1, 225, 293, 315
Diallo, Amadou 310–12, 314
Diallo, Din (Safoudiny) 290–1, 297, 298–302, 314
Diawara, Manthia 271–2
Diderot, Denis, *Les Bijoux indiscrets* 200
Dido, Queen of Carthage 146–82, *157*, Plates 10, 11
Diop, Wasis 271
Disney, Walt 75, 76
Disneyland 75–6
displacement, internal 7, 8
Diyab, Hannah 195
Doel, Marcus 2
Dome of the Rock, Jerusalem 28, 42, 63, 137, Plate 1a
Donatus, *Life of Virgil* 163
*Dosti* (1964 film) 267
Douglas, Mary 28
*Dream of the Rood, The* (Caedmon/Cynewulf) 80, 81
Drumgoold, Kate, *A Slave Girl's Story* 225
Dryden, John 282
Dupont, Florence, *The Invention of Literature* 268
Durham Cathedral 31, Plate 1b
dust, holy *115*, 116–17, 140–3

Egypt 51–77, 63–5, 69, 132, 176
*Egyptian Book of the Dead* 70
*Elene* (Cynewulf) 81–2
Elizabeth I 39, 101, 106, 135, 159
Emin, Tracey 107
empathy 98, 159, 170, 220, 223, 238, 316
Ephrem of Syria 131
*Epic of Gilgamesh, The* 287, 294–5, 313, Plate 16a

Equiano, Olaudah 225
Erasmus 120–1
Ernaux, Annie, *The Years* 236–7
Euripides 25, 238, 282
Eton College chapel 107, 342–3
'Europanto' (language) 262
Eusebius, Bishop of Caesarea 82–3
Evans-Pritchard, E. E. 68
exile 4, 36, 132, 138

fables 16, 199, 274, 277–9
 Arabic 62, 269, 284, 296–7
 classical 302, 309, 312
 contemporary 72–3, 258, 265–6
Fagles, Robert 150–1
fairy tales 17, 36, 57, 75–6, 183–211, 246–7, 262, 276–8, 296
*Farraj ba'd al-shidda (Joy after Distress)* 195
Faustini, Giovanni 172
feast days 30, 56, 78, 84, 85, 86, 93, 105, 128, 136
Fedda, Yasmin 238
*Festino della Santuzza*, Palermo 30
Fête de la Liberté 104
Fisher, Thomas 88, 107
Flaubert, Gustave, *Madame Bovary* 145
Flight into Egypt (Gospel of Matthew) 51–77, 68
folk practices 16, 70–2, 108, 201, 206, 272–3, 284, 314
folk singers 72, 74–5
folktales 17, 186, 188, 199
follies (Neuschwanstein castle) 76, *76*
forests 35–6, 43–4, 216
Francis, Pope 109
Frid Stol (Frith Stool, Peace Seat) *19*, 38
Frideswide, St 119
Friel, Brian, *Translations* 243
Frith, Chris 308
frith stools (Frid Stol) 38
*Frozen* (2013 film) 190
funeral songs 70
Furies, the 26–7

Galland, Antoine, *Les Mille et une nuits* 194–5, 196
games, playing 33–5
gardens 5, 59, 63–5, 84, 121, 291

Garland, Robert, *Wandering Greeks* 26
Gassimou, Maga (Magassouba) 291
Gaza Strip 215
Gell, Alfred 278
Genette, Gérard 277
Geneva Convention 45
Genio di Palermo 306–11, *311*, 372–374, Plate *14c*
Geoffrey of Monmouth, *History of the Kings of Britain* 92, 95
George, St and the Dragon, St 69, 105
Gide, André, *Les Nourritures terrestres* 274
Gill, Winifred 61
Gilroy, Paul, *The Black Atlantic* 177–8, 234–5
Giocherenda (cooperative association, Palermo) 296–7, 297, 310, 313–14
Girtin, Thomas 121
Glissant, Édouard 271
Goethe, Johann Wolfgang von 201
Goldoni, Carlo 200–1
Gonzenbach, Laura 296
Good Chance Theatre, *The Jungle* 224, 231
Good Friday 99
Good Thief, cult of the 62
Gormley, Antony 2
Gozzi, Carlo 199–202, *201*, 206
Greece, history of sanctuary in 21–8, 40
Gregory of Nyssa 131
Gregory of Tours 84
Grenfell Tower fire (2017) 235
grottoes 30, 76
Guild of the Holy Cross (Stratford-upon-Avon) 88, 105, 108
Gypsies 75

Hafez/Hafiz 257, 283
Haig, Alexander 93–4
Halbwachs, Maurice 252
hallowing (consecrate)
 hollowing and 2
 practice 15, 18, 63, 113, 141
 principle of 35, 71
 relics and 9, 82
Handel, George Frederic, *Giulio Cesare* 186
*Hansel and Gretel* 36
Hardy, Thomas 246

Hayden, Sally *My Fourth Time, We Drowned* 292–3
Headley, Maria Dahvana, *The Mere Wife* 280
Heaney, Seamus 102–3, 125–6, 268, 316
Heidegger, Martin 278
Helena, St 78–110
 background 89–91
 'Essex Girl' 91–7
Henry of Huntingdon, *Historia Anglorum* 92
Henry VIII 37, 41, 44, 120, 121
Henze, Hans Werner, *Il Re cervo (The King Stag)* 202
Herd, David 221–3
Herrick, Robert 238
heterotopia 2, 45, 64, 76, 337
Heti, Sheila, *How Should a Person Be?* 228, 230
*History of the Virgin* (Syriac text) 58
Hockney, David 357–8
holiness 25, 30–1, 99, 107, 160
hollowing 2, 106, 145, 250
Holy Houses 111–22, 127–33, 135, 136, 140
Holy Land 90, 97, 99, 105–6, 112, 116, 252–3
holy water 66
home regained 127–40
home, safety of 37, 42–7, 142–4
homelands 3–4, 108–9, 112, 247–8
Homer
 *Iliad* 153, 165, 247, 248, 275, 279
 *Odyssey* 46, 146, 153, 162, 239, 268–9
Hong Kong 8, 33
hospitality 1, 7, 14, 40–47, 148–9, 160–1, 181, 210, 309, 316
Howard, Deborah 254
Hughes-Hallett, Lucy 172–3
Hughes, Langston 144
Hughes, Ted 26, 275, 279
Hull, Katharine, *The Far Distant Oxus* 246
humanism 16
Hungary 215
'The Huntsman, the King's Son and the Enchanted Deer' 291, 297, 297, 298–301

Iarbas/Hiarbas, King 154, 155
Iman Riza *Plate 8*
immigrants/immigration
    numbers 326–7
    policies on 7, 42, 44, 170, 220
    workers 315
Innocent XI, Pope *133*, 135
internationalism 7
Irrealis, grammatical term 12, 110, 115, 233, 328
Ishiguro, Kazuo, *The Buried Giant* 258
Islam 53–8, 62–3, 68, 70, 98, 109, 117, 255
Italy 17, 44, 102, 232, 238, 250, 270, 315

James, Henry, 'The Figure in the Carpet' 257
James I 37
James, Marlon, *Dark Star* trilogy 270–1
James the Greater, St 250
Jarman, Derek 47
Joan of Arc 97, 100
Jolles, André 210
Jones, Claudia 71
Jordan 7
Joseph of Cupertino, St 111, *112*
Judaism 34–5, 56, 63, 88, 138, 257, 295
Julien, Isaac 12, 12–13, 179
Julius II, Pope 127
Justin, *Epitome of Pompeius Trogus* 153–4

Kaaba, the (Mecca) 131
Kafka, Franz 277–8, 279
*Kalilah wa Dimnah* (Arabic fables) 269, 297
Kameli, Katia 266–7
Kamppi Chapel, Helsinki 45
Kant, Immanuel 273
Keats, John 274
Kennedy, Philip 263
Khalili, Bouchra 227, 243
Khosravi, Shahram, *'Illegal' Traveller* 225
Kilito, Abdelfattah, 'Metaphor' 199, 265–6
King, Dr William, *The Persian and Turkish Tales* 199

Kleist, Heinrich von, *The Prince of Homburg* 289
Knausgaard, Karl Ove, *My Struggle* 228–9, 240
Kneebone, Rachel 45
knockers, door 31
al-Koni, Ibrahim 247
Korzybski, Alfred 242, 253
Kraus, Chris, *I Love Dick* 228, 229, 230
Kurkov, Andrei 184–5
Kyiv Opera House 183–4, 203–4

La Fayette, Mme de, La Princesse de Clèves 283
'La Solitude de Nazareth' 132–3
labourer, travelling 4
Laing, Olivia 228
Lamko, Koulsy 271
Lampedusa, Giuseppe Tomasi di, 12–13, 309–10
lamps, votive 161
Le Goff, Jacques, *In Search of Sacred Time* 83, 84, 129
Le Guin, Ursula K. *Lavinia* 179–81, 279
Lebanon 7, 225
LeCompte, Elizabeth 172
Lee, Sam 72, 74–5
Lerner, Ben 229
Levi, Primo, *If This Is a Man* 226
Lewis, C. S. 272
libraries 5, 46
Liguori, St Alphonsus 98

litany of Loreto 131
Literary Hotels (chain) 144–5
Lorde, Audrey 15
Loreto, Le Marche, Italy 43, 111–45, *114*, *126*, Madonna of Loreto statue 119, 128–30, *129*, 134–5
Lotto, Lorenzo 130, *130*
Louis XIV 119
Lubavitchers 138, *Plate 12*
Lucano, Domenico 'Mimmo' 315
Ludwig of Bavaria 76
Luke, St 29, 124
Lykophron, *Alexandra* 25

McCarthy, Justin Huntly 199
McPherson, J. W., *The Moulids of Egypt* 68–9, 70
Madame Tussaud's, London 105
Magdalene Laundries 133
de Maillet, Benoît 65
Malines, Archbishop of 94
Malouf, David, *Ransom* 247
Manchester 37
Mandé people 270
Mann, Thomas, *The Magic Mountain* 47
maps/mapping 131, 227, 242–59, 307–8, *Plate 13*
  ancient 244–5
  cities 257
  imaginary 244–7, 250, 252
  Santa Croce 98
  star 245–6
al-Maqrizi 57
Marani, Diego 262
Marcellus (nephew of Augustus) 164
Mardi Gras 71
Marlowe, Christopher, *Dido, Queen of Carthage*, 88, 158–9, 166
Mary I 37
Mason, Zachary, *The Lost Books of the Odyssey* 247
Mastrocinque, Attilio 161
Matarea (Matareya), Egypt 63–5, 64, 69
May, Theresa 219–20
Mayeur-Jaouen, Catherine, 'What Do Egypt's Copts and Muslims Share? The Issue of Shrines' 69–70
Mbembe, Achille 271
Mecca 55, 70, 98, 109, 131
Mediterranean, the 13, 27
Meloni, Giorgia 17, 315
mementoes 5, 132
memorabilia 105, 132, 137, 140–1
memorials 29–30, 75, 136–7, 145, 250, 308–9
Ménage, Gilles 194
Mexico 128
Michals, Duane, *The House I Once Called Home: A Photographic Memoir with Verse* 142

migrants/migration
  deaths 13
  Dido as 146–82
  economic 41
  'forced migrants' 6–9, 147, 178
  treatment of 28, 230, 271
Miller, Kei 234, 243–4
miracles 54–5, 58, 60–3, 77, 78, 84, 106–7, 136–7, 254
  *See also* Loreto, Le Marche, Italy
Moclès (Dervish) 195
Modiano, Patrick, *Dora Bruder* 133
Molière 194
Montaigne, Michel de 122, 128, 140
Montgomery, Lucy Maud, *Anne of Green Gables* 144
monuments 30, 101, 127, 130–1, 144, 145, 250, 295, 308–10
Morales, Helen, *Pilgrimage to Dollywood* 144
Moroni, Cardinal 124
Morosini, Francesco 29
Morrison, Toni, *Jazz* 234, 280
Moscati, St Giuseppe 102
Moubarac, Youakim 56
moulids (saints' festivals) 68–72
Mozart, Wolfgang Amadeus 200, 202
Mukherjee, Neel 222
multi-denominational chapels 46
Murasaki Shikibu, *The Tale of Genji* 246
Murphy, Joe 224
Musa, Hilda 139
museums 43, 46, 103–4
Muslims 53–8, 62–3, 68, 70, 98, 109, 117, 255
Al-Mutanabbi 284
Muybridge, Eadweard 258
Myers, Benjamin, *Cuddy* 31–2, 33
myths 17–18

Napoleon 99, 105, 111, 119, 135, 176
narratives, personal 221–9
nationalism 7, 16–17, 28
nativism 7
Nazareth 111, 113–14, 132, 139–40
Negev desert, Israel 243
'Nessun dorma' (*Turandot*) 186

Newton, Isaac 17
Nguyen, Viet Thanh, *The Displaced* 222–3
Nicholas, St 141
Nigeria 221–2
El Nizami, *Pavilion of the Seven Princesses* 188, 189, 192–3, Plate 9
No Man's Land 36, 215–41
nomadism 75, 155, 203, 243, 247, 260, 261
North Africa 171–9, 181, 266–7
Northern Ireland 46, 267
Notre-Dame de Paris 101–2
Notting Hill Carnival, London 71
Nova, João da 93
nursery rhymes 91–2

Octavia the Younger 164, 165
Okri, Ben, *The Famished Road* 270
Old King Cole 91–2, 95
Oldcorne, Blessed Edward 101
'One for You and One for Me', fable 302–6, 305, Plate 15
*One Thousand and One Nights* (*Arabian Nights*) 190, 193, 270
opera 171–5, 183–89, 200–7
  'chaos-opéra' 271–2, 313
oratories 30
Oratorio del Rosario di San Domenico, Palermo 30
Orlando, Leoluca 315
Orthodox Judaism 34–5, 90, 93
Oswald, Alice
  *Memorial* 248–9, 279, 282
  *Nobody* 238–41, 248
Ottoman empire 29, 113, 119, 134–5
Ovid 156, 159
  *Fasti* 160–1, 181
  *Metamorphoses* 26, 279

Pagano, Matteo, *Map of Cairo* 96
Palermo, Sicily 30, 43, 256, 290–1, 295, 306–11
Palestine 54, 112, 113, 138–40, 243, 260
Pamuk, Orhan, *The Museum of Innocence* 103–4
pardon tales 224–6
Parton, Dolly 144

Paul de Silva (Paul of the Wood) 124
Pavel, Thomas 75, 250, 274
Paz, Octavio 250–1, 259
Peacock, Thomas Love 272–3
performance 35, 237–9, 266–7, 271, 284–5, 306
  fabulism 268, 278
  poetry 231, 249
  workshop 312, 314
Perrault, Charles 210, 276
Perry, Grayson 107
*Peter Pan* 75
Pétis de La Croix, François, *Les Mille et un jours* 194, 195–9, 206
Phillip, Matthew 71
Piero della Francesca 86, 86–7, Plate 5b
pilgrimage 63–4, 252–4
  Canterbury 221
  Compostela 250
  Mecca 70, 98, 131
  Nile valley 54, 57
  secular 105, 144, 224, 237
  Soissons 255
  Walsingham 119–26
  ways 28
  *See also* Loreto, Le Marche, Italy; relics
Pincus, Anna 220–3
Ping, Wang 'Things We Carry on the Sea' 116
Pinkerton, Alasdair 216
*Pirates of the Caribbean* (Disneyland tableau) 75
Pitrè, Giuseppe 296
Pius V, Pope 135–6
Pius X, Pope 102
plague 29, 30, 35, 217
play, playing 29, 33–5, 290, 296–7, 332
Poetical Animals 31
poetry 81, 102–3, 116, 231, 238–41
Pollard, Clare 159–60
pollution 22, 27, 34
Popescu, Lucy, *A Country of Refuge* 222
precincts 34, 39, 43, 47, 63–4
  sacred 9, 22, 24, 117, 314
  'safe places' 44, 46
Presley, Elvis 144
Prince, Mary 225
Prochnik, George 138

Prokofiev, Sergei, *The Love for Three Oranges* 202
Protestantism 101, 104
Proust, Marcel 6, 246
Pseudo-Matthew, Gospel of 58, 59
Puccini, Giacomo, see *Turandot*
Pullman, Philip, *His Dark Materials* 142, 246, 274
Puppet Museum (Museo Internazionale delle Marionette A. Pasqualino), Palermo 290
Purcell, Henry, *Dido and Aeneas* 42, 173, 174, 180–1
Putin, Vladimir 270

Qasmiyeh, Yousif M. 225
Queen of Sheba 87, 105–6
Qur'an 54, 55–7, 60, 255, 260

Radjy, Omar-Hussein 70
*Rapunzel* 261
Ravenet II, Simon François 66
recitations 69, 104
Redonda, Kingdom of 359
Reeves, John 211
Reformers, Protestant 38, 85, 101, 105, 106, 118, 128
refugee camps 225, 292, 371
'The Jungle', Calais 42, 45–6, 224
*Refugee Tales* 221–3, 231
refugees (arrivants) 3, 7–8, 44, 116–17, 140, 284, 288–9
Dido as refugee 146–82
refuges 5, 14, 37, 43, 132–3, 136–7, 216
cities of 7, 22, 44–5
Reich-Ranicki, Marcel, *Mein Leben* 288–9
Reinhardt, Max 202
Relics *see* True Cross
footprints 79, 253–5, Plate 8
*Helena Dreams of the Cross* 78–110, Plate 4
Mar Tadros 69
primary 79, 93–4, 98, 101, 117
St John of Beverley 37
Santa Casa 111–19
secondary 5, 28, 98, 116, 117
shadow 255–6
St Mark's 126

*Titulus Crucis* 99, 113
Rembrandt 66–8, 67
replications 120, 128–9, 132, 136, 137–8, 364
retreats 5
Richeldis de Faverches 119–20, 121
Ricoeur, Paul, *Figuring the Sacred* 17, 77, 276
Rijeka, Croatia 117, 124, 136
Riley, Denise, *Lurex* 18, 240–1, 261
Ristelhueber, Sophie 217
Robbins, Bruce 286–7
Robertson, Jeannie 74
Robertson, Joe 224
Robertson, Stanley 74
Robin Hood 35–6
rocks 28–9
Rodney, Donald, *In the House of My Father* 143, *143*
Rohault de Fleury, Charles 84
Romanticism 121, 187, 201, 262, 273–4
Rosalia, Santa 29, 30, 308, 331, Plate 2
Rossini, Gioachino Antonio, *The Barber of Seville* 200
Rowling, J. K., *Harry Potter* series 39, 246, 274
Rucellai chapel, San Pancrazio, Florence 137
Rushdie, Salman 73, 263–4
Ruskin, John, *Ethics of the Dust* 141, 274
Ruthwell Cross, the 80
Rwanda 294

Sacchi, Antonio 201
Sacré Coeur, Montmartre 30
sacred spaces 28–42
'safe places', for groups 46
Said, Edward 15, 139–40, 190, 256–7, 287, 329, 348
Sainte-Chapelle, Paris 79
Sakha stone 57, 253
Sallustius 269
Salvini, Matteo 17, 315
sanctuary
history of 21–47
medieval law of 32, 37–42, 152, 332, 333
sanctuary (definition) 1–9

Sangallo, Francesco da 127
Sangallo, Giuliano da 126, 127
Sansovino, Andrea 126, 127
Santa Casa (Holy House), *see* Loreto 111–45
Santa Chiara, Palermo 43
Santa Maria della Salute, Venice 29
Santa Rosalia 29, 30, *Plate 2*
Sarkozy, Nicolas 283
Sartre, Jean-Paul, *Les Mouches* 26
Saudi Arabia 70
Saunders, George, *Lincoln in the Bardo* 236
Schiller, Friedrich, *Turandot, Prinzessin von China* 190, 201
Schneerson, Menachem Mendel 138
Schongauer, Martin 59
Schulz-Dornburg, Ursula, *The Land in Between* 216
Schwartz, Hillel 138
Scott, Walter 273
Sebald, W. G. 257
secondary worlds 100, 249, 272–4
Seeds of Hope, The (UN Refugee Agency) 116–17
Seferis, George 316
Sennett, Richard 108
Shakespeare, John 106
Shakespeare, William 7, 87–8, 106–7, 190
  *Hamlet* 121, 166, 210, 231
  *King Lear* 92, 93
  *Macbeth* 190, 231
  *Measure for Measure* 121
  *The Merchant of Venice* 190, 207
  *A Midsummer Night's Dream* 126
  *Othello* 166–71, 167, 172
  *Pericles* 107, 190, 207
  *Richard III* 40–1
  *Romeo and Juliet* 246
  *Sir Thomas More* 7, 326
  *The Tempest* 36, 39
  *Titus Andronicus* 107
  *Venus and Adonis* 26
  *The Winter's Tale* 36, 106–7
  *As You Like It* 35–6
Shamsie, Kamila 222
Shawcross, William 219
Shearman, Lee 302
Shehadeh, Raja 142–3

Sheikh, Fazal 243
Shelley, Percy Bysshe, *Defence of Poetry* 273–4
Shire, Warsan 227–8
shrines 28–30, 35–6, 43, 102–3, 254–5
  attacks on 109
  Coptic and Muslim 69
  demolished 70
  Dome of the Rock 28
  faith groups 4
  in literature 25, 180
  Marian 58, 63
  Qur'anic 57
  secular 47, 75–6, 204
  St Teresa of Shoubra 69
  Walsingham 119–26
  *See also* Loreto, Le Marche, Italy; pilgrimage; relics
Sicily 292–6, 312, 315
signs, planting 250–1, 253, 255–6, 259
Simone, Nina 144
Simoni, Renato 202, 204–5
simulacra 132, 136–7
*Sir Gawain and the Green Knight* (anon) 35
*Sleeping Beauty* 276
'small boats' 8, 27, 52, 223, 270, 292
Smith, Ali 222
*Snow White* 190
Solnit, Rebecca, *River of Dreams* 257–8
Al Solh, Mounira, *I Strongly Believe in Our Right to Be Frivolous* 227
Solzhenitsyn, Aleksandr 280
Sondheim, Stephen, *Into the Woods* 36
Soobramanien, Natasha, *Diego Garcia* 237
Sophocles, *Oedipus at Colonus* 21–4, 26, 27, 35
Southey, Robert 273
Spain 56, 58
Speed, John 36
spells, magic 39, 208
spories 186, 211, 266
springs, miraculous 9, 52–4, 59, 63, 65–6, 131, 161, 243, 255, 269, *Plates 3, 8*
Stace, Wesley 180–1
Stallings, A. E. 278

stately homes 43
Stations of the Cross 98–9, 113, 252
statues 24–5, 29, 97, 100, 103, 127, 128–30, 140, 308–10
Steinbeck, John 280
Stevens, Wallace, 'An Ordinary Evening in New Haven' 264–5, 275–6
Stewart, Susan, *The Ruins Lesson* 3, 52, 102, 132
stones 28–9, 39–40, 40, 57, 128, 131
Stories in Transit project workshops 13–14, 290–7, 306–16, *Plates 14a, b, c, 15*
Stories, Ocean of 262–72
story singers 312
storytelling 12–18, 28, 53–4, 83, 113, 116, 259, 288–9
  forewarning and forestalling 272–82
  persuasions of the craft 162–71
Stratford-upon-Avon, Warwickshire 105
Sturrock, John 229–30
Subin, Anna Della, *Accidental Gods* 276
Swift, Jonathan, *Gulliver's Travels* 213, 246
symbolism 131–2
  of blood 135
  Heaney and 103
  of *Terra nullius* 216–17, 233
  of water 239, 263, 293

Tacca, Ferdinando 62
'The Tale of the Old Man and the Snake' 311–12, *Plates 14a, b, c, 16b*
Tarnowska, Wafa' 314
Tate, Nahum 42, 173
tattoos 49, 116, 140
Taylor, Jeremy 273
Teale, Polly 231
Temple Church, London 136
temples 4, 5, 29, 330
'Teramano' (Pietro Giorgio Tolomei) 123–4
Teresa of Avila, St 101
territory 5, 40, 46, 131, 151
  *See also* No Man's Lands
*Terrore nello Spazio* (*The Planet of the Vampires*), 1965 film) 172–3
theatre 42–3, 231, 238

Thérèse of Lisieux, St 101
*Thousand and One Nights, The* 193–4, 313–14
  heroes and heroines of 265
  Kilito and 199, 266
  Solomon and 260
  tales from 62, 115, 207, 210, 270, 282, 289, 290
Tiepolo, Gianbattista, *Translation of the Holy House of Loreto* 125, *Plate 6*
Tiepolo, Giandomenico, *The Flight into Egypt* 52
Tillyer, William 239
Timaeus 153–4
Tofighian, Omid 226
Tolkien, J. R. R. 272
'Tom Tit Tot' 208, 209
tombs 62, 70, 84, 91, 109, 119
  *See also* Loreto, Le Marche, Italy
Touray, Numu 302–6, *Plate 15*
translations 125–6, 194–5, 260–1, 266–7, 282–3, 310–11, 370
  literary 92, 188, 199, 226, 236, 279–80, 293, 296
  mapping 246
  pattern books 108
  plays 201, 243
transluminations 282–8
*Treasures of Heaven: Saints, Relics and Devotion in Medieval Europe* (2012 exhibition) 101
Trías, Eugenio 104
Tribolo, Niccolò 127
Tring, Hertfordshire 61
Trogus, Pompeius 153
Troy 25, 29–30, 39, 130, 171–82, 247, 275
True Cross relics 78–110, *Plates 4, 5a, b*
Trump, Donald 7, 315, 316
*Turandot* 183–4, 185, 186–91, *187, 189, 191*, 193–4, 198, 200–11, 203, *Plate 9*
Truth and Reconciliation Commission, South Africa 225, 294
Turin Shroud 80

Ukraine 183–5, 255, 333
Ukraine–Russian war (2022–) 185, 204, 217, 233

Ukrainians 8
UNESCO 284–5

Vakhtangov, Yevgeny 202
Valdener, John, *The Legendary History of the True Cross* 106
Valeri, Domenico, *Pius V Gives the Earth of Rome to the Polish Ambassador* 135–6
Van Dyck, Anthony 30
Venezis, Ilias *Land of Aeolia* 349
Venice 29
Verdi, Giuseppe 185, 188
*Veronese, Paolo Cagliari* 66, 89, Plates 3, 4
Vietnam war 44
Virgil, *Aeneid* 146–58, 160–6, 171, 173–4, 175–81, 210, 248
Virgin Mary 29, 55–8, 60, 78, 107, 123–4, 135, 255, 293
Volok, Marina 202
Voltaire 73, 84
Volto Santo 80
Voragine, Jacobus de, *Golden Legend* 83–6, 87, 88, 89, 107
Vulliamy, Ed 75

Wagner, Richard, *Die Feen (The Fairies)* 76, 202
Wallen, Errollyn, *Dido's Ghost* 180–1

Walsingham Shrine, Norfolk 70, 119–26, 128
warfare, modern 217
Washburn, Anne 282
Waugh, Evelyn, *Helena* 94–5, 96–7
Weber, Carl Maria von 190
Wentworth, Richard, 'Making Do and Getting By' 40
White, Enos 74
Whiteread, Rachel, *Untitled (House)* 145
Whitlock, Pamela, *The Far Distant Oxus* 246
William of Worcester 120
Williams, Bernard, *Truth and Truthfulness* 224–5
Williams, Luke, *Diego Garcia* 237
Winnicott, D. W. 237
Winterson, Jeanette 282
Wistar, Caspar 210
*Wisteria* (plant) 210
Wittgenstein, Ludwig 209
Wood, James 4
Woolf, Virginia, *Jacob's Room* 71
Wordsworth, William 273
Writing Europe (British Council) 184

*Xenia* see hospitality

Zafer, Ibn, *Solwan; or, Waters of Comfort* 263, 296